THE GREAT BOOK OF MOVIE

THE GREAT BOOK OF MOVIE

VILLAINS

By Jan Stacy and Ryder Syvertsen

A Guide to the Screen's Meanies, Tough Guys, and Bullies

Contemporary Books, Inc.
chicago

Library of Congress Cataloging in Publication Data

Stacy, Jan.
   The great book of movie villains.

   Includes indexes.
   1. Villains in motion pictures—Dictionaries.
2. Moving-pictures—Plots, themes, etc.   I. Syvertsen,
Ryder.   II. Title.
PN1995.9.V47S73   1984   791.43'09'093510321   84-14254
ISBN 0-8092-5351-8

This book was produced by The Photographic Book Company

Published by Contemporary Books, Inc.
180 North Michigan Avenue
Chicago, Illinois 60601

Published simultaneously in Canada by Beaverbooks, Ltd.
195 Allstate Parkway, Valleywood Business Park
Markham, Ontario L3R 4T8 Canada

Manufactured in the United States of America

CONTENTS

Introduction 10

A 12

Aguirre • Alex • Rico Angelo • Bruno Anthony • Mrs. Appleyard • Martin
Arlington • The Assassin

B 24

Baby Jane • Bataiatus • Martha Beck • The Bey Officer • Colonel Nikita I.
Biroshilov • Black Tiger • Captain Bligh • Ernst Stavro Blofeld • Bonnie and
Clyde • Martha, Abby, and Jonathan Brewster • Buzz and the Gang

C 38

Peter Cable • Max Cady • Cal • Dr. Caligari • Calvera • Captain James and
Hector • Lily Carver • Coral Chandler • Sir Charles • Charlie • Alain Charnier •
Chauvelin • Nick Cherney • The Clanton Gang • The Clegg Family • Terry
Collins • Michael Corleone • Cottonmouth • Joan Crawford • Leslie Crosbie •
Noah Cross

D 62

Dalby • Danny • Mrs. Danvers • Dathan • Sandy Dawson • Sir Brian de Bois-
Guilbert • De Villefort, Mondego, and Danglars • Ulysses Diello • Dillon • The
Dirty Dozen • Fred C. Dobbs • Doc & Dix • Doctor No • Hugo Drax • Inspector
Dreyfus

E 80

Eichelberger • Einar, the Viking • Eve

F 85

Faber • Harry Fabian • Fagin & Sikes • Dr. Allen Fields • Jennie Finch • Frank
and Cora • Johnny Friendly • Fu Manchu

G 95

Elsa Gebhardt • Dr. George • German Captain of the *Louisa* • The Godfather •
Bert Gordon • Gray • The Gunfighter • Casper Gutman • Sir Guy of Gisborne

H 106

George Hally • Han • Dr. Hartz • Eddie Harwood • King Henry II • Homer • Matthew Hopkins and John Stearne • Hud • J.J. Hunsecker • Lieutenant Colonel Hyde

I 118

Tom Iverson and Paula

J 120

The Jackal • Frank and Jessie James • Earl Janoth • Cody Jarrett • Jaws • Johnny and Chino

K 128

Franz Kindler • Kongre • Kramer • Colonel Kurtz

L 132

Michael Landon • Clubber Lang • The Lavender Hill Mob • The Law • Leatherface • Harry Lime • Dad Longworth • Doyle Lonnigan • Rose Loomis • Luther of the Rogues • Waldo Lydecker

M 146

Margaret Macomber • Mad Dog Earle • Madeline • Magua • Mailer • Dave Mallory and the Gang • Moose Malloy • The Manchurian Candidate • Raymond and Connie Marble • Marie Antoinette • Martha and the Girls • Richard Mason • Mata Hari • Bobby Maxwell • Lewt McCanles • Nicholas Medina • Gerald Meldrick and Anya Von Duren • Dr. Josef Mengele • Enemy Agent Menlin • Messala • Frank Miller and Friends • Ming the Merciless • Misty • Admiral Mitamura • Mord • The Mountain Men • The Muranians

N 175

John Neville • Nuclear War

O 178

The Octopus • Odd Job

P 181

The Passengers • Grand Duke Peter • Phantom of the Paradise • Hjalmar Poelzig • Pretty Poison

Q 186

Judge Quincannon • Hank Quinlan

R   188

Nurse Rached • Captain Juan Ramon • Raven • Lonesome Rhodes • Rico • Johnny Rocco • Rochefort • Roy and the Driver

S   197

Colonel Saito • Sal and Sonny • Scanlon • The Scorpio Killer • The Scorpion • Hunt Sears • Alexander Sebastian • Leo Sellars • Ned and William Sharp • Long John Silver • Roger Simmons • Emma Small • Jimmy Smith and Gregory Powell • Perry Smith and Dick Hickok • Virgil Starkwell • Camilla Sternwood • Dr. Stevenson • Dr. Strangelove • The Stranger • Major Strasser • Szell

T   222

Bart Tare • Taxi Driver • Dr. Terwilliker • Bobby Thompson • Toecutter's Gang

U   227

Tommy Udo

V   228

Fred Van Ackerman • Philip Vandamm • Johnny Vanning • Mrs. Venable • Ventana Corp. • The Vigilante Cops

W   236

Mr. Wabash • Josey Wales • Walker • Matty Walker • Wallich Town Bigots • Walter and Phyllis • Wicked Witch of the West • The Wild Bunch • Wilkes and the Patients • Peter Willems • Professor Willingdon

Z   248

Zampano

Actor Index   250

Movie Index   254

Director Index   255

Studio Index   256

INTRODUCTION

What Is a Villain?

A villain is someone who encompasses more than the ordinary quotient of nastiness that is part of the nature of every individual. We all feel moments, hours, even days of anger, hate, and the desire for revenge. But the villain makes these darkest human emotions a way of life. He or she exists to carry out dark plans, dark acts, and to make life worse for others. The villain, like the hero, thrives on action. No villain is content to just sit around feeling mean. A villain actively seeks out ways to inflict his or her meanness on the world. Causing hardships for others is a way of life. In the most existentialist of senses, the villain does not become real until and unless he or she is causing trouble, evil, or pain. The film villain is the most lurid example.

Villains lie, cheat, attack, terrorize, murder, plunder, pillage, and destroy. Even worse, the villain does not necessarily strike at those he or she knows, but often gets a kick out of attacking total strangers. We are strangers, hence our fear and apprehension of the villain. Though we have done nothing, maybe never seen this person, group, or institution, in our unconscious is the thought that we could, may, or will be the next target. This is the dread of modern life. And yet, paradoxically, everyone loves movie villains. We might deny it, feeling it's wrong to enjoy someone's evil doings, but nonetheless it's true; we love to hate them.

There is a perfection to the film villain, a beauty, a smoothness of purpose. The villain knows just what he or she wants and pursues that goal without hesitation. In fact, the villain has as much a place in the deepest recesses of our unconscious center of moral decision-making as does the hero. Perhaps there is something about Americans, in particular, that makes us appreciate the villain for his special qualities of rebelliousness, individuality, and antisocial philosophies. After all,

many of us are descendants of so-called outcasts, rebels, cutthroats, and scoundrels. The people who founded our country, those who settled the West, and those who built the industrial empires that still chug and throb today all had a bit (or a lot) of villainy in them. Films reflect this heritage.

The villain has so many qualities that we admire that it's not surprising some misled people want to emulate them. The villain can do what he wants, go where he wants, and take what he wants. He is often loud, uncaring of others' feelings, tough, brash, all-knowing and self-confident to the supreme degree. Although many of these characteristics border on the negative, many of us would like to acquire them.

In fact, criminal villains have been popular for much of our history. It is widely known that Jesse James was protected by common people all over the West, and just the mention of names like Baby Face Nelson, Dillinger, and Machine Gun Kelly brings smiles to millions of faces. They were striking, poetic, romantic figures whose images still burn bright. Villains have, after all, stolen from the rich, struggled against the establishment, and fought back against the dehumanizing bureaucracy of power. For these reasons (whether right or wrong), villains have often become heroes to the oppressed and downtrodden. Some of the villains selected for this book are such hero/villains—a subtle blending of good and bad. In many instances, these characters often become villains by force of circumstance.

But no matter how much we admire a villain's attributes, his superficial attractiveness will lead to only one end: his destruction. One must pay the price for walking down the path of evil. The villain, through his actions, successes, and then failures, is acting out the most ancient of morality plays. We might want the villain's car, his mansion, his lover, or his power, yet when he must pay the price for his deeds we can say, "Thank God that wasn't me!" We realize we are more content to be just who we are. Vicariously, when watching villains on the movie screen, or reading of them in books and newspapers, we come face to face with our own darkest desires, let them surface (in the villain), defeat them, and put them back into chains.

Make no mistake about it, villains are philosophers of evil. They are not just musclemen or maniacs, but people who have chosen evil. They present evil as a viable alternative, a way of life. Of course, they have elaborate justifications for their choice ("I was wronged," "I was attacked," or "the world is corrupt."). They rationalize why the Earth would be better ruled by them ("the world must be controlled by someone, why not me?"). In reality they represent the ultimate development of the Darwinian concept of survival of the strongest (and toughest). With strength comes power; power corrupts; evil evolves in the form of the villain. If the villain is strong enough to rule and run things, (or so he or she thinks), well, why the hell not?

The Evolution of Evil

Villains can be found in almost every imaginable form, guise, and costume, reflecting man's changing consciousness as he developed through the ages. The motion picture industry has dramatically depicted the villain in all his various eras.

The earliest villain, of course, is the serpent in the Garden of Eden. He is shown tempting man and woman with what they should not do and should not touch. The serpent coaxes the man and woman into breaking the first basic moral code. In a sense all other villains have been based on this seductive, but terribly deadly, form of dark energy.

Other early villains depicted in films who left their mark on society include the Egyptian pharaohs, the cruel Sumerian slave drivers, and the cold Chinese emperors. The early Romans provided an extensive list of villains. There were the insane Caesars, the ruthless Centurions who ravaged Europe, and anyone and everyone who persecuted the early Christians. Somehow though, the later Romans became heroes as they became Christianized. It was then that the fierce Barbarians—Attila the Hun and Genghis Khan—began their reign of terror.

The era of middle villainy brought an onslaught of evil knights, conquistadors, Viking raiders, cannibals, headhunters, cruel Indians, pirates, and pretenders to the throne. As we move on in time, we see evil gunslingers, debauched Victorian lords, penny pinching industrial barons, and corrupt rulers.

With the 20th century, new movie villains arrived on the scene—organized gangsters, dictators, the Nazis, mad scientists, supernaturally powerful villains, super spies, power hungry media stars, psychopaths and psychiatric evildoers, corporations indifferent to human life, and even society and the law that governs all people.

Villains for the 1980s

Today's movie villains are, of course, more modern and up-to-date in their dress, mannerisms, goals, and weapons. The day of the mustache-twirling badmen is gone. Now, the villain can be seen smirking subtly as he pets a white cat or wears a swastika on his arm. No words even need to be spoken. The modern villain's main distinguishing features are his aims and tools of the trade. In the old days, all the villain wanted was the girl or the gold mine. Now the villain wants the world or a good chunk of it. The villain's appetite seems to have grown along with civilization. Of course, the weapons at the villain's disposal are a million times more frightening and powerful than the Black Knight's mace, the Viking's sword, or even the gangster's tommy gun. Today's villain uses laser rifles, atomic missiles, and germ warfare. He does not hesitate to use the most powerful weapons against us. The film industry has faithfully recorded this trend.

Perhaps this is another lesson for mankind. The villain gives us the opportunity to see that what we create today, in the name of defending ourselves, may well turn on us tomorrow.

Aguirre   13

Alex   14

Rico Angelo   16

Bruno Anthony   18

Mrs. Appleyard   19

Martin Arlington   21

The Assassin   22

Aguirre

Alias: Don Lope De Aguirre
Born: circa 1525
Died: 1560

Starred in:
Aguirre, The Wrath of God
New Yorker Films (Germany), 1977
Director: Werner Herzog
Played by: Klaus Kinski

The insane Aguirre (Klaus Kinski) gives Inez, the wife of the expedition's leader, the onceover in Aguirre, The Wrath of God.

Description: Tall blond man, deeply furrowed face, mad blue eyes. Wears metal helmet and breastplates, carries sword, Spanish.

Reason for Villainy: In 1560, the Conquistadores under Pizarro cross Peru. They send a small party onward to search for the City of Gold (the legendary El Dorado). Noblemen Pedrode Ursua (Ray Guerra) and Aguirre lead the party of 40 soldiers. Also accompanying them are Ursua's beautiful wife, Inez (Helena Rojo), Aguirre's silent 15-year-old daughter, Flores (Cecilia Rivera), and a priest, Gaspar. Perilous rivers, attacks by blowgun- and spear-wielding cannibalistic Indians follow. The 40 soldiers dwindle to 20, then 10. Aguirre becomes obsessed, takes over, and refuses to turn back. Everyone begins to catch a strange fever and hallucinate. They wander endlessly on the wide open river. Aguirre puts Ursua on mock trial, but he is given clemency by the others. The ridiculous, fat servant Guzman (Danny Andes) is made "Emperor" of the new world by Aguirre.

Evil Powers/Weapons: Psychotically obsessed with claiming the entire new area and its gold (non-existent). Carries a sword and gun and uses them. Creates a climate of ultimate fear in others who are terrified to even think of crossing him.

Occupation: Conquistador, soldier, madman.

Intelligence: Cunning, plotter, megalomaniac, visionary, bold explorer, but madness reigns over his faculties.

Strengths: Loves his daughter and has a great sense of purpose.

Weaknesses: Will never admit that they must give up their quest. Greedy.

Territory: Travels from Spain to the Amazon basin.

Idiosyncrasies : Wild-eyed; strange, sour smirks.

Friends: Pizarro, "Emperor" Guzman.

Enemies: His own men.

Relatives: Any megalomaniac who takes others down with him.

Evil Deeds: Cuts the head off of a dissenter. His insanity and power push his crew to their deaths.

Killed by: Their raft sails on to its doom. The food runs low—what little remains is fed only to "Emperor" Guzman. When the Emperor dies, Aguirre hangs Ursua, and Inez walks into the jungle and is never seen again. The crew continues to be hit by poisoned arrows from the Indians but they are not sure if they are not hallucinating the attacks since they have been drinking the disease-filled waters. Aguirre decides, in his fever, to marry his daughter, conquer Mexico, and found a dynasty. Flores gets hit with an arrow and dies. Aguirre continues to sail on with hundreds of chattering monkeys.

Current Status: Dead.

What to Do If You Meet: A character like this needs Bellevue. Don't go on expeditions with madmen.

Worthy of Note: Rivera is the one of the most beautiful women in any film ever. Kinski's real daughter is Nastassia Kinski, now a famous film personality in her own right.

Alex

Alias: The Head Droog
Born/Died: The future

Starred in:
A Clockwork Orange
Warner Bros., 1971
Director: Stanley Kubrick
Played by: Malcolm McDowell

Description: Handsome, devil-may-care, violent gang leader. Wears gang colors, white pants, striped shirt, bowler hat, huge plastic codpiece, suspenders, and cane.

Reason for Villainy: The film begins in a terrifying society of the future where gangs roam the streets fighting each other and attacking citizens. Alex and his "droogs" are one of the more vicious gangs who spend their time looking for kicks and acting out the "old

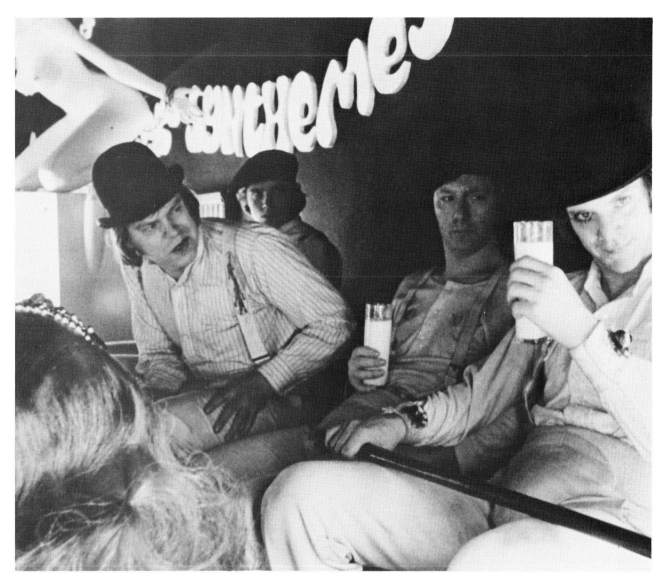

Alex (Malcolm McDowell, far right) and his droogs milk up on some delicious Molocko Plus before heading out for some of the "Old Ultraviolence" in Clockwork Orange.

ultraviolence." They first get high at the Korova Milkbar on Molocko Plus (a psychedelic drink) and then go out and beat up a drunk bum and fight a gang. They then break into the home of Mr. Alexander (Patrick McGee), a famous writer, and almost kill him. They also rape his wife (as Alex sings "Singing in the Rain"). Happy with the evening's violence, Alex goes home and plays "Ludwig B's" Ninth Symphony on the stereo. Another satisfying evening.

Evil Powers: Cruel, loves to torture and hurt people.

Weapons: Fists, feet, cane that he always carries, and whatever else is handy—including a giant plastic phallus.

Occupation: Gang leader, thief.

Intelligence: Extremely intelligent. A leader. Able to see through much of the hypocrisy of his society and to manipulate others.

Strengths: Fearless, aggressive, super fighter.

Weaknesses: No compassion, short-sighted.

Territory: London and countryside.

Idiosyncracies: Loves Beethoven's Ninth,

which he hums and plays over and over. Also sings "Singing in the Rain" as he smashes people's heads in.

Friends/Enemies: No real friends, but likes fellow gang members until they turn on him. Makes enemies everywhere he goes, who later attack him.

Evil Deeds: Lies, tortures, humiliates, beats, plunders, rapes, steals, wrecks, kills. . . .

Killed by: Alex is caught by the police after killing a woman (set up by one of his own gang members). He is sentenced to 14 years in prison, which he quickly grows to hate. The Minister of the Interior is seeking volunteers for treatment under the new "Ludovico Technique," in which prisoners are given injections of a miracle drug, shown pictures of violence which make them violently ill, and are conditioned to be unable to perform or even think any violence without vomiting and having severely painful cramps. Alex volunteers, undergoes the treatment, and is released. Whenever a violent feeling erupts, he screams. He is attacked and abused by everyone— bums, the old gang, and parents. He eventually returns to the home of Mr. Alexander by accident (badly beaten) and is taken in. Alexander recognizes his assailant as Alex hums "Singing in the Rain" in the bathtub. Alexander pumps in Beethoven's Ninth (doctors had used the symphony as background music when conditioning Alex) and the head "droog" goes insane with pain, finally jumping out the window. In the last scene, Alex is recovering in a hospital bed, but now cured of the conditioning. He can happily be violent again. Approached by the Minister of the Interior, who has tremendous political interests in the cure, Alex is bribed to keep quiet, and, at least, perform his violent acts discreetly. Alex, now part of the establishment, is free again.

Current Status: Alive, in the future, kicking ass.

What to Do If You Meet: Tell him you know where he can get some Molocko Plus. If he starts humming "Singing in the Rain," run!

Worthy of Note: Top notch apocalyptic picture of the future. Excellent writing by Anthony Burgess. McDowell is a wonder to behold.

Rico Angelo

Alias: The gangster
Born: early 1900s
Died: 1930s

Starred in:
Party Girl
MGM, 1958
Director: Nicholas Ray
Played by: Lee J. Cobb

Description: Rico Angelo is a tough, hard-bitten Chicago gangster in the days when Chicago was under the thumb of such villains. He wears—always—a white handkerchief in his suit pocket and the traditional gangster pin stripe. Well-groomed brown hair, manicured, cufflinks of gold, a constant sneer, looks sophisticated, but is a low life.

Reason for Villainy: Angelo is the head of a Chicago crime network. He has a powerful and corrupt attorney, Thomas Farrell (Robert Taylor), as his mouthpiece. Farrell is adept at springing Angelo's henchmen and making a mockery of jurisprudence. Farrell, who limps, meets nightclub performer Vicki Gaye (Cyd Charisse) through Angelo. Farrell falls for Vicki and they are off to her home. But when they enter—guess what?—a body, of course, and it's Vicki's roommate, Joy Hampton, who has committed suicide. Vicki isn't all that happy either, being a lost soul. Farrell and Vicki find what they need in life in each other. Now Farrell must spring one of Angelo's cronies from the slammer. When the crony, "Cookie," jumps his bail, the cops arrest Farrell for bribing a juror and pull a dirty trick. The cops release Farrell but put out the word—which isn't true—that Farrell has "squealed." Of course, Angelo and his goons are out to bump off Farrell—or worse, hit the dame. Farrell is afraid that Vicki will be hurt and he sings like a birdie to the coppers.

Evil Powers: Angelo has the tommy guns

that are trademarks of gangsters, a well-armed criminal militia to protect his interests. He also cannot stand squealers and has to make an example of them—or their "goils."

Occupation: Bloodthirsty and slick crime boss during the Prohibition in Chicago.

Intelligence: Angelo is a ruthless and highly intelligent gangster.

Strengths: He has his mob, the choppers, and the cars.

Weaknesses: He cannot stand up in a fair fight to Farrell.

Territory: Chicago in the 1930s.

Idiosyncrasies: Angelo wants to look slick, talk slick. He does, but there's an air of inauthenticity to it all—a small-timer looking big.

Friends: At first his mouthpiece Farrell, and the mob.

Enemies: Farrell, when he cooperates with the law.

Evil Deeds: Rampages through Chicago cutting out his piece of the action.

Killed by: Farrell finds Angelo and they have it out before the police close in. Angelo and his goons have captured Vicki and are holding her—it's up to Farrell to do something about it. Angelo has disfigurement in mind for the feisty dame and he lets Farrell know this. Farrell must act, but he is handicapped. However, his cane becomes a lethal weapon when the fate of the curvy tomato is concerned. Distraught and angry, Farrell lashes out at Angelo and is making some headway, but it is the police who make an end to the evil villain. Angelo falls, and the couple—sick and tired of the Rico Angelos of the world, the seedy

The party gets pretty rough for Rico Angelo (Lee J. Cobb) in Party Girl.

crime-ridden streets and smoky nightclubs of Chicago—make a beeline for the state border. They want to start a new life together and don't want to think about how they are going to do it. They'll just do it. In the inimitable style of 1950s Hollywood movies, it's a happy ending for Farrell and Vicki and "coitains" for our villain.

Current Status: Dead.

What to Do If You Meet: Angelo has backing. Be cool, leave Chicago. What is there in the big crime-ridden city anyway?

Worthy of Note: Isn't Robert Taylor great? Don't you wish they'd show him on TV more? This is Nick Ray's *piece de resistance* of crime.

Bruno Anthony

Born: 1900s
Died: 1950

Starred in:
Strangers on a Train
RKO, 1951
Director: Alfred Hitchcock
Played by: Robert Walker

"Suppose, just suppose, we exchange murders."
It's a suggestion between Strangers on a Train.

Description: A dapper young man, but weird. He is well-groomed and well-dressed in a woolen suit and sporty tie. He travels first class and drinks the best. Cufflinks and cigarettes are name brand.

Reason for Villainy: Bruno cannot stand his dad, and will inherit some money if the old guy is removed from his earthly domicile by the Grim Reaper. Bruno devises this dandy scheme, really. He's looking for somebody to swap murders with him. "It's so simple," he explains to Guy Haines (Farley Granger), a likable young man who detests his wife. Bruno says, "How about you murder my dad for me and I get rid of your old lady. Simple. We'll both have alibis and no one will have the faintest idea who did it because there's no motive. Then we each go our separate ways." Bruno conveys all this over some drinks on the dining car table as the train speeds along. Convinced that Bruno is serious and has a good idea, Guy thinks it over, talks it over, but finally turns it down. Too crazy. But Bruno goes ahead with his end of the deal, and kills Guy's wife anyway. Guy, a tennis pro, is short an alibi, and the police are watching him. Worse, the mad Bruno has Guy's lighter and threatens to plant it somewhere incriminating if Guy doesn't fulfill his part of the bargain. What to do, what to do?

Evil Powers: Clever and resourceful.

Occupation: Says he's a tennis fan. Really!

Intelligence: Must be bright to think this up.

Strengths: He follows up on what he thinks.

Weaknesses: Unwilling partner in crime.

Territory: Trains. Carnivals—for murdering other people's wives.

Idiosyncrasies : Carefree demeanor, disarming charm, batty ideas.

Friends: The night.

Enemies: The tennis pro.

Evil Deeds: Murder.

Killed by: Guy is at a tennis match, under scrutiny. He must get out of there and stop Bruno. Bruno is on his way to plant the lighter. Guy slams his way through a bizarre, tense match and bolts the usual post-game laziness in order to catch up to Bruno. He tracks him to a carnival. Meanwhile, Bruno has foolishly let the lighter slip down a drain and has been struggling to retrieve it for some time. Bruno's blunder gives Guy enough time

to catch him. Oddly enough, and typically Hitchcock in flavor, the audience is aghast when the lighter is hard to retrieve. Sympathy rests for a time with the villain. The McGuffen (the object of contention), which Hitchcock always uses, is just a little lighter. Bruno, in a *deus ex machina* ending, is crushed by a merry-go-round. Guy is free to bat his balls around.

Current Status: Dead—who wouldn't be when run over by a merry-go-round?

What to Do If You Meet: Don't get into a "suppose . . ." game with him.

Worthy of Note: Hitchcock in the prime rib phase of his career.

Mrs. Appleyard

Born: 1850s
Died: 1900

Starred in:
Picnic at Hanging Rock
Atlantic Releasing, 1979
Director: Peter Weir
Played by: Rachel Roberts

Description: She is a cool-looking matron, discipline etched on her controlled face. The only emotion that peeks through is a trembling of the lips. She is overdressed for all occasions and wears her hair up. She is the master of disapproving looks and walks like a ramrod is up her back.

Reason for Villainy: Appleyard runs the Australian boarding school, Appleyard College. The girls are rigorously instructed in the things necessary for a refined lady to know. They are denied fun whenever possible. Appleyard seems to be intent on squelching the girls' creativity and lack of conformity at every opportunity. The day of the picnic at Hanging Rock—a local attraction of bizarre cliffs and rock formations millions of years

Mrs. Appleyard (Rachel Roberts) the evil Headmistress at Appleyard College.

old—she forbids Sara (Margaret Nelson) to go. Sara did not memorize a dreadful poem. Sara prefers to write her own, but that is ridiculous, says the headmistress. Sara's best friend and roommate Miranda (Anne Lambert), a nice blonde with a far-away look, and the other students ride away on the wagon. It's St. Valentine's Day, 1900. When they arrive at the Rock, they stare up at its awesome presence. Miranda asks Mlle. DePontiers (Helen Morse) if she and two other girls could go closer. There is an electricity in the air, all the watches have stopped, perhaps due to a magnetic disturbance.

Evil Powers/Weapons: Her control over the school and its pupils is absolute. Several students are late in their tuition. The orphanage awaits them if their guardians don't pay up.

Occupation: Headmistress of a boarding school for teenage girls in turn-of-the-century Australia.

Intelligence: Very literate. Articulate.

Strengths: Her school is doing well.

Weaknesses: If something can go wrong, it will.

Territory: Australia, 1900.

Idiosyncracies: Likes "Wreck of the Hesperus," instead of romantic poems. Drinks heavily from a decanter. Loves Queen Victoria.

Friends: The instructors at her school for girls.

Enemies: The Hanging Rock, publicity.

Evil Deeds: She is the film's most obvious heavy. She is hardly reluctant to tell Sara that the school is not a charity. The girl will have to return to the orphanage because her fees are overdue. She's cold and calculating, she places money above human life. Her main concern is the adverse publicity from the girls' disappearances, not the girls' lives.

Outcome: Marion, Irma, and Miranda ascend the Rock. An overweight girl, Edith, tags along, but soon tires of the climb. They all fall asleep after philosophizing about human nature. Miranda says that everything begins and ends exactly on time. After they awaken, the three girls then continue to climb up the steep path. Fat Edith screams. We never find out why. She runs down the slope, and the wagon returns unaccountably late to the school. Three girls are missing, the fat girl remembers nothing of what happened. Miss McCraw is also missing after climbing about the huge cliffs. A search party is organized, and days later the huge search team of constables, aborigines, and townspeople gives up. The girls have seemingly been swallowed up and are presumed dead. The police interrogate all witnesses of the girls' climb. Michael Fitzhubert (Dominick Guard) said he saw them cross a brook and begin the ascent. He and his family's servant, Albert (John Jarratt), keep mulling over what happened. They return to the awesome cliffs and search. The rich young man finds a scrap of lace. Injured unaccountably, he passes the lace in a clenched fist to Albert, who later retrieves Irma (Karen Robinson), one of the missing girls. Irma is unhurt, just exhausted. She doesn't remember what happened either. Incredible. The townspeople are up in arms but have nowhere to turn their anger. Irma recuperates on the rich young man's estate. He demands to know what happened. Michael leaves for Queensland—the movie audience never hears Irma's explanation. Mrs. Appleyard believes that the girls have all been raped and murdered. Students begin dropping out of school, their guardians are withdrawing them because of the controversy. The staff resigns one by one. Irma returns briefly, and the schoolgirls surround her demanding to know the truth. Because of the pressure, Irma eventually runs away. Sara has been not eating or sleeping, mooning over Miranda's love scrapbook. Sara then commits suicide by jumping off the roof after Mrs. Appleyard confronts her with her large, unpaid tuition. The film ends with Mrs. Appleyard already dressed for a funeral before she is notified of Sara's death. The postscript to the film adds that this true story ended several months later when Mrs. Appleyard herself was found dead at the foot of Hanging Rock under mysterious circumstances.

Current Status: Dead.

What to Do If You Meet: Look for Miranda and friends.

Worthy of Note: We are giving this a large play because it is one of the finest films ever made. The mystical overtones, the music, the blurry color photography, and the intense drama of looking for the girls can only be implied here. See it. It's a must.

A poetry reading at the foot of the awesome Hanging Rock.

Martin Arlington

Born: Late 19th century
Died: Early 20th century

Starred in:
Tarzan and His Mate
MGM, 1934
Director: Jack Conway and Cedric Gibbons
Played by: Paul Cavanagh

Description: Arlington is a big lug. He's handsome to a point, but he is so caught up in the quest for riches, in the form of elephant ivory, that the sneering lust has invaded his dark features. He's tall, but not as tall as Tarzan. He carries a gun and wears a pith helmet.

Reason for Villainy: Arlington is a meanie from the word go. He's put a lot into his African expedition in order to get the ivory tusks from the legendary "Elephants' Graveyard." The place lies deep in the veldt, and Tarzan (Johnny Weissmuller), when he is approached to guide the expedition, is reluctant to disturb the elephants' resting place. After all, Tarzan is a friend to animals and won't do anything they don't like. The Mutia Escarpment, tusk site, is remote and guarded by beasts and Pigmies, who proceed to make mincemeat of the intruders. Jane Parker (Maureen O'Sullivan), the daughter of one of the explorers and Arlington's betrothed, is threatened by the mad Pigmies. Tarzan comes to her rescue, swinging through the trees. At first she's fearful of this English lord raised by great apes, but he's nice, swims great, and fights off crocs for her. Soon they are lovers. Of course, this doesn't sit well with her suitor.

Evil Powers/Weapons: Guns and rifles that can down elephants. He has a voracious poaching instinct.

Occupation: Hunter, poacher, bring-em-back-dead type.

Intelligence: He's a hot-shot explorer who is preoccupied with jungle treasures.

Strengths: His weapons.

Weaknesses: Many natives and wild animals stand in his way.

Territory: England and Africa.

Idiosyncrasies: He's ape over Jane, but he doesn't "suitor" (sorry).

Friends: Bang-bang stick.

Enemies: Rampaging Pigmies.

Evil Deeds: Arlington get's bummed out when he doesn't get what he wants. He wounds an elephant, so that the animal will walk to the secret cemetery. This guy should be reported to the SPCA.

Outcome: Arlington becomes enraged and shoots Tarzan. He finally claims the ivory in the elephants' cemetery. However, just as he thinks he has suceeded, the natives and lions

The great white hunters get directions at a local crossroad in search of the Elephants' Graveyard in Tarzan and His Mate.

attack and kill Arlington. Jane is rescued by Tarzan and decides to stay in the jungle.

Current Status: Dead.

What to Do If You Meet: Say you know where the elephants go to die and he won't shoot you. Lead him into quicksand.

Worthy of Note: This film surpasses all jungle films in its charm and spectacle. Weissmuller was an Olympic swim champion before the film and was hired by producer Irving Thalberg's intuition that he was right for the part. In addition, Tarzan and Jane were scantily clad throughout this film and it caused quite an outburst from censors. In subsequent films, Tarzan and Jane were more "covered up." A nude swimming was cut from this film in order to appease censors.

The Assassin

Born: Early 1900s
Died: 1934

Starred in:
The Man Who Knew Too Much
London Films, 1934
Director: Alfred Hitchcock
Played by: Peter Lorre

Description: Lorre is a sneaky young man with rolling big eyes and a squeaky voice. He is well trained in the art of disposal, and he is not a garbage person. He's short and nervous. He likes crowds because they hide his escape.

Reason for Villainy: The Assassin is to kill an unnamed prime minister when he attends an orchestral performance in Royal Albert Hall in London. But the story begins when two tourists, Mr. and Mrs. McKenna (Leslie Banks and Edna Best), are on a crowded train in the Arab part of French Morocco. Their young son, Hank, stumbles into an Arab woman and accidentally dislodges her veil, creating a cultural uproar that is silenced when a friendly and linguistically talented Frenchman, Louis Bernard, intervenes. Later, in the bazaar, a man in Arab clothing is killed. The dead man is Monsieur Bernard, exclaims Mr. McKenna, wiping some makeup from the dying man's face. Bernard whispers something about an assassination and "Ambrose Chapel" to the once-bored Mr. McKenna. McKenna goes straight to the police, but is dissuaded from telling his fantastic story because someone has kidnapped their little boy. Ben McKenna is suddenly the man who knew too much. Ben and his wife follow a trail of clues and red-herrings to London and discover that Ambrose Chapel is a place in Royal Albert Hall.

Evil Powers/Weapons: He has the kid under lock and key, and he has time on his side. He's a professional.

Occupation: An assassin, or otherwise known as a people terminator.

Intelligence: Slippery and sneaky and wily like a coyote. He's slimy as a rock covered with algae, but not too well read.

Strengths: He's fast and his face is unknown.

Weaknesses: He's got the McKennas against him.

Territory: London, Marrakesh, and wherever murder is the method most preferred.

Idiosyncrasies: Prefers anonymity.

Friends: Secrecy and the Draytons—"that nice couple."

Enemies: The McKennas.

Relatives: The Jackal.

Evil Deeds: Assassination is the game, you pay with the name, to me it's all the same, I shoot through the brain, they're never the same.

Outcome: The McKennas make their way to Royal Albert Hall. The wife manages to cause a disturbance and thwarts the Assassin, who plans to kill the foreign dignitary at the clash of the orchestra's cymbals. The "Storm Cloud Cantata," played by the London Philharmonic, is interrupted. The dignitary shifts in his seat and is spared a direct hit. Now to get the son back: The couple go to the minister's embassy, where he is held by that nice couple from Morocco—the Draytons. With little Hank in tow, the couple return to their flat.

Current Status: Dead.

What to Do If You Meet: Shift in your seat as he fires.

Worthy of Note: James Stewart and Doris Day (singing "Que Sera Sera") are in the 1956 remake. Most aficionados consider the Lorre film more moody and compelling, but Hitchcock chose to remake this film considering the 1934 work immature for his talents. See both.

Peter Lorre plays the Assassin in search of his target, The Man Who Knew Too Much.

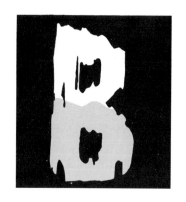

Baby Jane   25
Bataiatus   26
Martha Beck   27
The Bey Officer   28
Colonel Nikita I.
    Biroshilov   29
Black Tiger   30
Captain Bligh   31
Ernst Stavro
    Blofeld   33
Bonnie and Clyde   34
Martha, Abby,
    and Jonathan
    Brewster   35
Buzz and the Gang   36

Baby Jane

Alias: Jane Hudson
Born: Early 1900s
Died: Institutionalized 1962

Starred in:
What Ever Happened to Baby Jane?
Warner Bros., 1962
Director: Robert Aldrich
Played by: Bette Davis

Description: Weird. Her clothing is that of a child movie star and is as out of style as her ancient vehicle. This cutsey look and her overly made up and powdered face brands her as an A-1 looney.

Reason for Villainy: Baby Jane was a child star. In 1923, at the age of seven, she was making appearances all over the nation and was adored. She sings "I'm writing a letter to dadddddyyyyyyyyyyyy. . . ." and it brings down the house. However, tastes have changed. When Baby gets older, she loses her public, and her older sister, Blanche (Joan Crawford), becomes a rising star. Blanche becomes an ingenue and gets Baby minor parts. Returning one night from a party, they stop the big car. Baby gets out to open the gate. The car moves forward, crashes, and permanently cripples Blanche. Baby dedicates herself to caring for her wheelchair-ridden sister. Baby is guilt-ridden. She thinks she caused the accident in a jealous rage. With Blanche's money, they live together in their declining years in a big house. Baby constantly forges Blanche's signature to buy things and she imitates her voice to order things. Their only visitor is housekeeper Madie Norman. Baby drinks heavily and acts mucho weirdo. The maid realizes that Baby might not like finding out that Blanche intends to sell the old house. When Baby becomes aware of this, she turns Blanche into a prisoner, serving her rats under glass and strangled canaries. The housekeeper is worried after Baby fires her. When she comes back to look around, Baby smashes her with a hammer. Dead. She has finally flipped. She then decides to hire a publicist to revive her career singing "I wrote a letter to daddddddyyyyyy . . ." The publicist, Victor Buono, is an unemployed pianist. He figures, what the hell—if she has the money—he'll get to work on it. Buono comes for some cash and finds Blanche tied and gagged and starving upstairs.

Evil Powers: Baby is a regressed psychotic and her cruelty is unbounded. Her jealousy makes her starve her sister. She has use of Blanche's money and no one knows what's going on.

Occupation: Faded child star.

Intelligence: Mind of a child—but vengefully clever.

Strengths: Her ability to forge signatures and sound like Blanche on the telephone.

Weaknesses: She's a baby.

Idiosyncrasies : Thinks she can make a comeback as a child star.

Friends: Blanche—in a way.

Enemies: The housekeeper, Buono.

Evil Deeds: Hammers down Madie, the housekeeper, and tortures, starves, and makes her Sis watch reruns of Baby Jane flicks. Kills her sister.

Bette Davis plays Baby Jane, an aged child actress who has created a world of insanity for herself and her sister.

Killed by: Buono backs away saying, "Oh God," and Baby cannot stop him from escaping. He will tell the authorities. Baby loads her sister into the old roadster and takes off for the seashore. The woman is near death. Filthy and emaciated, she is forced to listen to Baby babble about her comeback. Baby spends the whole night on the beach with Blanche. Blanche is dying and tells Baby the truth about the accident that crippled her. Blanche had sent Baby out to open the gate and tried to run her down. Baby had staggered to the side and the car hit the gate so hard that Blanche, the driver, was severely injured. She was a monster, and had made Baby feel guilty all these years, driving her mad. Baby covers her ears like a child, then she relaxes and says "Do you mean all this time we could have been friends?" She goes off in the morning to buy them ice cream cones. A crowd gathers to look at the weird Baby and her little dance steps. The police arrive and break through the crowd to find Blanche's body spread out on the sand.

Current Status: Institutionalized, singing "I wrote a letter to daadddyyyyy."

What to Do If You Meet: Give her a lollipop and she'll be your friend.

Worthy of Note: After a long hiatus, Bette was a box office hit again.

Bataiatus

Born: 100 B.C.
Died: 72 B.C.

Starred in:
Spartacus
Universal-International, 1960
Director: Stanley Kubrick
Played by: Peter Ustinov

Description: Piggy, always with something in his mouth. Ingratiating, sycophantic hedonist with avaricious, eager eyes. He wears a white embroidered toga and sandals, sometimes a laurel sprig around his fat head and curly dark hair. His fat fingers have some chicken grease on them. He's the eternal exploiter, incarnate.

Reason for Villainy: Bataiatus is the owner of a gladiator training camp and exhibition stadium outside of Rome. For a sum, he has his best gladiators put on a display. For larger sums, he has them fight to the death. He sells the gladiator-slaves, and carefully controls them and has the best trainers for them. The venal slave dealer had spotted Spartacus (Kirk Douglas), a road-construction slave, at work. He has a keen eye for talent and takes him to be trained. The training is intense and comprehensive. The gladiators are strong and good fighters. Occasionally, women-slaves are thrown into the cell of a good gladiator as a reward. Spartacus gets such a treat, but doesn't take "advantage" of her. It's love at first sight. The woman-slave, young Varinia (Jean Simmons), is sold to a fat Roman politician but escapes. Spartacus begins organizing the slaves. In a fight to the death for Bataiatus's fortune with Draba (Woody Strode) there is a revolt. The spectator Crassus (Laurence Olivier) almost gets killed by Draba. The gladiator slaves go into rebellion, and Bataiatus's camp is empty.

Evil Powers: Uses slave against slave. The 'state' condones him.

Occupation: Professional slave-trainer, exhibitor, salesperson.

Draba gives Spartacus a hard time in Bataiatus's gladiator pit.

Intelligence: Clever in negotiations, hasn't read Hellenic texts.

Strengths: He's good at driving a bargain.

Weaknesses: He underestimates the slaves he owns.

Territory: Rome area. Capua in particular.

Idiosyncrasies: Taste for the ladies.

Friends: The powerful rich who purchase slaves.

Enemies: Spartacus.

Evil Deeds: The whole system of slavery is sick. He is its outstanding proponent and a profiteer on human flesh.

Outcome: Well, the slave rebellion gets out of hand. Spartacus is joined by defectors from many estates, including that of Crassus, whose handsome, lute-playing, servant boy, Antoninus (Tony Curtis), is one of the first nongladiator slaves to join. But where is Varinia? Here she comes, telling Spartacus how she just ran away and the fat fool couldn't catch her. Based on a real revolt in 73 B.C., the action goes on. Only the Roman legions can save the estates and the system. They do. Spartacus is nailed to a cross. Thousands are crucified along the roads as a warning to other slaves. But Varinia is pregnant, gives birth, shows the free baby to Spartacus as he hangs there dying. Fade to black. And what happened to Bataiatus? Oh, some of the slaves made their former masters fight to the death for their amusement. Evidently, he was among the fat losers!

Bataiatus shows his slaves who's the boss in Spartacus.

Current Status: Dead.

What to Do If You Meet: Look weak.

Worthy of Note: True adventure—Kirk Douglas style.

Martha Beck

Born: 1940s
Died: Still alive, in jail

Starred in:
The Honeymoon Killers
Cinerama Releasing, 1970
Director: Leonard Kastle
Played by: Shirley Stoler

Description: Huge, 200-pound creature, who likes to wear bathrobes and underwear around the house.

Reason for Villainy: Martha is a lonely head nurse living with her senile mother. She joins a correspondence club and begins exchanging letters with Ray Fernandez, a Spaniard from New York. She falls in love with him and he comes to visit her. He sleeps with her, gets her to give him some of her money, and then leaves town. Not being able to stand losing this handsome man who had given her such sexual pleasure, Martha follows Ray to New York where she joins him in his livelihood of swindling lonely old women.

Evil Powers: Willing to commit any act, even murder to get her man.

Weapons: Pills, hammer.

Occupation: Head nurse, swindler, murderer.

Intelligence: Moderate intelligence, but insanely jealous of Ray.

Strengths: Strong, smart, ruthless.

Weaknesses: Sex, the prospect of love from Ray.

Territory: Mobile, Alabama; New York City.

Idiosyncrasies: Can't keep her hands off Ray.

Martha Beck, one of the Honeymoon Killers, uses her lethal hammer.

Friends: Ray.

Enemies: Ray's victims.

Evil Deeds: Kills several people. Helps Ray rip off lonely women.

Outcome: The lovebirds, Ray and Martha, fleece Doris and head for Arkansas, where Ray begins to pay too much attention to Myrtle. Martha poisons her with lethal doses of sleeping pills. Then she kills Janet, Ray's next wife, with a hammer. Ray and Martha next hop to Grand Rapids, Michigan, where Ray becomes engaged to Delphine Downing, who has a young daughter. Martha finds out that Ray slept with Delphine and gives her pills, putting her in a daze. Ray returns and finishes the woman off by strangling her and then drowns her daughter in a washing machine. Realizing Ray will never be faithful to her, Martha turns them both in to the police. In jail, they begin writing love letters to one another again.

Current Status: In prison for murder.

What to Do If You Meet: If you seduce him, don't get her jealous.

Worthy of Note: Shirley Stoler later appeared as a Nazi commandant in Lina Wertmuller's *Seven Beauties.*

The Bey Officer

Born: 1880s
Died: Presumably in the 1920s

Starred in:
Lawrence of Arabia
Columbia Pictures, 1962
Director: David Lean
Played by: Jose Ferrer

Description: The Bey Officer has an oily complexion. He walks about with a swagger stick in his hands. He taunts and sneers. He is constantly building up his own importance in the scheme of things. He does this by intimidating prisoners. He is fond of torturing the captured Arabs.

Sex: Male (but . . .).

Reason for Villainy: The Bey is a petty official of the Turkish army in Arabia. Though most Turks are honorable, hard fighters, who ask for and give no quarter, this officer is sick. He is not met in this film for some time, however, so let us summarize the plot before he appears: It is 1916 and Lieutenant Lawrence (Peter O'Toole) is serving as a clerk in the Cairo office of the British Empire. He loves the desert and the Arab way of life. This comes to the attention of the high command, particularly the head of the Arab Bureau (Claude Rains). Lawrence is sent to King Feisal (Alec Guinness) to further the British cause among the Arabs, who hate the Turks. In the desert, his riding companion, an Arab guide, is shot down as he drinks from another tribe's well. Later, the gunslinger befriends the Englishman—it is their only way to defend their well. The new friend, Sheriff Ali (Omar

Sharif), helps the uncannily astute Lawrence unite the Arab tribes. Lawrence is a fabulous organizer and fighter. He is superbly brave and the Arabs call him El Orrence and follow him zealously. He is unstoppable, and the Arabs, without much British back-up, take the important city of Aqaba. But Lawrence is captured and finds himself brought before The Bey Officer, who "likes" pale young men. He has Lawrence flogged mercilessly and then does much worse to him. Lawrence is changed by all of this, and is sadistic to all he opposes.

Evil Powers: Absolute power over life and death for prisoners.

Occupation: Interrogator of prisoners.

Intelligence: Dumb—he thinks the Englishman is a blue-eyed Arab.

Strengths: He has absolute sway over prisoners.

Weaknesses: The prisoner is the brave Lawrence.

Territory: The Middle East.

Idiosyncrasies : "Likes" fair-haired, pale young men.

Friends: The fellow officers who allow this to happen.

The cruel Bey Officer doesn't know he's got Lawrence of Arabia at his whip-tip. Lawrence, when released, will hold quite a grudge.

Enemies: The Arabs, Lawrence.

Evil Deeds: Does unspeakable things to Lawrence after having him flogged.

Outcome: The Bey Officer is stupid. He doesn't realize who Lawrence is, and eventually has him thrown out in the mud of the streets where he had been first picked up for questioning. Had The Bey Officer known who he had in his custody, he would have been a hero. As it is, the swaggering fool made a great enemy for his people, much greater and more sadistic than before. Lawrence and the Arabs go on to win, killing all prisoners on his orders. The Turks lose and the English and Arabs have an uneasy peace. Lawrence returns to England and dies in a motorcycle accident. His funeral is immense.

Current Status: Probably died in an Arab attack later on—though not shown.

What to Do If You Meet: Get a suntan first.

Worthy of Note: Superb! One of the most acclaimed films of all time and rightly so. The perfect adventure film. It won Academy Awards for Best Picture, Best Director, and Best Cinematography.

Colonel Nikita I. Biroshilov

Born: 1900s
Died: Still alive

Starred in:
Prisoner of War
MGM, 1954
Director: Andrew Marton
Played by: Oscar Homolka

Description: He's a mean Russian officer in Korea, advising the evil Commie enemy on ways of extreme torture and brainwashing that can rob men of their sanity and souls. Tall, hefty, sneering monster from the iron land of Stalin. This beast is all that we fear—intelligent, cunning, cruel, and an atheist to boot.

Colonel Biroshilov, (Oscar Homolka), tortures his prisoner of War.

Reason for Villainy: The Colonel is in charge of brainwashing the Americans that have been captured during the Korean War. Captain Web Sloane (Ronald Reagan) is all that an American officer should be—big, brave, and spirited. In a documentary approach, this film chronicles the attempts of the Red menace to program our heroes into automatons. We see the death march north, the Pavlovian brainwashing, and the appendectomies without anesthesia to recalcitrant GIs. Naturally some of our guys' inner stuff gives out and they sign confessions of war atrocities for the slimy reds. Sloane feigns acceptance of the Communist line and plays along. He's an intelligent intelligence officer who volunteered for this hell to better equip our guys for the rigors of the Red rape of the mind.

Evil Power/Weapons: Cold, heat, knives, psychological torture, turning one against another, probing for weaknesses, starvation, hopelessness, the works.

Occupation: Torturer—the Red kind.

Intelligence: Memorizes Lenin and denies he has heard of Trotsky.

Strengths: He's well up in the ranks.

Weaknesses: He's shallow like all atheistic Reds.

Territory: North Korea and Moscow.

Idiosyncrasies: Vacations in Siberia.

Friends: The Red menace.

Enemies: Sloane and the GIs.

Relatives: Ivan the Terrible.

Evil Deeds: Torture and cheating at cards.

Outcome: The Red officer gets his from the bullets of loyal Americans. Sloane's triumph over psychological and physical torture will go down in the record books.

Current Status: Korean dogfood.

What to Do If You Meet: Don't mention Trotsky.

Worthy of Note: Prime Red-scare movie.

Black Tiger

Born: 1909
Died: 1940

Starred in:
The Shadow
Columbia Pictures, 1940
Director: James W. Horne
Played by: J. Paul Jones

Description: The Tiger is a slouch-hatted villain of the gangster era. Yet, no one outside of his own gang has seen his face and lived. We will know that he looks like Stanford Marshall, a gray-templed industrialist, because that is who he really is!

Reason for Villainy: Airplanes crash, railroads are wrecked—sound familiar? No part of the vast nation is safe from the clawing hand of the Tiger. Yet there is hope. The Shadow (Victor Jory) is on the prowl. He knows what evil lurks in the hearts of men. Yes, he does. He's everywhere—that's why he's the Shadow. He'll get the Tiger by the tail.

Who knows what evil lurks in the hearts of men? The Shadow Knows.

The police under Commissioner Weston (Frank La Rue) make arrests but the Shadow is needed to crack the case. Lamont Cranston, master criminologist and scientist, is the Shadow. He also disguises himself as Lin Chang, a merchant. The Black Tiger is stealing vast quantities of chemicals and electrical stuff for his evil aims. What are they? The Shadow knows. The "Chinese merchant" infiltrates the gang and finds the secret hideout—sound familiar? The Black Tiger is trapped, and it turns out to be millionaire industrialist Stanford Marshall, attempting to perfect a death ray and rule the nation. Marshall fights free, however. Will he escape? The Shadow knows.

Evil Powers/Weapons: Axes, bombs, electricity, goons, guns, anonymity.

Occupation: Scientist, industrialist, criminal.

Intelligence: Well read.

Strengths: He's got money and goons.

Weaknesses: The Shadow knows.

Territory: The City.

Idiosyncracies: Hangs around warehouses.

Friends: His gang and his mother, Tigermamma.

Enemies: The Shadow.

Evil Deeds: Kills a lot of innocent people in his quest for power.

Outcome: The Shadow chases the escaping madman through the vast warehouse. The evil man is deft, runs like a cat, like a Tiger as a matter of fact. But he falls against an electrical control panel and is electrocuted. A sparkling end to a charming evening. The Shadow slips into the shadows, laughing madly. Silly, but who *does* steal all that electrical stuff?

Current Status: Full of current.

What to Do If You Meet: Bring marshmallows.

Worthy of Note: This was also a popular radio show—and better when you used your imagination to visualize it. Still, great Saturday matinee kid stuff.

Captain Bligh

Born: 1750s
Died: Still alive . . . maybe

Starred in:
Mutiny on the Bounty
MGM, 1935
Director: Frank Lloyd
Played by: Charles Laughton

Description: Middle-aged captain of His Majesty's Ship *Bounty*. He is dressed appropriately, sometimes wearing a tricorner hat, frilly shirt. Carries a one-shot flint pistol. His hair is long and brown, pulled back into a ponytail, as is the custom. He slouches, waddles a bit when he walks. He is a tough, hard-bitten character, cruel and arbitrary to his crew, expecting hard work and no fun.

Reason for Villainy: The *Bounty* is on a voyage to bring back breadfruit and other plants from the South Seas. The crew dislikes Bligh, but likes masters mate Fletcher Christian (Clark Gable). Bligh goads Christian, and he makes midshipman Roger Byam (Franchot Tone) sick with his cruelties. Half rations for the crew means more money in Bligh's pocket. He is a crook. Tahiti is sighted. Christian goes ashore and Hitihiti, the native chief, likes the young stranger. Christian spends some time with Tehani (Movita), a gorgeous Tahitian girl, then falls in love with the chief's granddaughter, Miamiti (Mamo). The time for the ship to depart arrives. The sailors are distressed. Here is paradise—the ship is hell. Five crew members slip away. They are flogged when caught. The old ship's surgeon, forced to watch this brutality, dies. The crew turns against the Captain. Bligh is charged with murder and set adrift. Christian takes the ship back to Tahiti and all is well for several months. No one knows if evil Captain Bligh is even alive.

Evil Powers: The Captain is super commander at sea. Mutiny means death to the mutineers when they are brought to justice—unless. . . .

Occupation: Captain H.M.S. *Bounty*.

Intelligence: Rule book sort of mind, still he cheats.

Strengths: He's captain.

Weaknesses: He's a thief of Crown property.

Territory: The South Pacific.

Idiosyncrasies: Cruelty.

Friends: Supposedly Byam, until he can take no more.

Enemies: Christian.

Evil Deeds: Floggings, throwing sailors in the brig, limiting shore leave, cutting rations to steal for himself.

Outcome: Bligh indeed has gotten to safety. One night the British frigate *Pandora* arrives at Tahiti with Bligh. Christian and his men flee on the *Bounty*. They bring their girls. Byam, figuring he really had no part in the whole thing, stays. But Byam is clapped in irons. The *Pandora*, taking off after the *Bounty*, is wrecked on a reef. The crew is rescued and taken to England. Christian and his men land on Pitcairn Island, the *Bounty* is burned. They will go native. Byam, in England, stands trial. But the trial is fair, Bligh is exposed and Byam goes free. He rejoins the Navy.

Current Status: Alive at the end of film, in disfavor with the King.

Captain Bligh (Charles Laughton) tries to prevent a Mutiny on the Bounty *with chains.*

What to Do If You Meet: Go ashore and stay there.

Worthy of Note: Remade in 1962 with Marlon Brando as Christian. The myth of getting away from it all is what's appealing in the story.

Ernst Stavro Blofeld

Born: 1928
Died: 1969

Starred in:
On Her Majesty's Secret Service
United Artists, 1969
Director: Peter Hunt
Played by: Telly Savalas

Blofeld peeks through a curtain of beads and sees Bond, who's On Her Majesty's Secret Service.

Description: Blofeld is bald, wears a pea jacket, sometimes carries a pistol with a silencer. Long nose, arched eyebrows make him a stern-looking villain. He is an allergist, a world-famous doctor. Sometimes he wears a doctor's white outfit. He is often surrounded by beautiful, rich women patients from all over the world.

Reason for Villainy: Blofeld is head of SPECTRE, a secret multi-national criminal conspiracy. His plan is to give all the brainwashed women in his Piz Gloria Swiss resort atomizers. They will return to their nations and spray deadly germs that will destroy all the world's crops. He will have the antidote—for a price. James Bond (George Lazenby), British secret agent, is on his case. But first Bond rescues beautiful Tracy (Diana Rigg) from goons on the beach. She is the daughter of Marc Ange Draco (Gabrielle Ferzetti), a Corsican criminal who opposes Blofeld. With Draco's help, Bond, using a super device, opens Blofeld's safe easily and gets his plans. Exposed, Bond is trapped in the wheelhouse of a cable car high on the mountain retreat. He

crawls out and onto the cable. He jumps to the approaching cable car and is again free at the mad Blofeld's resort. Donning skis, he leads Blofeld's mad machine gun army on an incredible daredevil ski chase through the Alps. One by one they are wiped out. He survives to meet Tracy. Blofeld, however, is still on the loose.

Evil Powers/Weapons: Millions of dollars, secret germs, beautiful women.

Intelligence: Super genius. Can cure allergies like *that*.

Strengths: His mountain retreat is nearly impregnable.

Weaknesses: 007 is on to him.

Headquarters: Piz Gloria—a Swiss Mountain retreat.

Idiosyncrasies: Big plans.

Friends: His snow troops.

Enemies: Bond.

Evil Deeds: Plans to destroy the world's food. If that isn't enough, as a SPECTRE mastermind he's destroyed rockets, sunk ships, etc.

Outcome: Draco's helicopters—disguised as Red Cross rescue squads—blast the heck out of the resort. Bond and Tracy escape in their red sports car into a speedy car rally. The drivers find themselves outclassed by Bond, and by the madman's Mercedes which is chasing them. Bond survives, Blofeld's Mercedes rolls over and explodes. The carnage is terrific.

Current Status: Dead. Burned beyond recognition.

What to Do If You Meet: His type will always be with us. Call Bond.

Worthy of Note: How many Bonds will there be before this series is over? Lazenby? You must be kidding! The ski sequences make this film.

Bonnie and Clyde

Born: 1900s
Died: Gunned down 1930s

Starred in:
Bonnie and Clyde
Warner Bros.–Seven Arts, 1967
Director: Arthur Penn
Played by: Faye Dunaway and Warren
   Beatty

Description: They like to dress well for their bank robberies, etc. She in a tight-fitting sweater, he in a dapper pinstripe suit and snap brim hat. You would think that they would try out for fashion pages.

Reason for Villainy: We rob banks, states the pair. That is true. Together with Clyde's grim brother, Buck (Gene Hackman), and rube, C.W. Moss (Michael J. Pollard), who they pick up on their travels, the pair tear through the Depression-ravaged Southwest plundering and plugging. At first Bonnie and Clyde are more interested in violence and money, but as their sexual relationship takes off with gusto, they drop their desire to kill— the message? Alas, they have sown the wild oats of lead that they now must reap. The

Bonnie and Clyde are sure to die for the pair is being trailed by the FBI.

police are hot on their trail, often pulling up to motels and houses that the pair and their cronies have vacated moments before.

Weapons: The pair sport sub-machine guns, pistols.

Occupation: They rob banks.

Intelligence: Clever, fast, but not bright.

Strengths: Their weapons.

Weaknesses: The law won't rest until it eliminates them.

Territory: The Depression-era Southwest U.S.A.

Idiosyncrasies: She writes him crude love poems. He goes *shucks* a lot.

Friends: Brother Buck, C.W. Moss.

Enemies: The law.

Evil Deeds: If robbing banks wasn't enough, the pair and their buddies kill a few tellers, guards, and cops in the process, as well as some people walking by. Shame on them.

Killed by: Finally, the police have them, and this time they intend to kill them. The cops plunge in on Bonnie as she waits for loverboy to return with some milk. They open up mercilessly with sub-Thompsons as the pair and their remaining friends grab mattresses as shields and blast back. The carnage is unbelievable, and the motel court is filled with spinning bullets. One by one they fall. Fate closes in and Bonnie, Clyde, and C.W. are trapped in a field after their car is riddled with thousands of bullets. The death scene is graphically presented in slow-motion and freeze-frame camera work. Moral: Don't break the law, because it can get mean. All through the film we got the idea that the pair was somehow admirable in their amiable insanity, now comes the come-uppance.

Current Status: Dead, but stylish models for today's hip killers.

What to Do If You Meet: This kind is best not met.

Worthy of Note: Some of action in the film was borrowed—performed by Dillinger in real life. Bonnie and Clyde were actually country bumpkin killers without much class.

Martha, Abby, and Jonathan Brewster

Born: 1900s
Died: Happily committed to an asylum 1944

Starred in:
Arsenic and Old Lace
Warner Bros., 1944
Director: Frank Capra
Played by: Josephine Hull, Jean Adair, Raymond Massey

Description: The ladies are old spinster types, with shawls and stooped-over postures. Jonathan looks like Karloff. They are all smiles and very friendly.

Reason for Villainy: Insanity runs in the family, real, stark-naked insanity. It isn't discovered until Mortimer Brewster visits his zany aunts with the news of his marriage. Mortimer (Cary Grant) is aghast when he finds a dead body in his aunt's window seat. Together, Martha and Abby have helped 12 elderly, lonely gentlemen to their graves with their strychnine-laced elderberry wine. Teddy (John Alexander), who is Mortimer's younger

The Brewsters gather together in their Brooklyn home in Frank Capra's Arsenic and Old Lace.

brother, thinks he's Teddy Roosevelt, and buries the "yellow fever" victims in the "Panama Canal Zone" (the cellar) for his aunts. Mortimer fears for his own sanity. Meanwhile, Mortimer's insane older brother, Jonathan, arrives with the crazed doctor Einstein (Peter Lorre). Jonathan is a mass murderer and brings his twelfth victim home. He is angry that he no longer holds the record for murders in the family. To get back in first place, he ties up Mortimer, who is a drama critic, and plans to slowly torture him to death. But dumb cop O'Hara (Jack Carson) arrives and uses Mortimer's "tied up" situation to read him a horribly boring play he has written. Smarter cops eventually arrive and arrest Jonathan, but they don't believe Mortimer's story about all the killings.

Weapons: The old ladies use poisoned wine, and Jonathan uses the "Melborne Method" of slow death on his victims.

Occupation: Killers.

Intelligence: Really clever, but insane.

Strengths: The old ladies use subterfuge, while Jonathan uses changes in his face courtesy of plastic surgeon Einstein, and the "Melborne Method."

Weaknesses: They keep killing—sooner or later one gets caught!

Territory: Brooklyn, of course.

Idiosyncrasies: The old ladies care for their insane nephew, Teddy, but they kill all other guests; Jonathan likes to kill too, along with sidekick Doc.

Friends: The old ladies are so kind that everyone is their friend; however, Jonathan only has the mad doctor.

Enemies: The police and Mortimer.

Relatives: Norman Bates.

Evil Deeds: Twenty-four murders between the three of them.

Outcome: The police see to it that both Teddy and Jonathan are put in the asylum. However, nobody can convince the cops that Martha and Abby did any harm. To everyone's surprise, however, the two old ladies decide to accompany Teddy on his "safari" to the "happy" house. Doc Einstein signs their commitment papers and slips away just as the cops find out he's involved in all this lunacy. Meanwhile, Mortimer is convinced he'll go insane just like his family. Happily, he soon

discovers that he's really the son of an errant sea cook and not related to the Brewster side of the family.

Current Status: Cutting out paper victims at the "happy" house.

What to Do If You Meet: Call the cops, and don't drink elderberry wine.

Worthy of Note: Boris Karloff played Jonathan in the original Broadway stage production.

Buzz and the Gang

Alias: The chicken-racers
Born: 1940s
Died: 1955 (Buzz)

Starred in:
Rebel Without a Cause
Warner Bros., 1955
Director: Nicholas Ray
Played by: Corey Allen

Description: Buzz is a teen punk with a D.A. (duck's ass) haircut and his collar up. He's spoiled, surly, callow, insolent. He sneers and combs his hair a lot.

Reason for Villainy: On the first day at his new school (his well-to-do parents just moved to this town), Jim (James Dean) tries to pick up cute Judy (Natalie Wood). Judy is in with the school's tough crowd, run by drag race champ Buzz. She is Buzz's girl and Buzz doesn't take well to the newcomer. Buzz and Jim get into a switchblade fight and that ends inconclusively. Jim, being alienated, meets Plato (Sal Mineo), another disaffected youth. Plato and Jim become friends. Buzz, to prove once again he's not chicken (cowardly), challenges Jim to a chicken race. Chicken is played by driving stolen cars at each other as fast as possible; the first guy to swerve is chicken. Buzz is chickened-out by Jim, has no time to swerve, and goes off the cliff. The whole mob runs from the arriving cops. Jim, Plato, and Judy then break into a large house and wander

James Dean, the Rebel Without a Cause, gets a slap from Buzz (Corey Allen) as the kids look on.

around feeling empty and useless. Finally, Plato is picked off by a cop's sniper bullet.

Evil Powers: Buzz is so intent on being head honcho at the high school that he will do anything, including die, to not look chicken.

Weapons: His car is a lethal weapon.

Occupation: Teen degenerate.

Intelligence: Below average, especially in geometry.

Strengths: He's a tough guy. Good with a blade and with a car.

Weaknesses: His souped-up ego.

Territory: Smalltown, U.S.A., in the juvenile delinquent era (1950s).

Idiosyncrasies: Wears a leather jacket with the collar up to formals.

Friends: Carburetors, hot chicks.

Enemies: Jim, society, himself.

Relatives: Elvis in *Loving You.*

Evil Deeds: Vandalism, hooliganism, car theft, speeding, disrespect for elders.

Killed by: Buzz was killed by wrecking his car. He died a victim of the alienation of America's youth in the 1950s. There was a scene in this movie that summed up the angst and ennui the youth of this era shared. The youths watch a planetarium display of the sky—well, it's all so big, Daddy-O, and we are all so small. We are nothing. Our parents' values are stupid and worth nothing. So Buzz, being a nothing, throws away his life to prove nothing. After Plato is killed for no good reason, Judy and Jim are taken away by the cops. They are nothings also. They mean nothing to themselves. What is happening to our youth? Middle-class kids who have everything to live for according to their parents are throwing their lives away. For nothing.

Current Status: Dead.

What to Do If You Meet: Youth must be given a reason to behave. Offer him a carburetor with fuel injection and he'll put his switchblade away.

Worthy of Note: Naturally, this film made Dean a superstar and every kid in the U.S.A. wanted to be a zero like him.

Peter Cable   39
Max Cady   39
Cal   40
Dr. Caligari   42
Calvera   43
Captain James
  and Hector   44
Lily Carver   45
Coral Chandler   46
Sir Charles   47
Charlie   48
Alain Charnier   49
Chauvelin   50
Nick Cherney   51
The Clanton
  Gang   52

The Clegg Family   54
Terry Collins   55
Michael Corleone   56
Cottonmouth   57
Joan Crawford   58
Leslie Crosbie   59
Noah Cross   60

Peter Cable

Alias: The Sadist
Born: 1930s
Died: 1971

Starred in:
Klute
Warner Bros., 1971
Director: Alan J. Pakula
Played by: Charles Cioffi

Killer and prostitute (Jane Fonda) grapple in Klute.

Description: Male sadist murderer. Handsome, distinguished-looking. Wears a suit.
Reason for Villainy: Cable kills research scientist Tom Gruneman, who has uncovered his perverted habit of beating and hurting prostitutes. Detective John Klute (Donald Sutherland), who was Gruneman's friend, tries to track down the killer.
Evil Powers: Pervert, sadist. Whips, punches, loves inflicting pain.
Weapons: Guns, fists.
Occupation: Research scientist.
Intelligence: Highly intelligent, but twisted.
Strengths: In control of things. Good liar,
Weaknesses: Perversion leads him to commit acts which do him in.
Territory: New York.
Idiosyncrasies: Loves to cause pain. It gives him sexual excitement.
Friends: Pretended to have been Gruneman's friend.
Enemies: Klute, Bree.
Evil Deeds: Whips, tortures, murders.
Killed by: Klute gets on the trail of the murderer. He meets Bree, a prostitute, and the two slowly fall in love. Bree has been receiving dirty letters and phone calls, possibly from one of her past clients. As a prostitute she has done some pretty strange things. Klute reanalyzes one letter, supposedly from Gruneman, and discovers that it's actually from Cable's typewriter. Bree gets a terrifying call from the pervert who has been after her and flees to the offices of one of her clients,

Mr. Goldfarb. She is cornered by Cable, who tries to kill her, but Klute arrives in the nick of time. In a struggle, Cable falls through the window to his death.
Current Status: Dead.
What to Do If You Meet: Don't let him whip you.
Worthy of Note: Jane Fonda won an Oscar for her portrayal of Bree.

Max Cady

Born: 1920s
Died: 1962

Starred in:
Cape Fear
Universal International, 1962
Director: J. Lee Thompson
Played by: Robert Mitchum

Description: Dapperly dressed in a white Panama hat, white clothes suitable to Southern climates. Tall, dark hair, charming—like the Devil.

Max Cady (Robert Mitchum) won't leave Sam's family alone in Cape Fear.

Reason for Villainy: Max Cady had been in jail for a long time, thanks to prosecuting lawyer Sam Bowden (Gregory Peck). Bowden lives in a small Southern town with his wife and young daughter. Cady comes back to seek revenge on them all. Bowden is threatened obliquely by Cady. He terrorizes the family, follows the child Nancy (Lori Martin) until she panics. Cady is seen everywhere the Bowdens go. Sam goes to the law but their hands are tied unless Sam can come up with something concrete. Sam hires a private investigator, Dick Sievers (Telly Savalas), and Sievers finds out Cady is shacking up with a bar girl and abusing her. The cops raid the place with Sam but Cady has left the scene. What he did to the girl was so horrible that she refuses to testify in order to save her family grief. She then leaves town. Sam goes beyond the law and hires goons to beat Cady. But under a boardwalk, Cady wipes out his attackers. He now has a case against Sam. He's going to get Sam disbarred and arrested.

Evil Powers: Psychotic revenge motive drives him. He's strong as a bull and slippery as a snake.

Weapons: Guns and terror.

Occupation: Sadistic ex-con, criminal, woman beater.

Intelligence: Clever as hell.

Strengths: The guy knows the law and its limits inside out.

Weaknesses: He thinks that his prey will not be as vicious.

Territory: Cape Fear, a small town in the South. The swamps.

Idiosyncrasies: Smooth talk, refuses money to stop the madness.

Friends: Lax justice.

Enemies: Sam and his wife and daughter, Sievers, ultimate justice.

Relatives: The Scorpio Killer.

Evil Deeds: Terrorizes Sam's wife, Peggy (Polly Bergen), and little Nancy. He does unspeakable things to women. Flaunts the law, uses it to protect his criminal activity. Murder.

Killed by: Sam hides his family in a swampland cottage, knowing that Cady will come there. Sam pretends to board a flight to Miami and secretly doubles back. Using his family as bait is the only way. When Cady shows up he kills an officer helping Sam protect his wife and daughter. Sam appears and a struggle ensues. Cady soon has Sam at his mercy. Cady tells Sam what his plans are for the daughter and wife and what he's going to do to him. The two begin to fight in the mud and slime of the swamp and the law comes to get Cady. They have him dead to rights now. Finally.

Current Status: Executed after a brief trial.

What to Do If You Meet: Say "Hi" and leave town. If he follows you, hire some extra tough goons to stop him.

Worthy of Note: Gripping drama, tension builds and builds, as does a sense of outrage.

Cal

Born: 1950s
Died: Jailed 1980s

Starred in:
Resurrection
Universal, 1980
Director: Daniel Petrie
Played by: Sam Shepard

Description: Cal is a lanky, good-looking farmboy who has straight black hair, crude but

Cal (Sam Shepard) comes to believe he's sleeping with someone literally divine, the result of a Resurrection. He'll shoot her, and if she lives, maybe she is.

effective manners, a seductive grin, and a passionate nature. Sometimes he acts confused.

Reason for Villainy: Cal is a person that really doesn't believe too much in religious hocus pocus. However, Edna (Ellen Burstyn) has died and literally been awakened from death after several minutes of being beyond it all. You see, Edna had a terrible car crash and only today's incredible medical machinery pulled her back. Well, Edna, who was just an ordinary Christian before the accident that left her paralysed, is now able to lay her hands on herself and cure herself gradually. People flock to her for cures and some are indeed cured. It all is because of her contact with the unknown. She saw lights, beautiful lights, dead relatives beckoning, heavenly music—but she was brought back to life. "What about Jesus?" asks some religious farmer. She didn't see him, but nothing that happened denies he's real, she replies. They say she'd better make sure she is not fooling around with Devil stuff. Here's where Cal comes in. He's a Bible reader and he's also on the make for Edna. They have a normal sexual relationship, but he gradually becomes convinced she's the Lord or somebody like that. In a twisted way he struggles with her, demanding that she reveal herself. She insists she is just an average person.

Evil Powers: Cal has a Bible and a gun. The Bible is heavily underlined and leads him to misinterpret his mission in life.

Occupation: Ne'er-do-well, farmworker, truck driver.

Intelligence: Cal ain't too bright.

Strengths: He's not a bad shot.

Weaknesses: He drinks and thinks he's on to some secret of the Bible.

Territory: Farmtown of the Western U.S.

Idiosyncrasies: Cal is crazy, period.

Friends: Edna.

Enemies: Edna.

Evil Deeds: Up until now, he's just busted up a few bars.

Killed by: Well, it all comes to a head. Edna is having her tent meetings and curing people. Sometimes she takes on the symptoms of the person, then throws them off. It's tiring work and she doesn't do it for profit. People don't know what to make of her, but she makes sure to attribute all her work to the Lord so that the people are of the opinion that her cures are all right. Cal has split from Edna, refusing to believe she's quite human. He's been hitting the Good Book and probably the bad bottle, too. He gets his big old pistol and decides to shoot Edna. He has the twisted idea that she will have to reveal herself—if she doesn't die. Or something like that. He comes tearing down the road trailing smoked rubber, jumps up with a gun as Edna is doing her thing and blasts her. Well, she's wounded all right—she's human. She manages over the next few weeks to get well mighty fast though. What did he prove? That he can get himself in a lot of trouble.

Current Status: Undergoing psychiatric treatment.

What to Do If You Meet: Keep it platonic.

Worthy of Note: Jeez, this is a good movie. Kinda profound you know? It isn't preachy, nor is it a condemnation of tent mysticism. It's really great, honest. It makes one think that we're only here for just a short time and what's really beyond?

Dr. Caligari

Alias: The "Director"
Born: Late 19th century
Died: Unknown

Starred in:
The Cabinet of Dr. Caligari
Decla-Film-Ges, 1919
Director: Robert Wiene
Played by: Werner Krauss

Description: Vicious, mad, cantankerous old man, with stringy white hair. Wears black coat and cape, large black tophat, spectacles balanced low on nose, and carries a walking stick.

Reason for Villainy: Insane director of an insane asylum who believes he is (or may be) the famous hypnotist of the 18th century—Caligari. Francis and Alan (both in love with Jane) visit a carnival whose top attraction is Dr. Caligari, who presents an eerie perfor-

Dr. Caligari raises Cesare from his coffin to give him some food in The Cabinet of Dr. Caligari.

mance with his zombie slave Cesare. He also tells fortunes and tells Alan he has only until morning to live. The next day, Francis discovers that Alan has been killed. Soon people are being killed all over the place and Francis is sure that Caligari is behind it.

Evil Powers/Weapons: Hypnotist, magician, zombie master, murderer. Uses Cesare to kill.

Occupation: Carnival performer, head of asylum.

Intelligence: Extremely intelligent, perceptive, understands the human mind and can manipulate others easily.

Strengths: Powers of the insane.

Weaknesses: Loses self in own fantasy world.

Territory: North Germany.

Idiosyncrasies: Mean, mumbles.

Friends: Cesare.

Enemies: Humanity.

Relatives: The White Zombie.

Evil Deeds: Has killed or caused scores of innocent people to be killed through the years. Kidnapper, uses power of asylum directorship to further evil ends and to experiment on inmates.

Killed by: Caligari sends his zombie to kidnap Jane, but she screams and her father (a doctor) rushes in. Cesare drops dead from the effort. Francis confronts Caligari but the master criminal escapes to the asylum. Francis follows him and discovers that the real Caligari was an 18th-century hypnotist and Cesare his subject. The "Director" has gone insane and taken Caligari's place. Francis confronts the "Director" with Cesare's body and the "Director" confesses and is led away by police.

Current Status: In the film's last scene, the viewer discovers that Francis has been telling the whole story to an inmate of the asylum where he himself is an inmate. The "Director" (Caligari) says that the cause of Francis's madness is that he believes that the "Director" is Caligari. Who is insane and who isn't?

What to Do If You Meet: Don't visit insane asylums.

Worthy of Note: One of the most famous of all horror/fantasy films. The use of bizarre settings created a truly nightmarish atmosphere.

Calvera

Alias: The Bandit
Born: Mid 19th century
Died: Turn of the 20th century

Starred in:
The Magnificent Seven
United Artists, 1960
Director: John Sturges
Played by: Eli Wallach

Description: Cruel, constantly laughing, then screaming. Mexican bandito, wears sombrero, goatee and mustache, fancy needlework jacket.

Reason for Villainy: Seven gunfighters are hired by a group of Mexican peasants from the small town of Ixcatlán to save them from the ravages of the ruthless Calvera, who annually comes to their village with his army of bandits and takes half their belongings and crops. The seven cowboys, led by Chris (Yul Brynner), are Vin (Steve McQueen), Chico (Horst Buchholz), O'Reilly (Charles Bronson), Lee (Robert Vaughn), Harry (Brad Dexter), and Britt (James Coburn). They all head down to Mexico to help.

Evil Powers: Controls evil band of killers who follow his bidding.

Weapons: Guns, intimidation of peasants, torture.

Occupation: Mexican bandito leader.

Intelligence: Quite intelligent, has commanding presence, powerful personality, knows how to use people to get what he wants.

Strengths: Unafraid.

Weaknesses: Fights the Magnificent Seven.

Territory: Ixcatlán, Mexico.

Idiosyncrasies: Likes to think he's not such a bad guy.

Friends: His own bandits.

Enemies: Hates the Magnificent Seven, although he does respect them.

Relatives: Goldhat *(Treasure of the Sierra Madre)*.

Evil Deeds: Plunder and rape all the small villages in this section of Mexico. Have killed hundreds of peasants who got in their way, razed whole towns.

Killed by: The bandits, under Calvera, attack the town. Three of them are killed and the rest retreat. The villagers decide to listen to the Magnificent Seven and learn how to defend themselves with guns and barricades. The enraged Calvera makes a major assault

Calvera (Eli Wallach) rides toward Ixcatlan with his banditos behind him ready to face The Magnificent Seven.

but is driven back. The villagers and the Seven think it's over, but Calvera sneaks back in. takes over the town, and captures the Seven. He releases them, feeling generous, but they are magnificent. A furious battle erupts in which Calvera and most of his men are killed, but so are Harry, Britt, and Lee. The remaining heroes ride off into the sunset. Ixcatlán is now free of terror.

Current Status: Dead, but Mexican bandits still roam those mountains.

What to Do If You Meet: Promise him anything! Tell him he's the meanest looking bandit you ever saw.

Worthy of Note: One of the most popular American westerns. Based on Kurosawa's *Seven Samurai.* An all-star cast in which almost every hero went on to become a superstar.

Captain James and Hector

Born: 200 years in the future
Died: Dismantled soon after

Starred in:
Saturn 3
Associated Film Distribution, 1980
Director: Stanley Donen
Played by: Harvey Keitel, and "Unknown"

Description: Hector is a shade under eight feet tall, shiny metal and various wires, sensing devices and gauges. Hand laser, superhuman strength and speed, somewhat human in shape. Captain James is a human space pilot. Definitely off the wall.

Reason for Villainy: Hector was performing correctly until crazed, psychotic space pilot Captain James (Harvey Keitel) arrived on the third moon of Saturn–Titan–and repro-

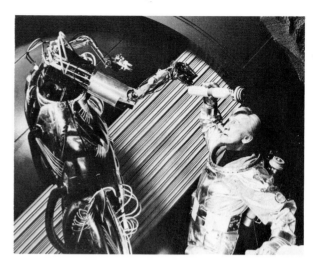

Hector, programmed by Captain James, attacks Kirk Douglas on Saturn 3.

grammed it. Now, during the 22-day eclipse of Titan by its mother planet Saturn, the darkness is penetrated by the evil presence of the robot. Hector was sent up by shuttle to help the researchers produce new foods for Earth's overpopulated continents. Now the robot terrorizes the veritable Garden of Eden that Alex (Farrah Fawcett-Majors) and Adam (Kirk Douglas) are working in. A vast lab shielded from the poisonous, volcanic surface of Titan becomes a hide-and-seek hell for the duo. Worse, the eclipse cuts all radio contact with any possible help. Earth is several astronomical units away anyway, but the space stations could do something, if they only could be called.

Evil Powers/Weapons: Hector can squeeze you with his pincer hands, crush you with his feet, laser you, phaser you, mazer you. It can chase you down.

Occupation: A normal helper robot specializing in food production technology.

Intelligence: Programmed with all pertinent data.

Strengths: It is superhuman.

Weaknesses: It is not human and cannot understand them fully.

Territory: Research station on Saturn 3.

Idiosyncrasies: Likes to hold Alex.

Friends: Captain James.

Enemies: Alex and Adam.

Evil Deeds: Terrorizes Saturn 3, endangers research to find food for Earth's masses.

Killed by: After the small shuttle craft

arrives with "helper" Hector, all hell breaks loose. Captain James has a small node on his head that he can insert in Hector to transmit his ideas to the mighty space villain. When Captain James dies the robot is on its own. Once again Earth can only gasp at how close they were to losing the hope of humanity—Saturn 3.

Current Status: Deactivated.

What to Do If You Meet: Pull the plug—wherever it is.

Worthy of Note: Enormous sets and production costs, but little box office success. Still, it's a nice little film.

Lily Carver

Born: 1920s
Died: 1955

Starred in:
Kiss Me Deadly
United Artists, 1955
Director: Robert Aldrich
Played by: Gaby Rodgers

Description: Blonde sexpot in slinky dress. She's always looking at you like she wants something. She is a slinky walker and a silky talker.

Reason for Villainy: Lily is Christina's roommate. Christina (Cloris Leachman) is hitching rides—without shoes on—and Mike Hammer (Ralph Meeker) picks her up. She says that if anything happens to her, "remember me." Something does happen; the car is sideswiped and she dies. While in the hospital Hammer begins to think of how she was murdered. He's going to get those behind her death. The trail leads to Carl Evello (Paul Stewart), a gangster. Carl tries to buy Hammer off. No go. Then Hammer is roughed up. Still no go. Hammer finds Lily Carver, and thinking that she's in danger, hides her. Slews

Lily Carver (Gaby Rodgers) refuses to tell Mike Hammer the truth in Kiss Me Deadly.

of people connected to Christina are dying. Hammer is drugged and abducted. Evello is behind it, and Hammer manages to overpower him. More mayhem. Lily and Hammer find Christina's locker key. She was involved in something. Lily disappears. Hammer is met by the cops, who tell the ace detective that the box contains atomic stuff of a secret nature.

Evil Powers: Guile, charm, seduction.

Weapons: A gun, a body, and a brain.

Occupation: Double-dealer from the bottom of the deck. Deadly dame.

Intelligence: Great at lying, clever in general. When she turns on the sex appeal, you get careless.

Strengths: Her looks and her flair for sex.

Weaknesses: Greed.

Territory: California.

Idiosyncrasies: Kiss and kill.

Friends: Gangsters.

Enemies: Mike—but not until she doesn't need him.

Relatives: The women in *The Beguiled.*

Evil Deeds: Lily kills, tortures, and maims to get the box.

Killed by: Hammer discovers that Christina's killers have been killed by Lily.

But it's not revenge, it's to get the box. Lily now turns on Hammer and wounds him, and opens the box. Instantly she bursts into flames. That stuff inside is radioactive. She is blown up with the house. Hammer narrowly escapes.

Current Status: Dead, in tiny radioactive pieces.

What to Do If You Meet: If she were around she'd wrap you around her finger. Call Mike, he's more experienced with this type.

Worthy of Note: Nasty.

Coral Chandler

Born: Circa 1920
Died: 1947

Starred in:
Dead Reckoning
Columbia Pictures, 1947
Director: John Cromwell
Played by: Lizabeth Scott

Description: Long, wavy, blonde hair. A knockout. A dame with a classy chassis and an eager transmission, a hot tomato, a cool cookie. A woman you want to hold, who whispers sweet dreams of paradise in your hot ears, and then pulls a gun on you.

Reason for Villainy: You're Rip Murdock (Humphrey Bogart), and you're a heroic war veteran. She's the girl of your dead pal, Johnny. It all began a short while ago . . . you were on the train into Washington—you and Johnny were going to get decorated by the President for standing a few of the enemy on their ears. Suddenly Johnny gets a notion to hop aboard a train going in the opposite direction. You tried to catch the train, but he waved goodbye. What gives? You trace down his old pals, and his girl, after you find out that Johnny bought it in a fiery car crash. You give it to her straight—to see if she flinches. She

Coral Chandler (Lizabeth Scott) entices Rip Murdock with her version of paradise in Dead Reckoning.

seems like a true blue tomato, so why the buzzing in your head, what's wrong about this jasmine smelling blonde? She whispers things in your ear—things about going away together; about it being a blue, dark world; and how you both can start over—and you buy it—almost. This woman you're crazy about (just like Johnny was) is named Coral, and you gradually find out she belongs to Martinelli (Morris Carnovsky), a nightclub owner who has a way of slipping you snake-eye dice and Mickey Finns. He introduces you to Kraus (Marvin Miller), who likes to hurt people.

Evil Powers/Weapons: You believe her when she's lying through her pearly teeth. You really want to believe her. All your life you've been aching for a sweet one like this.

Occupation: A pretty face who hangs out in nightclubs singing songs of doomed love.

Intelligence: She has smarts.

Strengths: Her chassis.

Weaknesses: Rip is tough.

Territory: Nightclubs.

Idiosyncrasies: She says it's a blue, dark world, and you love it when she says that.

Friends: No one really.

Enemies: Maybe Martinelli, but who can figure the dame?

Relatives: Just whistle—you'll find out.

Evil Deeds: She's pumped six bullets into many a man.

Outcome: You begin living for her touch, buying that story about how Johnny didn't want the medal because he was a fugitive. She had been attacked by a man, Johnny shot him in self-defense, joined the Army—she says it's a long story. You believe that line about how there's a lot of night-blooming jasmine around here. (You had smelled her jasmine perfume before you were slugged while looking through Martinelli's office.) Then she tells you another story once you prove to her the pieces don't fit together. She says she shot the man and Johnny took the rap and went on the lam to save her. Martinelli controls her because he has the gun with her fingerprints on it. You break into Martinelli's safe, slug him and his mean pal, Kraus—all for her. You begin driving away with Coral in the rain, buying that paradise bit again that she does so well. She shoots you, but you floor the pedal. Next thing, you're in the hospital, you have a broken arm, and she's dying in the other room. She asks for you. You hold her hand and she says, "Rip, I'm afraid." You say, "Listen, sister, you're going out the jump door, hold your breath, don't fight it, just let go, you got plenty of company, Mike (that's her nickname) . . . Geronimo, Mike." In the final scene of the film, as "The End" flashes on the screen, there is a parachute descending, descending. . . .

Current Status: Made the final jump.

What to Do If You Meet: If you're a guy, you'll probably buy any story she tells you.

Worthy of Note: One of the finest examples of film *noir*. A must-see. We'd put this on our ten best films list.

Sir Charles

Born: With a silver spoon in his mouth, 1930

Died: Lives on

Starred in:
The Pink Panther
United Artists, 1964
Director: Blake Edwards
Played by: David Niven

Description: Suave, urbane, thin. Elegant manners and suit, debonair raconteur with the ladies, delicate deceiver of desperate dowagers, facile flatterer of flabby femmes, handsome thief of the wealthy's delicate diamonds.

Reason for Villainy: Sir Charles is the man who is stealing the necklaces of the rich all over Europe. Can anyone find out his secret identity? Perhaps the great Inspector Clouseau (Peter Sellers) can. Clouseau stumbles his way to the exclusive play spot of the royalty and rich, the Cortina D'Ampeozo, hidden in the Alps—hidden unless you are classy enough to get there. In the meantime, Sir Charles has begun to charm the pants off the best of the European beauties. He also sets up his plan to steal the Pink Panther—a diamond with an imperfection in the shape of a pink panther. (In the film's sequels, the fantastic cartoon creation begun here—wherein the Pink Panther comes to life and wreaks havoc with the lettering in the opening titles—makes one forget the Pink Panther was originally a diamond.) Princess Dala (Claudia Cardinale) has the Pink diamond and Charles intends to get it, if Clouseau doesn't stumble upon his careful plan. Clouseau has brought along his wife—a sort of vacation/business trip. His wife Simone (Capucine) is soon cozy with Charles and Clouseau can't even find that out.

Weapons: Charm, stealth.

Occupation: Rich jewel thief, seducer of beauties, lover of the finer things in life, comfortable con man.

Intelligence: Went to the best schools in England, but was better at extracurricular activities.

Strengths: Nimble charmer.

Weaknesses: Diamonds puts him in danger.

Territory: All the watering holes of society.

Idiosyncrasies: Leaves a monogramed glove at the scene when he departs with the family jewels.

Friends: His secret identity is his best defense. Who would think . . .

Inspector Clouseau accuses Sir Charles of being the jewel thief. He shows him the monogrammed glove left at the scene of every crime in The Pink Panther.

Enemies: Clouseau, but he's not much of a threat, is he?

Evil Deeds: Steals from the rich for the rich. The poor? Who are they?

Outcome: Why does the debonair knight-of-the-realm go about robbing the ladies of their big bangles? Maybe it's the only fun a man who has everything can have. In any case, Charles quickly goes about his dastardly deeds. (If you've seen the other Pink Panther movies first, you might be surprised at how much this film depended upon Niven.) Sir Charles, of course, succeeds with his pursuit. The bumbling Inspector is due to become a star—eclipsing all—in the sequel *A Shot In The Dark*, and then in innumerable Pink Panther movies. This character of Sir Charles is the lightest villain you will ever find. After all, theft is a sport to him. Clouseau is only looking to keep his job and his sleuthing is not to be believed. It's all in fun for a change. Bravo.

Current Status: Still doing his thing somewhere among the rich.

What to Do If You Meet: Rattle your jewelry, he'll flatter you.

Worthy of Note: Niven is really the ultimate, one-of-a-kind lady killer. Sellers became more than an art-house favorite with the Pink Panther series. The Pink Panther also became the best cartoon creation since Donald Duck and Mickey Mouse. Suave, very suave.

Charlie

Born: Long ago
Died: Just now–maybe

Starred in:
The Last Wave
World Northal, 1977
Director: Peter Weir
Played by: Nanjiwarra Amagula

Description: Charlie is a gray-bearded Aborigine (native Australian) with intense eyes. He wears western clothes most of the time, and is quiet and observant. His broad nostrils smell the air for danger. He's a witch doctor and carries the down under version of a ju-ju stick. Chris is his 'brother'. Articulate, young and strong. A man without tribal roots, an 'urban' native.

Reason for Villainy: It's complicated. Charlie and Chris are tribal blacks living in Sidney. Their group is trying to prevent the whites from knowing certain things—things that are secret and sacred. One of Charlie's tribe members, Chris, seems to penetrate David Burton's (Richard Chamberlain's) mind when he sleeps. Burton got involved in this whole situation as a court-appointed lawyer for Chris (Gulpilil) and his friends, who were accused of killing another black. Burton has done research suggesting that Charlie killed the man with a sorcerer stick merely by pointing it at the man. Chris pleads with the lawyer not to reveal that the dead man had stolen certain sacredly inscribed rocks from a secret place. But the lawyer is intent on proving the group innocent and reveals some of the tribal "myths."

Evil Powers/Weapons: Charlie is a sorcerer. He can turn himself into an owl and can project his mind anywhere. He also can move between "real" and "dream" time. Chris can be in Burton's dreams at will.

Occupation: Aborigine sorcerer.

Chris (Gulpilil) and Charlie (Nandjiwarra Amagula) are tribal aborigines in The Last Wave.

Intelligence: Supernatural.

Strengths: Sorcery.

Weaknesses: There are things above all men.

Territory: Sidney, Australia.

Idiosyncrasies: He turns into an owl. Isn't that enough?

Friends: Chris and his brothers—most of the time.

Enemies: Burton—in a way.

Evil Deeds: Charlie's deeds are really beyond good and evil. Still, in the end, he sure scares the hell out of everybody. He can move through dream time, float into your bedroom, your mind, your. . . .

Outcome: Burton and Chris have a special relationship. Chris often shows Burton things in his dreams. In the meantime, all over Australia, weird water phenomena are occurring—huge storms and weird rainbows. Burton has flashes (when he is driving his Volvo through titanic storms) of a flood. He is learning that there is something beyond "everyday" and that something is "Dreamtime." Chris takes Burton to an underground temple—accessible only through half-constructed storm sewers. Once there, Charlie hypnotizes Burton and discovers that Burton is not a human being but a "Mulcrul," a supernatural being that appears at the end of a "cycle." Then Burton discovers what the end really is—a huge wave. The Last Wave will be thousands of feet high and wipe out everyone in this era. It's all in the sacred paintings in the temple. But then Charlie appears once again, all painted and half naked. He threatens Burton. In a scuffle, Burton kills Charlie and stains the sacred stone. All of this fulfills a dream he had. He staggers out of the temple, lost for hours underground, and comes out on a beach. There the "Mulcrul" envisions the Last Wave coming, coming. The End. Literally.

Current Status: Dead in normal time, but . . .

What to Do If You Meet: Get in a jet and don't land anywhere.

Worthy of Note: This supernatural thriller is too good to miss. One of the best films ever made. It's impossible to describe how weird and profound this film is, or to explain its juxtaposition of our time with dream time. See this as a cure to the everyday world around you—when it needs to be all washed away.

Alain Charnier

Alias: The Frog
Born: 1920s France
Died: 1975 Marseilles

Starred in:
The French Connection
20th Century Fox, 1971
Director: William Friedkin
Played by: Fernando Rey

Description: Dapper Frenchman, white trimmed beard, always extremely well-dressed in designer clothes. Elegant, refined tastes. Suave, sophisticated.

Reason for Villainy: The brilliant, French heroin smuggler Alain Charnier is setting up a huge drug deal in NYC. Popeye Doyle (Gene Hackman) is a half-crazy, tough-as-nails narco cop. He pursues the Frog relentlessly throughout the film, trying to pin something on the elusive Frenchie, but the Frog is too clever and

Alain Charnier (Fernando Rey), the French drug dealer, does a little sprint to lose Popeye Doyle who's trailing him in The French Connection.

seems to just slide out of every trap. In a terrifying chase sequence, Doyle kills one of Charnier's assassins, but he just can't get the main man.

Evil Powers: Clever, vicious, will do anything to further his drug trade.

Weapons: Has thugs who work for him, who will kill for him.

Occupation: Heroin cutter and smuggler.

Intelligence: A master criminal. One of the top drug smugglers in the world. Always one step ahead of the cops and other crooks.

Strengths: Ruthlessly clever.

Weaknesses: Underestimates "dumb" cops.

Territory: Marseilles, NYC.

Idiosyncrasies: Loves fine women, food, can't stand "dumb" Americans.

Friends: Gourmet restaurant owners.

Enemies: Popeye Doyle.

Evil Deeds: His drug activities have hooked tens of thousands of young Americans. He has "eliminated" competitors, shot innocent bystanders, bribed corrupt officials, smuggled heroin.

Killed by: Charnier meets with organized crime biggies in NYC. The big dope deal is arranged—more than 70 pounds of pure high-grade heroin. The exchange of cash for drugs is made in a sanitation department garage on Randall's Island. But it's suddenly raided by Doyle and other narcos. The Frog gets away, though most of his men are caught or killed.

Current Status: Alive, but in sequel, *French Connection II*, he is killed by Doyle.

What to Do If You Meet: Say "Excusez moi" and beat it.

Worthy of Note: Based on a real happening. Eddie Egan, the real cop on the case, played a bit part here.

Chauvelin

Born: 1750s
Died: 1790s

Starred in:
The Scarlet Pimpernel
London Films, 1934
Director: Harold Young
Played by: Raymond Massey

Description: Chauvelin is a thin, dark, handsome, angular man with a military bearing and an elaborate waistcoat and pantaloons. He wears a scarlet or white sash at his waist, and generally looks like a French Revolution ambassador to England.

Reason for Villainy: The French Revolution is taking its toll. One after another, innocent and relatively innocent royalty and nobles of pre-revolutionary power in France are being guillotined or worse. The nobles in England feel for their own and have arranged safe passage for the embattled rich of the continent. Central to the plot is the role of The Scarlet Pimpernel, who is a master at subversive activities in France as well as at derring-do. The silly, foppish Sir Percy Blakeney (Leslie Howard) is secretly the wily Pimpernel. He courts the affections of his reluctant wife, Marguerite (Merle Oberon) to no avail. Meanwhile, the French terror masters send their best spy, Chauvelin, to England to find out who the Pimpernel is. His life will be forfeited if he does not succeed. Rightly, he thinks the Pimpernel must be an aristocrat, and engages Marguerite in his work by telling her he will see to it her brother is released by

The Revolution rounds up its aristocratic victims whom The Scarlet Pimpernel will try to save.

the French if she helps find the Pimpernel. She reluctantly agrees, and she finds out that a maneuver to rescue nobles is to take place in Calais. The spy swings into action, and arranges a trap for the mysterious Pimpernel.

Evil Powers/Weapons: Chauvelin has his foppish manners, his cunning wiles, his position to worm his way into the parties of the aristocrats. Plus he has Marguerite's brother as a hostage.

Occupation: Ambassador, spy.

Intelligence: Superior.

Strengths: The Ambassador is backed by the French.

Weaknesses: He could fall prey to the excesses of the rabble, or the Pimpernel could turn the tables on the spy and end up holding all the souffles himself. Oh, the truffles of a French diplomat—it's parfaitly unbearable.

Territory: England, France.

Idiosyncrasies: Big ears.

Friends: The Reign of Terror in France.

Enemies: The Pimpernel.

Evil Deeds: The Ambassador supports the French Reign of Terror, the excesses of a revolution gone to rack and ruin, killing the cream of the nobility. The San-Culottes rule and he follows the orders.

Outcome: Chauvelin, having detained Percy, strikes a deal. For the release of his wife and her safe passage back to the cliffs of Dover (England), Percy will surrender. Chauvelin agrees, and soon Percy is facing a firing squad and saying "too bad." Percy must

have been shot down, because bullets whistled in the other room. But Chauvelin is surprised when the redoubtable Percy, a.k.a. the Pimpernel, returns unharmed. You see, all of the firing squad was on the Pimpernel's payroll. Now it's our villain's turn to face justice.

Current Status: Lost his head.

What to Do If You Meet: Chauvelin dies if you don't feed him Napoleons.

Worthy of Note: Leslie Howard, brilliant here as Percy, was shot down by the Nazis (in real life) over Portugal. They thought Churchill was on the plane. Howard was on a goodwill trip to neutral Portugal.

Nick Cherney

Born: 1920s
Died: 1950

Starred in:
Red Light
United Artists, 1949
Director: Roy Del Ruth
Played by: Raymond Burr

Description: Nick is a sinister man. Often during his villainy in this film we see only his shoes, the view of him stalking his victim. The stocky, dark man's motive is revenge. His method is murder. He likes to dress up in a suit because it makes him look clean and responsible. However, he's not clean, and the only thing he's responsible for is murder!

Reason for Villainy: Nick is an ex-employee of a Los Angeles freight company. He was an embezzler and got his just desserts—a stretch in the pen. Now he's back seeking revenge on Johnny Torno (George Raft), the boss. Nick's plan is to kill Jess, the boss's brother, a chaplain just back from the war. Jess (Arthur Franz) will be killed in such a way as to place the blame on Johnny. Indeed, his plan works. Nick commits the murder, but Jess is not quite

Nick Cherney (Raymond Burr) has accomplished exactly what he set out to do in Red Light.

Outcome: Johnny, obsessed, leaves Warni Hazard (Gene Lockhart) in charge of the company to pursue Nick, who becomes the likely suspect. Johnny searches for the Bible. When he finds it only the words "Vengeance is mine . . . saith the Lord" are underlined. What does that mean? We find out soon enough, but not before Warni is killed. She is pursued by smiling Nick through the garage. When she stumbles, Nick topples a jack and crushes her. Later, Johnny chases Nick to the roof of the freight company, where a huge neon sign is blinking brightly. Johnny has Nick lined up in his sight, but he doesn't shoot. At that moment he understands the meaning of his dead brother's underlined biblical message. Nick, however, is accidentally electrocuted by the neon sign. The smiling, smoking villain is all hung up in neon. What a way to go.

dead when Johnny arrives. Gasping from the effects of the shooting, Jess utters only one phrase: "In the Bible . . . ," then he dies. Johnny, seeking the meaning, believes that the Gideon Bible from the hotel room holds the evidence against whoever killed Jess. He enlists the aid of Carla North (Virginia Mayo)

Evil Powers/Weapons: He's an unknown and has the advantage of surprise. He uses a hand-gun and is good at killing.

Occupation: Killer, embezzler.

Intelligence: Sure, he's crafty. But did he go to accounting school? Perhaps he forged those references to put himself in the position to embezzle!

Strengths: The power of evil and his surprise tactics.

Weaknesses: He has God against him.

Territory: A freight company, hotel rooms, and the streets around L.A.

Idiosyncrasies: Laughs when he kills.

Friends: Stealth.

Enemies: Johnny.

Relatives: Tommy Udo.

Evil Deeds: He kills and embezzles. He has a sadistic streak, and likes to frighten his victims first.

The Clanton Gang

Born: 1850s
Died: Three died, October 1881

Starred in:
Gunfight at the O.K. Corral
Paramount, 1957
Director: John Sturges
Played by: John Ireland, Lyle Bettger,
    Lee Van Cleef, Dennis Hopper

Description: Dusty worn boots, mean looks on faces, crude manners. Illiterate, no good, cow-dung smelling ruffians slouchy from carrying too many rifles, shotguns, and .45 Colt repeaters.

Reason for Villainy: It's Tombstone, Arizona Territory, 1881. In just 25 years horseless carriages will ply the streets. But it is time for the final gasp of the West—the greatest gunfight ever. The protagonists: Wyatt Earp (Burt Lancaster), Doc Holiday (Kirk

Doc shows that he has no hidden weapons at a meeting with the Clanton Gang. That meeting is not enough, though, to prevent the Gunfight at O.K. Corral.

Douglas), Bat Masterson (Kenneth Tobey), and Virgil Earp (John Hudson). This downbeat adult western is historically inaccurate to the extent of the action and the personalities. There are wide-screen shots of glistening spurs, close-ups of Doc, a consumptive alcoholic, downing his whiskeys, and Frankie Laine's haunting soundtrack. All these aspects were calculated to build the mood of destiny confronting men. And it works. Enter the antagonists. The Clantons feel wronged by the Earps. They hate *all* Earps and their friends. And they're mean. A meaner bunch of sidewinders there's never been, and they don't intend to fight fair. A drunken challenge, a background of cattlemen (represented by Earp's forces), and sheepmen (the Clanton's), leads to trouble with Wyatt's brother. Doc and Wyatt hold back, but Wyatt's and Virgil's brother Jimmy is gunned down. Now there will be a confrontation.

Evil Powers: Good with shotguns, rifles, repeater revolvers.

Occupation: Gunslingers.

Intelligence: Ain't never went to no school.

Strengths: Their triggers are hairtriggers, their fingers itchy.

Weaknesses: Up against the West's best shots.

Territory: Tombstone, Arizona Territory.

Idiosyncrasies: Believe a big town isn't big enough for the Earp men.

Friends: Their blazing guns.

Enemies: Earp and his men.

Evil Deeds: In the range wars that ripped the West, they bushwacked a lot of folks. Brawl in bars, cheat at cards, maltreat horses.

Outcome: The meeting is set: There will be a gunfight on the outskirts of town at the O.K. Corral. Holiday steels himself with whiskey. Virgil and Wyatt oil their revolvers, and the women beg them not to go, but they are men, and must do what men must do. The Clanton Gang ride to the O.K. Corral. The scene is set. Who will win? "There the outlaw band make their final stand . . ." sings the cowboy on the soundtrack. Tension mounts. Here come the Earps, Doc. Boot Hill awaits the losers. The sun burns down, the horses stir restlessly, sensing the slaughter to come. Guns blaze, men fall. The fight sweeps through the streets. Another man is down. Doc is hit. Three Clanton Gang members fall dead. It is over. History will record this day as the climax of the Western legend. But wait, Billy Clanton, the youngest, who Wyatt begged to not get involved, is drawing a bead on Wyatt. Wyatt had let him live, but he's not returning the favor. Doc spots the desperado and shoots him down in the nick of time to save his lawman friend, Wyatt.

Current Status: Three are buried in Boot Hill's rocks. They died with their boots on.

What to Do If You Meet: In real life, Virgil

was picked off some time after the fight by some remaining gang members. So don't go about saying the Clantons are no-good, dirty criminals. Keep your boca buttoned.

Worthy of Note: A famous episode of the defunct, super popular TV series *Star Trek* had Chekhov, the Captain, Spock, and Doc as Clantons in a time warp. It seemed to be a take off on this dramatic movie, with weird camera angles and odd music. Compare this film with that TV episode for some good fun.

The Clegg Family

Born: 1800s
Died: Late 1800s

Starred in:
Wagonmaster
RKO Radio, 1950
Director: John Ford
Played by: Charles Kemper, James
    Arness, Hank Worden, Fred Libbey,
    Mickey Simpson

Description: The Cleggs are the meanest sons of the West that ever attacked good Mormon folk and their companions on the great western plains. They are shootin' and fightin' fools out for plunder.

Reason for Villainy: The story begins as a group of Mormons engages Travis Blue (Ben Johnson) to guide them west. They soon meet a stranded group of actresses on the trail, and Travis insists they not be left to fend for themselves. Among the actresses are comely Denver (Joanne Dru) and Prudence (Kathleen O'Malley). Prudence finds favor with a young Mormon named Sandy (Harry Carey, Jr.) and Denver has a thing for Travis. At a dance while at camp, the Cleggs invade the festivities. Trouble is brewing. The Cleggs take all of the Mormons' guns and begin to rule the wagon train. Floyd Clegg (James Arness) harasses Denver while the other Cleggs create more mischief.

Evil Powers/Weapons: They have ornery dispositions that are hard to stop.

Occupation: Mean old outlaws.

Intelligence: Some are smart enough to add.

Strengths: Guns and plenty of experience in robbing and meanness help them out.

Weaknesses: They underestimate the power of the united group.

Territory: The old West.

The Clegg family watch the approaching wagontrain which they plan to attack in Wagonmaster.

Idiosyncrasies: Their loyalty to the family goes beyond money.

Friends: Each other.

Enemies: Everyone on the wagon train.

Evil Deeds: Rob, cheat, and abuse women.

Outcome: The Mormon group slowly becomes fed up with their unwelcome guests. Using all their gumption, they cleverly disarm and surround the intruding gang and send them packing—what's left of them. The group then moves on toward the promised land.

Current Status: Still terrorizing but on a smaller scale.

What to Do If You Meet: Don't surrender your guns.

Worthy of Note: One of the best John Ford westerns.

Terry Collins

Born: 1929 or thereabouts
Died: 1946

Starred in:
The Dark Mirror
Universal, 1946
Director: Robert Siodmak
Played by: Olivia de Havilland

Description: She's a twin, and her sister's name is Ruth. Terry's insane, but looks exactly the same as her adorable, sane sister. She has dark hair and nice doe-eyes. But watch out, she's a killer.

Reason for Villainy: Lieutenant Stevenson (Thomas Mitchell) has a murdered doctor on his hands. One of the twins was seen leaving the building. She did it. But upon interviewing the twins, one is covering up for the other. Hoping that the mystery can be sorted out by a psychologist, the lieutenant goes to Dr. Scott Elliott (Lew Ayres). He pays the sisters to undergo testing—the Rorschach test—for a re-

Olivia de Havilland plays the twins Terry and Ruth Collins in The Dark Mirror.

search project. He confides shortly thereafter that one of the twins is psychotic. He starts romancing Ruth, the sane one. This makes Terry jealous. (Both sisters are played by De Havilland.) Terry starts to drive Ruth crazy accusing her of things she didn't do. Stevenson convinces Elliot to tell Ruth that her sister is insane and he makes an appointment with Ruth to tell her. But Terry, pretending to be Ruth, keeps the appointment. Drive you nuts yet?

Evil Powers/Weapons: Double trouble.

Occupation: Twins.

Intelligence: Sharp as a knife.

Strengths: Confusion.

Weaknesses: Resolution.

Territory: Various places.

Idiosyncrasies: Split personality. Does that make triplets?

Friends: Herself.

Enemies: Her sister—maybe.

Evil Deeds: Murdering Dr. Peralta and trying to drive her sister nuts.

Outcome: Elliot knows that Terry is masquerading as Ruth, but he tells her anyway that Terry is sick. "Ruth" resists Elliot's suggestion that her sister undergo treatment. Then

Elliot says he knows she's Terry, and that she killed Peralta because he was in love with Ruth. Then, suddenly, Elliot gets news that Ruth killed herself. Looking over Ruth's cooling body, Terry reveals herself and admits that she killed Peralta. Ruth, not dead, awakens. Ruth's "death" was planned in order for Terry to admit her crime. Get it? They seem to understand, and in the end Ruth gets her guy, Elliot.

Current Status: Doing time—concurrent sentences.

What to Do If You Meet: Get them together; they're safer as a threesome.

Worthy of Note: Nothing.

Michael Corleone

Born: 1920s
Died: Still alive at end

Starred in:
The Godfather, Part II
Paramount, 1974
Director: Francis Ford Coppola
Played by: Al Pacino

Description: Michael is now the Capo, the Godfather of an extended crime family. He is handsome and dresses in expensive suits. His swept-back hairstyle is contemporary. He looks around carefully when he enters a room, as did his father Don Vito.

Reason for Villainy: Michael has inherited the reins of his extended crime family. He manages to fend off the opposition of a U.S. Senator (G.D. Spradlin) by finding a skeleton in the senator's past. Then Michael moves in big on Las Vegas. He also travels to pre-Castro Cuba to set up operations with Roth (Lee Strasberg), a Jewish gangster he distrusts. Sure enough, Michael's resentful older brother Fredo (John Cazale) has set him up for a hit by Roth's goons. He survives. Michael's wife (Diane Keaton) has an abortion because she hates his crime world. She

will not raise a son to that hell. Michael abandons her. He plans revenge upon those who tried to kill him and take over his operations. Before this, however, the film has some beautiful flashbacks to the elder Vito Corleone's beginnings in old, pushcart New York. It makes this film in some ways better than the original *Godfather*. Later, Michael is summoned before a Senate hearing on organized crime. A disillusioned former associate, Franki Pentangeli, is to testify against him. However, Michael sends for Pentangeli's brother and has him sit in the audience. The squealer won't squeal. The Senate is baffled.

Evil Powers: He has the men, the will, and the violence in him to run the Mafia.

Occupation: Godfather.

Intelligence: Bright.

Strengths: He is suspicious, careful.

Weaknesses: He is a revenge-seeker.

Territory: The U.S.A., particularly Nevada.

Idiosyncrasies: He is more violent than his father ever was.

Friends: His extended family.

Enemies: Roth, brother Fredo.

Evil Deeds: Runs a notorious crime family.

Outcome: Michael's violence was somewhat deferred out of respect for his mother's feelings. After her death he goes on a rampage. He has his brother Fredo done away with and Roth is hit at the airport. Then Pentangeli is

In The Godfather II, Michael Corleone talks with his father's old crony, Frankie Pentageli, who will later betray him and, at Michael's suggestion, commit suicide.

convinced to commit an honorable suicide by Michael's *consiglieri*, Tom Hagen (Robert Duvall). Michael is now supreme.

Current Status: Alive.

What to Do If You Meet: Speak well of Don Vito, show some respect.

Worthy of Note: A special combined *Godfather* and *Godfather II* was produced and aired on television. It had additional scenes and some altered scenes. That version, lasting many hours, is really the best.

Cottonmouth

Born: 1870s
Died: 1920?

Starred in:
Wind Across the Everglades
Warner Bros., 1958
Director: Nicholas Ray
Played by: Burl Ives

Description: Cottonmouth is a chubby denizen of the Everglades. He is full of mosquito bites and is greasy and dirty. He is most often seen with his band of feather-pirates on swamp boats and handles a mean old gun very well. He can also imitate birds.

Reason for Villainy: It is shortly after the turn of the century, and the women of high society are crazy for exotic plumage in their bonnets. Cottonmouth is the head of a feather-poaching group in the Florida Everglades. He is responsible for the deaths of thousands of birds. However, the Audubon Society's fanatical investigator, Walt Murdock (Christopher Plummer), is intent on rooting out the feather poachers. George Leggett (Howard I. Smith), a merchant, is in league with Cottonmouth. Murdock, smoking and drinking at the local whorehouse, looks formidable enough to tackle Cottonmouth. Billy (Cory Osceola), an outcast Seminole, is assigned by Cottonmouth to kill Murdock. He likes Murdock and refuses. This makes Cottonmouth angry and he kills Billy by tying him to a poisonous tree. Murdock is later captured by Cottonmouth deep in the swamps.

Evil Powers/Weapons: He knows the 'Glade like the back of his hand. He's also aware of its poisonous creatures.

Occupation: Lusty feather-poacher, and both a lover and despoiler of nature.

Intelligence: Likes music and bawdy songs.

Strengths: Cottonmouth is much like Murdock—a vibrant, fun-loving, strong, and robust man.

Cottonmouth (Burl Ives) is the head of a feather-poaching group in Florida in Wind Across the Everglades.

Weaknesses: He's killing the nature he loves.

Territory: The Florida Everglades.

Idiosyncrasies: He likes his enemy.

Friends: The merchants, the ladies, and, eventually, Murdock.

Enemies: Murdock and the law.

Relatives: Swamp rats.

Evil Deeds: Kills to protect his domain.

Outcome: As a sporting gesture, after a night of jawing and reveling deep in the 'Glades, Cottonmouth makes an offer to his captive. Cottonmouth agrees to turn himself in if Murdock can find his way out of the maze of the Everglades. The challenge is accepted, and days of bewildering rowing ensue. Yet, the farther they row, the more lost they become. The men also become quick friends. Cottonmouth, however, moves to quickly pick up his hat and is bitten by a deadly snake. He gasps out in pain that he was wrong to destroy the beautiful birds and that Murdock is a wonderful friend. He also tells Murdock that he's in the right channel to escape the 'Glade. Cottonmouth insists that Murdock continue his journey, although Murdock is reluctant to leave the dying man.

Current Status: There are others like Cottonmouth living with nature and destroying it.

What to Do If You Meet: Prepare some bawdy stories in advance.

Worthy of Note: Stunning plumage.

Joan Crawford

Born: 1905
Died: 1978

Starred in:
Mommie Dearest
Paramount, 1981
Director: Frank Perry
Played by: Faye Dunaway

Faye Dunaway gives a remarkable performance as Joan Crawford in Mommie Dearest.

Description: Well bred and obviously high class from her demeanor. She's a bit cold though, if you can see through her superficial warmth. She's also a bit of a stickler when it comes to her ego, and she doesn't like kids much. She's graying, but still a striking middle-aged woman.

Reason for Villainy: It is 1939 and Crawford is twice divorced (from Franchot Tone and Douglas Fairbanks, Jr.). She is also about to undergo a steep fall in her career. She adopts Christina and Christopher. Then she subjects the children to Draconian measures of discipline and scolding. She's so severe she's like the ice she immerses her still beautiful complexion into daily for beauty reasons. Christina, it seems, has endured much. Joan lectures her on how life is unfair. When Christina applies makeup she has her locks shorn. When she eats a forbidden steak she is starved and criticized for being like a Hollywood agent. When Joan is drunk at night, which is quite often, she destroys the plants in the yard with an axe. She beats Christina with a clothes hanger because the child used a wire hanger.

Evil Powers/Weapons: She's the mommie and the kids have to bear it.

Occupation: Famous movie star, but fading fast.

Intelligence: Very smart and attractive, but mean.

Strengths: She's adored by the public.

Weaknesses: She's an angry drunk.

Territory: Hollywood and Brentwood, California.

Idiosyncrasies: She has a love/hate relationship with Christina.

Friends: Christina, the public, and her boyfriend, Greg Savitt (Steve Forrest).

Enemies: Christina.

Relatives: The Wicked Witch of the West, perhaps.

Evil Deeds: Beats Christina, chops down bushes, and rants and raves.

Outcome: Christina is a testing and cagey child, but that is glossed over and we follow Joan's tirades. The woman pulls Christina out of private school when she is found petting with a boy, then almost strangles her in front of a visiting reporter. Christina is sent for two years to a convent. Christina grows up to be quite pretty and lands a job on a soap opera. While she is in the hospital having a real operation, Joan steals the role. Somehow Joan stabilizes a bit, marries an exec, and some sort of reconciliation between her and Christina is in the wind. Joan dies, however, and the will disinherits Christina. But, somehow, Christina gets the last words in.

Current Status: Dead.

What to Do If You're Adopted: Get a lawyer and take cover.

Worthy of Note: This film is based on Christina Crawford's book. In this film, Faye Dunaway gives a remarkable performance as Joan Crawford and gives credit to the story line. Whether the movie is fact or fiction doesn't really matter. Would you believe Zefferelli was supposed to direct this one? If he had it might have come out as a serious study of how abused children grow up and have a go at child abuse themselves. As it is, this is a tremendously weird film. Shades of Baby Jane?

Leslie Crosbie

Born: 1900s
Died: 1940

Starred in:
The Letter
Warner Bros.–First National, 1940
Director: William Wyler
Played by: Bette Davis

Description: She's an elegant, alabaster-skinned beauty, often wearing formal clothes for parties and social occasions in the tropical plantation world. Sometimes this articulate, well-educated woman carries a gun, too. Sensuously moving, seductively charming, scorpion-like mind.

Reason for Villainy: Leslie cannot take rejection. Not without mayhem anyway. She's been having an extramarital affair with someone. He's leaving her for a dragonlady-type local girl. She protests, he's adamant. Then

Leslie Crosbie's attractive but deadly. She'll do anything to keep The Letter from surfacing.

he's dead, and she's holding the revolver. Howard Joyce (James Stephenson) is a lawyer friend of Leslie and her husband. He takes the case. However, there is the embarrassing presence of a love letter to the dead man in Leslie's handwriting. The lawyer goes to Leslie's husband (Herbert Marshall) and says he needs a lot of money to free his wife. Crosbie agrees to a blank check. The letter is bought back from the native girl who was the dead man's other lover. First, however, the native girl, Sen Yung (Ong Chi Seng), makes Leslie crawl a bit before returning the letter. Leslie crawls, but somehow with dignity. The trial goes on. It is a tough case. There is some other circumstantial evidence, but without the letter, it's really all in Leslie's favor. The lawyer tells Mr. Crosbie that most of his money was spent to get the letter back—and the husband, shocked, insists that he read this letter that cost a fortune.

Occupation: Housewife on a plantation.
Intelligence: Wily.
Strengths: She's a good liar.
Weaknesses: She writes too much.
Territory: Southeast Asian plantation.
Idiosyncrasies: She's angered easily.
Friends: The lawyer.
Enemies: The truth.
Evil Deeds: Murder, cover-up, perjury, conspiracy, deceit.
Outcome: Leslie's husband gets a gander at that infamous letter and is naturally distraught. Further, it appears that his wife was at the scene of the crime. She said in court that the man hardly knew her, he tried to rape her, and she shot him. Now all that's down the drain. But Leslie's able to wrap her poor, loving husband around her finger and he soon comes to rationalize the whole thing and still wants her. Poorer, but not wiser. Sen Yung and her native friend, however, wait for Leslie to step out for air at a party in the plantation ballroom. The party is to celebrate her release. Leslie steps outside, and Sen Yung removes a long native dagger from her clothing and plunges it into Leslie. Of course, the local constable catches the two natives outside the gate and asks them what they are doing there. They too will die for their crime. But it is done; Leslie's murder avenges the dead man. Sen Yung is happy.

Current Status: Dead.
What to Do If You Meet: Remind her she wrote you letters, and tell her if you die they will be turned over to the police.
Worthy of Note: Isn't Bette charming?

Noah Cross

Born: 1890s
Died: Alive

Starred in:
Chinatown
Paramount, 1974
Director: Roman Polanski
Played by: John Huston

Description: Sixtyish, heavy-jowled man with froggy complexion, and an evil voice. He is a well-dressed land baron and schemer. Stands rather stiffly, deadpans to good or bad news.
Reason for Villainy: It's 1937 Los Angeles and there is a drought. The reservoir is way down. Private eye J.J. Gittes (Jack Nicholson) is hired by a certain Mrs. Mulwray to get the divorce goods on her philandering husband, the water commissioner. Gittes photographs Mulwray with a young girl and turns it over to Mrs. Mulwray. The next day the story hits the newspapers. The *real* Mrs. Mulwray (Faye Dunaway), who is the daughter of tycoon Noah Cross, threatens to sue Gittes. But when the commissioner is killed, she hires the gumshoe to find her husband's killer. Gittes finds out that someone connected with Noah is monkeying with the water level in the reservoir. He confronts Noah and the old guy admits he's planning to profit from the drought, but denies any wrongdoing. Gittes gets it on with Evelyn Mulwray and he believes she is holding out on him about something. He slaps her around and she says that the girl that was with her husband was both

Noah Cross (John Huston) uncharacteristically needs support in Chinatown.

her daughter and her sister. She reveals that Noah had raped her and she begat little Kathryn. Sick.

Evil Powers: Wealth, status, cops in his pocket.

Occupation: Land baron, crook, child rapist, incestuous father.

Intelligence: Devious mind bent on passions of the lowest sort.

Strengths: He's rich and influential.

Weaknesses: He thinks he can buy everyone or scare them off.

Territory: Los Angeles and the surrounding area.

Idiosyncrasies: He doesn't think evil desires are wrong.

Friends: Corrupt cops and politicians.

Enemies: J.J. Gittes.

Evil Deeds: Rape, incest, child abuse, the murder of Mulwray, conspiracy, kidnapping, bribery, etc.

Killed by: Noah had Mulwray killed because the commissioner knew about the water scam and might squeal. Noah is now determined to do to Kathryn what he did to Evelyn. Gittes can't go to the cops, he's hot. He must spirit Kathryn away to save her. Gittes is trailed by the corrupt cops. In Chinatown it all comes down hard. Evelyn wounds Noah slightly. Gittes is nabbed and cuffed by the cops. As he looks on, Evelyn is shot in the back of the head as she tries to escape. Kathryn is turned over to her daddy the rapist. Sick.

Current Status: He's won.

What to Do If You Meet: Suspect the worst. It's worse than that.

Worthy of Note: Sad and sicko. Try some lighthearted Sherlock Holmes flick after this.

Dalby   63
Danny   64
Mrs. Danvers   65
Dathan   66
Sandy Dawson   67
Sir Brian
   de Bois-Guilbert   68
De Villefort,
   Mondego, and
   Danglars   69
Ulysses Diello   70
Dillon   71
The Dirty Dozen   72
Fred C. Dobbs   73
Doc & Dix   74
Doctor No   75
Hugo Drax   77
Inspector Dreyfus   78

Dalby

Born: Circa 1912
Died: 1965

Starred in:
The Ipcress File
Universal, 1965
Director: Sidney J. Furie
Played by: Nigel Green

Dalby (Nigel Green) pretends that he doesn't understand the contents of The Ipcress File.

Description: Dalby is chief of civilian intelligence for Great Britain. He is a pleasant man, as opposed to the head of military intelligence, Ross, who is mean and sharp. Dalby will speak softly and seems concerned for his operatives. He's tall, smoothly dignified, with all the right moves a British intelligence man should have.

Reason for Villainy: It all begins when Harry Palmer (Michael Caine), a maverick army intelligence agent under the command of Ross (a man he hates), is blackmailed into working again for the West. (Palmer had done illegal currency dealings.) He is assigned to civilian intelligence where he's well rid of Ross, an ascerbic, demanding man. He is assigned by Dalby to pursue leads in finding a kidnapped scientist and arranging for the scientist's release from East Germany. He quickly tracks down "Bluejay" (Frank Gatliff), and although nothing seems wrong, he orders a surprise attack on a warehouse where he suspects the scientist is located. The scientist is not there, only a tape labeled the "Ipcress File" and full of incoherent noises is found. Palmer should be admonished for his blunder, but nice old Dalby shields him from criticism.

Evil Powers/Weapons: Dalby's pretense of friendship is amazing.

Occupation: Double agent.

Intelligence: Very intelligent, or so it would seem.

Strengths: Secrecy.

Weaknesses: Palmer's hunches.

Territory: Britain.

Idiosyncrasies: He's oh so nice.

Friends/Enemies: Palmer starts out as a friend but soon discovers Dalby's plan.

Relatives: Judas.

Evil Deeds: He's helping the other side drain our scientists' brains. Torture and murder add spice to his nasty, nasty record.

Outcome: Palmer succeeds in making the exchange for the missing scientist after his initial attempt. But the scientist's brain is scrambled—drained of its knowledge. Why those dirty Commies! Palmer tells Dalby he suspects his old boss Ross is a double agent. Dalby encourages him to be careful and investigate. Later, Palmer is seized and drugged. When he wakes up he thinks he is in a prison inside the Iron Curtain. He is subjected to torture—intense noises that drain one's brain. Palmer recognizes the noise as the mysterious sounds from the Ipcress file tape. He also realizes that he is being drained of his will and hurts himself so the pain will block the brainwashing. After he is released, Palmer discovers that his prison was really the British warehouse he had raided earlier. Dalby and Ross confront Palmer, who is convinced that one of them must be the double agent. From the vantage point of Palmer's gun, we look at both men. Palmer instinctively picks Dalby to shoot. Ross walks away without even a thank you, saying that Palmer is paid well for making correct decisions.

Current Status: Dead.

What to Do If You Meet: Erase any tapes you find.

Worthy of Note: This film, from a Len Deighton novel, and screenplay by Bill Canaway and James Doran, was well made. It is quite the opposite of the gadget-ridden Bond films.

Danny

Alias: Danny Boy
Born: 1900s
Died: Arrested and in jail

Starred in:
Night Must Fall
MGM, 1937
Director: Richard Thorpe
Played by: Robert Montgomery

Description: Danny, who is fond of singing "Danny Boy," is a charmer. He's good looking, sweet, and kind. Above all, he's innocent looking, and that's the worst kind of killer.

Reason for Villainy: Danny Boy is a servant at a resort hotel in England. In nearby Essex, a cantankerous, wheelchair-bound widow lives

Danny (Robert Montgomery) and Olivia do not bother to hide their suspicion of each other in Night Must Fall.

all alone while being a tyrant to her servants. The resort is rocked with the news of the woman's disappearance. Mrs. Bramson (Dame May Whitty) is also shocked to find out her maid, Dora (Merle Tottenham), has been foully seduced by Danny. Dora hopes the old lady will force Danny to marry her, but conniving Danny convinces and charms the old lady into believing that Dora was at fault. Meanwhile, the police find the missing widow's body sans the head. The only clue— her killer whistles "Danny Boy."

Evil Powers/Weapons: Good at garroting, and sings a mean "Danny Boy."

Occupation: Bellboy, seducer, charmer, and killer.

Intelligence: He's charming and witty, but not too schooled.

Strengths: He's handsome and charming.

Weaknesses: He likes to kill.

Territory: Essex, England, and environs.

Idiosyncrasies: "Danny Boy" is *his* tune.

Friends: The old ladies.

Enemies: The old ladies.

Relatives: The Boston Strangler is a cousin on his mother's side.

Evil Deeds: Danny kills for the fun, and then kills again.

Outcome: Mrs. Bramson's niece, Olivia (Rosalind Russell), is beyond succumbing to Danny's charms, even though she is amused by him. Danny has an equal suspicion of Olivia because she knows he can look a person straight in the eyes when he lies, and only the most heinous criminals can do that. One day while she was off with her boyfriend, Justin (Alan Marshal), Olivia hears Danny whistling the mysterious tune the police are warning everyone about. Fascinated that Danny can be a killer as well as a charmer, Olivia goes searching through Danny's box and discovers the garrotted head of the old lady. Olivia confronts him with her findings. He admits to his crime and plans to do the same to her. However, the police are standing by outside and hear his confession. They are quick to escort him away.

Current Status: Life imprisonment.

What to Do If You Meet: Whistle yourself up a bobbie.

Worthy of Note: Superb performances by all.

Mrs. Danvers

Alias: The Witch
Born: 1890s
Died: 1940

Starred in:
Rebecca
United Artists, 1940
Director: Alfred Hitchcock
Played by: Judith Anderson

Description: Witchlike, bitchy, sneaky, cold, cruel, mysterious housekeeper. She always wears high choker-collared dresses and blouses, tight black outfits with long sleeves. Her black hair is in braids tied up in a bun. Severe face, large nose, thin eyes.

Reason for Villainy: The quiet, withdrawn, and lovely young bride of Maxim de Winter (Laurence Olivier), a wealthy but intolerant and overbearing man, comes to Manderly. The new Mrs. de Winter (Joan Fontaine) meets her nemesis in Mrs. Danvers (Judith Anderson). Danvers is cold and intimidates the new bride, who tries her best to get along and run the huge mansion as her husband would expect. Mrs. de Winter discovers that Maxim's first wife, Rebecca, died in a boating accident. She believes that her husband adored his first wife and finds her somewhat lacking. She wanders the beach and house seeking clues to the death. It isn't exactly clear as to how it occurred. Mrs. Danvers keeps telling her how wonderful Rebecca was, and that she is greatly lacking.

Evil Powers: Mean, constantly puts down the new bride, innuendo.

Weapons: Her vile tongue.

Occupation: Housekeeper of Manderly.

Intelligence: Malicious, cunning.

Strengths: Good at sneaking about.

Weaknesses: Obsessed with the past.

Territory: Manderly, one of England's "stately homes."

Idiosyncrasies: Devoted to her dead mistress. Keeps the dead Rebecca's room in perfect order and worships the objects within it.

Friends: The deceased Rebecca.

Enemies: The new wife.

Relatives: Wicked Witch of the West.

Evil Deeds: Skulks around, snaps at Mrs. de Winter. Interrogates, cajoles, pressures the girl to near insanity, all for the love of her past mistress.

Mrs. Danvers (Judith Anderson) refuses to accept the new bride of her employer, remaining faithful to the memory of her first mistress Rebecca.

Killed by: Driven to distraction by Mrs. Danvers, the new bride finally cries out to Maxim that she's sorry he still loves Rebecca. He says she's wrong, that he hated her intensely. When Rebecca died accidentally, he scuttled his yacht at sea and dumped the vile body. The haunting is over for the young bride. But then the mansion erupts into flames. The husband and wife escape, but Mrs. Danvers runs from burning room to burning room in a fit of madness, unable to leave the past. She dies in agony, consumed along with the evil memories of the old house.

Current Status: Dead, cremated in Manderly fire.

What to Do If You Meet: Crank housekeepers like this should be replaced by young French maids with short skirts who say "Mais oui!"

Worthy of Note: Daphne du Maurier's cult classic, rich in atmosphere and mystery. See it only without commercial interruption.

Dathan

Born/Died: Early Biblical times

Starred in:
The Ten Commandments
Paramount, 1956
Director: Cecil B. DeMille
Played by: Edward G. Robinson

Description: Dathan is resplendent in his leopard skin and toga-like outfit, elaborately decorated with pagan signs. He stands, not so tall, but resplendent with rings and his well-trimmed, modified, biblical goatee. His hair is long, dark, but receding. He is confident.

Reason for Villainy: Dathan is disgusted with Moses. After all, Moses has been wandering around the Sinai desert for years now and he still can't come up with the Land of Milk and Honey. The Hebrews, in exodus

Dathan discusses Moses with the Egyptian Pharoah Ramses in Cecil B. DeMille's great epic The Ten Commandments.

from captivity of Pharaoh Ramses's (Yul Brynner) Egypt, are about to receive the Ten Commandments. Moses (Charlton Heston) ascends Mount Sinai and the rest is prehistory. God Himself writes—with elaborate balls of fire—the Commandments. But what does Moses find at the foot of the slope? His people, many of them at least, are worshipping the golden calf. Blasphemy. The leader of these sexual revellers is Dathan. Edward G. is here at his worst (sounding like Rico in *Little Caesar*) extolling the virtues of the golden calf. Of course, if Moses's rod could part the Red Sea, a little miracle like casting the blasphemers into hell isn't much to ask.

Weapons: Treachery, licentiousness.

Occupation: Priest of the golden calf, reveller, traitor to his people.

Intelligence: Not too bright. After Jehovah parted the Red Sea (via Moses), what's this turkey doing following a lesser god?

Strengths: He's a good speaker—and revels sound like fun after the dusty trip into Sinai.

Weaknesses: You don't challenge Moses.

Territory: Sinai, Egypt.

Idiosyncrasies: Dramatic stances.

Friends: Worshippers of the calf.

Enemies: Moses.

Evil Deeds: Turned many Israelites against Moses.

Killed by: Well, the minute you mess with Moses, it's scary. What happens? The ground opens up and the correct path of Moses is accepted by the survivors. Needless to say, old Dathan doesn't make it. He falls, the golden calf statue falls, the revellers fall. Moses and the righteous go on to the Promised Land. That's in the Bible, but in this stunning remake of *The Exodus*, earlier Moses had been vying for the hand of Princess Nefertiti (Anne Baxter) with none other than Ramses. That's probably news to biblical scholars, but it's entertaining. The movie, spectacular for its giant panoramas of the pyramids being built, the Red Sea parting, and the tablets being inscribed by the hand of God, takes some liberties. Special effects seem simplistic by later standards.

Current Status: Worse than dead.

What to Do If You Meet: You're in the wrong place, but there isn't much you can do about that now.

Worthy of Note: The majesty of this production was never duplicated; this was the last Biblical spectacle filmed on such a vast scale. The moods and emotions are emphasized in later films, not the spectacle.

Sandy Dawson

Born: 1900s U.S.A.
Died: 1955 Tokyo

Starred in:
House of Bamboo
20th Century Fox, 1955
Director: Samuel Fuller
Played by: Robert Ryan

Description: Sandy is tall, well-groomed, and well-dressed. He has a perfect haircut, a manicure, and lots of yen in his pockets. He likes cigars, and often has one in his hands.

Reason for Villainy: Sandy is an ex G.I. in occupied Japan. He's used his skills from the war to start a vicious criminal gang in Tokyo. Eddie Kenner (Robert Stack) is sent by the

Sandy Dawson (Robert Ryan) looks on as his supposed gang member questions Mariko, the widow of another gang member, in House of Bamboo.

U.S. Army to infiltrate the gang. The infiltrator gets involved with Mariko (Shirley Yamaguchi), a gang member's widow. After a factory robbery, forays in the Pachinko galleries of the underside of Tokyo, and various other seamy raids, Sandy discovers that Eddie is an informer. Sandy tries to set Kenner up so that the Army will shoot him by mistake. It doesn't work, however, because Kenner is careful, clever, and lucky.

Evil Powers: Sandy Dawson is the head of a huge gang of thugs and racketeers in post-war Tokyo. He has lots of fire power.

Occupation: Gangster.

Intelligence: Dawson is shifty and fast. He has quick instincts, but is not very brilliant otherwise.

Strengths: His organization.

Weaknesses: Greed. Becomes so big the Army is interested in him.

Territory: Tokyo.

Idiosyncrasies : Smokes cigars, cool demeanor.

Friends: Thinks Kenner is his friend.

Enemies: The U.S. Army, the Japanese authorities.

Relatives: Cody in *White Heat*.

Evil Deeds: Smuggling, gun running, drugs, extortion, graft, theft, diversion of military supplies. Murder, too.

Killed by: Kenner and Dawson play cat and mouse in a daring game for the highest stakes –life–in a Japanese amusement park. The two blaze at each other in a struggle to the death amidst the weird, garish atmosphere. It ends when Kenner wins the duel and Mariko is in Kenner's arms. The whole tawdry atmosphere of alienation and ennui in a conquered nation is displayed before us. Symbolically, Kenner is a part of the disillusionment of victory. We all thought it would be so great after the war, but it's just more violence and struggle.

Current Status: Dead.

What to Do If You Meet: Dawson is best left alone.

Worthy of Note: The real star of the film is the carnival sleaze and the underside of Oriental society.

Sir Brian de Bois-Guilbert

Born/Died: Merrie olde England

Starred in:
Ivanhoe
MGM, 1952
Director: Richard Thorpe
Played by: George Sanders

Description: Ivanhoe's foe, Sir Brian, is a knight, with armor and chain mail covering his head and neck. He also carries a lance when in combat. Otherwise he wears a loose, flamboyant, escutcheoned blouse, and stockings. He's tall, with long and flowing hair. He has a big nose and chin, a beard and moustache.

Sir Brian De Bois-Guilbert (George Sanders) sits on the right of the Norman usurper of the English throne Prince John in Ivanhoe.

Reason for Villainy: Sir Brian supports evil Prince John against Richard the Lionhearted, true and just King of England, who is in captivity in Europe. Ivanhoe (Robert Taylor) is on his way home to England from the Crusades. Ivanhoe, disowned by his father, vows to stop Prince John from usurping the throne. Lovely Rowena (Joan Fontaine) has been waiting for him and he rekindles the flames of passion. Ivanhoe goes to a prominent Jew for ransom money to free Richard. The Jew, Isaac of York (Felix Aylmer), gives him the bounty, because Richard, unlike the Norman viper John, is fair to all races and creeds. Ivanhoe then falls for Isaac's daughter Rebecca, and subsequently Sir Brian arrests Ivanhoe and his followers. The rebellion is not quelled, because Sir Robin of Locksley (Robin Hood) besieges the castle, and Ivanhoe sets fires that help the Saxon attack. Brian steals away with Rebecca in his arms. Rebecca is to be tried as a sorceress because she is a Jew who "compromised" the virtue of a knight of Christendom. Ivanhoe appears and chivalrously demands to defend her—though he is not well. Brian will ride against him in the joust.

Evil Powers: He's the right-hand man of usurper John.

Weapons: Mace (not the aerosol type), lance, armor, fleet horse, ax, shield, helmet.

Occupation: Knight.

Intelligence: Master of the joust and its rules and strategies. Knowledge of the laws of the Church affecting Jews and sorcerers. Has a knowledge of intrigue and knows where the power lies—with Prince John (he thinks).

Strengths/Weaknesses: Sir Brian has pull with the Prince. He also has the advantage of his strength and ability in the joust for fair Rebecca's life. He is good with a sword, lance, shield, and mace.

Territory: Brian rides for the Normans and Prince John throughout England, although he must be wary in Sherwood Forest, because Sir Robin lurks there. Yet, in his castle, the infamous Torquilstone Fortress, he feels secure.

Idiosyncrasies: Sir Brian is chivalrous, and fights fair despite the advantages he could take if he didn't go by the rules.

Friends: The Prince and his forces.

Enemies: Ivanhoe, Richard's men, the Saxons, and the Jewish merchants.

Evil Deeds: Imprisons Ivanhoe, holds Rebecca on the false charge of sorcery, and covets powers rightly belonging to Richard's forces. Slaughter of peasant Saxons, oppression, and taxation without representation.

Outcome: The duel is fierce. The riders fall from their horses and engage in swings of sword, chains, and mace. Ivanhoe wins. The dying villain sees Richard's men arriving. Ivanhoe's cause is now secure. Ivanhoe then bids adieu to Rebecca, who, with her father, is to leave for the Continent. The ever-chaste and faithful Rowena falls into Ivanhoe's arms once more, and he assumes his place at the height of the Saxon leadership, reconciled with all, and blessed by God, etc., etc.

The Count of Monte Cristo encounters two of the evil conspirators.

Current Status: Sir Brian is maced-out at the moment.

What to Do If You Meet: Brian fights fair—but is strong. Get a token of your beloved to wear on your helmet for luck. You'll need it.

Worthy of Note: It's lovely to see these jousts and fair maidens, the honor of knighthood, the noble death of a worthy opponent, and the triumph of good. Chivalry is so lacking in our urban streets. The castle fight is incredible. The pageant and spectacle make this a must-see.

De Villefort, Mondego, and Danglars

Born: 1700s
Died: Mondego dies, Danglars becomes insane, De Villefort is arrested.

Starred in:
The Count of Monte Cristo
Reliance Films, 1934
Director: Rowland V. Lee
Played by: Louis Calhern, Sidney Blackmer, Raymond Walburn

Reason for Villainy: Edmond Dantes (Robert Donat) is a young French naval officer about to be married to Mercedes (Elissa Landi). Suddenly he is arrested and accused of being a supporter of the now deposed Napoleon. He is imprisoned in the notorious Chateau d'If. Many years of deprived, miserable existence pass without hope. Eventually he discovers that he is the victim of a plot by a civil servant, De Villefort. Dantes was unknowingly carrying a traitorous dispatch for him when arrested. De Villefort was in league with Mondego, who has now married Dantes's fiancee, and Danglars, a jealous naval officer who also conspired to frame him. One day, years after being put in solitary, Dantes hears tapping in the wall. A year passes, and an old, bearded man, the Abbé (O.P. Heggie) crawls through a hole. The old man teaches Dantes science, philosophy, religion. They try to continue digging an escape. But the Abbé dies. Dantes buries the Abbé in the wall and sews himself into the Abbé's body bag. The guards toss the supposedly dead body into the surf. Dantes is free. He goes to the isle of Monte Cristo, where the Abbé had an immense treasure buried. He becomes a rich, intelligent, and powerful count. Twenty years have gone by since Dantes was first imprisoned. Our conspirators have been successful. However, the Count will now try to destroy our villains.

Evil Powers: These three are good at deception, and they are wealthy, influential, and successful.

Occupation: Mondego, a general; De Villefort, a government minister; Danglars, a great banker.

Intelligence: The three are cunning.

Strengths: They have power.

Weaknesses: They don't expect the return of Dantes—in great wealth and power.

Territory: France.

Idiosyncrasies: They are too complacent.

Friends: They have influence on people.

Enemies: Dantes (The Count).

Evil Deeds: Unlawful imprisonment, conspiracy, meanness.

Outcome: All three seek to serve—and profit by association with—the new, mysterious Count of Monte Cristo. He inveigles them in schemes, and then pulls the bottom out from under them. He exposes Mondego's scandals and the villain takes his own life. Then the Count ruins Danglars's bank. Finally he has himself arrested and charged by De Villefort, but turns the tables in court brilliantly. The villain is condemned by the law. Dantes returns to Mercedes and lives happily ever after.

Current Status: De Villefort is incarcerated, Mondego is dead, and Danglars is broke.

What to Do If You Meet: Don't trust them.

Worthy of Note: One of the most dramatic adventures ever filmed. Three cheers for the Count. A rags-to-riches scheme with which everyone can identify.

Ulysses Diello

Alias: Cicero
Born: 1900s
Died: 1945

Starred in:
Five Fingers
20th Century Fox, 1952
Director: Joseph L. Mankiewicz
Played by: James Mason

Description: Dark and handsome, but almost bald. He has gold teeth and strange eyes. He's an employee at the British Embassy in Ankara, Turkey. Because of his position he wears decent duds, and they hide his evil.

Reason for Villainy: Diello has access to every scrap of paper that crosses the British ambassador's desk in Ankara and he offers to

Ulysses Diello (James Mason) is one of the best German spies ever in Five Fingers.

copy these papers for the Germans and their master spy Von Pappen (John Wengraf). The Germans pay him, but are wary of following up on the information thinking it might be a trick. The reason Diello wants the money is to make a life for himself with the impoverished Countess Staviska (Danielle Darrieux) in Rio. However, she slaps him when he implies that she can be bought. Royalty above money, it seems. Meanwhile, British Intelligence sniffs something foul and agent Travers (Michael Rennie) flies to Ankara and informs Ambassador Sir Frederick (Walter Hampden). An alarm is placed on the safe. On the German side, Gestapo spy chief Von Richter (Herbert Berghof) is intrigued by all the references in the secret material to "Operation Overlord." He orders Diello to get more documents on this secret invasion plan of the Allies.

Evil Powers/Weapons: He is good at his spying thing, der Fuehrer will be pleased.

Occupation: Spy, traitor, fugitive.

Intelligence: Diello is clever, but so is the devil.

Strengths: He's well paid.

Weaknesses: He is pursued by British Intelligence.

Territory: Ankara, Turkey.

Idiosyncrasies: Greedy, greedy, greedy.

Friends: He thinks the countess is his friend.

Enemies: The British.

Relatives: Mata Hari is a distant cousin.

Evil Deeds: Helping the mad dictator with his plan for world domination.

Outcome: Diello realizes that the British are on to him and he decides to flee with the countess, who has finally let him call her Anna. But the Countess disappears with all the money he had saved. So much for *noblesse oblige!* Penniless, Diello decides to steal the "Overlord" secrets for the Nazis anyway. He partially disarms the alarm, but the darned cleaning lady reconnects the fuse so she can vacuum. Diello flees with the info, but Travers is in hot pursuit. In Istanbul, he hands over the film to Moyzisch (Oscar Karlweis), his contact, and plans to board a ship with his Nazi payoff and go to Rio. Eluding the Nazis who have no use for him now, and the British, Diello fades away. But wait, will the Nazis use this great information? No. You see, the countess, who doublecrossed Diello, has written the Nazis saying Diello is a British agent feeding them false information. The foolish Germans destroy the authentic plans.

Current Status: Starved to death in 1945—the Nazi money was counterfeit.

What to Do If You Meet: Call Interpol.

Worthy of Note: Based on true incidents. How close we were to losing the second World War!

Dillon

Alias: Eddie's best friend
Born: 1930s
Died: Still alive

Starred in:
The Friends of Eddie Coyle
Paramount, 1973
Director: Peter Yates
Played by: Peter Boyle

Description: Dillon is bald, chunky, and about six feet tall. He has darting, beady eyes and a quick, insincere smile. The only place he looks comfortable is in the stands at a sporting event. What hair he has is black, and he favors sports clothes over suits.

Reason for Villainy: Eddie Coyle (Robert Mitchum) is a friend of Dillon. However, Dillon, a professional hit man, is contracted to kill his buddy because Eddie is cooperating with the Feds in a criminal investigation. Eddie is a three-time loser. He's up for his third jail stint for a serious crime. In the less liberal American days, that meant you were behind bars for life. To avoid jail, Eddie agrees to cooperate with the law. He hopes for a "break." He informs on many criminals to T-man, Dave Foley (Richard Jordan). Eddie was involved in transporting stolen goods across state borders. This makes him a good source for information. Meanwhile, the mob contacts Dillon, and arrangements are made with the callous gunsel to eliminate his buddy. Dillon plays up to Eddie, and they make the rounds together. The slimy bum makes Eddie think that he's still his best friend by treating him to shows, drinks, a last fling at life—like a lamb being milk-fed just before it's slaughtered. Don't you hate this kind of insincerity? Isn't this the worst kind of villainy—betrayal of a good friend?

Evil Powers: Dillon is sneaky, real sneaky. And he's good with the tool of his trade—the gun.

Occupation: Hit man, mob style.

Intelligence: Smart like a weasel.

Strengths: Dillon likes his work.

Weaknesses: He also likes Eddie.

Territory: Boston.

Idiosyncrasies: Dillon has to take his sweet time setting up his hits.

Friends: Eddie.

Enemies: Eddie.

Evil Deeds: Are you kidding? Numerous "hits."

Outcome: Dillon goes with Eddie to a great hockey game (it's all part of the palsy-walsy bit). They go for a spin afterwards. That is when Dillon plans to make his move. Hey Eddie, let's go to some dark, deserted place so's I can bump you off, he says to himself. Yup, Eddie's earthly time is up, and Dillon is the messenger of death. Eddie Coyle, small time hood up for some big time in the big

Dillon (Peter Boyle) isn't really interested in the game; he's intent on gaining Coyle's confidence then killing him in The Friends of Eddie Coyle.

house winds up pushing the bell on the pearly gate. Eddie experienced an ignominious end that befalls all who fall in with the wrong company. I guess that's the message. And Dillon, not surprisingly, gets away with it all.

Current Status: Dillon is still pursuing higher goals in life (better hits for the mob, that is) at end of the film.

What to Do If You Meet: Don't take rides to lonely spots with him.

Worthy of Note: This 1973 film has the mood and demeanor of some of the great 1940s crime films. Bravo!

The Dirty Dozen

Born: 1900s
Died: Most died 1944

Starred in:
The Dirty Dozen
MGM, 1967
Director: Robert Aldrich
Played by: Lee Marvin, Charles Bronson, Jim Brown, John Cassavetes, Telly Savalas, Clint Walker, Donald Sutherland, Tom Busby, Ben Carruthers, Stuart Cooper, Robert Phillips, Colin Maitland, Richard Jaeckel, Trini Lopez

Description: The meanest, most hostile bunch of khaki-clad killers this side of Hitler's bunker. Sneering hunks of muscle and madness.

Reason for Villainy: It is Europe, World War II, and an impossible mission needs to be accomplished. The Allies need expendable men who can accomplish the impossible plus men who will think nothing of killing women and children. The answer: Prisoners sentenced to death for various despicable crimes. Their reward, if they survive, is freedom. According to his superiors (played by Robert Ryan, Ernest Borgnine, and Robert Webber), the

The Dirty Dozen attack ferociously, sparing none of the enemy.

man to head this despicable crew is Major Reisman (Lee Marvin). The challenge: Whip the sadistic bunch into an effective commando team and go blow up the underground bunkers of German officers and their families. Soon the war games begin. The Dirty Dozen learn that Major Reisman can bend the best of them. The men form a sort of odd camaraderie, but they all hate the insanest and cruelest of the bunch, Maggot (Telly Savalas). However, since he is one of the best fighters, they are glad to have him.

Weapons: Sub-machine guns, armored vehicles, flamethrowers, bombs.

Occupation: Suicide commandoes.

Intelligence: Below average to way-below average.

Strengths: Insane penchant for violence and cruelty, nothing to lose.

Weaknesses: They detest the high command as much as the Nazis.

Territory: Wartime Europe, 1944.

Idiosyncrasies: Stubborn, reckless, cruel.

Friends: Their guns.

Enemies: The Nazi army.

Evil Deeds: Aside from killing, raping, and robbing half the people on our side, what they do to the Germans shouldn't be done to cockroaches. They burn entire German families alive.

Killed by: Now it's time to go and accomplish the impossible. They attack a German-occupied villa and drive the Germans into the safety—or so they think—of their underground bunkers. But spies have smuggled out the plans of these bunkers. The Dirty Dozen use the ventilation ducts to pour down hellfire and incinerate all below—a dastardly deed performed with skill, and sometimes glee. The opposition is fierce, after all it's a suicide mission. Getting there has taken its toll. The attack kills off most of the rest of the crazies. Should the few left alive be decorated for killing civilians along with the officers? Hardly. This movie breaks new ground in showing the cruelty of war—as opposed to the glory. Perhaps it reflects the new Viet Nam era consciousness about warfare—it's dirty.

Current Status: Dead. The few survivors of the mission died a few months later in fights unrelated to the war.

What to Do If You Meet: Stay away.

Worthy of Note: Both Savalas and Bronson in one movie—with Lee Marvin! It was bound to be a tough action movie, and it was.

Fred C. Dobbs

Born: Turn of the century
Died: 1930s

Starred in:
Treasure of the Sierra Madre
Warner Brothers, 1948
Director: John Huston
Played by: Humphrey Bogart

Description: A mangy American drifter and two-bit hustler, greedy, petty, dirty. Always has half-grown beard and sweaty clothes. Wears hat.

Reason for Villainy: Stranded in Mexico without a centavo, Fred C. Dobbs joins up with another American, Curtin (Tim Holt), in an effort to prospect for gold and scrape up enough money to get back to the U.S. They buy the necessary equipment and take on another partner, Howard (Walter Huston), an eccentric old prospector who knows the area. While traveling from Tampico to Durango, they're attacked by Mexican bandits led by the evil Gold Hat (Alfonso Bedoya), but they drive them away with the help of soldiers on a train. After getting supplies and mules, the three men head up into the Sierra Madres.

Evil Powers: Paranoia and greed makes him go mad and plot to cheat his partners.

Weapons: Uses rifle and pistol.

Occupation: Drifter, construction worker, prospector.

Intelligence: Intelligent, but mostly cunning—like a rat.

Strengths: Strong personality, brave.

Goldhat approaches Dobbs, taunting him. Within seconds he will pull out a machete and kill the other villain in Treasure of the Sierra Madre.

Weaknesses: Mad, filled with a fatal, all-consuming greed.

Territory: America, Mexico, the Sierra Madres.

Idiosyncrasies: Becomes increasingly paranoid, edgy. Hears things, sees things in the dark, talks to himself more and more.

Friends/Enemies: Other men try to befriend him (Howard tells him of the corrupting effects of gold), but he becomes hostile to them. He's sure that they're plotting to kill him.

Evil Deeds: Tries to kill Curtin, steals gold.

Killed by: The men do find gold and prospect it, putting it away in their saddlebags. But Dobbs becomes increasingly suspicious of his partners and starts muttering accusations. On their way home, the partners are approached by tribe of Indians seeking help for a sick boy. Howard goes and saves his life. Meanwhile, Dobbs goes over the edge and shoots Curtin, taking all the money. Wounded, Curtin crawls to Howard and the Indians. The now completely demented Dobbs stumbles on, with the gold on a mule. But before he gets very far, he is attacked by Gold Hat, who taunts the prospector and kills him with a machete. The bandits rip open the sacks of gold not knowing the value and the dust blows away in the desert wind.

Current Status: Dead, halved by Mexicans.

What to Do If You Meet: Tell him you know where there's more gold, but don't turn your back on him for one second.

Worthy of Note: One of the best. Bogart rarely talked about any of his films, but whenever *Treasure of the Sierra Madre* was mentioned he would shrug "Yeah, that wasn't a bad one." The film won two Academy Awards.

Doc & Dix

Alias: The Thieves
Born: Doc–turn of century
      Dix–1920's
Died: Doc–in jail
      Dix–1950

Doc (Sam Jaffe) shows the stolen jewels as the crooked Alonzo smiles greedily and Dix (Sterling Hayden) looks on suspiciously in The Asphalt Jungle.

Starred in:
The Asphalt Jungle
MGM, 1950
Director: John Huston
Played by: Sam Jaffe, Sterling Hayden

Description: Doc Riedenschneider is an aging crook in his 60s. He is charming and well-dressed, always in a suit and tie, hat and gloves. Dix is a small-time hood, slightly scruffy looking, with his collar up, and stubble on his face. Neither man is truly evil, they just happen to be crooks.

Reason for Villainy: Dix just wants enough money to return to his namesake—Dixieland—the green hills of Kentucky. Doc wants to return to his life of crime, even though he's just got out of prison. It's what he knows best; it's his element. Doc plans a jewel robbery with the financial help of crooked lawyer Alonzo D. Emmerich (Louis Calhern). Doc assembles a small group of low-level criminals and proceeds with the jewel robbery. It is a success. The plan, however, is doomed from the start because Doc has been set up by Alonzo to be double-crossed.

Evil Powers: Will do what is necessary to get what they want.

Weapons: Dix carries a gun.

Occupation: Doc is a master criminal, the leader and brains of the gang. Dix is a "hooligan" brought in just in case of trouble.

Intelligence: Doc is a genius at crime. Dix is of medium intelligence, but lost, cynical.

Strengths: Aggressive, focused on robbery.

Weaknesses: They are in beyond their depth. They are not quite corrupt or tough enough to compete with others.

Friends/Enemies: The group of thieves don't trust one another, but Alonzo is their real enemy.

Relatives: Ocean's Eleven, The Gang that Couldn't Shoot Straight.

Evil Deeds: The gang has stolen, cheated, and killed.

Killed by: Dix discovers that Alonzo plans to take the jewels and run. He kills a private eye hired by the crooked lawyer to sabotage the disposal of the loot. Dix is wounded in the gunfire. As the police move in, Alonzo commits suicide. Dix, who has come to like Doc, tries to convince him to take some of the money and helps him escape before the cops arrive. Dix escapes to the farmland of Kentucky, where he dies. Doc is captured by police.

Current Status: Dix is dead. Doc, if he's still around, would have been released from jail by now; he would be in his 90s, and probably planning another crime.

What to Do If You Meet: Tell them you know an easy score. But don't go!

Worthy of Note: One of the first and finest *films noirs*—set a tone for gangster and anti-hero films to come.

Doctor No

Born: 1920s
Died: 1963

Starred in:
Dr. No
United Artists, 1963
Director: Terence Young
Played by: Joseph Wiseman

Dr. No (Joseph Wiseman) is head of the criminal organization SPECTRE and it is James Bond's job to stop him.

Description: Dr. No is six feet, four inches tall and has an Oriental cast to his looks. He wears plastic gloves a lot and sometimes an anti-radiation suit. Neat uniforms with Nehru collars are his sartorial trademarks. His dark hair is swept back. Altogether, he's severe looking—the "military kimono" look.

Reason for Villainy: Dr. No is head of SPECTRE, a criminal organization acronym for "Special Executor for Counterintelligence, Terrorism, and Extortion." He has built a fortress on the mysteriously shrouded Crab Key Island. The fortress contains a huge reactor, and thousands of radiation-suited men work there. Plus, stunning women of all nationalities inhabit the island for diversion. There is a lot of guano (bird shit) on the island and it is used as a cover for the operations Dr. No is conducting. It seems that this island, near Jamaica, is famous for its great guano, used worldwide as a preferred fertilizer. But Dr. No is really using his giant dish-shaped weapon to shoot down U.S. missiles as they fly over the island. Dr. No also has quite a collection of great art treasures, including a missing Goya and other prizes that no honest man can afford. James Bond (Sean Connery) is introduced in this, the first of a long line of great Bond films. Perhaps this is the best Bond film because 007 is not so gadget-ridden here.

The film opens with Bond winning heartily at a casino. The lovely Sylvia Trench (Eunice Grayson) approaches the superspy, whose back is to us. She says "I admire your good luck, Mr. . . . ?," and a new era in film excitement is born when Bond turns, lights a cigarette, and says "James Bond." Other women, friendly or not, are enraptured by the suave spy. He later meets seductive Honey Ryder (Ursula Andress), who is on his side, wearing a wet T-shirt and a bikini of minute proportions. Bond also meets and charms deadly Miss Taro (Zena Marshall), who, as Dr. No's girl, lures Bond into the mountains to meet his end.

Women are not the only things that drop into Bond's bed. A tarantula is supplied by Dr. No. It crawls on him and wakes him up. Bond disposes of it and is then jumped by Dr. No's goon. Bond dumps him into the bathtub and drops in an electric fan. "Shocking," says Bond. Wry? Yet, Dr. No has other surprises up his sleeve.

Intelligence: Dr. No is a scientific genius, cultured, a real talent at arranging murder and mayhem.

Strengths: He's got all of SPECTRE behind him.

Weaknesses: Bond's in his way.

Territory: The guano-covered island of Crab Key.

Idiosyncrasies: The man likes power, especially of the nuclear variety. He's built an elaborate reactor station that really should be checked out by the N.R.C. before going into operation. It seems unstable.

Friends: His henchmen.

Enemies: Royal Navy Commander James Bond, 007—licensed to kill.

Evil Deeds: Hey, he's knocking down all those great missiles of ours. Do you know what that costs us taxpayers? Besides, he murders.

Killed by: There is a boiling hot pool—to cool the reactor perhaps—on the island. Dr. No sees it as a perfect way to get rid of the pesky Bond. But, in a switch, he himself gets dumped and drowns in the bubbly liquid. What an end. Yech! Bond, of course, gets the girl, Ursula Undress—er, sorry about that. And the whole damned island, of course, blows up—or this wouldn't be one of those massive, overkill-type films that are the trademark of the Bond series.

Current Status: Probably exported as part of the guano fertilizer.

What to Do If You Meet: Call M, Miss Moneypenny, anyone in MI-5 (the British Seret CIA-type agency). Ask for 007. Tell him a SPECTRE agent is haunting you.

Worthy of Note: The first of the Bond flicks with Connery. The film caused quite a sensation when it opened. Box office was so good that the producers knew they had hit on a gold mine. However, don't expect to find the same plots in Ian Fleming's books. For one thing, Bond is much more amusing in the films.

Hugo Drax

Born: 1950s
Died: Probably 1987

Starred in:
Moonraker
Eon Productions, 1979
Director: Lewis Gilbert
Played by: Michael Lonsdale

Description: Drax is dressed futuristically, of average height and weight. He is clean, very clean, and considers himself a superior being. Van Dyke beard, sports clothes, swept-back dark hair make him a neat, hip scientist.

Reason for Villainy: Drax wants to repopulate the world with a superior group of people. Of course, since the world is now populated with "inferior" types, he must first cleanse the Earth. He decides to launch hundreds of exterminating globes from space. He builds an enormous gravity-controlled space station that is invisible to detection by NASA and the Reds.

Let us now pick up Special British Agent James Bond (Roger Moore), who has been tracking Drax because the American Space Shuttle has been stolen. Drax had six Moonraker shuttlecraft ready to go into space. However, one shuttle was damaged, so he stole the Space Shuttle as a replacement in order to bring people up to the space station to start his new master race.

Dogging Bond's heels is Chang, Drax's manservant. The two engage in a fight that leaves the precious glass in the Venetian museum in shards. Drax then plants another surprise for Bond, who has teamed up with American CIA spy Holly Goodhead (Lois Chiles) in Rio. It is none other than favorite villain Jaws (Richard Kiel), the seven-foot-tall, steel-toothed strong man popular from another Bond flick. Jaws tries to bite the cable off of Bond and Goodhead's cable car, but only winds up hung up himself. However, all has not been for naught. Jaws meets and falls in love with a diminutive lady (Corrine

Hugo Drax (Michael Lonsdale) is James Bond's arch-nemesis in Moonraker.

Clery). The pair are all smiles from that point on. What does little pigtailed Corinne see in Jaws?

Evil Powers/Weapons: Drax, a genius, has a space station, space commandoes, laser guns, space shuttles, labs, poison gas made from orchids, Jaws, Chang, and an invisibility ray—whew!

Occupation: Mad scientist, orchid lover.

Intelligence: Genius-plus, with a touch of madness.

Strengths/Weaknesses: Drax is too confident that his scheme will work. However, he forgets that Bond is resourceful and a student of elementary psychology. Bond's casual remarks can turn the tables—or space station—around.

Territory: Outer space, Brazil, Venice.

Idiosyncrasies: Likes orchids.

Friends: Jaws—for a while, Chang, and his troops.

Enemies: Bond and Goodhead.

Evil Deeds: Kills pilots, steals Space Shuttle, conspires to put up unauthorized space station, conspires against U.N. charter forbidding genocide, and attempts to cremate Goodhead and Bond.

Outcome: Drax captures Bond and Goodhead, and thinks he's disposed of them at the rocket base, but they replace two of his shuttle pilots, fly up to the space station, and create havoc by destabilizing it. Bond and Goodhead destroy the station's invisibility long enough for NASA and the international community to send up some spacetroopers. Caught again, Bond has Drax explain his plans for the master race in front of Jaws and Corinne. Obviously, they are on the wrong side because they are not super race material. Helping Bond, Jaws wreaks havoc, the space troopers battle, and the day is saved. The station breaks up, supposedly dooming Drax. Bond and Goodhead take a shuttle and pursue the deadly orchid-gas globes, destroying them with laser guns. They make love in space, it's heavenly.

Current Status: Dead?

What to Do If You Meet: Get Jaws. (Jaws and his girl survived in a spinning piece of the space station that landed in the ocean.)

Worthy of Note: Good space battle, but weak James Bond film. Too much like a comic book.

Inspector Dreyfus

Born: 1930s
Died: Going mad, 1976

Starred in:
The Pink Panther Strikes Again
United Artists, 1976
Director: Blake Edwards
Played by: Herbert Lom

Description: Dreyfus used to be a neat, dapper inspector for the Sûreté in Paris. That's before he met his underling, Clouseau. Clouseau has made the man disheveled, although he still wears a three-piece striped suit and striped shirt. However, now he often has injuries caused inadvertently by Clouseau.

Reason for Villainy: Dreyfus has had it up to here with the mad antics of his worst employee, Clouseau. The trouble is that Clouseau accidentally succeeds in smashing difficult cases—literally. Dreyfus is forced to keep him on the police force. But the time has come, he decides, to kill the insane snoop. Clouseau, disguised as a sailor (with a statue of a parrot on his shoulder) or as Toulouse Lautrec, or fighting his houseboy Cato (Burt Kwouk), is damned lucky he doesn't get killed by Dreyfus, who is hiding nearby.

Dreyfus, in the apartment downstairs, is nearly crushed when Cato and Clouseau start doing their sparring and the ceiling falls. Clouseau always tells his servant to attack without warning so he can keep up his karate practice. The servant always attacks at a most inopportune time. This time, however, it thwarts the hostile Inspector's attack. Dreyfus goes over the edge. Clouseau has driven him mad. Dreyfus decides to force the world to kill Clouseau for him, and builds a Doomsday Ray machine. He makes his demands on worldwide TV: Kill Clouseau or else!

Evil Powers/Weapons: He's got the Doomsday Ray machine. It was built for him by the most brilliant scientist in the world when Dreyfus threatened the scientist's daughter.

Inspector Dreyfus (Herbert Lom) blames Clouseau for all his problems and fires a gun at him. That "gun" turns out to be a cigarette lighter, another mishap in The Pink Panther Strikes Again.

Occupation: Madman, former police inspector.

Intelligence: Clever, mad.

Strengths: He has a doomsday machine to threaten the world.

Weaknesses: Clouseau is incredibly lucky.

Territory: France, the Alps.

Idiosyncrasies: His one desire in life is to kill Clouseau.

Friends: His machine.

Enemies: Clouseau.

Evil Deeds: Kidnapping, plays the organ badly, attempted murder.

Outcome: The world must respond to the madman who possesses the Doomsday Ray. The President of the United States and the presidents of all other nations send their dead-liest agents to the Munich beer-guzzling Oktoberfest with orders to kill Clouseau. Otherwise Dreyfus will destroy many cities. But the agents, tracking Clouseau into a bathroom stall and surrounding him on both sides of the stall, all kill one another as Clouseau bends to retrieve a roll of toilet paper. Other agents meet their death in a similar way. Clouseau infiltrates Dreyfus's castle, disguised as a dentist, and drills at Dreyfus badly. Clouseau is unkillable, and Dreyfus is moved to a padded cell as the film ends. Presumably, Clouseau will get a higher police post, perhaps replacing his insane boss. You just can't win.

Current Status: Down at the asylum.

What to Do If You Meet: Don't mention you-know-who.

Worthy of Note: Although played for laughs, this villain still represents the way we feel about certain people at certain times. The film is doubly hysterical for its jokes, sight-gags aplenty, and subliminal truth: There are times when we want to kill somebody who's particularly annoying.

Eichelberger 81
Einar, the Viking 83
Eve 83

Faber 85
Harry Fabian 87
Fagin & Sikes 88
Dr. Allen Fields 89
Jennie Finch 91
Frank and Cora 92
Johnny Friendly 93
Fu Manchu 94

Elsa Gebhardt 95
Dr. George 96
German Captain
    of the *Louisa* 97
The Godfather 98
Bert Gordon 100
Gray 101
The Gunfighter 102
Casper Gutman 103
Sir Guy
    of Gisborne 104

Eichelberger

Born: Circa 1920
Died: Indicted 1952, outcome unknown

Starred in:
The Turning Point
Paramount, 1952
Director: William Dieterle
Played by: Ed Begley

Description: A distillation of all the ethers of evil, Eichelberger is the ultimate corrupt man. As his feral eyes and sweaty face reveal, he stops at nothing. He is dark and somberly dressed, often in a muted tie and suit. An ideal description has him calmly drinking a glass of fresh water while he plans the arson of an inhabited tenement.

Reason for Villainy: The scene is a midwestern city. Our story begins when John Conroy (Edmond O'Brien), an aggressive lawyer/politician, heads up an organized crime investigation. A reporter friend, Jerry McKibbon (William Holden), discovers that Conroy's father was a mob-controlled cop. McKibbon doesn't tell his friend the truth about his dad. But the syndicate chief, Eichelberger himself, begins to put the screws on Conroy, ordering him killed if he persists in his investigations. The committee has its eyes on the gangster's records, which are stored in a tenement, and they subpoena them. Eichel-

Ed Begley (far right) plays the syndicate chief Eichelberger in Turning Point.

berger, committing a heinous act, destroys the building with fire, killing the poor slobs inside. McKibbon then walks into a trap at a ring fight. Conroy learns of the trap, but will he be in time to warn McKibbon.

Evil Power/Weapons: Eichelberger has his mob, and he uses arson freely. He's also good with a gun.

Occupation: Gangster.

Intelligence: Feral finesse.

Strengths: Utter contempt for life lets him burn, burn incriminating evidence.

Weaknesses: Brutal men meet just desserts.

Territory: Midwestern city.

Idiosyncrasies: Inhuman conscience.

Friends: The mob.

Enemies: The reporter and the lawyer.

Relatives: Big Al out of Chicago.

Evil Deeds: Cremates men, women, and children alive and plans murders for his aides to carry out. He's the top man in the mob, and the mob does every bad thing you could imagine.

Outcome: Eichelberger cannot be stopped—or can he? McKibbon walks into the trap before Conroy and the police arrive, but now they have, over McKibbon's body, more damning evidence against Eichelberger. A witness to one of the gangster's murders is also singing like a canary to the investigating committee. With all the pieces together, Eichelberger's career as a professional criminal comes to an end.

Current Status: Indicted for murder, and probably fried in the electric chair.

What to Do If You Meet: Keep out of tenements.

Worthy of Note: This film was probably inspired by the Kefaufer committee hearings going on in Washington, D.C. in the early 1950s. The semi-documentary fashion of the film adds to its realistic portrayal of an atmosphere of corruption which was much in the news.

Einar, the son of the leader of The Vikings, hurls his weapon in a fit of rage.

Einar, the Viking

Born: 10th century Norway
Died: About 35 years later

Starred in:
The Vikings
United Artists, 1958
Director: Richard Fleischer
Played by: Kirk Douglas

Description: One-eyed, tall, blonde, rugged features. Full of Viking vitality and fearlessness. Wears chain armor and brightly colored vest.

Reason for Villainy: Einar was raised to be a Viking warrior, and taught to be tough as nails. He worships Odin, the god of war. Taunted by a slave, Eric (Tony Curtis), Einar fights him and loses an eye. Eric is punished by being thrown into a slop pool filled with giant crabs, to be eaten alive. Egbert, an English ally, notices that Eric has the royal stone of the English Queen and persuades Einar's father, Ragnar, the Viking leader, to save him. (It seems that the Queen had been raped by Ragnar and that Eric is Einar's half brother, without either of them knowing it.) Later after a raid on England, Morgana (Janet Leigh), an English princess, is brought back to Norway where, to the consternation of Einar, she falls in love with Eric. The lovers escape to England and Ragnar pursues. He is captured by Eric, who hopes to exchange him for Morgana, who is being forced to marry a nobleman she hates. When Ragnar is thrown into a wolf pit, Eric throws him a sword to die like a Viking. For this, Eric too is thrown in and loses a hand. Saved from death by Morgana's pleas, he is cast adrift by Morgana's fiancé and gets back to Norway. When he explains to Einar what happened they set aside hatred and attack England.

Evil Powers/Weapons: Swings a huge broadsword, uses ropes, axes, daggers. The Viking longboat is swift and more powerful than English ships.

Occupation: Viking raider, warrior prince.
Intelligence: Cunning, swift, single-minded at getting what he wants.
Strengths: Fierce beyond belief. Willing to withstand anything.
Weaknesses: Believes death as a Viking is the best goal in life.
Territory: Lives in Norway but raids England.
Idiosyncrasies: Wants to die with a sword in his hand to enter Viking heaven, Valhalla.
Friends: Eric is an ally when it serves both of their purposes.
Enemies: Hates the English and all weaker races.
Relatives: Both Einar and Eric are sons of Ragnar, King of the Viking clan, but they don't know it.
Evil Deeds: Kills and rapes scores of English. Cruel.
Killed by: Now united, Eric and Einar and their forces attack King Aella's territory. In bloody hand-to-hand combat they vanquish the English. Einar reaches Morgana first and claims her, but she rejects him. He says he'll kill Eric and take her. She, however, reveals that Eric is his brother. Eric attacks and stabs Einar when the Viking, for the first time in his life, hesitates to take advantage of an opponent's weakness. Mortally wounded, Einar demands the right to die with a sword in his hand and Eric hands him one. In a shout to the gods, Einar enters Valhalla. His funeral is like all great Viking endings—he's put in a warboat which is set afire and sent out to sea.

Current Status: Einar is separated from us by about 1,000 years. Be glad!

Worthy of Note: One of Kirk's own productions, and one of his, (and one of our) favorite movies.

What to Do If You Meet: Tell him you hate King Aella, Morgana has a soft spot for him, and that you worship Odin.

Eve

Born: 1920s
Died: Unknown

Starred in:
All About Eve
20th Century Fox, 1950
Director: Joseph L. Mankiewicz
Played by: Anne Baxter

Description: Striking young woman, brunette, open, an innocent-looking face, filled with naiveté. Has a quality that draws people to her, mixture of child and woman. She's ruthless, ambitious, and wants to be a star. She will do anything to get there.

Reason for Villainy: Eve Harrington is found by Karen (Celeste Holm) outside the theater where Margo Channing (Bette Davis), a great star, is performing. She brings her to meet Margo and other assembled greats—playwright Lloyd Richard (Hugh Marlowe), Bill Sampson (Margo's boyfriend), and the play's director (Gary Merrill). They are all taken by Eve's seeming openness and are spellbound. Margo asks her to come stay with her. Eve becomes a servant around Margo's home, but beneath the surface she is watching and absorbing all of Margo's skills.

Evil Powers/Weapons: Her personality is somehow a mixture of charm and child that draws people magnetically to her. She uses her beautiful body and face to attract men and get what she wants.

Occupation: Farm girl, actress.

Intelligence: Appears to be quite intelligent and an amazing storyteller. As the movie progresses, we see that she is, in fact, quite empty inside, without real depth, just the illusion of it.

Strengths: Charm, looks, acting ability.

Weaknesses: Emptiness, amorality.

Territory: New York City, Broadway theaters.

Idiosyncrasies: Observes her mentor, Margo Channing, and learns her acting tech-

Theater critic Addison De Witt is spellbound upon meeting Eve (Anne Baxter) while a jealous Margo Channing and a friend look on in All About Eve.

niques and motions down to the minutest detail.

Friends/Enemies: Everyone loves her at first, but later they realize her deceptiveness.

Evil Deeds: Uses people as steppingstones to further her own career. Tries to wreck marriages and seduces any man who can help her.

Outcome: Eve does all of Margo's housework and appears to love the older star. But Margo, at 40, is sensitive to her age and begins believing that Eve is trying to steal Bill. However, after fighting over Eve, Bill and Margo decide to marry. Eve eventually becomes Margo's understudy. When Margo can't go on one night, Eve steps in and is a huge success. Eve then hooks up with the dastardly theater critic Addison De Witt (George Sanders), who helps further her career through his columns. (He wrote that Margo should give up her part to Eve.) Eve then tries to attract Lloyd Richard, but Addison finds out and threatens to expose her if she doesn't come back to him. With her play a huge success, Eve wins the coveted Sarah Siddons Award. But Eve has lost all of her friends. Not one even attended the awards' banquet. Returning to her dressing room Eve meets Phoebe, an aspiring actress. Phoebe begins coming on to Eve as Eve once did to Margo. Eve's days are numbered.

Current Status: Alive, an aging actress.

What to Do If You Meet: Don't let her seduce you or you'll regret it!

Worthy of Note: Classic. One of the more intelligent and meaningful films made of the world of theater. Sparkling dialogue and a cast of true all-stars. The film won an Academy Award for Best Picture.

Faber

Born: Around 1910
Died: 1944

Starred in:
Eye of the Needle
United Artists, 1981
Director: Richard Marquand
Played by: Donald Sutherland

Description: Faber is the ultimate effective German spy. Even Hitler has heard of him. If you see his face and recognize him, his knife flashes and you're dead. He's tall, charming, though a bit cold. He has a moustache, soulful eyes, and brown-blond hair.

Reason for Villainy: World War II is on. The Allies are creating a fictitious invasion fleet, complete with thousands of cardboard airplanes, for Patton. Faber is in England to verify if it is indeed a real invasion force. The Nazis for the most part think it is—it seems logical that Patton wouldn't be running around playing make believe in the countryside—and the area is heavily patrolled. Faber is surprised by his landlady while listening to his secret radio. He kills the landlady even though she dropped by with an offer to make love. He also kills a young Nazi sent to give him his mission—he's expendable. Then, he steals a canal boat, eludes the patrols, and discovers that the whole invasion force under Patton is a fake. He must somehow get to the U-boat rendezvous point to tell Hitler that the real invasion will be at Normandy, not Calais. He'll kill, rob, or love anyone that can help. His stolen ship is wrecked and he crawls out on a small island inhabited by a seriously crippled pilot and his young bride, Lucy (Kate Nelligan). They suspect nothing. He makes love to Lucy, and the husband becomes suspicious—of other things.

Evil Powers: The most cunning spy for the Nazis—reliable.

Weapons: His knife, his strength, his will.

Occupation: Hitler's trusted spy.

Intelligence: Brilliant, paranoiac mind.

Strengths: His willpower.

Weaknesses: British counter-intelligence is after him.

Territory: Scotland, Germany.

Idiosyncrasies: The need for love versus his duty is in battle.

Friends: The Germans on the U-boat.

Enemies: Lucy's husband.

Evil Deeds: Kills the landlady, home-guard river patrollers, the other German spy who he feels is expendable, and Lucy's husband.

Outcome: Faber roams the sheep-filled island. He must contact the U-boat, or Germany herself. He finds a shepherd who has a small radio and kills the old man. But then

Faber, the sly German spy, makes love to Lucy who has given him shelter on her remote Scottish island in Eye of the Needle.

he is surprised by Lucy's husband who confronts him on the cliffside. There is a struggle for survival. The ex-pilot has, at last, something he can do for his nation. Unfortunately, he fights too fair and Faber dumps him off the cliff. There is no mercy for the enemies of the Reich. Faber returns to the house. Lucy has boarded it up and stares frantically from inside. Faber says he loves her and that she should let him in. Lucy struggles with her emo-

tions and stalls. A team of Britishers is on the way; she must detain him. Finally, there is nothing to do but battle Faber and kill him. The commandoes arrive, survey the damage and the carnage. One woman had done the dirty work alone. The U-boat submerges. The Nazis will never know about the real invasion set for Normandy, June 6, 1944.

Harry Fabian

Born: 1920s
Died: 1950

Starred in:
Night and the City
20th Century Fox, 1950
Director: Jules Dassin
Played by: Richard Widmark

Description: Sleazo type of fight promoter, hanger-on, chump. Wears a snap brim hat, has acne scars, and a slouchy countenance. This guy is a gutter-type hustler in a suit. What's with the lapel flower? Who's his tailor? Shoot the guy.

Reason for Villainy: Fabian is interested in being big time, making big bucks. He will do anything to get it. He doesn't deliberately murder anyone to reach the top of the wrestling-promotion field, but his manipulations lead to a great man's death. Not to mention his own. It all starts in merry old England, circa 1950. Harry is out of luck and out of cash. He's a tout for the Greek's London Club—a sin spot with not enough sin to keep customers coming back. His girl friend, singer Mary

Harry Fabian (Richard Widmark) is lucky to have a girl who will stick with him whatever he does, but he'd still rather have a lot of money in Night and the City.

Bristol (Gene Tierney), is a sucker for this lout. Fabian tells her that he wants to be like Kristos, a big, important, wrestling promoter. Fat chance. But Harry tries. Through slimy maneuvers he manages to find out that the great wrestler Gregorius—who is so great he doesn't wrestle much anymore—is Kristo's father. Well, what a match it would be—and what money it would make for Fabian—to have Gregorius's protégé Nickolas wrestling for him. Can he pull it off? Our villain sets up the match with funding from a nightclub owner's wife, Helen Nosseros. (Don't you dig these names?) Mr. Nosseros (Francis L. Sullivan) doesn't like the cozy relationship between Fabian and his wife, and to make things worse, she leaves Nosseros.

Evil Powers: Fabian is amoral and conniving. If he stopped to think. . . .

Occupation: Hustler, tout, schemer, dreamer.

Intelligence: Schemer, but you can tell by the outcome that he doesn't work things through too well.

Strengths: He knows what he wants.

Weaknesses: He wants the wrong things, and causes damage in the world.

Territory: The sweaty gyms and locker-rooms of London.

Idiosyncrasies: Dames somehow fall for him.

Friends: He uses people. Gregorius thinks he's a friend.

Enemies: Kristo, anyone in his way.

Evil Deeds: He has quite a record of betrayals. He will do anything to get his way. He steps on people. What he does to Gregorius —he has the simple-minded old pro killed—is unforgivable, if anything is.

Killed by: Nosseros won't take Fabian's deceitful tricks lying down. He goes to Kristo (Herbert Lom) and offers his services to trap the schemer. Nosseros tells Fabian that Nickolas must wrestle the "Strangler," an insane, mad brawler who is highly valued to audiences. Fabian is bewildered. How to make Nickolas do this is a problem. For the Strangler, as Nosseros well knows, hates Gregorius. Fabian lures the Strangler to the gym to set up a confrontation. At the gym he will say to the two angry wrestlers, "Let Nickolas and the Strangler settle it in the ring." But Gregorius and the Strangler get into a tiff, and they fight to the death—without even one seat sold. What a waste. Fabian can do nothing. Gregorius wins, but dies of exhaustion. Kristo puts out a contract on Fabian. Our villain dodges the entire underworld of London and winds up on a barge in the river. Mary eventually finds him. The Strangler, realizing that Fabian had maneuvered him into murder, grabs Fabian, kills him, and throws him in the river.

Current Status: Dead, floating down the river.

What to Do If You Meet: Fabian should learn that money isn't everything. Tell him to meditate for a year, then go back to his sweetheart. He blew it all for a few lousy bucks.

Worthy of Note: Exhausted, wheeling through light and harsh shadow, the ratlike Fabian is well portrayed by your favorite and ours, the great Widmark.

Fagin & Sikes

Born/Died: 19th century England

Starred in:
Oliver Twist
Gineguild, 1948
Director: David Lean
Played by: Alec Guinness, Robert Newton

Description: Fagin is a long-bearded, ragged old man with a huge nose and a somber expression. He is often seen, as is Sikes, in the company of a rag-tag army of mini-thieves. Sikes is a sweaty, swarthy, non-gentleman who wears a battered top hat and carries a flintlock pistol.

Reason for Villainy: This film is true to the book—as much as time allows. A grizzled Robert Newton is loathsome as Sikes. Guinness, lisping and rasping across the screen, is convincing as the master of the little criminals.

The myriad details of the grubby back streets of London are very adequately portrayed here. We see Oliver Twist (John Howard Davies), an orphan, learning at an early age the cruel vicissitudes of life. He runs from an orphanage into the clutches of criminal Fagin. Fagin teaches Oliver the art of pickpocketing and other nefarious skills. Later, Oliver is rescued by Mr. Brownlow (Henry Stephenson), but is quickly abducted back to Fagin by Sikes.

Evil Powers/Weapons: Fagin and Sikes are the leading figures in a ring of child-using thieves in the slums of London. For shame!

Occupation: Criminals.

Intelligence: Crafty nasties.

Strengths: They're hidden in the vast slums of London, and they have an army of larcenous brats.

Weaknesses: Kind people will intervene.

Territory: The London slums.

Idiosyncrasies: Not your typical court-appointed guardians.

Friends: Each other.

Enemies: Decency.

Sikes (Robert Newton) is a cohort of Fagin and together they head a rag-tag army of juvenile thieves in Oliver Twist.

Relatives: Scrooge could be a cousin to Fagin.

Evil Deeds: Innumerable. Taking advantage of young kids is not nice. Particularly heinous was Sikes' crime of murdering the poor doxy Nancy.

Outcome: The kindhearted doxy is beaten to death by Sikes when she tries to help Oliver get away. She, at least, had been kind to Oliver. As Sikes and Oliver escape over the roofs of London, Sikes is confronted and killed. The authorities—and the mob—have also surrounded Fagin's premises. He will get his just desserts if they get him. So ends our villains, ultimately.

Current Status: Dead.

What to Do If You Meet: Grow up fast.

Worthy of Note: Davies is a very believable Oliver here. Guinness' portrayal of Fagin was considered by many to be an affront to Jews. This version was not given wide play in the U.S.A. until 1951 and the only full version of the original Fagin portrayal was shown at the Museum of Modern Art in a David Lean retrospective in 1970.

Dr. Allen Fields

Alias: The Thief
Born: 1920s
Died: Received maximum sentence for espionage in 1952.

Starred in:
The Thief
United Artists, 1952.
Director: Russell Rouse
Played by: Ray Milland

Description: He wears an overcoat and a snap brim hat that he pulls down in crowds. He looks furtive. He keeps his nervous hands in his pockets. He wears a suit just like all nuclear scientists/spies did back in the McCarthy era.

Dr. Allen Fields (Ray Milland), alias The Thief, passes on microfilmed documents to a Communist agent.

Reason for Villainy: This traitor is passing our vital atomic secrets on to the insidious Red menace. The whole film, incidentally, is without benefit of dialog. Could it be that the lack of dialog was due to a fear on the part of the production company? These were hot days of Red-baiting. When this brilliant picture came out, there was a Communist under every bed, or so they said.

Fields photographs documents—and almost gets caught—at the Atomic Energy Commission in Washington. When a Communist whom he passes the microfilm to, in exchange for good old American dollars, is killed, Fields is exposed. The man was found with the microfilm and the FBI, that nemesis of evil, is called in. Working secretly, they start checking on AEC personnel. Fields gets a telegram in code advising him to leave. The FBI is suspicious and checks out the telegram. They trail the amateur spy to New York City. As Fields is about to make contact with a woman who has his ticket out of the country, an FBI agent closes in.

Evil Powers: Works for the heinous Reds—nemesis of the free world.

Weapons: Stealth, the Communist conspirators.

Occupation: Spy, scientist, traitor.

Intelligence: Atomic scientists ain't dumb!

Strengths: He's got the Commies to back him up.

Weaknesses: He's never killed a person, and doesn't want to do so.

Territory: Washington, D.C., the Atomic Energy Commission, New York.

Idiosyncrasies: Nervous as hell.

Friends: Commies.

Enemies: The FBI.

Evil Deeds: Turns over our most vital national secrets to those who would make us eat borscht for breakfast.

Killed by: Fields opens a locker at Grand Central Terminal where he finds the instructions to meet his contact atop the Empire State Building. She will get him his ticket out of the U.S.A. At the observation deck, his contact (Rita Gam) gives him the ticket, but the FBI man tries to apprehend him. In the struggle, the good guy plummets to the sidewalk. Back downstairs, Dr. Fields is disgusted as he passes the sticky mess on the sidewalk, and moves on, remorseful as all hell. Our villain returns to the dingy neon-lit hotel room where he is hiding out until the ship is ready to sail. He can't get that FBI man's eyes out of his head. He decides, after a gruelling time of it, to throw away his ticket, let the ship sail, and turn himself in to the FBI. Another good citizen led down the ill-starred path of global

Communism bites the dust. He never meant to kill anyone he wails. Yeah sure, you Commie bum. What do you suppose they do with atomic secrets? Make better pumpkins?

Current Status: After the McCarthy years, he was released and became a horticulturist.

What to Do If You Meet: Take him to the top of the World Trade Center.

Worthy of Note: Silent intrigue is part of this spy's world. He doesn't get to make quips like James Bond. Realistic propaganda.

Jennie Finch

Alias: Reiner
Born: 1900s
Died: 1940

Starred in:
Charlie Chan in Panama
20th Century Fox, 1940
Director: Norman Foster
Played by: Mary Nash

Description: Jennie is mysterious, but only in her guise as master enemy spy "Reiner." As Jennie she is a vacationing schoolteacher from the States; a bit mawkish, but otherwise of no special notice.

Reason for Villainy: "Reiner" is the master spy-saboteur who is creating havoc with our defenses against attack. Charlie Chan (Sidney Toler) is the redoubtable inspector from Honolulu who is assigned to crack the case in Panama, the Canal Zone. The enemy plans to blow the canal up. Chan's "number two son," Jimmie (Sen Yung), isn't much of a help, but he's a good foil for Chan's fortune-cookie philosophical statements. The characters under investigation are typical of that period. They all act extremely suspicious and one by one eliminate themselves from consideration as spies by getting themselves killed by the real spy—whoever that may be. Kathi Lenesch (Jean Rogers) is suspicious as a Czech refugee without a passport, but Charlie eliminates her due to some obscure oriental point or another. Next suspect, please.

Evil Powers/Weapons: The Reich is behind the master spy.

Occupation: Nasty saboteur.

Intelligence: Wily dame.

Strengths: Surprise.

Weaknesses: She's on the wrong side and pursued by the profound, inscrutable Charlie.

Territory: The Third Reich and Panama.

Idiosyncrasies: Though she's from Chicago, she doesn't know how to get to the Loop.

Friends: Nazis and other parasites of humanity.

Enemies: Charlie Chan and his most bungling son.

Relatives: Mata Hari.

Evil Deeds: She plans to blow up the canal, and has blown up plenty of other stuff. She also killed those in the party who found out the truth about her.

Outcome: There are lots of juicy suspects. Take Cliveden Compton (a made up name for sure) played by Lionel Atwill. He's an English mystery novelist, or so he says. Next there's Manolo, who, in a subplot, is blackmailing the lovely Czech woman. Manolo (Jack LaRue) owns the nightclub where the Czech woman performs, even without her papers. Richard Cabot (Kane Richmond) is a U.S. government engineer—someone in an ideal position to

Jennie Finch (Mary Nash) confuses the Chinese detective in Charlie Chan in Panama.

blow up the canal! But who is the spy? Charlie says, "Prease assemble in the main loom, and I will say name of most dishonorable climinal." The atmosphere is tense, the lights go out, and bullets sail through the air. Charlie says he's set the bomb to go off and the spy sweats, then cracks. Lo and behold it's Jennie. Number Two son sweats a brick, but it is all a bluff because the bomb has long since been disarmed.

Current Status: Up the canal without a paddle.

What to Do If You Meet: Ask how the Cubs are doing.

Frank and Cora

Born: Early 20th century
Died: 1940s

Starred in:
The Postman Always Rings Twice
MGM, 1946
Director: Tay Garnett
Played by: John Garfield, Lana Turner

Description: Frank is a handsome, uneducated, passionate man. Cora is a sexy blonde looking for kicks.

Reason for Villainy: Sex. Frank Chambers, a drifter, meets Cora when he gets a job sweeping Nick Smith's diner. Cora is married to Nick, an older man. There is an immediate and powerful attraction between Frank and Cora. They fall in love and begin a tempestuous affair. Greedy for Nick's wealth and insurance, they plot to kill him. After several unsuccessful murder attempts, the three of them get in a car where Frank and Cora have arranged an auto accident in which Nick will be killed. But Frank gets stuck as the car goes over a cliff and is seriously injured. Nick is killed.

Evil Powers: Cunning, greed.

Weapons: They use the auto as a weapon.
Occupation: Cora is a waitress in the diner. Frank is a sweeper, an odd job man.
Intelligence: Average, but boy are they passionate.
Strengths: Love, determination.
Weaknesses: Their planning is not the greatest. Greed.
Territory: Midwest U.S.A. Roadside diner and environs.
Idiosyncrasies: Obsessive love for one another.
Friends: Each other.
Enemies: Nick (who's in the way), cops, lawyers, the D.A.s, who are after them, and, ultimately, fate.
Relatives: All greedy adulterous couples bent on murder.
Evil Deeds: Husbandcide.
Killed by: Nick is dead and the couple sweat out their lies. The D.A. wants to fry Cora and tries to get Frank (in the hospital from the crash) to testify against her. But Cora gets off for lack of evidence and marries Frank. However, a crooked lawyer is blackmailing them with a signed confession he tricked out of Cora when she thought Frank was ratting. They take off to start a new life, and Cora is killed in a real car accident. The cops go after Frank for her murder and he's fried in the electric chair.

Frank (John Garfield) meets Cora (Lana Turner); The mutual attraction is instantaneous and, ultimately tragic, in The Postman Always Rings Twice.

Current Status: She gets her neck broken. He's steamed in the hot seat.

What to Do If You Meet: If you're an old guy, don't marry a young hotpants. If you're a drifter like Frank, skip odd jobs with blondes.

Worthy of Note: Excellent *film noir*. Moody, gripping. Remade in the 1980s, but not as well.

Johnny Friendly

Alias: Mr. Friendly
Born: Between 1910-1920
Died: Probably alive, in prison

Starred in:
On the Waterfront
Columbia Pictures, 1954
Director: Elia Kazan
Played by: Lee J. Cobb

Johnny Friendly (Lee J. Cobb) tries to buy Terry Malloy's loyalty while Charlie Malloy looks on in On the Waterfront.

Description: Racketeer labor boss. Big man, big face, seemingly friendly, but ruthless and cold as ice when he wants something or someone out of the way. Wears dark, double-breasted suits.

Reason for Villainy: It's the mid-1950s on the New York waterfront. Johnny Friendly rules the docks and the longshoremen's union with an iron fist. He doles out work to those who obey him, and has his thugs rough up anyone who interferes. Terry Malloy (Marlon Brando) is an ex-boxer who hangs around the docks doing favors for Friendly. Friendly throws him enough money to live halfway decently. Terry unknowingly sets up a man to be murdered by Friendly's goons and then meets and falls in love with the dead man's sister, Edie (Eva Marie Saint), who asks his help in tracking down the murderers. But the killers are Friendly and Terry's own brother, Charley (Rod Steiger). Terry slowly realizes the truth and cuts his relations with them. Meanwhile, Father Barry (Karl Malden), a tough, anti-gangster priest, tries to convince Terry to testify against the whole rotten crew. Friendly orders Terry to keep his yap shut!

Evil Powers: He's strong, but his main power is his control of the work on the waterfront. Through his henchmen and his control of jobs he has created an atmosphere of fear in all the workers. They are terrified to oppose him.

Weapons: Thugs—use fists, pipes, meathooks, and guns.

Occupation: Labor racketeer.

Intelligence: Smart, knows how to use fear to get what he wants.

Strengths: Power over the waterfront, gang of thugs.

Weaknesses: Megalomania, thinks he's unstoppable, thinks money can buy anyone off.

Territory: New York waterfront.

Idiosyncrasies: Likes to pretend he's a nice guy.

Friends: Pretends to (and in some ways does) like Terry Malloy.

Enemies: Hates Father Barry, the waterfront commission, and, later, Terry.

Relatives: Gangster from *Slaughter on Tenth Avenue*.

Evil Deeds: Has had countless men beaten and killed to maintain his control of the docks. Bribed politicians and cops.

Killed by: Friendly sends out Charley to silence Terry. In one of greatest (and most emotional) scenes in film history, Charley pulls a gun on Terry in a car, threatening to shoot him. Terry just looks sadly at his brother. Realizing that he's been used and that he sold out his chance to become a top boxer years earlier, Terry says, "I coulda been something, Charley. I coulda been a contenda, instead of a bum, which is what I am!" Charley can't shoot and lets Terry go. That night Terry finds Charley dead, draped on a meathook. He heads to the waterfront the next morning and confronts Friendly in a huge fight in which he pummels the gangster before being beaten to a pulp by Friendly's goons. But with the urging of Father Barry and hundreds of dockworkers watching, Terry manages to walk up the gangplank from Friendly's headquarters onto the dock, showing that, symbolically, he's stronger than the gangster. His will has won, the men turn away from Friendly in disgust, refusing to work for him anymore. His power broken, the gangster vainly threatens the longshoremen as they walk away en masse.

Current: Alive, but probably in jail, since Father Barry convinced Terry to testify against Friendly in front of the commission investigating waterfront crime.

What to Do If You Meet: Smile, act dumb, say "Gee Mr. Friendly, could I, I mean, would you let me unload some of dem bananas from da dock!"

Worthy of Note: One of the greatest, if not the greatest, American films ever made. Made Brando a superstar.

Fu Manchu

Alias: The Evil Master
Born: 19th century
Died: Still alive

Starred in:
The Face of Fu Manchu
Seven Arts, 1965
Director: Don Sharp
Played by: Christopher Lee

Fu Manchu (Boris Karloff) looks over his laboratory in The Face of Fu Manchu.

Description: Chinese superhuman warlord. Wears brightly decorated silk robes and a velvet hat. He has a long, thin mustache hanging down on his chin and long, sharp fingernails.

Reasons for Villainy: The ultimate reasons for his villainy are shrouded in the distant past. Fu Manchu is a villain par excellence, intent on controlling the world through any means. In his many film appearances he attacks the forces of civilization as a representative of pure evil and the will to supreme power. In "The Face of Fu Manchu" the action begins with Fu Manchu being executed on a huge chopping block. Although he appears to die, the Chinese archvillain soon returns and is plotting once again. Fu Manchu and his daughter, Fah Lo Suee (Tsai Chin), plan to take over the world by using a super poison made from a flower "found only in the inaccessible mountains of the north." Fu Manchu forces a scientist to help carry out the plan by kidnapping the scientist's daughter. Soon, Commissioner Nayland Smith of Scotland Yard (Fu's longtime foe and pursuer) is on his trail and the sparks fly.

Evil Powers/Weapons: Super intelligent, vast array of both ancient and modern weaponry—daggers, poisons, flying knives, numerous springing traps, rays, torture chambers, hypnotic powers. During the course of his career he has used countless torture devices, including giant bells, giant walls bristling with spikes where victims are skewered, hourglass tortures with victims slowly fed to crocodiles, snakes, or spiders.

Occupation: Master of evil—with millions of devotees.

Intelligence: Extremely intelligent, possibly one of the most brilliant villains of all time.

Strengths/Weaknesses: Very strong, armed with an arsenal, hidden fortress, army of followers everywhere. Immortal. Perhaps his only weakness in his supreme ego.

Territory: His headquarters are in his own mini-kingdom in a remote region of China. But he operates on a worldwide scale—London, Europe, Tibet. . . .

Idiosyncrasies: Loves to torture. He also loves newfangled weapons. Fascinated by the technology of violence.

Friends: His daugther Fah, who is his right hand, is the only person on earth that he cares about.

Enemies: Nayland Smith is his eternal nemesis.

Relatives: Ming the Merciless; Charlie Chan is his "good" cousin.

Evil Deeds: Countless evil deeds over the years. He has tortured and killed thousands, tens of thousands. He has stolen, plundered, and destroyed. You name something bad, Fu has done it.

Killed by: Fu Manchu creates the poison. He comes to London to release the poison gas from an underground chamber near the Thames. But Nayland Smith foils the dastardly plot at the last moment. Fu flees to Tibet, but Smith follows. In a climactic explosion, Smith blows up Fu and Fah in their castle. However, as the film ends, Fu's face looks down from the smoke and fire and he says, "The world shall hear from me again."

Current Status: Eternal, immortal (has magic potion). Fu Manchu always returns.

What to Do If You Meet: Watch out for his long fingernails—they're poisoned. Don't drink anything. Don't fall for his daughter or accept free trips to China from thin-mustached men.

Worthy of Note: Many other Fu Manchu movies have been made. The first group was produced in the 1920s, directed by Warner Oland. In 1932, Boris Karloff gave a stab at playing Fu in *The Mask of Fu Manchu. The Face of Fu Manchu* is considered by many to be the modern classic.

Elsa Gebhardt

Alias: Mr. Christopher
Born: 1919
Died: 1945

Starred in:
The House on 92nd St.
20th Century Fox, 1945
Director: Henry Hathaway
Played by: Signe Hasso

Description: We don't know what Gebhardt looks like. We see "his" shoes walking, we see "his" shadowy presence. Finally, we see Elsa, dressed as a man to escape the FBI. She is dirty blond, stern looking, slim. She moves fast.

Reason for Villainy: Gebhardt is the top Nazi spy in New York City. Isn't that reason enough? *Plot*—A brilliant student named Bill Dietrich (William Eythe) is asked by the Nazis to join their cause. He informs the FBI and they ask him to be a double agent. He agrees and is asked to discover the big mystery of who is passing atomic secrets, through a bookstore front, to the Nazis. With every move he makes the mysterious presence of the unseen super spy Gebhardt is felt. Dietrich has forged papers supposedly from Berlin granting him access to top secrets of the ring. They are being checked. In the meantime he is privy to enough information to visit the house on 92nd street. (This film is based on real events, but the house was really on 91st street, according to local residents.) He attends cell meetings, gets the name of the agent passing the secrets

Elsa Gebhardt (Signe Hasso) and her accomplice confront Bill Dietrich whom they've discovered to be a counter-spy for the FBI in House on 92nd Street.

and calls in the FBI, who start moving in on the agent.

But in the meantime, Gebhardt discovers Dietrich's secret. He's supposed to be transmitting to Berlin but the Nazis note that his radio device can't reach that far. Of course, he's broadcasting to the good old FBI.

Evil Powers/Weapons: Gebhardt is a suspicious, ruthless spy with a luger, hatchetmen, radio-transmitting devices, poisons, etc.

Occupation: Nazi super spy.

Intelligence: Cunning and good at changing her identity. Familiar with several languages, codes, espionage procedures.

Strengths: She has the might of the Reich behind her.

Weaknesses: She's up against the greatest counterespionage network ever devised: the Federal Bureau of Investigation.

Territory: 92nd street, New York City and environs.

Idiosyncrasies: She dresses as a man.

Friends: Der Fuehrer.

Enemies: The FBI, Inspector Briggs, counterspy Dietrich.

Evil Deeds: Passing atomic secrets to the Nazis, sabotage, killing, illegal possession of classified materials, smuggling, impersonation, lewd sexual impersonation.

Killed by: Gebhardt has checked out Dietrich and finds his credentials don't jibe. He's captured, and is about to be killed when the FBI comes in. Gebhardt must escape, but

how? She dresses up as a man and hopes to pass for one of the agents—anybody except herself. However, one of her Nazi pals spots her before she can identify herself, and he shoots her dead thinking that she was an FBI agent. Gebhardt had been done in by the same trick that had kept her alive up till now—impersonating a male. Inspector Briggs (Lloyd Nolan) has made a fine catch in this bunch of Swastika-suckers.

Current Status: Dead.

What to Do If You Meet: Watch for the luger, and don't make a pass.

Worthy of Note: This is a good thriller.

Dr. George

Alias: Dr. George Harris
Born: 1920s
Died: Still alive, but in jail

Starred in:
Coma
MGM, 1978
Director: Michael Crichton
Played by: Richard Widmark

Description: Suave, distinguished head of surgery at Boston Memorial Hospital. His gray hair, kind, benevolent demeanor and face disguise the evil that lurks beneath.

Reason for Villainy: Money, of course! *Plot*—Surgical resident Dr. Susan Wheeler (Genevieve Bujold) works at Boston Memorial. She feels terrible when her friend Mary emerges from simple surgery in a brain-dead coma. She investigates and discovers that many such cases have occurred in the last year. Susan breaks into the offices of chief anesthesiologist Dr. George (Rip Torn) and finds that all the coma cases had been operated on in OR 8. A maintenance man, Kelly, tells her that he has a secret and to meet him later. But when Susan arrives, Kelly is dead and a mysterious figure tries to kill her. She narrowly escapes. She tells Dr. Mark Bellins (Michael Douglas) but he won't believe her.

Evil Powers/Weapon: Powers of a totally trusted surgeon. He uses carbon monoxide to put patients in coma. Almost above suspicion because of his position.

Occupation: M.D., Chief of Surgery.

Intelligence: Extremely intelligent, cunning, very smooth operator.

Strengths: His medical position. He has access to drugs and machines that can kill.

Weaknesses: Thinks he's unreachable.

Territory: Boston Memorial Hospital and the Jefferson Institute.

Friends: Other doctors who are involved in his horrifying scheme.

Enemies: Dr. Susan Wheeler, who discovers the truth.

Relatives: Dr. Death, Jack the Ripper.

Evil Deeds: Responsible for putting hundreds of people into irreversible comas and then selling their organs.

Killed by: Susan visits the Jefferson Institute where the coma victims are stored and is able to sneak in. She discovers a vast life-support chamber in which the coma victims are kept alive, suspended by wires and tubes from the ceiling. But even more horrifying is the discovery that the victims' organs are sold throughout the world to the highest bidder. A factory of human flesh exists and Dr. George is in charge. She rushes back to the hospital to tell her superior, Dr. Harris. Much to her chagrin, Dr. Harris's first name is George, and it is he who runs the Institute. He gives her a drug that simulates appendicitis and sends her to OR 8. Mark, meanwhile, becomes suspicious and runs to the generator room and finds a carbon monoxide generator that feeds into the oxygen mask of OR 8. He destroys it, saving Susan's life as her face is covered with the mask. After calling the police he runs back to the operating room. Dr. George is arrested as Mark and Susan tearfully embrace.

Current Status: Alive, in jail.

What to Do If You Meet: Cough, act sick. Tell him all your organs are diseased and no one would want them.

Worthy of Note: A frightening and tension-filled movie that did big biz at the box office.

Dr. George (Richard Widmark) tries to convince Susan that everything is alright and that she's imagining things about Operating Room 8 in Coma.

German Captain of the *Louisa*

Born: Late 1800s
Died: 1914

Starred in:
The African Queen
Horizon-Romulus, 1951
Director: John Huston
Played by: Peter Bull

Description: He is middle-aged and mid-sized. He wears a white, but stained, officer's uniform and a captain's hat. He often sits at his desk aboard the *Louisa* giving orders. He will listen to anyone—once—and then shoot them. He has dark hair, and is always sweaty because of the insufferable African heat.

Charles Allnut tries to explain to the German captain of the Louisa how he and Rose Sayer "accidently" came upon the ship in The African Queen.

Reason for Villainy: The Captain is patrolling the lakes of East Africa for the Kaiser. The war has just started in earnest, and his orders are to hold down the area. He does. German soldiers arrive at the settlement of Rose Sayer (Katharine Hepburn) and her brother the Rev. Samuel Sayer (Robert Morley). They burn the church and scatter the native worshippers, the shock of which kills the pastor. Charlie Allnut (Humphrey Bogart), a trader, takes Rose on his miserable bark, the *African Queen*. She is constantly after him for his appearance and manners, but comes to respect his honor, determination, and fortitude. After pouring all Charlie's gin into the river, Rose manages to straighten Charlie out. They fall in love. Rose convinces Charlie to attack the German warship *Louisa*. They shoot the rapids, conquer heat and leeches and mud, and enter the lake to attack where the *Louisa* is patrolling. They plan to fix torpedoes on the *Queen's* bow and ram the warship, but a storm sinks them. The *Louisa* picks them up and they are interrogated by the Captain, our villain. He's never seen such crazies and sentences them to death. While they are about to be hanged, Charlie asks the Captain to marry them first.

Evil Powers: He's a cold one, and he's determined to hang the spies he's caught for the Kaiser.

Occupation: German ship's officer in wartime.

Intelligence: Reads Nietzsche at night.
Strengths: He's the captain.
Weaknesses: He has a streak of morality.
Territory: The Lakes of East Africa.
Idiosyncrasies: He actually likes to be a captain, and to marry people.
Friends: The Kaiser.
Enemies: Charlie and Rose.
Evil Deeds: Blasts natives, kills British civilians and soldiers, fights for the evil, pointy-hatted Kaiser.
Outcome: The captain temporarily postpones the hanging in order to marry the dirty-looking couple. When it comes around to hanging time again, the *Queen*, submerged but still torpedo-loaded, smashes against the *Louisa* and sinks her. The lovers embrace in the water—they did need a good cleaning—and swim off. Everything is okay now, and they are even legal. Miss Staight-lace is now a bit untied.
Current Status: The old German is drowned.
What to Do If You Meet: Stall for time.
Worthy of Note: Bogie can do more than play criminals and nightclub owners, and Kate is great as always. The triumph over high odds thrills all.

The Godfather

Alias: Don Vito Corleone
Born: 1920s
Died: 1972

Starred in:
The Godfather
Paramount, 1972
Director: Francis Ford Coppola
Played by: Marlon Brando

Description: Don Vito is a tall, emotional, sincere man with strong family ties. He believes in honor and retribution against the dishonorable. He's often at formal affairs—

like weddings—dressed in a tux, but when he's at home, he likes to walk about in an old shirt and pants and tend to his backyard garden, especially the grapes. Although he has graying, receding hair and a wrinkled brow, he's still a dominating presence in a room full of younger Cosa Nostra members.

Reason for Villainy: The Godfather is the chieftain of one branch of the extensive syndicate that controls crime in the U.S.A. Another "family," the Tattaglias, wants to go into narcotics, and asks Don Vito to approve and to join in. The Godfather says no dice and shortly thereafter he is seriously wounded by Tattaglia-financed gunmen. The Godfather's son Michael, who had never intended to go into the family business, vows revenge. Michael (Al Pacino) shoots down the Godfather's assailants in a local restaurant. To protect Michael, Don Vito sends him to Sicily where he falls in love with and marries pure, but sexy, Apollonia (Simonetta Stefanelli). Old rivalries flair, and a bomb meant for Michael kills his bride. He then returns to New York. His older brother Sonny (James Caan), who was to become Don Vito's successor, is killed. A peace conference is set up among the rival Mafia families. Will Don Vito be able to keep his empire—and his life? Will this "honorable" crime boss survive?

Evil Powers/Weapons: Are you kidding? The Mafia!

Occupation: Capo di tutti capi.

Intelligence: A no-nonsense, old-world, survivor type.

Strengths: He's the capo.

Weaknesses: Other, more modern families vie with him for power.

Territory: New York, U.S.A. in general.

Idiosyncrasies: Likes to putter in his garden and attend family events like weddings. He often conducts business at these family events.

Friends: His family.

Enemies: The other families.

Evil Deeds: All the crime that a capo controls—extortion, bribery, illegal possession of firearms, tax evasion, conspiracy, perjury, murder, prostitution, etc. But not narcotics.

Outcome: Don Corleone tries to get narcotics off the minds of the other families. In the end, however, he relents as long as they keep the narcotics in the ghettos. The Don realizes he is too old to fight his enemies and avenge Sonny's death. That job will be left to Michael. While playing with his grandson in his favorite garden, he suffers a fatal heart attack. The new capo is Michael, who promptly kills off all the other family heads. The sequel is Godfather II.

Current Status: Dead.

What to Do If You Meet: Show some respect.

Worthy of Note: An Academy Award for Best Actor went to Brando. Many other nominations honored this picture. Surprisingly, the sequel is nearly as good.

The Godfather stands at his daughter Connie's wedding with his sons and the rest of his family.

Bert Gordon

Born: 1930
Died: Still alive

Starred in:
The Hustler
20th Century Fox, 1961
Director: Robert Rossen
Played by: George C. Scott

The Hustler (Paul Newman) gets roughed up by pool players who don't like to be hustled.

Description: Bert is a gangster. He is seldom seen, except at pool halls where he is a promoter/advisor. He is very silent, except after he makes an analysis of a pool hustler's chances for the big time. He's tall, a bit chunky, strongly built, and plays cards a lot. Most of all he's an astute, cynical pool-player's manager. He'll train you and take you.

Reason for Villainy: Eddie Felson (Paul Newman) is a pool hustler—one of the best. He is young and brash. He wants to break into the big time, and play the great Minnesota Fats (Jackie Gleason). Eddie's manager, Charlie (Myron McCormick), is encouraging and treats him like a son. Bert looks at Eddie in a different way. Bert thinks Eddie is a born loser but a potential winner. He offers to handle Eddie for a whopping 75 percent of the take. Eddie refuses. After Eddie is beaten badly by Fats, he drops Charlie as his manager and takes off for another city. Eddie meets lonely, handicapped, and drunk Sarah Packard (Piper Laurie) in a bus station. She takes the loser in. Later, when Eddie's fingers are broken at a local joint where he hustles pool players who don't like to be hustled, she cares for him while his fingers heal. She knows nothing about him, and when Bert comes on the scene again, she realizes she will lose him. She eventually does. Bert isn't good enough for Eddie now.

Evil Powers/Weapons: He's conniving, interested in profit, and uses that drive for winning above humanity and caring. He also gets Eddie in that same winning frame of mind.

Occupation: Pool players' manager and shady customer.

Intelligence: Calculating.

Strengths: Cynical appraisal of whether someone can make a buck.

Weaknesses: Inhuman.

Territory: Pool halls.

Idiosyncrasies: He will wait for you. You'll come to him someday.

Friends: Money.

Enemies: Caring individuals.

Evil Deeds: Bert uses people for profit.

Outcome: Bert listens to Eddie's loser philosophy, then informs him of the truth as he sees it: Determination, self-esteem, and not letting overconfidence get to you. In the return match with Fats, Eddie plays superbly. Fats senses the match is lost—unlike Eddie who refused in the first match to admit he was licked. Fats goes off in dignity. Eddie beats Fats to prove that he can make money and to psychologically pay back himself and everybody for all the trouble when his star rose and fell and rose again. Oddly, Bert, who has never let humanity interfere with profit, lets Eddie walk off with the entire pot.

Current Status: Hanging out in some pool hall sizing up more players.

What to Do If You Meet: Play the percentage.

Worthy of Note: This is a good film. A particularly good scene takes place in the bus station between Newman and Laurie.

Gray

Alias: The Body Snatcher
Born: 1790s
Died: 1832

Starred in:
The Body Snatcher
RKO Radio, 1945
Director: Robert Wise
Played by: Boris Karloff

Description: Tall, hulking, sideburned man in a long, gray coat. Sometimes he wears black. He wears a top hat as part of his disguise as a horse-carriage cabbie and is often seen carrying a heavy bag containing you know what.

Reason for Villainy: Gray is the assistant to Dr. MacFarland (Henry Daniell), a surgeon in Edinburgh, and a notorious experimentor. MacFarland has an insatiable need for more bodies for his work and Gray obliges by opening fresh graves and occasionally taking a shortcut by killing someone. The latter cuts down on the long trip to the cemetery and all that digging. Gray has some uncanny influences on the bad doctor, though. Gray develops a goal in life; he wants the Doc to save a crippled girl and make her walk again. Great, says the Doc, but I'll need some spare parts. Gray goes into action to procure the parts—body parts. Where are the police? Are they hiding themselves on these foggy nights, or are they afraid of the strange, hulking shape that walks the streets with a big, big bag.

Evil Powers: Gray is good at stabbing, especially good at clubbing, and great at carrying loads.

Occupation: Body snatcher.

Intelligence: Below average intelligence, but he has some sort of sixth sense.

Strengths: Knows how to get parts for mad doctors.

Weaknesses: Crippled kids make him sob.

Territory: Edinburgh, especially when it's foggy.

Idiosyncrasies: Likes the smell of freshly turned soil.

Friends: The dead, and the Doc, when he pays well and helps the kid.

Enemies: Joseph, the man-servant.

Evil Deeds: Kills people and desecrates graves in most unchristian behavior! Both Joseph and the Doc are done in by Gray.

Killed by: Joseph, the servant (Bela Lugosi), has an idea to blackmail the Body Snatcher. He, of course, is promptly and efficiently killed by Gray. The doctor is disturbed by this happening. He decides to kill Gray, and then he uses Gray's body for dissection. (Incidentally, Gray and the doctor had a falling out because the little girl did not get better.) MacFarland is safe at last from this maniac, and to hell with the spare parts. But wait. What was that noise? MacFarland is sure that the ghost of Gray is following him, speaking to him. It's probably just in his demented mind, but the Doc thinks it's real. He thinks Gray is coming to get him. No, no, no. The Doc rushes off a cliff and dies. Even in death Gray kills.

Current Status: Dead.

What to Do If You Meet: Don't say anything, but if he asks if you are alone, say 500 friends expect you around the corner in five seconds.

Worthy of Note: The last time Lugosi and Karloff worked together.

Gray smothers another victim to provide his master Dr. MacFarland a fresh supply of bodies for his work in The Body Snatcher.

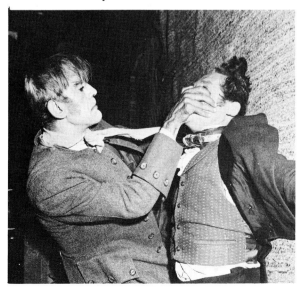

The Gunfighter

Alias: Jimmy Ringo
Born/Died: 19th century

Starred in:
The Gunfighter
20th Century Fox, 1950
Director: Henry King
Played by: Gregory Peck

Description: Tall, handsome, cowboy gunslinger with a mustache. He wears a jacket, a dark hat, and two guns. Plus he seems tired of his life of gunfighting.

Reason for Villainy: Ringo rides into a frontier town and enters a saloon where he is forced into drawing by a punk kid, Eddie. Eddie wants to make a name for himself by killing the legendary Ringo. Eddie draws and Ringo drills him dead. He then goes to a nearby town to hide from what he senses is his approaching end. Eddie's brothers are hunting down.

Evil Powers: Very fast with a gun.
Weapon: Two six-shooters.
Occupation: Gunslinger.
Intelligence: Highly intelligent. Ringo realizes that the life of a gunman is getting him nowhere. He sees things through the macho needs of other would-be gunslingers and his own stupidity.
Territory: The West.
Idiosyncrasies: He wants to retire.
Friends: Peggy Walsh, his wife, son Jimmi, Sheriff Mark Stone.
Enemies: Eddie's three brothers.
Relatives: Johnny Guitar, *High Noon*.
Evil Deeds: Jimmy Ringo has killed many men in his life as a gunfigther. But he repents now; he's tired of the violence.
Killed by: Ringo visits his wife and son and vinces her to come with him. His wife also agrees to tell his son that Ringo is his real father, if Ringo does not get into a gunfight for one year. Ringo gladly agrees and heads out of

The Gunfighter gets a moment of rest as he cleans up.

town. The sheriff also cooperates by arresting Eddie's three brothers, giving Ringo time to get away. But as he rides out, another would-be punk killer (Hunt Bromley) forces Ringo to draw. Knowing he can't escape his life of blood, Ringo lets himself be killed in the street. "Now, you're the fastest gun alive," he says to his killer, before dying.

Current Status: Dead.

What to Do If You Meet: Don't draw on him. He doesn't like to fight anymore.

Worthy of Note: One of the first "adult" westerns with a realistic atmosphere and an examination of psychological motives.

Casper Gutman

Alias: The Fat Man
Born: Circa 1900
Died: Unknown

Starred in:
The Maltese Falcon
Warner Bros., 1941
Director: John Huston
Played by: Sydney Greenstreet

Description: Fat, slow-moving, lounges around in silk robe or smoking jacket. Frowns a lot. Eats a great deal.

Reason for Villainy: Casper Gutman (Sidney Greenstreet) seems to be the central figure in the death of Sam Spade's (Humphrey Bogart's) partner, Miles Archer. Archer was meeting a man named Thursby for a client when he was killed. Now Spade is looking for the killer. Archer was meeting Thursby for a Miss Wonderly, a.k.a. Brigid O'Shaughnessy (Mary Astor). Spade finds that the dame is searching for a figurine of a falcon. Gutman and his sometime associate, Joel Cairo (Peter Lorre), are also after it. Gutman's two-bit gunsel, Wilmer (Elisha Cook Jr.), killed Thursby and a ship's captain in an attempt to secure the falcon. However, the captain lived long enough to get the bird to Spade. Heavy negotiations among all parties ensue, each offering a share to the other, but not planning to share at all. When the bird is produced, it's found to be a fake. They scratch its surface and the coated bird doesn't contain jewels. It seems that the murders, abductions, all the machinations and intrigues were for nothing. In the meantime, Spade becomes involved with Brigid and gets her to admit that she killed Miles Archer.

Evil Powers: Gutman has his gunman, the snivelling Wilmer. He also has an intense capacity for cruelty. Cairo works with him, but only when it suits him.

Casper Gutman (Sidney Greenstreet) returns a gun to his man Wilmer after Sam Spade berates the man in front of Gutman in The Maltese Falcon.

Weapons: Standard .38 and .48 caliber handguns.

Occupation: International intriguer.

Intelligence: Scholarly. Gutman had researched the history of the bejeweled Falcon through history. Well-traveled.

Strengths: Determination, cunning.

Weaknesses: Wilmer is a pathetic gunman.

Territory: The Near East, Corsica, U.S.A. Wherever the trail leads. Hotel rooms and apartments near fine restaurants.

Idiosyncrasies: Wants the bird more than life itself.

Friends: Wilmer, Cairo, even Spade—if they can get the bird.

Enemies: Anyone that stands in his way—the sea captain, Spade, Thursby, etc. He will strike a temporary deal with the person most knowledgeable as to the bird's location.

Evil Deeds: Murder, abduction, theft, conspiracy.

Outcome: Brigid, it seems, intended the murder of Archer to be pinned on Thursby, her partner in the pursuit of the precious falcon. Spade pretends that he loves Brigid more than doing the right thing—having her fry in the electric chair. She is desperate enough to spend the rest of her life with the detective. However, Spade would always have to watch his back if she were with him. She's treacherous. Besides, he owes it to his partner to turn her in, and he says so. Still, Gutman and Cairo have a new lead. Gutman says it's been fun and invites Spade to accompany them to the Middle East to continue the search. Spade declines. He's had it. When this involved plot concludes, the pair of crooks (Gutman and Cairo) are off on a new adventure. Presumably they are still out there looking for the Maltese Falcon. The real one.

Current Status: Following leads in the Middle East, Turkey, etc.

What to Do If You Meet: Say you know where the bird is and ask for some money to give him a map, a locker key, anything. But watch out—if he thinks you're crossing him, it's curtains for you.

Worthy of Note: This film is often parodied on comedy shows. No wonder.

Sir Guy of Gisborne

Born/Died: Merrie olde England

Sir Guy of Gisborne (Basil Rathbone) is cornered by Robin Hood as the merry men fight on in The Adventures of Robin Hood.

Starred in:
The Adventures of Robin Hood
Warner Bros., 1938
Director: Michael Curtiz
Played by: Basil Rathbone

Description: Sir Guy is tall and wiry. He wears an elaborate, gold-embroidered short kilt and blouse and a long velvet cape. He has a van dyke-styled beard and long, flowing, swept back brown hair. A long nose, a long stride, a long, hard look, and a long sword complete the picture!

Reason for Villainy: Sir Guy is the co-conspirator with Prince John to usurp the throne of England while Richard (Ian Hunter) is away battling the infidels in the Crusades. They discover that King Richard has been captured on the way back to England and is being held for ransom. Prince John (Claude Rains) welcomes the news, intending not to pay the ransom. Instead he raises taxes and declares himself Regent. Sir Guy enforces the rule of terror. At a banquet, Robin Hood (Errol Flynn) challenges the prince's rule. Robin is the Earl of Locksley, but is declared an outlaw. He escapes, however. Robin's hoods ambush Guy in Sherwood Forest, but let him go to tell the evil prince that Robin now has the ransom Guy had collected. Robin knows that they never intended to pay it out, merely collect it for their own use. The prince is outraged. He knows, however, that Maid Marian (Olivia de Havilland) is sweet on Robin and vice-versa, so he holds an archery contest, with Marian giving out the prize. Robin attends, outshoots everyone, and is arrested. He escapes with Marian's help. Guy is now more adamant about destroying our hero.

Evil Powers/Weapons: Has the ear of the usurping brother John. He also is a mighty swordsman.

Occupation: Assistant usurper.

Intelligence: Sharp.

Strengths: Supports the best-positioned "King."

Weaknesses: Richard is free and on his way; Robin holds Guy at bay.

Territory: England.

Idiosyncrasies: Enjoys hearing screams from the dungeon.

Friends/Enemies: Prince John is a friend, Robin is an enemy.

Evil Deeds: Usurious taxation, oppression, unfair swordplay, plotting against the fair and just King Richard, suppression of the Saxons.

Outcome: Sir Guy is incensed that Robin has thwarted him. He arrests Maid Marian and condemns her to death. Sir Guy knows Robin will try to rescue Marian, and when he does he will be slaughtered. But, secretly, disguised as monks, King Richard and his troops have landed. They join Robin and his men and enter the castle still disguised as monks, because Richard knows Prince John and Sir Guy plot against him. Just as Prince John is to crown himself, the men attack. Robin sets his sights on Sir Guy. The evil man is pressed to defend himself with his sword. He makes a good effort, but Robin is not only good with a bow and arrow. He also is the best swordsman around. He wins, stabbing Guy to death with the broadsword. Marian falls into Robin's arms, and he is no longer declared an outlaw. Merry old England is once again merry.

Current Status: Dead.

What to Do If You Meet: Say you're a holy father and he will be cursed if he harms you.

Worthy of Note: This is still the best of the Robin Hood films.

George Hally 107
Han 108
Dr. Hartz 109
Eddie Harwood 110
King Henry II 111
Homer 112
Matthew Hopkins and John Stearne 113
Hud 114
J.J. Hunsecker 115
Lieutenant Colonel Hyde 117

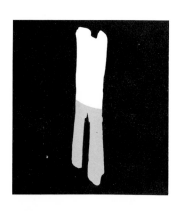

Tom Iverson and Paula 118

George Hally

Born: Early 1900s
Died: Early 1930s

Starred in:
The Roaring Twenties
Warner Bros., 1939
Director: Raoul Walsh
Played by: Humphrey Bogart

Jeffrey Lynn, James Cagney, and Humphrey Bogart look deadly as gangsters during The Roaring Twenties.

Description: Hally is a dapper gangster, with creases in his pinstriped sleeves from carrying a tommy gun. He made his mind up during service in WW I not to be nobody's chump, see? So George won't let no wet-behind-the-ears punks tell him what to do.

Reason for Villainy: George, Eddie Bartlett (James Cagney), and Lloyd Hart (Jeffrey Lynn) return as buddies from the great war, but job pickins ain't too good back stateside. George goes into bootlegging, Lloyd returns to his poor, unstable law practice, and Eddie is lucky to get a spot driving a cab. One night Eddie goes to Panama Smith's (Gladys George's) nightclub with a delivery and is caught in a raid. Panama takes a liking to the honest young man and makes him dishonest. Panama soon becomes wild about Eddie, but Eddie only has eyes for Jean Sherman (Priscilla Lane), a girl who once wrote letters to him in the Army. Eddie builds up a lucrative cab fleet that really delivers liquor, not passengers, he finds out that old pal George is in the other gang. They get together, make a deal, and set the gangster, Nick Brown (Paul Kelly), up for a fall by informing the feds of a shipment, then hijacking the liquor once it's in government hands. Hally has recognized his old army sergeant is one of the guards and kills him. Eddie is upset, but they go on. Lloyd, who had joined his buddies up till now, splits off. George is prevented from killing him by Eddie's assurances that Lloyd won't rat on them.

Evil Powers: George will kill to protect his racket—he has no scruples. He will get what he wants any way he can, even over the bodies of his pals.

Occupation: Bootlegger and gangster.
Intelligence: Shifty.
Strengths: He's wily.
Weaknesses: He's a rat, and time wounds all heels, and traps all rats.
Territory: Mineola, New York; Panama Smith's club; and Italian restaurants.
Idiosyncrasies: A bit paranoiac.
Friends: Eddie and Lloyd—if he'd let them be his friends.
Enemies: The law.
Evil Deeds: George bumps off countless people, but the dirty rat is out to get his buddies, too, and that's not nice.
Outcome: After the Stock Market crash in 1929, Eddie's out of business. To save anything at all, he sells what he has left to Hally, who leaves his old pal with just one cab. Eddie drinks and drives, and is crushed also by Lloyd, now a law-enforcement lawyer, when he makes off with Jean, the love-of-his-life. Eddie lets Panama comfort him. She's singing in a down-and-out dive now. A chance meeting with Jean and her four-year-old son gets Eddie the news that Lloyd, now the district attorney, is after George. George has threatened Lloyd, and for Jean's sake Eddie goes to warn George. This only makes George

decide to kill old pal Eddie, too. Eddie, however, shoots George and two of the gangster's henchmen. Eddie, though, is mortally wounded. He crawls to the steps of a church and dies in Panama's arms.

Current Status: Dead as a doornail.

What to Do If You Meet: Don't trust the punk.

Worthy of Note: The classic.

Han

Alias: The Pimp
Born: 1930s
Died: 1973

Starred in:
Enter the Dragon
Warner Bros., 1973
Director: Robert Clouse
Played by: Shih Kien

Description: Evil master criminal, Chinese, martial arts expert. About 45 years old, with slicked-back black hair. He wears a black kung-fu styled suit, covering neck to ankles, a black glove, and a tiger claw.

Reason for Villainy: Han runs an island fortress from where he directs a ring of prostitutes and a heroin trade. He also holds a semiannual martial arts contest which Lee (Bruce Lee), Roper (John Saxon), and Williams (Jim Kelly) all enter. Lee has been hired by the Hong Kong government to collect evidence on Han, and he also knows that Oharra, Han's right-hand man, tried to rape Lee's sister, Su-Linn, forcing her to commit suicide. On the island, all the martial arts contestants are greeted by Han at a banquet and given girls for the night. Lee sneaks out and makes contact with Mai Ling (an inside agent) and beats up a number of Han's men.

Evil Powers: Mean, top master of martial arts. He uses a steel-clawed tiger paw with which he can rip a man open. He has an army that works for him and a castle with secret tunnels and plenty of torture devices.

Occupation: Head of prostitution ring and drug organization.

Intelligence: Highly intelligent, well organized. Rules island and gang with an iron fist (claw).

Strengths: Feared by his men. He, however, is totally fearless. Very tough fighter.

Weaknesses: Thinks he can take on Bruce Lee.

Territory: Private island near Hong Kong.

Idiosyncrasies: Loves to watch men fight one another to the death.

Friends: No friends, his men all fear him.

Enemies: Lee, Roper, and Williams.

Relatives: Dr. No, The Man With the Iron Claw.

Evil Deeds: Han has forced hundreds of young Chinese girls into lives of prostitution and has spread heroin throughout the world. He's murdered, tortured, and raped. . . . Not someone you would want to bring home to mom.

Killed by: The next day, the guards who let the unknown prowler escape are forced to fight the awesome Bolo, who kills them. Lee fights Oharra, who uses broken bottles, but Lee destroys him with a kick to the neck. Han tries to get Williams to join him and kills him when he refuses. Roper also declines Han's invitation even after seeing Williams's dead

Han (Shih Kien) is the brutal, claw-fisted syndicate chief in Enter the Dragon.

body. Meanwhile, Lee radios his contact Braithwaite for help. He is attacked by hundreds of Han's men and kills them all. Roper fights Bolo, killing him. Mai Ling frees the prisoners who fight and vanquish the guards. Lee and Han fight it out. Lee is badly wounded by Han's steel claw, but finally succeeds in impaling the Chinese master criminal on a spear.

Current Status: Dead, but may have some sons from prostitutes.

What to Do If You Meet: Tell him you're Bruce Lee's cousin.

Worthy of Note: The biggest budgeted of Lee's films and one of the best.

Dr. Hartz (Paul Lucas) has the whole train in confusion in The Lady Vanishes.

Dr. Hartz

Born: 1890s
Died: Still alive at the end of film

Starred in:
The Lady Vanishes
Gainsborough Pictures, 1938
Director: Alfred Hitchcock
Played by: Paul Lukas

Description: He's a dapper society doctor, with a patient swathed in bandages in his compartment and a "sister" as a nurse who wears high-heels! He's a suave and suspicious character who wears a pinstriped suit. He's well groomed, but full of villainy.

Reason for Villainy: Miss Froy (Dame May Whitty) is a friendly old lady on a train bound for trouble. The train is traveling through the unsettled Balkan countries and is full of intrigue. Suddenly, Miss Froy disappears and Iris (Margaret Lockwood), the young woman she befriended, is ridiculed by all the passengers because they don't believe this old woman was even abroad. Is she going mad? Handsome Gilbert Redman (Michael Redgrave) doesn't think so. They join forces and discover that a passenger, Signor Doopo (Philip Leaver), who shared the compartment with the missing woman, is a magician famous for his disappearing act. The magician was working in league with the dapper Dr. Hartz, the sinister head of a counterspy ring. To everyone's surprise the vanished Miss Froy was a British spy carrying vital information for the home office. The bandaged patient in the doctor's compartment is none other than Miss Froy! What are they to do?

Evil Powers/Weapons: Guns, drugs, and an army of accomplices. He can talk his way out of any accusation.

Occupation: Doctor and enemy agent.

Intelligence: Clever at poisoning drinks.

Strengths: His organization.

Weaknesses: His nurse is half British and not to be trusted.

Territory: The Balkans.

Idiosyncrasies: Spends a lot of time in the baggage car.

Friends: The Magician, whom he pays well.

Enemies: The young couple and Miss Froy.

Evil Deeds: Slips drugs into drinks, kidnaps brave Miss Froy, has his men attack and shoot the passengers on the train, and breaches international etiquette.

Outcome: Iris and Gilbert are not to be thwarted. They bop the magician on the head and put him in a trunk. Unfortunately, it's a trick trunk and he escapes to inform Dr. Hartz. Upon meeting, the doctor talks the couple into having a few drinks in the dining car, and then poisons their drinks. But, unknown to the doctor, his nurse has switched the powerful drug with a harmless substance and is now in league with Iris and Gilbert. The couple feign collapse in the doctor's presence. He has rid himself of his opponents, or so he thinks. With the doctor out of his compartment, Gilbert and Lisa replace Miss Froy with one of the doctor's accomplices. The doctor leaves the train at the next stop in an ambulance thinking he has succeeded in with his mission. To his displeasure, he soon discovers the deception and that he has been thwarted. Miss Froy and the couple think they are safe until the train is sidetracked and the unfriendly country's troops begin to fire on the train. Miss Froy escapes out the other way and everyone meets happily in the British Home Office in London. Iris, ditching her former fiancee at the station, has decided to marry Gilbert.

Current Status: He was sort of glad the brave couple got away.

What to Do If You Meet: Switch drinks.

Worthy of Note: Redgrave's first go at the silver screen. Well done, old chap.

Eddie Harwood

Born: 1906
Died: 1946

Starred in:
The Blue Dahlia
Paramount, 1946
Director: George Marshall
Played by: Howard da Silva

Description: Harwood is a typical nightclub owner, with a lot going on under the surface both in his personality and in the club. He is suave, cool, dapper, and has a quick temper. This dark-haired, rakish millionaire has it made—or does he?

Reason for Villainy: This film is a mystery, of the *noir* variety. We don't know who the bad guy is, and we are thrown "red herrings" throughout the plot. The film begins with a group of war-buddies returning home. Johnny Morrison (Alan Ladd) and his friends Buzz (William Bendix) and George (Hugh Beaumont) go to Johnny's wife's place. She is at a

Johnny Morrison tries a dangerous stunt with Eddie Harwood, who is actually a murderer, in The Blue Dahlia.

motel, and is a "hostess" at a large party there. Johnny spots her kissing Eddie Harwood and complains. The party breaks up. The wife, Helen (Doris Dowling), scoffs at returning to a normal marriage. She also admits that their young son did not die as she had told Johnny in a letter. Instead, she tells Johnny that their son died because she was drunk-driving. Johnny walks out quietly. Later, Helen is mysteriously murdered. Johnny discovers that he is wanted for her murder, and he slips into the shadows. What's worse is that Buzz, who has a war-related head injury, had gone to Helen to "talk to" her and can't remember what happened next. Did Buzz flip and hear buzz saws and kill her?

Evil Powers/Weapons: He can lie to your face easily, plus he's been known to frame several guys.

Occupation: Nightclub owner.

Intelligence: Cool and cunning.

Strengths: He owns the club, and he can lie and cheat under pressure.

Weaknesses: Guilt. Time wounds all heels.

Territory: The Blue Dahlia.

Idiosyncrasies: Hidden anger at dames.

Friends: Hidden henchmen.

Enemies: Johnny.

Evil Deeds: Murder, deceit, crooked gambling, and vice.

Outcome: Joyce Harwood (Veronica Lake) is Eddie's doll, but she is fed up and takes it on the lam in her car. She stops for a hitchhiker, and it's Johnny. The two fall for each other, but they don't realize how connected they already are. Later, at a seaside resort, they meet again. Without telling each other, they are both returning to the big city. Johnny, on the run, trusts nobody, even this swell dame. In the meantime, George and Buzz are trying to uncover the events of the evening when Helen was killed. They discover that Buzz could have committed the murder in a fit. But it is also discovered that Dan Newell (Will Wright), the motel owner, is blackmailing Harwood. Newell is then found murdered. It slowly becomes clear who committed the murders—or more confusing. Huh? Anyway, Johnny eventually ends up with Joyce. The end.

Current Status: Dead. The nightclub is up for sale.

What to Do If You Meet: Don't get involved, it's too complicated.

Worthy of Note: Alan Ladd is stiff as always, and Veronica Lake is sumptuous.

King Henry II

Alias: The King
Born: 1133
Died: 1189

Starred in:
Beckett
Paramount, 1964
Director: Peter Glenville
Played by: Peter O'Toole

Description: A tall, handsome, hedonistic king. Wears riding clothes when out carousing, and kingly garb at castles—long, embroidered robe, crown, jewels, gloves.

Reason for Villainy: Beckett (Richard Burton) is King Henry's closest friend. They do everything together: ride, hunt, whore, and share gallivanting adventures, laughing all the way. Beckett will do anything for his king and Henry listens closely to his advice. But when it becomes opportune for the king to dump the Archbishop of Canterbury for political reasons, and replace him with Beckett as if the whole thing were a joke, he expects Beckett to do whatever he requests.

Evil Powers: All the powers of a king.

Weapons: Knights, swords, maces, executioners with big axes.

Occupation: King of England.

Intelligence: Highly intelligent. A gifted and cunning ruler.

Strengths: Strong-willed, benign (up to a point).

Weaknesses: Egomaniac.

Territory: England, various castles and countryside.

Henry II is amused by Beckett's proclamation of Church independence in Beckett.

Idiosyncrasies: Doesn't like to be opposed.

Friends: Loves Beckett like a brother until he kills him.

Enemies: The Pope.

Relatives: A Man For All Seasons.

Evil Deeds: He has done many of the nasty things kings tend to do. He has cheated, double crossed, stolen, kidnapped, manipulated, tortured, killed, sold the family jewels. . . .

Outcome: Beckett begs Henry not to appoint him Archbishop, fearing trouble. Once Beckett is anointed he searches his heart and finds that he has no choice but to obey the Church and follow the commands of God and not Henry. He defends his position from Henry's encroachments. Henry becomes depressed and torn, realizing, too late, how much he loved Beckett and that their relationship has split irrevocably apart. When a final appeal to Beckett fails, the King has him executed.

Current Status: Dead eight centuries.

What to Do If You Meet: Swear allegiance to the crown. Tell him you know a great brothel.

Worthy of Note: Excellent, unusually well-written and acted movie.

Homer

Alias: Clumsy
Born: 1890s
Died: 1930s Hollywood

Starred in:
Day of the Locust
Paramount, 1975
Director: John Schlessinger
Played by: Donald Sutherland

Description: Shy, tender soul. Wealthy enough to support someone. Short, cropped hair, parted on right. He's very tall, six feet, three inches at least, and gaunt. He's got a neat moustache and wears pinstriped suits.

Reason for Villainy: Homer is a sensitive soul in an insensitive world. He takes in bit-part actress, Faye Greener, and they have a platonic relationship. She's hardly platonic with other men though, determined to sleep

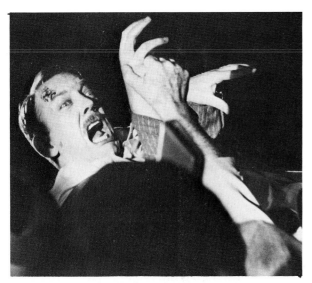

Homer (Donald Sutherland) is crushed to death by a rampaging mob after he stomps his actress friend to death in Day of the Locusts.

her way to the top, with some others on the side just for fun. She is beautiful but shallow and vain. Her closest male friends are Miguel (Pepe Serna), Tod (William Atherton), and Earle (Bo Hopkins). Tod is the only one who befriends the awkward Homer. The others taunt him. Still, Homer is not destroyed until he sees Miguel having sex with Faye. Tod sympathizes with Homer. It's a tough life. Slimy types like Miguel make out, Homers don't. Later, Tod goes to a sensational film premiere where he finds Homer wandering outside. He realizes Homer has flipped and wants to take the dazed guy home. However, Tod gets caught up in the hysteria of the crowd, trying to catch a glimpse of the celebrities.

Evil Powers: He's always near insanity. He goes over the edge. Look out for his feet.

Occupation: Upper-middle-class Mr. Lonely.

Intelligence: Intellectual, but slow-witted in practical matters.

Strengths: Financially secure.

Weaknesses: Mentally unbalanced.

Territory: Hollywood.

Idiosyncrasies: Can't adjust to a harsh, uncaring world.

Friends: Tod—but even he is somewhat callous.

Enemies: Faye, though he wants her.

Evil Deeds: Tries to be nice, but Faye

makes him kill her. She taunts him a little too much and she gets stomped.

Outcome: After Tod leaves Homer, Faye comes along. She is in one of her nasty moods and is cruel to Homer. She hits Homer with a rock and taunts him. He goes berserk and stomps the pretty actress right then and there. Someone in the crowd screams that he's killed a little girl and the crowd attacks Homer. The "child murderer" is thrown down and torn apart. Tod is injured by the rampaging mob, too. The mob forgets what it is doing and just keeps on going, like locusts. They are more the villain than Homer. However, stomping Faye was no act of compassion either.

Current Status: Dead.

What to Do If You Meet: Be nice to Homer, the guy needs a shrink and maybe the world does, too.

Worthy of Note: Nathanael West wrote this, but in the 1930s it was too hot to handle.

Matthew Hopkins and John Stearne

Alias: The witch hunters
Born: 1600s
Died: 1645 (The actual historical characters retired in the 1650s.)

Starred in:
The Conqueror Worm
American International, 1968
Director: Michael Reeves
Played by: Vincent Price, Robert Russo

Description: Hopkins is a neatly dressed Puritan. He wears an all black outfit, high black hat, long hair, scruffy beard. Stearne wears a leather-studded vest and a frilled shirt. His hair is bowl cut.

Reason for Villainy: The pair are witch hunters in not so merry old England at the time of Oliver Cromwell's rebellion. In reality, the pair killed more than 200 people by accusing them of witchcraft. They tortured people until they confessed. In the film, Hopkins and Stearne ride from village to village, paid by the authorities to rid villages of unwanted witches—sort of an exterminating angel pair. They pick on an old clergyman, John Lowes (Rupert Davies), and torture him, stopping only when his niece, attractive young Sara (Hilary Dwyer), offers sex for the forgiveness of her uncle. Hopkins is distraught when Stearne takes advantage of Sara's offer and continues to torture Lowes in the dungeon. When Sara's fiancee, Richard Marshall (Ian Ogilvy), returns and learns of these events, he vows to kill the witch hunters. With some soldiers, Marshall catches the torturers, but he and Sara are overpowered and end up being tortured in prison.

Evil Powers/Weapons: The long needles of cruelty, the pervasive superstition rampant in England, and the fear that if you oppose them you will be called a witch. If you have a birthmark watch out. That's the sign of the witch!

Occupation: Witch hunters, witch executioners.

Intelligence: Well read, but only in superstition.

Strengths: The power of religion gone mad.

Weaknesses: Those they harm—if they live—seek revenge.

Territory: Brandiston and other small towns in England.

Idiosyncrasies: They suspect everyone of witchcraft.

Friends: Fearful community leaders.

Enemies: Marshall.

Evil Deeds: Rape, murder, torture, blasphemy.

Killed by: Sara is attacked with long needles on her spine while she is chained in the dungeon, and Marshall is forced to watch. She might be spared if Marshall confesses that he is a devil worshipper, but he refuses. When Hopkins is branding Sara, Marshall strikes out with his boot, smashing and blinding Stearne. A soldier friend of Marshall comes in and shoots Stearne. Marshall also manages to grab an ax and does some chopping at Hopkins as

Matthew Hopkins (Vincent Price) and John Stearne (Robert Russo) are the dreaded witchhunters in The Conqueror Worm.

the villain vainly tries to fend off the blows. Angry that Stearne suffered so little, Marshall rants at the soldier as Sara screams. (In reality Hopkins and Stearne retired gracefully, wrote their memoirs of a brilliant career of witchfinding, and died comfortably.) But of course—after death—there comes the conqueror worm.

Current Status: Dead down there.

What to Do If You Meet: Hide your birthmarks.

Worthy of Note: The director, Michael Reeves, died at age 25, the year after the film was released. A promising talent.

Hud

Alias: Hud Bannon
Born: 1930s
Died: Still alive

Starred in:
Hud
Paramount, 1963
Director: Martin Ritt
Played by: Paul Newman

Description: Handsome, smiling, blue-eyed hunk of man. Cool, amoral, macho, with cowboy boots and hat. He always wears his denim jacket and jeans. An unregenerate heel.

Reason for Villainy: He rejects everything, even his friends and children. Sarcastic, amoral. Hud is an anti-hero, an existentialist of darkness. Life is only for him and no one else matters.

Evil Powers: Tough, cruel, egocentric.

Weapons: Fists, cold heart.

Occupation: Modern-day cowboy.

Intelligence: Smart, cunning, devious, but always for his ends.

Strengths: Good looks, macho image, strong.

Weaknesses: Cynicism, alienation, selfishness.

Territory: Bannon Ranch, Western U.S.A.

Idiosyncrasies: Likes to rape and get into fights.

Friends/Enemies: Idolized at first by his younger brother, Lon Bannon. Hud's crude behavior eventually alienates the youth.

Hud loads his rifle with Lon by his side as they prepare to shoot down hundreds of infected cattle.

Relatives: Homer Bannon, Lon Bannon, and Fast Eddy of "The Hustler." A "Non-hero" classic, too.

Evil Deeds: Uses people and doesn't care who he hurts. He's constantly fighting, is totally dishonest, attempts rape, and is no good liar.

Outcome: As the movie progresses and Hud gets into fights, con various people, and mistreats everyone around him, he slowly alienates all his friends and family. After trying to rape Alma Brown (Patricia Neal) and driving her off, when she actually liked him, he ultimately drives Lon away, the person he probably cares more about than anyone. As the film ends, Lon walks off into the sunset (a marked contrast to the usual happy-cowboy ending in which hero rides off), tearfully coming to grips with his revulsion and rejection of Hud and everything that he stands for. Hud yells after him, "There's so much crap in this world you're going to wallow in it sooner or later."

Current Status: Still alive, trying to live up to his macho image.

What to Do If You Meet: Don't mess with him. He's just itching to get into a good brawl.

Worthy of Note: An anti-hero classic that set the tone for the movies of the 1960s. Totally turned around the myth of the cowboy hero.

J.J. Hunsecker

Alias: Brother J.J.
Born: 1920s
Died: Lives on

Starred in:
Sweet Smell of Success
United Artists, 1957
Director: Alexander Mackendrick
Played by: Burt Lancaster

J.J. Hunsecker tries to cajole his sister to stop seeing her musician boyfriend in Sweet Smell of Success.

Description: A big guy with a taste for expensive lounging robes, fine liquor, and getting his own way. He's suave and powerful. He weighs 230 pounds and is six feet, three inches tall. His extreme monomania makes him not well liked, but people still fawn on him because he is powerful. All of this, of course, feeds his excessive ego.

Reason for Villainy: Hunsecker is incensed that his sister Susan (Susan Harrison) is going out with Steve Dallas, a guitarist. Sidney Falco (Tony Curtis) is a desperate publicity agent. Since Hunsecker is the top Broadway columnist, he could do something for Falco—for a price. Hunsecker makes a proposition to Falco: Get Steve Dallas (Marty Milner) away from my sister and I will throw some good vibes your way. Up until now Falco has been doing most of Hunsecker's work without payment. Sidney begins spreading rumors that the guitarist is a doper and a card-carrying Communist. The items of destructive character assassination appear in the papers and Hunsecker tells Steve he will help him out. Susan believes that Hunsecker is a good joe. Steve, however, suspects that the whole thing was set up by Hunsecker, but he can't prove it. Steve tells Susan to choose between her family and him. This angers Susan and she tells Hunsecker that she will not see the guitarist anymore. But she does. To retaliate, Hunsecker gets Falco to plant marijuana in the guitarist's place.

Evil Powers: Influence peddling, egomania, frame-up, and conspiracy.

Occupation: Columnist.

Intelligence: Sharp as a hypodermic.

Strengths: His position.

Weaknesses: Egomania always is self-defeating.

Territory: Broadway, NYC.

Idiosyncrasies: He thinks he can do anything, and loves to manipulate people.

Friends: Sycophants.

Enemies: Steve, the guitarist, and, later, Falco.

Evil Deeds: Innumerable. He twists the truth to destroy people, makes Falco frame Steve, and is a sinister egomaniac.

Outcome: Steve is arrested for marijuana possession and Falco is called to Hunsecker's place to celebrate. Upon arriving at Hunsecker's, Falco discovers that Susan is so distraught about Steve's arrest that she is about to do away with herself. She isn't wearing much in the way of clothing either, preparing to exit this vale of tears the way she came into it—stark naked. At this point, bad boy Hunsecker steps in and assumes that Falco has done something indecent to Susan. Falco rushes out. Hunsecker calls the police and tells them that Falco had planted the marijuana. Susan, is no longer planning to commit suicide anymore, she just leaves her insane, megalomaniacal frere. As she leaves, she sees Falco being beaten and taken into custody by the cops. Steve, the small-time jazz guitarist, will be freed. Whatever motive—jealousy a la Freud perhaps—Hunsecker had for hurting Steve is not revealed. As for Sue, she's through with being dominated. Hunsecker has finally failed in his manipulations of other people's lives.

Current Status: Fixing himself a martini, very dry.

What to Do If You Meet: Don't kowtow to creeps. Stand on your own two feet.

Worthy of Note: Hunsecker is one of that new breed of villains—the media-created villain. His nationally powerful syndicated column made him a dictator of sorts.

Lieutenant Colonel Hyde

Born: 1910 or thereabout
Died: 1950

Starred in:
The League of Gentlemen
Allied Film Makers, 1960
Director: Basil Dearden
Played by: Jack Hawkins

Description: The ex-soldier was trained to be efficient, and he looks it. He's got good thews, sharp falcon-eyes, and is quick-witted and shifty. He looks every bit the military man.

Reason for Villainy: Hyde summons a group of seven desperate war vets by sending them five pound notes cut in half. He meets them for lunch at the Cafe Royal. They are: Race (Nigel Patrick), the driver; Mycroft (Roger Livesey), disguise expert; Stevens (Kieron Moore), the combat expert; Weaver (Norman Bird), explosives man; Porthill (Bryan Forbes), the con-man; Lexy (Richard Attenborough), radio wiz; and Rupert (Terrence Alexander), smokescreen expert. Hyde reveals that he knows their secret crimes. He has a dossier, it seems, on all of them. He then dangles the carrot—the London Bank and its one-million pound contents. They agree to participate in a military-style robbery of the bank. Weapons are acquired by raiding the army supply depot. Next, a truck is stolen—a large lorry as they are called in Britain. They are ready to attack the bank.

Evil Powers/Weapons: Know-how and weapons, good planning and guts. Besides, if the team refused, Hyde does have that dossier.

Occupation: Hyde is a redundant war veteran. (Redundant means unemployed over in fish and chips land.)

Intelligence: Oh, he's a smart one.

Strengths: He has all the stuff and the right men.

Weaknesses: He should have splashed mud on the license plates!

Territory: Britain.

Idiosyncrasies: Provides jobs for veterans.

Friends: The vets.

Enemies: The bobbies.

Evil Deeds: Blows up a lot of stuff, holds people captive, steals ammo and weapons, grand theft, and, of course, bank robbery.

Lieutenant Colonel Hyde (Jack Hawkins) is the military expert who gets together a squad of war vets to rob the London Bank in The League of Gentlemen.

Outcome: The event was planned well, but it failed. They got through the alarms all right, they held the staff off with machine guns, they sealed off the area with smoke, they loaded the bullion into the lorry, but. . . . A little boy saw the license plates. Hyde, thinking he alone has been caught, enters the police wagon to find all the other members of his team. The end.

Current Status: Jolly good at doing time.

What to Do If You Meet: Keep your money in the mattress.

Worthy of Note: All the blokes in this film were ripe for male adventure, being hampered and kept in the doghouse by various females. It's one of those films about the need for men to be men. See *The Wild Geese* instead.

Tom Iverson and Paula

Alias: The Smugglers
Born: 1940s
Died: 1975

Starred in:
Night Moves
Warner Bros., 1975
Director: Arthur Penn
Played by: John Crawford and Jennifer
    Warren

Description: The two killers are a "wild," middle-aged couple who live in the south of Florida. They both have light hair. Paula's is shoulder-length and Tom has an overgrown crewcut. They often have drinks in their hands and wear ragged "beach" clothes.

Reason for Villainy: This pair is involved in smuggling Columbian art treasures into the country. Private investigator Harry Moseby (Gene Hackman) has a nose for this sort of thing. Initially he is hired to find Arlene Iverson's missing daughter Delly (Melanie Griffith), who had run off with a no-good stunt

pilot. Moseby tracks the girl to the south-Florida seaside home of her stepfather Tom Iverson. Iverson's home is a sick, drunken scene with very unpleasant sexual overtones. Moseby convinces Delly to go back with him, but first he has to fight off Tom, and not before he becomes romantically involved with Paula. Delly, very anxious to leave, spots the wrecked plane and the no-good stunt pilot's dead body in shallow water near her stepfather's house. Moseby whisks the promiscuous teen back to L.A., where he returns to his estranged wife. Is the case solved? Moseby's nose is twitching. Not yet.

Evil Powers: Tom Iverson is a cunning, immoral murderer. He and Paula have the advantage of being completely guiltless and ruthless.

Weapons: Guns, planes, ships, and sex.

Occupation: Smugglers—though we don't know that till the end.

Intelligence: Tom is mean as a sidewinder, or rather, a water moccasin. Paula uses her sexual charms and all the powers of subterfuge.

Strengths: They kill anybody who threatens them, so they have no opposition.

Weaknesses: They are into sex, drugs, and liquor.

Territory: South Florida.

Idiosyncrasies: They are a horny pair.

Friends: Other smugglers who help them.

Enemies: Moseby and anyone who knows their secrets like the dead stunt pilot.

Evil Deeds: They kill the stunt pilot who was working with them, do unkind things to Delly, and commit several murders to cover up their smuggling.

Outcome: Back in L.A., Delly takes off again to a movie location where she is killed while involved in a stunt. She went for wild times, now she's dead. Moseby watches the footage and is convinced that Delly was murdered. Harry is off to Florida again, even though it's on his own time. Tom and Paula, our villainous pair, have a little welcoming celebration for the nosey guy. They plan to murder him. After all, that's what they do best. Harry and Tom have a fistfight, there is a wild sea chase, and Tom and Paula wind up dead in a plane crash while attempting to get away with it all. Harry is not too well off

Harry Moseby punches Tom Iverson (John Crawford) in Night Moves.

either. He's circling around and around helplessly wounded in a motor boat. One can only hope that our ever-vigilant Coast Guard will find him, but it's such a small boat and such a big ocean. Maybe Tom and Paula have managed to kill one more person—Harry.

Current Status: Tom and Paula are dead as doornails.

What to Do If You Meet: Try not to let Paula wrap you around her finger. Avoid Tom's fists and bullets. Keep your nose straight ahead and leave.

Worthy of Note: Black times in south Florida. An excellent film full of sleazy eroticism.

The Jackal   121

Frank and
   Jessie James   122

Earl Janoth   123

Cody Jarrett   124

Jaws   125

Johnny and
   Chino   126

Franz Kindler   128

Kongre   129

Kramer   130

Colonel Kurtz   131

Michael Landon   132

Clubber Lang   134

The Lavender
   Hill Mob   135

The Law   136

Leatherface   137

Harry Lime   138

Dad Longworth   139

Doyle Lonnigan   140

Rose Loomis   141

Luther of the
   Rogues   143

Waldo Lydecker   144

The Jackal

Alias: The Assassin, Calthrop
Born: Around 1930
Died: 1963

Starred in:
Day of the Jackal
Universal Pictures, 1973
Director: Fred Zinnemann
Played by: Edward Fox

Description: Good-looking blonde killer, about six feet, two inches tall. Debonair, suave, ruthless. Dresses in suits, often wears an ascot. Always extremely well-groomed. Very charming, but icily cold and efficient when it comes to killing.

Reason for Villainy: It's 1963, and members of the OAS (a right-wing organization) are plotting to assassinate Charles de Gaulle. They bungle one execution attempt, and all but three of the terrorists are captured and executed. The remaining OAS members plan another attack but this time they hire the world's most ruthless assassin, the Jackal, to do the job right. After OAS secures false pass-

The Jackal (Edward Fox) inspects the rifle specially made for him by one of the world's best gunsmiths, who he's about to kill in Day of the Jackal.

ports and a special rifle that shoots exploding bullets at long range, the Jackal sets out to kill De Gaulle.

Evil Powers/Weapons: Cunning, an incredible actor, can fool almost anyone. Master of disguise. Expert in all weapons, particularly the sniper rifle. Karate expert, will kill anyone who gets in his way.

Occupation: Hired assassin. Gets half a million dollars a job, *prix fixe*. Job guaranteed.

Intelligence: Extremely intelligent. Expert in all the necessary tools of assassination, including planning, mapping, organization. Speaks several languages. Smarter than almost anyone he has to deal with.

Strengths: Cold-blooded, focused, strong.

Weaknesses: Psychopathic, over-confident.

Territory: Works all over the world, but is located in England. The film takes place in France as he pursues De Gaulle and the police pursue him.

Idiosyncrasies: Kills everyone who might identify him, leaving a trail of bodies behind, even the people who help him.

Friends: He has no real friends. Although he pretends to be friends with people, he only uses them for his own evil ends and then disposes of them.

Enemies: Inspector Lebel of French Intelligence.

Relatives: Black Sunday Terrorists, Manchurian Candidate.

Evil Deeds: He has assassinated countless famous and infamous people around the world. Murders innocent bystanders, steals, lies. Not a nice fellow.

Killed by: The French Sûreté have captured an OAS member who confesses that a man known as "The Jackal" is preparing to hit De Gaulle. The French Minister (Alan Badel) tells Inspector Lebel (Michel Lonsdale) to check all assassinations of the past five years and find out who the Jackal is. Lebel learns that a Charles Calthrop recently killed a South American. He also realizes that the first letters of this killer's first and last name spell *chacal*, the French for Jackal. Realizing the authorities are onto him, the Jackal disguises himself as a schoolteacher and evades capture. On Liberation Day, the authorities block off the entire area where De Gaulle is to speak, but the Jackal sneaks into a building disguised as an old war veteran. As the Jackal aims his rifle on De Gaulle from a window, a cop informs Lebel that a strange man entered the building. The Inspector runs up into the building as the Jackal gets off a shot. Luckily, De Gaulle decided to bend over and the bullet missed him. Before the Jackal can shoot again, Lebel smashes the door and blasts the Jackal to bits with a submachine gun.

Current Status: Dead, but there are other "superkillers" like the Jackal plying their trade.

What to Do If You Meet: Tell him you're a terrorist, too, and talk shop. "Hey, that's a nice Kalashnikov you've got there, pal."

Worthy of Note: Big money-making movie from a best selling book by Frederick Forsyth.

Frank and Jessie James

Born: 1840s
Died: Jesse died in the 1870s, Frank a little later

Starred in:
The Long Riders
Warner Bros., 1980
Director: Walter Hill
Played by: Stacy and James Keach

Description: They both wear long, camel-colored wool riding coats. They have wide brimmed, black cowboy hats and are quite trail-dusty. Frank sports a long moustache, and both are armed with six-shooters. As did all men of their time, they wear round-collared shirts, boots, and riding gloves. Garrison belts and Levis complete the look.

Reason for Villainy: The James Brothers are teamed with the notorious Cole Younger and the Miller Boys in this film. Together with the gang, they rob a train, blowing up the baggage car, and nearly killing the guard when he refuses to open up. The cruelty, as well as

Frank and Jesse James (Stacy and James Keach) rob another train in The Long Riders.

the friendlier side of the brothers, is shown in this well-made film. The whole scene looks like the real 1870s to this viewer's eye. There are references to the suffering of the post-Civil War Missouri homesteaders and the desperate plight of the sharecroppers. But in the end, the ruthless gang decides to pick on these people, the common folk. The next big raid is planned for a wealthy bank in Minnesota. Those Swedes and Norwegians have a lot of money. The town, however, expects the gang to make the long ride up to rob their bank, and they've prepared a counterattack. When the gang rides in and pulls their guns in the bank, a teller wisecracks that they will all soon be dead. For his idiotic bravery he's shot point-blank in the head. As the gang makes its escape, the town erupts in gunfire, and many are wounded. Desperate, the gang convenes out of town and the James Brothers desert their "friends."

Evil Powers/Weapons: An organized gang, equipped with solid plans, rifles and six-shooters.

Occupation: Train robbers, bank robbers, farmers.

Intelligence: Not well read, but clever dirt farmers.

Strengths: They are viewed by some as modern Robin Hoods.

Weaknesses: There is a big reward out for them.

Territory: The Midwest—from Missouri to Minnesota.

Idiosyncrasies: They want one big haul to retire.

Friends: Their gang.

Enemies: Anyone seeking the reward on their heads.

Evil Deeds: Kill innocent people, rob banks, trains, shoot Pinkertons.

Killed by: Most people know the line "dirty little coward shot Mr. Howard, and laid Jasse James in his grave." As it turns out, Jesse is shaving, or straightening a mirror, or something like that and the coward out for the reward money shoots him in the back. It is the end of an era. Frank escapes for a time. The days of robbing banks and pestering honest folks are drawing to a close. So be it.

Current Status: Dead folk heroes. But they were pretty mean, really.

What to Do If You Meet: Say you hate the law.

Worthy of Note: This picture was made in an attempt to revive the Western. It didn't. Very few Westerns are made nowadays. People just don't go to see them. Hollywood steers its production money into more sure-fire successes now.

Earl Janoth

Alias: The Tycoon
Born: 1910s
Died: 1947

Starred in:
The Big Clock
Paramount, 1948
Director: John Farrow
Played by: Charles Laughton

Description: Hefty, but not portly, tycoon in double-breasted, hand-tailored outfit befitting his stature. Dapper, three-pointed hanky extending from his breast pocket (Irish lace). He's six-feet tall with a moustache, some crow's-feet, a fat chin, fat lips, and a receding hairline.

Reason for Villainy: The Big Clock is the immense central timer in the lobby of the *Crimeways* building, from which the compulsive time-watcher Janoth rules his empire. He spies on coffee breaks and it's curtains for those who come in late. Janoth has a multi-million-dollar publishing outift. He is publisher of *Crimeways* magazine, a crusading track 'em down rag. The brilliant and handsome editor of *Crimeways* is George Stroud (Ray Milland). George is having marital difficulties with his wife, Georgette, (Maureen O'Sullivan). It's the old "you never come home" bit. It's been five years now that George has been postponing his honeymoon. He becomes enraged and quits when Janoth wants him to cancel his trip and begin work on some hot new case. George is really the pivotal person on the magazine. He charts the crimes, the personality of the criminals, and often comes up with the perpetrators and turns them over to the authorities. The magazine would be in bad shape without him. The slave-driver Janoth naturally is enraged, but lets George go.

Evil Powers: Janoth has money. He has wily intelligence and knows the city, the building, and the offices of his empire. His gun, and framing the wrong man make him formidable.

Occupation: Publishing tycoon.

Intelligence: Very intelligent and good at business, and murder, too.

Strengths: Cunning, money, familiarity with the scene.

Weaknesses: Up against the brilliant crimefighter George.

Territory: The *Crimeways* Building.

Idiosyncrasies: He "times" everyone— you'd best be on time.

Friends: Time is on his side, usually.

Enemies: George and the truth.

Evil Deeds: He kills Pauline, his mistress.

Killed by: Although George is anxious to meet his wife, he dillydallies and picks up Pauline (Rita Johnson) and takes her home after a night of wildness. He does all of this without knowing she's Janoth's mistress. Janoth arrives on the scene and is enraged that she had a male visitor. He is so flustered he kills the luscious blond. Janoth then becomes

Compulsive time-watcher Earl Janoth (Charles Laughton) poses in front of The Big Clock, the immense time-keeper in his building.

George, falls in his madness down the elevator shaft. The end.

Current Status: Keeping Satan Standard Time.

What to Do If You Meet: For heaven's sake, be on time.

Worthy of Note: The Clock is nice. Name all the movies that clocks have appeared in—if you can spare the time.

Cody Jarrett

Born: 1900s
Died: 1949

Starred in:
White Heat
Warner Bros., 1949
Director: Raoul Walsh
Played by: James Cagney

distraught. He's never even killed time (ouch), but now he's killed a person. Our villain seeks advice from his assistant and friend Steve Hagen (George Macready). Hagen suggests they find a patsy—the man that was seen leaving Pauline's moments before Janoth killed her. Janoth puts his entire staff on the assignment. Good idea. In the meantime, George is at the vacation resort getting back in his wife's good graces. Janoth calls him back to work on the case, and he goes. His wife says that it is really quits for them. George, however, finds he has a bigger problem. He must throw his resourceful team off the track of the missing man—because it is him. He must instead track down the real murderer. He soon finds out that Janoth was keeping Pauline and deduces the rest. He goes to Hagen and convinces him that Janoth will double-cross him. Hagen then gets into a tiff with our villain and Janoth shoots Hagen. Janoth, knowing that George is onto him, begins chasing George about the offices. Janoth, however, doesn't know that George is hiding in the Big Clock. It's a tense moment or two, with time ticking away, for George has tripped up the mechanism. Finally, Janoth, continuing his pursuit of

Description: Cody is short, cocky, wild-haired. A tough guy with a sharp and snappy no-nonsense voice. Wears convict suits or the pinstripes of a well-dressed mobster.

Reason for Villainy: Cody is a little hood with a big idea: to be on top of the world. He also has this thing for his mother, whom he idolizes. In short, he's a fruitcake. Jarrett, his mom, and his gang have pulled a train robbery. They iced one railroad guard. Then Jarrett cops a plea on a lesser charge to beat the heat. But the cops know that Jarrett is a killer. They plant a detective, Hank Fallon (Edmond O'Brien), to win his friendship. Hank and Jarrett bust out of the joint. Cody's Ma, meanwhile, has been bumped off by gang members Big Ed and Verna, Cody's wife. Big Ed (Steve Cochran) has taken over the mob. All of this action has given Cody lots of real, real bad headaches. He's ready to kill anyone that harmed mother. Verna somehow convinces him that she had nothing to do with the killing. However, to reassert his power over the gang, Cody guns down Big Ed.

Evil Powers: Spunky, tough guy, who will shoot you dead if you look at him the wrong way.

Weapons: He uses a pistol, and he doesn't miss.

Occupation: Professional criminal, convict, psychopath.

Intelligence: Not too bright. His brain needs a retread. But he's a wily guy, and sneaky.

Strengths: He has his heater, and uses it.

Weaknesses: He gets these bad, bad headaches, and he wants to please his Ma.

Territory: U.S.A.

Idiosyncrasies: Needs aspirin.

Friends: He thinks that Verna and Hank are his friends, but actually he has no one except his Ma.

Enemies: Big Ed, Hank, the coppers, society.

Relatives: Could Rocco of *Key Largo* be his cousin?

Evil Deeds: He kills, steals, speeds, breaks out of jail, and violates his parole.

Killed by: Cody and Hank have planned a new robbery. Hank, of course, tells the coppers, and the gang and Cody walk into a trap. This is the old days, folks, and the cops shoot first and ask questions later. The gang is mercilessly gunned down. But Cody escapes. He climbs to the top of a giant, gas-filled tank. There he takes a stand, shooting it out. He shouts to his dead mother that "I'm on top of the world." Then he is blown to kingdom come as the tank explodes when it is hit by bullets.

Current Status: Dead (atomized).

What to Do If You Meet: He's dangerous. Pen him and he busts out. Forget parole, he can't go straight. He has to be shot down.

Worthy of Note: *THE* gangster movie with Cagney.

Jaws

Born: 1940s
Died: Thought to still be alive.

Starred in:
The Spy Who Loved Me
United Artists, 1977
Director: Lewis Gilbert
Played by: Richard Kiel

Description: Giant of a man, more than seven-feet tall, hands as big as your head, huge, gleaming metal teeth fill his entire mouth. Not a nice fellow.

The giant Jaws holds James "007" Bond from carrying out his mission in The Spy Who Loved Me.

Reason for Villainy: James Bond is on assignment again, investigating the disappearance of two nuclear-powered submarines (one British, one U.S.). He discovers that the subs have been stolen by a powerful shipping magnate, Karl Stromberg (Curt Jurgens), by using a huge tanker, the *Liparus,* that can open up the entire forward section and literally swallow ships. Stromberg wants to blow up the world with the nuke missiles and build his own empire under the sea. When he discovers that Bond is on his trail, he sends out Jaws, his meanest killer, to take care of the secret agent.

Evil Powers/Weapons: Strong as five men. His hands can break a man's back. His teeth are a powerful weapon—can bite through necks, boards, steel. Totally fearless.

Occupation: Hired killer.

Intelligence: Not that smart, but mean.

Strengths: Powerful, intimidating, sneaky.

Weaknesses: Not too fast.

Territory: Works all over the world, wherever he is sent.

Idiosyncrasies: Smiles, most alarmingly, as he comes at you to attack.

Friends: Stromberg.

Enemies: James Bond.

Evil Deeds: Has killed scores of spies, agents, and innocents with those snapping teeth.

Outcome: Jaws follows Bond all over the world as the agent tries to prevent Stromberg's dastardly plans from succeeding. Jaws attacks Bond several times, trying to murder the agent with those razor-sharp teeth. Somehow Bond manages to outwit the killer each time. First he jams an electric wire into Jaws's teeth and nearly electrocutes the villain. A second time, after Jaws traps Bond in a train, Bond manages to knock Jaws off the top of the train as it goes through a tunnel. Jaws is presumed dead. Bond then boards a British sub and allows himself to be captured by Stromberg's tanker. Once in the madman's undersea fortress, he escapes, stops the missiles which are about to be launched (to start a war between the superpowers), shoots it out with Stromberg, killing him, and blows up the villain's headquarters.

Current Status: Jaws just can't be stopped. He is more than mortal. He is still hiring himself out to whoever needs his services.

What to Do If You Meet: Tell him you know where he can get dental work cheap!

Worthy of Note: One of the best Bond films. Jaws has also appeared in other Bond and adventure/spy films playing the same terrifying character.

Johnny and Chino

Born: 1900s
Died: Motorcycle crashes without helmets probably left them basket cases.

Starred in:
The Wild One
Columbia, 1954
Director: Laslo Benedek
Played by: Marlon Brando, Lee Marvin

Description: Chino is tall, lanky, and in his mid-thirties. He sports a wasp-pattern, blue-and-white-striped shirt under a dusty, sleeveless leather jacket. Johnny wears a beat-up motorcycle jacket and a captain's style hat.

Reason for Villainy: Johnny is the leader of a raucous, mad, motorcycle gang that rides from town to town on their Harleys causing havoc. They give the sport a bad name. Chino's gang of drunken hoods cycles into the same town (Wrightsville) that Johnny and his Black Rebels Motorcycle Club have just invaded. Johnny is persuaded to keep the peace because he is enamored of a local waitress, Kathie (Mary Murphy). She is the daughter of Wrightsville's constable, Robert Keith (Harry Bleeker). There is drunken confrontation between the town and the two gangs. People are afraid. Chino will not adhere to any civilized standards and is looking for a rumble. He even covets Johnny's motorcycle-contest trophy. (Actually, Johnny stole the thing when his group was thrown out of a legitimate contest.) Both gangs ride in tight formation through the town and its environs making all God-fearing people pull down their shades. Johnny gets Kathie to ride with him, and they begin to talk about life—in a

Johnny keeps his beloved stolen trophy firmly attached to his beloved motorcycle in The Wild One.

cemetery, of all places. They become lovers. Chino just wants trouble and he continues to tumble about the street with his enemy.

Evil Powers/Weapons: Lethal cycles, clubs, fists, guns, beer bottles. They are a gang of uncouth highway savages.

Occupation: Motorcyclists.

Intelligence: They fight dirty and are not smart.

Strengths: Backed up by gang.

Weaknesses: Not capable of besting an aroused citizenry.

Territory: Wrightsville; the highway; everywhere, man.

Idiosyncrasies: Argumentative with the law and most other people.

Friends: The road.

Enemies: The law.

Evil Deeds: They're out to have fun, a wild time, to really terrorize the town.

Outcome: Chino and his gang continue to terrorize the town. After stealing Johnny's stolen trophy, Chino and Johnny engage in fistfights. But Chino is arrested, and the gangs join forces against society. Johnny and Sheriff Bleeker drink together, saddened at their inability to stop the gangs. Johnny rescues Kathie from the gangs. They drive to the cemetery where he makes advances to her. She slaps him. In a moment, townspeople surround and menace Johnny. Johnny gets on his cycle, but is cut off by the townsfolk who are now a mob. Someone throws a tire iron at him and he's thrown off the cycle. The cycle, however, plunges into the mob, killing the old bartender. The sheriff takes Johnny in, but after learning the circumstances lets him ride out of town. On his way out of town, he stops at Kathie's cafe, but he can't articulate his feeling. He smirks and gives her his proudest possession—the stolen trophy. Then he rides. He's the wild one. Chino takes off, too. Good thing.

Current Status: Probably had an accident by now.

What to Do If You Meet: Give them a speeding ticket, or better yet, don't meet.

Worthy of Note: While merely depicting a certain lifestyle, the picture seemed to idolize the senseless, restless youths who ride motorcyles. This film spawned gangs of the type seen in the film.

Franz Kindler

Alias: Charles Rankin
Born: 1900s
Died: 1948

Starred in:
The Stranger
RKO Radio, 1946
Director: Orson Welles
Played by: Orson Welles

The foreign poster for the Stranger shows Orson Welles as Franz Kindler, on the left.

Description: Kindler looks just like your ordinary, small town, history teacher.

Reason for Villainy: The War Crimes Commission is meeting in Germany. One of the members, Wilson (Edward G. Robinson), seeks the release of Konrad Meinike (Konstantin Shayne) in order to capture more war criminals. Meinike is released and Wilson tracks him to Connecticut. Meinike's first stop is the home of Charles Rankin, a history teacher. Rankin is actually the notorious Franz Kindler, the mastermind of many atrocities during the war. Kindler has successfully lived under his alias and is even engaged to an unsuspecting woman, Mary Longstreet (Loretta Young), the daughter of a judge. He thinks this will be the perfect cover "until ve vill rise again in ze Fourth Reich." Meinike has actually sought out Kindler in the hope of having him repent. Meinike, it seems, has become truly repentant and religious. Kindler, however, strangles Meinike for being so foolish as to lead the authorities to him. Kindler hides the body in the woods on the way to his marriage ceremony. Wilson successfully tracked Meinike to Harper, Connecticut, but is still unsure of Kindler's identity. Mr. Potter (Billy House), the town druggist who knows and sees all, has an intense conversation with Wilson on the many possibilities. Wilson, befriending Mary's parents, is invited to a party which the newlyweds also attend. Danger looms.

Evil Powers/Weapons: His obsession with a Nazi triumph and his murderous hands.

Occupation: War criminal, school teacher.
Intelligence: Evil brilliance.
Strengths: He went underground very successfully.
Weaknesses: He loves Naziism so much that he can't keep his mouth shut.
Territory: Harper, Connecticut.
Idiosyncrasies: Takes the dog for a walk, but then kicks it.
Friends: The mad housepainter—Adolf Hitler.
Enemies: Wilson and democracy.
Relatives: *The Boys from Brazil.*
Evil Deeds: Countless war atrocities, plus he kicks dogs and strangles people.
Outcome: Wilson casually swings the discussion at the party to the topic of the recent war. Kindler as Rankin is a vehement supporter of democracy, as are all the other guests. Wilson begins to think he has hit a dead end. Meanwhile, Meinike's body is uncovered by Mary's dog while Kindler was taking the animal for a walk. Kindler is so upset he kicks the

dog. Wilson, still out to get his man, remembers that "Rankin" had referred to Karl Marx as a Jew, not as a German in their conversation. This makes him very suspicious. How can Wilson make the man reveal himself for certain? Wilson decides to tell Mary all he knows. She doesn't believe her husband is the Nazi criminal and refuses to incriminate him. "Rankin," however, realizing that his wife is too much of a gamble decides it is time to kill her. He climbs the town's clocktower and saws a set of rungs off the stairs. He then phones his distraught wife and asks her to meet him there so he can explain his innocence. He will be playing checkers with Potter—the perfect alibi. But Mary, on the maid's urging, doesn't go and "Rankin" is surprised to find her alive when he goes home. The evidence soon becomes too apparent and Mary and the angry townspeople go after "Rankin," now revealed as Kindler. Trapped in the clocktower, Mary climbs the stairs to kill her husband. He keeps shouting that he was only following orders. The clock has moving metal soldiers and Kindler gets tangled up in one of the lifesized figures and a sword impales him.

Current Status: Dead.

What to Do If You Meet: Discuss Karl Marx.

Worthy of Note: Dramatic tour de force, only a bit overdone.

Kongre

Born: 1830s
Died: Late 1860s

Starred in:
The Light at the Edge of the World
National General, 1971
Director: Kevin Billington
Played by: Yul Brynner

Description: Kongre is a pirate cutthroat through and through. Filthy, over-adorned with baubles, booted, carrying sword and dagger and a single-shot musket. The sea rogue stands six-feet tall and is the bald scourge of the south Atlantic and Pacific. He likes black—the color of the Jolly Roger (pirate flag).

Reason for Villainy: The Argentine government has set up a huge lighthouse, manned by three different types of men, to warn ships of the dangers off the turbulent Cape Horn of South America. The three are Denton (Kirk Douglas), an American drifter; Moriz (Fernando Rey), a driven ex-sea captain; and his assis-

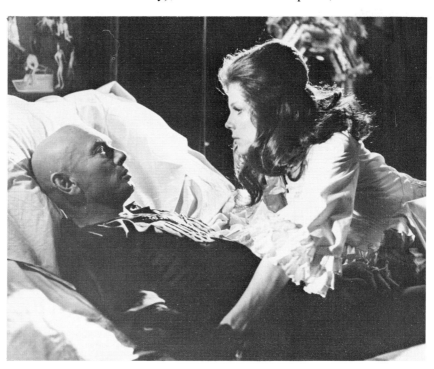

Kongre (Yul Brynner) listens impassively as his captive Arabella makes a plea in The Light at the Edge of the World.

tant, Felipe (Massimo Ranieri). The three do not get along and Denton decides to leave. Then fate intervenes. Kongre arrives, determined to destroy the lighthouse and send ships to their doom to be plundered by his pirates. The black pirate schooner is in the bay. Moriz and Felipe board it and are murdered. Denton hides out in a cave watching with spyglasses from afar. Eventually he's caught, degraded by Kongre, but escapes. Before he can be recaptured, a ship arrives. It follows the pirate's false light, runs aground, and all on board are horribly murdered—except the lovely noblewoman Arabella (Samantha Eggar) and the ship's engineer, Montefiore (Renato Salvatori). The two are captured and used as bait for Denton. Denton tries to rescue Arabella, but only gets away with Montefiore. Kongre admires Denton's bravery and wants him to join the pirates.

Evil Powers/Weapons: Kongre has ships, men, swords, pistols, and enough swashbuckling bravado to win the day.

Lew Kramer (Anthony Perkins) takes over the ship Esther in ffolkes.

Occupation: Bloodthirsty pirate, plunderer, and a mistreater of women.

Intelligence: Narrowly concerned with gold and other booty, but smart.

Strengths/Weaknesses: Denton is just one man but is also a real man.

Territory: The south Atlantic and Pacific. Cape Horn.

Idiosyncrasies: Likes an opponent with spunk.

Friends: His crew.

Enemies: Denton and all civilized peoples.

Evil Deeds: Forget it! These are not the jolly pirates of yore, but Jules Verne's killers-of-the-seas. They're not nice to anyone or anything.

Outcome: It finally comes down to a contest between Denton and the villain. Kongre does the worst thing imaginable; he turns Arabella over to his desperately deprived crew of cutthroats for their pleasure. Due to this, she eventually dies. No more need be said. Denton secures a big cannon and fires on the black schooner, sinking it. Kongre meets him at the lighthouse for a duel to the death. A shot from the pirate's pistol sets the lighthouse on fire. Kongre falls and burns alive. Drawn by the flames, a ship arrives and takes on Denton. He leaves, watching the flames recede on the horizon.

Current Status: Dead.

What to Do If You Meet: Most pirates have torture on their minds. Don't meet them unless your country will post reward for your safe return.

Worthy of Note: A mean movie, perhaps too mean for Saturday-matinee kids interested in a jolly pirate movie. Grim. Another Jules Verne-based great. Kirk is excellent in this one. See all of Verne's Disney films too.

Kramer

Born: 1940s
Died: 1980

Starred in:
ffolkes
Universal, 1980
Director: Andrew V. McLaglen
Played by: Anthony Perkins

Description: Kramer wears nautical blue, and often holds a pair of binoculars, looking nervous. He's thin, drawn, his fingers move about uncontrollably as he frets. He also wears a warm woolen cap against the cold sea air. He's described as a "neurotic homosexual."

Reason for Villainy: Seven hijackers led by Kramer and his "friend" Shulman (Michael Parks) board the *Esther*, a Norwegian ship bearing cargo to Ruth, a North Sea drilling station. Jennifer is a nearby petrol-producing platform anchored above the cruel waves. Kramer plants high explosives all over Ruth and Jennifer and demands 25 million pounds sterling while threatening to blow them up. Ffolkes (Roger Moore), a counterterrorist team leader, is secretly placed aboard a supply ship near *Esther*. The Prime Minister of Britain (Faith Brook) orders Ffolkes and his team to stop Kramer. Kramer believes the Brits won't pay up and tries to blow up Ruth. However, Ffolkes's team diverts the explosion by using frogmen to remove the explosives. Kramer, however, thinks he destroyed Ruth and that now Britain will accede to his wishes. Meanwhile some of the *Esther* crew attack Kramer's men, but fail.

Evil Powers/Weapons: Lots of explosives rigged in a deadly and complicated array.

Occupation: Terrorist. (Terrorists, following actual news trends, seem to be a favorite, new supervillain in the films of the late '70s and early '80s.)

Intelligence: Oh, he's clever all right. Bloody clever.

Strengths: Lots of explosives.

Weaknesses: His psychological profile is known and Ffolkes is after him.

Territory: The North Sea.

Idiosyncrasies: He's a bit swishy.

Friends: Shulman.

Enemies: Ffolkes, the Brits, and the Norwegians.

Evil Deeds: Kramer is itching to blow every-thing up. He forces a crewmember to drink poisoned coffee. He is nasty over the radio. He's an all around blighter, he is.

Outcome: Admiral Brindsen (James Mason) says Britain will pay even though they are really stalling to let Ffolkes do his thing. The admiral boards the terrorist's ship with Ffolkes who is disguised as an aide. Kramer is too careful, however, to let Ffolkes do him in. First wanting them as hostages, Kramer now orders them off the ship. Ffolkes boards the *Esther* in a wetsuit with his men following. Sanna (Lea Brodie), a female crewmember in hiding, saves him when he is surprised by Kramer's man. Ffolkes has always thought women to be incompetent, but was now forced to admit they have their place. The good guys eventually take over, and Kramer is killed. Knowing that Ffolkes won't take a monetary reward, the prime minister presents him with a box of white kittens.

Current Status: Dead.

What to Do If You Meet: Talk about redecorating the explosives.

Worthy of Note: Wet and cold. See it.

Colonel Kurtz

Born: 1920s
Died: Late 1960s

Starred in:
Apocalypse Now
United Artists, 1979
Director: Francis Ford Coppola
Played by: Marlon Brando

Description: Insane, totally bald, renegade U.S. Army colonel. Thick, muscular, sloppy, aura of powerful darkness.

Reason for Villainy: It's the late 1960s in Saigon, Vietnam, and Captain Willard (Martin Sheen) of the Intelligence Division, is destitute and badly in need of a mission. He has nightmarish memories of the last war, a time when he saw incredible ugliness. He is pulled out of his depression when he is ordered to "terminate with extreme prejudice" an insane American officer, Colonel Walter E. Kurtz. It appears that Kurtz has gone completely psychotic and created a bloody kingdom for himself on an island in remote Cambodia.

Evil Powers/Weapons: A superior military strategist. He commands a group of fanatic soldiers and has strange powers over natives. He understands the uses of terror and pain and has access to heavy field weapons.

Occupation: Rogue colonel, warlord.

Intelligence: Extremely intelligent, well versed in military techniques.

Strengths: He controls a whole section of a country and is meaner than a junkyard dog.

Weaknesses: Insane.

Territory: A little kingdom of army barracks and Cambodian hovels.

Idiosyncrasies: Mumbles incoherent philosophies of nihilism, about the beauty and necessity of violence, and pain in the world.

Friends: His own troops.

Enemies: Captain Willard, who is sent to kill him.

Relatives: The Deer Hunter, The Warlord.

Evil Deeds: Takes over part of Cambodia, kills soldiers and natives who oppose him by severing heads and hanging the corpses. Ruthless, sadistic.

Colonel Kurtz expounds upon his philosophies with Captain Willard in Apocalypse Now.

Killed by: Willard heads into Cambodia on a gunboat with a four-man crew. Their first stop is a U.S. chopper base, commanded by the slightly demented Lieutenant Colonel Kilgore (Robert Duvall), who "loves the smell of napalm in the morning." Willard and crew accompany Kilgore on a raid of a Viet Cong village and then head on to Kurtz's island. Willard is greeted with some hostility by the native tribesmen and runaway American soldiers who have become Kurtz's followers. Willard then meets and talks with the mad colonel. He is impressed by the powers of the would-be god and disgusted by his cruelty. Kurtz talks endlessly of the need for horror and moral terror in the world. Though secretly admiring Kurtz, Willard knows what he must do. He kills the roque officer by calling in an air strike and blowing the compound to bits.

Current Status: Dead, but military madmen are always popping up.

What to Do If You Meet: Tell him you agree that the world needs more horror and back slowly out the door. Don't disagree!

Worthy of Note: This film captures much of the horror/beauty of war. Considered the best of the Vietnam flicks. Based loosely on Joseph Conrad's famous novelette, *Heart of Darkness*—transplanted from 19th-century Africa to 20th-century Asia.

Michael Landon

Alias: The Blimp Pilot, Black Sunday Terrorist
Born: Around 1937
Died: 1977

Starred in:
Black Sunday
Paramount, 1977
Director: John Frankenheimer
Played by: Bruce Dern

Description: Psychotic Viet Nam veteran, with deep, insane eyes and a twisted smile.

Now a blimp pilot. Usually wears a pilot's suit, jacket, tie, and sunglasses. Good-looking, about six-feet tall.

Reason for Villainy: Landon feels he was screwed by the U.S. government after the Viet Nam War. He lost his wife, and wasn't given any real psychiatric or support help upon returning from Viet Nam. He wants revenge and is easily manipulated. At a training camp in Lebanon, Black September terrorists Na Geeb (Victor Campus) and Dahlia (Marthe Keller) plot an attack on the U.S. to stop its support of Israel. Dahlia wins Landon over by sleeping with him and twisting his mind even further against the U.S. Their plan is to kill hundreds, perhaps thousands, of people at the Super Bowl by attaching an explosive device that will shoot steel darts from the underside of a blimp. The terrorists record their plan of attack on cassette (in a very general way so that it's not clear just what they plan to do). That night Israeli commandos, led by Major David Kabakov (Robert Shaw), attack and blow up the training camp. Kabakov kills Na Geeb but lets Dahlia survive (finding it hard to shoot a woman in cold blood). Later, after hearing the tape, he realizes his mistake and flies to Washington to work with the FBI on stopping the dastardly plot, although no one is sure exactly when or where the evil will occur.

Evil Powers: The terrorists and Landon are half crazy, burning with desire for revenge against the U.S. They are ruthless and steel cold.

Weapons: Use guns, knives, explosives, and steel darts to destroy.

Occupation: Psychotic Viet Nam veteran.

Intelligence: Landon is quite twisted but smart. High IQ, good blimp pilot.

Strengths: Burning desire to wreak havoc.

Weaknesses: Too crazy! Can hardly function sometimes. Goes into catatonic-like states.

Territory: The terrorists work out of Lebanon but the story takes place in Los Angeles at the Super Bowl.

Idiosyncrasies: Talks to himself, laughs, gets strange looks, has fits of rage.

Friends: Landon thinks Dahlia loves him and he will do anything for her.

Enemies: The terrorists and Landon hate America and all her citizens violently.

Relatives: The terrorists of *Ten Days to Munich* and *Operation Thunderbolt*.

Evil Deeds: Kill, mutilate, torture, hurt everyone around them. Double-cross each other. Bribe, smuggle. Inject poison (Dahlia kills an Israeli with a lethal injection). Mount explosives and darts on underside of blimp. Attack Super Bowl, America's most sacred institution.

Killed by: Dahlia and Landon decide to go ahead with their plot even after they realize that the authorities are after them. Cops have already gunned down one member of their group. Other problems soon arise. They discover that Landon is being replaced by another pilot on the day of Super Bowl. Dahlia

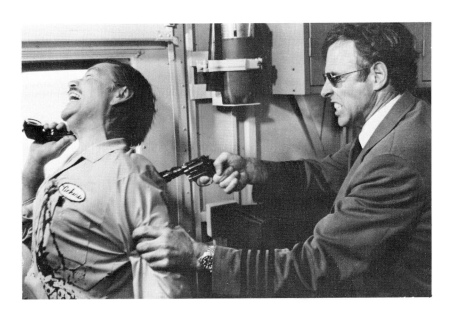

Wanting to take control of the blimp, Michael Landon (Bruce Dern) shoots one of the ground crew in Black Sunday.

fixes the situation by killing the other pilot. Landon shows up and takes pilot's place, after slaughtering half the crew. Dahlia and Landon place the killing device beneath the blimp and head toward the Super Bowl. Meanwhile, Kabakov, figuring out the plan, pursues the pair in a jet helicopter. Firing his Ouzi into the pilot's cabin of the blimp, he kills Dahlia and wounds Landon, who sets the fuse to fire the death darts. The blimp heads for the stadium. Kabakov swings down on a tow line and hooks it to the blimp's tail. After nearly crashing the blimp in the Super Bowl, the helicopter tows it to sea where it explodes.

Current Status: Dead, but these terrorists just grow like Topsy.

What to Do If You Meet: Tell them you agree that the U.S. is imperialistic and a warmonger, and that you would love to join their terrorist group as long as you could go home and get your toothbrush first.

Worthy of Note: Considered a cut above the usual thriller because of director Frankenheimer and the stars of the cast. Sometimes called the "thinking man's" thriller.

Clubber Lang

Alias: Mr. T
Born: 1950s
Died: Still alive

Starred in:
Rocky III
MGM/United Artists, 1982
Director: Sylvester Stallone
Played by: Mr. T

Description: Mean, mean, mean, black boxer. Dark, menacing eyes, mohawk hairstyle. Exudes aura of violence. Weighs 237 pounds at the time of the fight.

Reason for Villainy: Raised in a *tough* neighborhood where you had to fight just to survive, Clubber Lang vowed to get to the top the only way he knew how—fighting. Clubber is the number one challenger who is undefeated and even sent one opponent into a coma. Mickey, Rocky's manager, has avoided setting up a match between Rocky (Sylvester Stallone) and Clubber. At the dedication of Rocky's statue in Philadelphia for winning the heavyweight championship, Clubber shows up and shouts insults at Rocky and his family, demanding a chance to fight him. Mickey refuses the offer, even though Rocky is game. Mickey had been giving Rocky good but not insanely violent opponents. As Mickey, Rocky, and Adrian, his wife, are leaving the ceremony, Clubber gruffly tells Adrian to show up in his bedroom if she want to see what a real man is like. That does it! Rocky goes mad. The fight can no longer be avoided. Mickey admits, however, that Rocky might lose because he's been going soft.

Evil Powers/Weapons: A powerhouse puncher, a leftie, who can nearly take a man's head off with a swing. Mean, incredibly tough fighter.

Occupation: The contender for the heavyweight crown.

Intelligence: Though a street person, Clubber is smart as a fox. Cunning, believes totally in himself.

Strengths/Weaknesses: The desperation of coming up from terrible poverty.

Territory: NYC, Madison Square Garden.

Idiosyncrasies: His mohawk. He keeps predicting pain for Rocky and hates most people, and they hate him in return.

Friends: Donut, his manager, is his only friend.

Enemies: Apollo Creed, who Rocky defeated in *Rocky II*, hates Clubber.

Evil Deeds: Even before he gets in the ring, Clubber swings at old Mickey, Rocky's trainer, and the guy has a heart attack. He wants more than just to win, he wants to massacre Rocky.

Outcome: In their first match, Clubber Lang blasts Rocky right off his feet and wins the title. Apollo Creed hates Clubber so much he decides to help Rocky train for a rematch. He teaches Rocky that he has to recapture *The Eye of the Tiger*, that intense desire to crawl up from the gutter and survive that he once had. It works. Rocky trains harder and harder and gets mean as hell. Back in the ring again, Clubber tears into Rocky. But this time Rocky responds to the pain by getting even meaner. After an incredibly brutal fight, Rocky finally wipes out Clubber Lang and regains his title.

Current Status: Clubber Lang is as mean as ever, licking his wounds and just waiting to get back at Rocky again.

What to Do If You Meet: Tell him you have the keys to Rocky's Maserati and will let him borrow them if he doesn't shake hands with you, touch you, or even get near you.

Worthy of Note: Rocky movies get better and better. The saga of the little guy and his struggles making it to the top touches every one.

Mr. T portrays Clubber Lang, the vicious heavyweight who wins the championship, then loses it, to Rocky in Rocky III.

The Lavender Hill Mob

Born: Various times during 20th century
Died: All still alive at end

Starred in:
The Lavender Hill Mob
Ealing Film, 1950
Director: Charles Crichton
Played by: Alec Guinness, Stanley
   Holloway, Sidney James, Alfie Bass.

Description: They are a motley lot. Holland (Guinness) is a timid bank messenger, bespectacled, innocent, and weak—so it seems! Sculptor Pendlebury (Holloway), and Cockney crooks Shorty (Bass) and Lackery (James) round out the diverse crew.

Reason for Villainy: Holland has an idea: Wouldn't it be nice to be rich and live in Rio (which is, he proclaims, a paradise for a well-heeled Englishman)? Holland, who works for a bank, is regularly entrusted with a fortune in gold bullion. This time, however, he never makes his delivery. He commissioned the sculptor Mr. Pendlebury, to melt it down and reform it. Holland also employs two cockneys to help with the rough stuff. While radios are blasting reports about how impossible it will be to get the bullion out of the country, our villains are making the gold into little Eiffel Tower souvenirs. The figurines pass customs without a hitch, but when Pendlebury and Holland try to claim them in Paris, six little towers have been sold to touring children. Five of the towers are retrieved, but one tyke gives one to a cop. A towering chase ensues, one of several dizzy escapades in this comedy of trial and error. Holland and Pendlebury even steal a police car.

Evil Powers/Weapons: They can reform bullion, have stolen millions in a desperate, madcap robbery, and have illegally exported stolen goods.

Occupation: Meek clerk, sculptor down on his luck, and petty thieves. They've all gone into big time robbery—and if they're caught will Do big time.

Intelligence: Holland and Pendlebury are fumbling but clever at retrieving the gold.

Strengths: Their plan.

Weaknesses: The things that happen by accident.

Territory: London, Paris, and Rio.

Idiosyncrasies: Should the meek become so bold?

Friends: Each other.

Enemies: The police.

Evil Deeds: Theft, smuggling, stealing cars, making illegal "police" broadcasts, speeding, failing to signal at turns, and bothering children.

Outcome: The film began while Holland was relating his exploits in a lush Rio nightclub, and ends with a fade back to him sitting there trying to impress his companion. Before that, however, we hear the rest of the story. In a parody of an earlier Ealing film *Blue Lamp*, the police and Holland with Pendlebury match wits as the crooks speed about in a stolen car. By giving phony location leads by car radio, the pair manage to get all the police cars to crash. Did Holland and Company get away with it? Evidently not, for as Holland gives an enormous tip to his companion, we see that he is handcuffed and taken away.

Current Status: Probably still in jail. Holland had a fling though. The others were also apprehended and didn't even get to Rio.

What to Do If You Meet: Don't trust clerks with large sums of money.

Worthy of Note: Hysterical.

The Law

Alias: Society
Born: Not applicable
Died: Still making mistakes

Starred in:
The Wrong Man
Warner Bros., 1956
Director: Alfred Hitchcock

Description: Amorphous tentacles of society embodied in cops, judges, cells, and the lonely wait before execution.

Sex: Justice is female?

Reason for Villainy: The Law is wrong. Someone thinks they recognize Manny Balestrero (Henry Fonda), a bass player in a New York club, as a stick-up man so he is picked up and arrested. Manny is told to block print a note by the detectives. He mispells the word "drawer" the same way that the criminal did, spelling it "draw." The print looks alike, too. A common mistake that spells his doom. His wife, Rose (Vera Miles), gradually slips into insanity as he is handcuffed and remanded to prison and trial. Manny's lawyer, O'Connor (Anthony Quayle), is convinced he has an innocent client, but he is unable to do anything. Worse, Manny, and Rose keep trying to come up with an alibi, but it keeps slipping through their fingers—and it doesn't look good.

Evil Powers: The Law has all the power of the system behind it—the weight of evidence, the leap to conclusions in search of a solution to a heinous crime. All these things add up to a long stretch in the pen for our hapless victim.

Weapons: Cops, judges, prosecutors, circumstantial evidence, eyewitnesses with bad eyes.

Occupation: Upholder of civilization, occasionally commits errors.

Intelligence: Plodding good sense, but blind justice can make mistakes.

Strengths: It's The Law.

Weaknesses: It's not a good judge of character.

Idiosyncrasies: It's relentless.

Friends: The cops.

Enemies: The innocent man accused of a crime.

Evil Deeds: The Law is ready to sentence the wrong man.

Outcome: The Law lives on and on, helping the average citizen survive, keeping the lid on the jungle underneath civilized society, and occasionally making mistakes. In this case,

poor Manny is up the creek without a paddle until the real guilty party just *happens* to be caught in the nick of time. Manny is finally a free man. But for his faithful wife, the strain has been too much. When Manny visits Rose in the mental asylum, she is happy that he is free, but it's too late for her, she's not the same. Manny, perhaps, had been saved by his prayers, but God has forgotten his wife, it seems—if God can forget anything. Manny's first trial ended in a mistrial, and it was on the way to the second trial, when Rose cracked. How could anyone go through this sane? Hitchcock expertly lets us go through the experience of being wrongly accused. It works and it's very unpleasant. Life doesn't seem so great when things like this happen to innocents. Maybe it's their karma from previous existence or just bad luck. Maybe it's our faulty law.

Current Status: The law lives on, constantly changing, evolving.

What to Do If You Meet: Get a good lawyer and take the Fifth Amendment. Don't incriminate yourself, others will do it for you!

Worthy of Note: There is no hint early in the film that the faithful wife is ready to crack—and Hitchcock makes it a wrenchingly sad twist.

The Law shadows The Wrong Man.

Leatherface

Alias: The Chainsaw Killer
Born: 1940s
Died: Still alive

Starred in:
The Texas Chainsaw Massacre
Bryonston Pictures, 1974
Director: Tobe Hooper
Played by: Gunner Hansen

Description: Absolutely horrific looking murderer about six-feet tall, wearing blood

Leatherface poses with his infamous chainsaw beside his equally repulsive grandfather in The Texas Chainsaw Massacre.

splattered butcher's smock and mask made of a flayed human face. Huge arms and neck. He's an insane, psychopathic killer from an insane, psychopathic family.

Sex: Male (if you can call it that).

Reason for Villainy: Hearing that vandals have wrecked her grandfather's grave, Sally (Marilyn Burns) heads out by van to her childhood Texas home with her fat, wheelchair-bound brother Franklyn, her boyfriend Jerry, and friends Pam and Kirk to check it out. They reach rural Texas and stop in a Gulf station for some "delicious sausage." Later, Pam and Kirk go looking for a swimming hole, but are distracted by buzzing noise from a house. Kirk goes in to investigate and his head is quickly smashed in by Leatherface's sledgehammer. The happy travelers soon enter a world of unending horror.

Occupation: Murderer, butcher, cannibal. Sells human sausage at roadside stand.

Intelligence: Not very smart, but a good killer. He is super at butchering human flesh.

Strengths: Unafraid, and will kill anyone who comes near him.

Weaknesses: He can't hang out with normal folk.

Territory: The backroads of Texas.

Idiosyncrasies: He has bones and flesh everywhere in his home. His chairs are made of human arms. Messy, messy.

Friends: Only his family.

Enemies: Everyone else.

Relatives: *Psycho, Halloween* killers.

Evil Deeds: You name it, he's done it. Knifed, tortured, chopped, stabbed, sawed, mutilated, cannibalized, turned good people into sausage. . . .

Killed by: Pam goes to find Kirk and walks into a room filled with bones and flesh. Leatherface suddenly appears and carries her to a butchering room where he hangs her on meathook and proceeds to cut up Kirk with a chainsaw. Jerry comes looking for his friends and finds Pam blue, hanging in a deep freeze. Suddenly Leatherface does him in too. That night, Sally wheels Franklyn through the woods searching for the others. Again, Leatherface charges out and saws Franklyn in half. Sally runs away, is captured, escapes, and is recaptured. She is attacked with a hammer by Leatherface's corpselike granddad. She escapes again, and finally makes it to the highway where a trucker picks her up.

Current Status: As Sally drives off, Leatherface spins around and around holding his chainsaw high in air, squealing in anger at his escaped food.

What to Do If You Meet: Don't meet!! Go to Disneyland, go to Miami Beach, go to Lebanon, but don't go to the backroads of Texas unless you have a burning desire to become sausage!

Worthy of Note: This film was the Grand Prize winner at the Avoriaz Film Festival, and is now part of the Museum of Modern Art's permanent film archive. Originally made for $200,000, *Texas Chainsaw* has gone on to become one of the largest grossing horror flicks of all time. Also one of the grossest. If you see it, bring a barf bag.

Harry Lime

Born: 1900s
Died: 1949

Starred in:
The Third Man
London Films, 1949
Director: Carol Reed
Played by: Orson Welles

Description: Harry Lime wears a homburg against the damp night air of Vienna. He is seen furtively in glimpses scurrying through back alleys and storm sewers. He has a knowing look, the look of a man's dark features who believes all is corrupt, and that a buck—dirty or not—is still a buck.

Reason for Villainy: Harry is supposedly dead in Vienna, shortly after World War II. His friend Holly Martins (Joseph Cotten) comes to believe that Harry is still alive. He searches for Harry in war-ravaged Vienna, and tantalizing glimpses of the man appear. It turns out that the accident that "killed" Lime was faked. Lime, a big-time black marketeer, wants the authorities to think him dead. Anna Schmidt (Valli) is Harry's old lover. Holly tries to take up where Harry left off with Anna. It isn't working very well. Meanwhile, Harry becomes responsible for hundreds of deaths because he has been selling diluted penicillin to desperate people. Is there no end to the mystery man's desire for profit? What has this war done to people?

Evil Powers/Weapons: Harry is supposedly dead. His primary weapon is his anonymity.

Occupation: Black marketeer.

Intelligence: Very shifty, furtive. Good at running the black market.

Strengths: He's invisible, or so it seems.

Weaknesses: Holly's on his trail.

Territory: Vienna, after World War II.

Idiosyncrasies: He uses the sewers to escape.

Friends/Enemies: Holly was his friend but becomes an enemy.

Evil Deeds: The callous black marketeer is responsible for thefts, murders, and for people dying because they received useless penicillin.

Outcome: Holly is hot on Harry's trail, but he can't stop him. On what must be the world's tallest ferris wheel Holly and Harry have a bizarre rendezvous. Lime is incorrigible. Holly realizes that it's now time to get the authorities. Amidst titanic strumming of a zither (the *Third Man* theme), the film concludes as Holly, Major Calloway (Trevor Howard), and Sergeant Paine (Bernard Lee) close in on the sewer rat. A police trap is set with Holly's help. When Harry appears he is gunned down. In the brilliant fade-out, Holly is at the cemetery with Anna. She ignores him and walks away like a zombie down the avenue filled with bare trees.

Current Status: Dead, dead, dead, dead, dead!

What to Do If You Meet: Save your money because the penicillin is no good.

Worthy of Note: Michael Rennie later starred in a TV series based on this story.

Harry Lime (Orson Welles) looks furtively about him to see if he's being followed in The Third Man.

Dad Longworth

Born: 1800s
Died: 1885

Starred in:
One-Eyed Jacks
Paramount, 1961
Director: Marlon Brando
Played by: Karl Malden

Description: Dad is an outlaw par excellence. He rides a palomino, or any horse he's stolen that can run like the wind from lawmen. Together with Rio, he plunders mucho and is not above deceit. He has black hair and is very mean.

Reason for Villainy: Dad, Rio, and their gang rob a small bank in Sonora, Mexico during 1880. When they are pursued by the efficient Federales (Mexican police-army), the gang decides to split up. Dad decided to find fresh mounts for the gang before they split up but instead takes off with all the loot. However, Rio (Marlon Brando) is caught and spends five years in prison before he can escape. Rio then goes into partnership with Harvey Johnson (Sam Gilman) and Bob Amory (Ben Johnson), and they plan to rob the town where Dad is now masquerading as a sheriff. Upon their arrival, they discover that the bank is closed for fiesta. Dad thinks he's still friends with Rio when Rio convinces him he's just been partying down in Mexico and hadn't been caught at all. Dad for his part swears he got hung up trying to find horses, and says that he felt bad. Meanwhile, Dad's wife, Maria, has a lucious daughter by a previous man, and the comely senorita Louisa (Piña Pellicer) is seduced by Rio. The mother is in favor of it, and Dad doesn't know.

Dad Longworth (Karl Malden) runs a tight town now that he's supposedly on the right side of the law in One-Eyed Jacks.

Evil Powers/Weapons: A six-shooter, and the badge.

Occupation: Thief, betrayer, covered up lawman.

Intelligence: A bit thick.

Strengths: He's the law now.

Weaknesses: He's in for a surprise.

Territory: Mexico, Texas.

Idiosyncrasies: He's on both sides of the law, and has a dual character.

Friends/Enemies: Rio.

Evil Deeds: Whips Rio with a horsewhip, betrayed Rio, forces Rio into a shootout, theft, and deceit. Dad's treachery is unforgivable.

Outcome: Dad surprises Rio and Louisa and horsewhips Rio. He then smashes Rio's gun hand in sudden anger. Rio flees to a Chinese settlement and recuperates. Then Bob and Harvey, Rio's partners, rob the bank and blame it on Rio, who is arrested, tried, and sentenced to death for something he didn't do. Rio is tortured by sadist deputy Lon (Slim Pickens) but Louisa frees him. In a final bow, Dad forces Rio into a shootout and Dad dies. Rio gets the girl.

Current Status: Deep in Boot Hill.

What to Do If You Meet: You go get the horses.

Worthy of Note: Brando's first and last try at direction. The film is good, but he had a real hard time directing and gave it up.

Doyle Lonnigan

Alias: The Patsy
Born: Early 1900s
Died: Stung in 1936

Starred in:
The Sting
Universal, 1973
Director: George Roy Hill
Played by: Robert Shaw

Doyle Lonnigan (Robert Shaw) gives John Hooker a hard time after he's been conned by the small-time hood in The Sting.

Description: Tall, wears expensive pin-striped wool suits and suspenders. Although he's well-groomed and manicured, he snarls. He has a mustache and slicked-back hair.

Reason for Villainy: Doyle Lonningan (Robert Shaw) is a Chicago racketeering boss. Swindled by Luther Coleman (Robert Earl Jones) and John Hooker (Robert Redford), Lonnigan has his hoods kill Luther. Johnny then hooks up with Henry (Paul Newman), another hustler who Luther called the world's greatest con man. Together, they locate the best con artists they know and train them for the big sting (scam) on Lonnigan. They want to break the villain for having Luther killed. They set up a phony horse betting parlor and Lonnigan starts placing bets there. They make sure he wins. Hooker, befriending Lonnigan, says Lonnigan should put all his bucks on a horse named Syphon.

Evil Powers: He will kill anyone who messes with him. He's also the gang boss and leader of the Syndicate in Chicago with lots of goons, guns, and bucks backing him up.

Occupation: Big-time gangster.

Intelligence: He's clever, but he thinks he's more clever than he is, and that's why he gets stung!

Strengths: Has a mob.

Weaknesses: Greed.

Territory: Chicago.

Idiosyncrasies: A compulsive gambler.

Friends: Mobsters, and his molls.

Enemies: Hooker and Henry.

Evil Deeds: He'll have his gang break an old lady's legs if she owes him two cents. He had old Luther killed when he was taken by the old man, plus he's committed countless other violent crimes. Also, bootlegging and prostitution.

Outcome: The "Feds" (actually pals of the con men) burst in as Lonnigan is placing a million-dollar bet in the phony betting parlor. Henry and Johnny "shoot" each other and Lonnigan rushes out to avoid arrest by the Feds. Lonnigan thinks he has escaped, but actually he's just lost a million. The raid was a phony and the two con men have successfully scammed the toughest man in Chicago.

Current Status: Alive, seeking revenge.

What to Do If You Meet: Don't try to con him.

Worthy of Note: A super hit. It pulled in big bucks at the box office.

Rose Loomis

Alias: The Wiggle
Born: 1920s
Died: 1953

Starred in:
Niagara
20th Century Fox, 1953
Director: Henry Hathaway
Played by: Marilyn Monroe

Description: Need we say that Monroe is one of the greatest beauties to ever grace the screen. Tight dress, full figure, youthful exuberance, open toed, high heels, big, round gypsy-type earrings. In her 20s.

Reason for Villainy: Rose is plotting with her lover, Patrick (Richard Allan), to bump off her husband, old George (Joseph Cotten). George has recently been released from the

Rose Loomis (Marilyn Monroe) poses enticely by Niagara Falls with murder on her mind in Niagara.

Veteran's hospital where he was having a head checkup—and failed. Rose and Patrick have it all doped out: They will make Georgie's demise look like suicide. But fate intervenes. The plan is flawed, and George is not so easily disposed of. Rose is called to the city morgue to view a body. She thinks Patrick has done away with old George. But the body she sees is Patrick's. George has done Patrick in, not the other way around. Rose doesn't admit knowing the corpse and leaves. But she is now being pursued by cuckold George, and boy is he mad. Now just the thought of Niagara Falls gets Rose upset. She becomes so upset by the whole thing that she winds up in the hospital. It is a shock, you can imagine.

Evil Powers: Wiggle, jiggle, boom.

Occupation: Unfaithful wife.

Intelligence: If she's as intelligent as she is attractive, Einstein move over. But she's not. Not that she's dumb either.

Strengths: The wiggle.

Weaknesses: The mind.

Territory: Niagara Falls and environs.

Idiosyncrasies: She's the real view.

Friends: Patrick.

Enemies: George.

Evil Deeds: Conspiracy to murder and looks that could kill.

Killed by: The minute Rose leaves the hospital, hubby George is back to wreak vengeance. He finally confronts her and strangles her to death. Couldn't George have made some sort of better choice? After all, maybe a reconciliation would be possible. It's just such a pity. It's like smashing a work of art. To finish up, however, George has some problems. He's stolen a boat with a woman named Polly (Jean Peters), aboard. George heads out into Niagara River. Everyone knows, of course, that you don't go out in the Niagara River above the falls and expect to live very long unless you know what you are doing. George doesn't. He manages to put Polly safely on a rock before he goes over the falls. Polly is united with her boyfriend Ray and the happy couple make a striking contrast to George and Rose.

Current Status: Dead.

What to Do If You Meet: What the hell, go for it.

Worthy of Note: Niagara Falls.

Luther of the Rogues

Born: 1950s
Died: 1979

Starred in:
The Warriors
Paramount, 1979
Director: Walter Hill
Played by: David Patrick Kelley

Description: Teen hoodlum with sleeveless leather jacket with "Rogues" written on the back. Sweatshirt underneath. Wild blonde hair, longish nose, paranoiac disposition, and constantly darting eyes. Leader of the Rogues.

Reason for Villiany: Luther assassinates Cyrus (Roger Hill), the leader of the Gramercy Riffs, who had called all the gangs of New York together to make peace and work together. Luther shoots Cyrus in Riverside Park and points at the Warriors, another gang, screaming that they killed Cyrus. The Warriors evade the other gangs and the cops and head back to Coney Island, their home turf. Swan, the Warriors' leader (Michael Beck), leads the way. The Warriors encounter incredible obstacles as they fight back against New York's countless gangs who have been called out over the radio to stop them—the Baseball Furies, The Orphans. . . .

Evil Powers/Weapons: Trickery. Especially good at getting all the other gangs to rumble with the Warriors. Uses knife, gun, any weapon. Vicious, good, and mean fighter.

Occupation: Teen gang leader.

Intelligence: Cunning but uneducated. Speaks in a mocking, insulting way.

Strengths: Good with a gun and with his feet. He rules his gang with an iron hand.

Weaknesses: Not so good with a blade.

Luther (David Patrick Kelly) points his gun at rival gangleader Swan as The Warriors prepare to fight.

Territory: New York City streets, subways, and beaches.

Idiosyncrasies: Jumpy, wild-eyed.

Friends: The other gangs until they find out the truth.

Enemies: The Warriors.

Relatives: *Wild in the Streets, The Defiant.*

Evil Deeds: As a gang leader he's harassed storekeepers, ripped off supermarkets and bodegas, been a graffiti artist, vandalized, and committed all punk activities. You can also add assault and cold-blooded murder to the list. Plus he incites all gangs to destroy the Warriors.

Killed by: The Warriors make it to the sands of Coney Island at dawn. They are approached by Luther and the Rogues, who are armed with guns. Swan jabs his switchblade into Luther as hundreds of gang members swarm down from around them. But they're not out to get the Warriors—they know that Luther killed Cyrus. The other gangs salute the Warriors as the best gang in New York for fighting their way back to Coney Island. As the Warriors walks away, the other gangs slowly surround Luther and the Rogues. . . .

Current Status: Probably fish food.

What to Do If You Meet: Look out, he's packing a rod.

Worthy of Note: When first shown in movie theaters, the film caused riots around the country as teens tried to act out gang fantasies on their own.

Waldo Lydecker

Born: Early 1900s
Died: 1945

Starred in:
Laura
20th Century Fox, 1944
Director: Otto Preminger
Played by: Clifton Webb

Description: Waldo is tall, the smooth type, distinguished looking, well-groomed, dark hair kept cropped. He's a columnist and very articulate. He is also good at hiding things—as you'll find out. And his anger flares easily.

Reason for Villainy: Although we don't find this out till the end of the film, Waldo was the mysterious killer who blasted Diana Redfern down, thinking that she was Laura (Gene Tierney). Everyone thinks Laura was killed, who were the bullets meant for? Laura? Diana's face was blown apart when she was killed so everyone thinks it was Laura's body. Laura hopes that she and detective Mark McPherson (Dana Andrews) can trap Diana's killer. (The detective, who fell in love with Laura's picture—thinking what a shame she's dead—finds out that she isn't and they fall in love.) The problem: where is the shotgun (the murder weapon)? The killer was not carrying it when he left, and there was too little time to dispose of it. (They should call Ellery Queen—really!) The detective questions suspects, not letting on that Laura lives. Waldo says he was just a platonic friend of the "deceased!" A good suspect is Shelby (Vincent Price), a character with a shady background who dated Diana.

Evil Powers/Weapons: Good at hiding things and lying. He uses a shotgun.

Occupation: Columnist with a pithy radio show of his own. He can be on the air when committing a crime due to new invention, recording.

Intelligence: Smarty pants.

Strengths: Smooth manner, charms Laura.

Weaknesses: Jealousy and conceit. "My self-admiration is justified", he says. Yeah sure, you cold fish.

Territory: Waldo is "on the air." He makes the rounds of wealthy society and hangs out in the hangouts of the rich.

Idiosyncrasies: Types and uses the phone while taking baths.

Friends: Pretended he was Laura's friend and she believed him.

Enemies: The cops and the truth.

Evil Deeds: Killed Diana by mistake—he wanted to blast Laura. He also conceals evidence and lies to the authorities. Deceit, deceit, deceit.

Outcome: Waldo is the killer, but who

Waldo Lydecker (Clifton Webb) jealously confronts Laura, his supposed murder victim, and Mark, the detective investigating the case.

knows? Laura is awakened by Mark, the detective, who explains the complicated case. Mark figures the weapon was dumped in the grandfather-clock casing and it turns out to be true. The detective removes the shells from the gun and puts it back. Only the killer and he know where the gun is. Waldo checks the gun later and reloads it. He confronts Laura and Mark and shoots at Laura in jealousy! She ducks, thankfully, and the cops cut him down.

Current Status: Dead.

What to Do If You Meet: Don't break into his apartment while he's on the air.

Worthy of Note: The plot isn't important. It's good acting and the principals are interesting characters. You figure it out!

Margaret Macomber 147
Mad Dog Earle 147
Madeline 148
Magua 149
Mailer 150
Dave Mallory and the Gang 152
Moose Malloy 153
The Manchurian Candidate 154
Raymond and Connie Marble 155
Marie Antoinette 156
Martha and the Girls 157
Richard Mason 158
Mata Hari 159
Bobby Maxwell 160
Lewt McCanles 161
Nicholas Medina 162

Gerald Meldrick and Anya Von Duren 163
Dr. Josef Mengele 164
Enemy Agent Menlin 166
Messala 167
Frank Miller and Friends 168
Ming the Merciless 169
Misty 170
Admiral Mitamura 171
Mord 172
The Mountain Men 173
The Muranians 174

John Neville 175
Nuclear War 176

Margaret Macomber

Born: 1900s
Died: Still alive

Starred in:
The Macomber Affair
United Artists, 1947
Director: Zoltan Korda
Played by: Joan Bennett

Margaret Macomber (Joan Bennett) practices her aim which she later puts to use in The Macomber Affair.

Description: She is a looker, but she is also a loveless and deceitful woman.

Reason for Villainy: Margaret and her husband, weak, cowardly Francis (Robert Preston), are rich. The idea of going to Africa on safari means little to them, but they set off. They hire the best bearers, buy the best guns, and they acquire the services of the best guide, Englishman Robert Wilson (Gregory Peck). Wilson is a real man according to Margaret. He's noble and sportsmanlike. Margaret repeatedly berates her husband in front of Wilson. When they are hunting, Francis panics and runs. This further enrages his wife, who compares Francis to Wilson contemptuously. Margaret even throws herself into Wilson's tent, charming him with her feminine ways. On their next hunting spree, three wildebeests are shot, but one is only wounded, not dead. Where will this leave our threesome?

Evil Powers/Weapons: She's determined to have a real man, plus she has access to a big blunderbuss of a gun. She can shoot, too.

Occupation: Rich, cuckolding wife.

Intelligence: Clever at deceit.

Strengths: She's all woman.

Weaknesses: Her need for a "real" man.

Territory: Her many mansions and Africa, on safari.

Idiosyncrasies: She has to keep herself pretty in the jungle.

Friends: Virile men.

Enemies: Her hubby.

Evil Deeds: Kills her husband, bitchiness.

Outcome: Francis, this time showing no fear in order to prove a point, goes into the bush with Wilson to find the wildebeest. They discover the wounded animal and Francis shoots the enraged beast. A second later, Margaret puts a bullet through his head. Hysterical—or faking, we never know—Margaret falls on her husband's body. It will now be up to a court of law to determine if she killed him deliberately. She herself said she hated him and wanted him dead. Now she says she doesn't know if she did it deliberately or not.

Current Status: Probably beat the rap and living in Scarsdale.

What to Do If You Meet: Don't turn your back.

Worthy of Note: Hemingway on screen, and not bad. Good screenplay by Eric Ambler.

Mad Dog Earle

Alias: Roy Earle
Born: Turn of the century
Died: 1940s

Starred in:
High Sierra
Warner Bros.-First National, 1941
Director: Raoul Walsh
Played by: Humphrey Bogart

Description: Attractive, moralistic, with a short prison haircut, suit, and jacket. Mild mannered but tough.

Reason for Villainy: Earle (Bogart) escapes from prison with the help of criminal Big Mac. Earle is to go supervise a resort stickup. He meets Velma (Joan Leslie) and her family on the way. Velma is clubfooted and needs an expensive operation. Earle arrives at the hideout, meets Red and Babe, his cohorts, and Marie (Ida Lupino), a wordly woman who falls in love with him. A clerk at the resort is in on the job. The robbery goes awry and Babe and

Marie clings to Mad Dog Earle, the man she loves like no other in High Sierra.

Red are killed along with a guard. The clerk squeals. Earle pays for Velma's operation but she dumps him for another guy and Earle gives the engagement ring to Marie. They're two of a kind—losers.

Evil Powers: Criminal, stick-up artist.
Weapons: Gun.
Occupation: Professional robber.
Intelligence: Intelligent and actually quite moral, except when it comes to getting money.
Strengths: Has a sense of values.
Weaknesses: Softhearted.
Territory: Sierra Country, prison.
Idiosyncrasies: Softhearted when it comes to dames.
Friends: Marie, Velma, and Big Mac.
Enemies: Cops, squealers.
Evil Deeds: A born loser. He can't stop robbing and go straight.
Killed by: Earle realizes the cops have his "ticket" and goes on the lam. He leaves Marie for her own good. He climbs into the Sierras for safety but he gets trapped. The cops are going in for the kill. Marie hears it all on the radio and rushes to the scene. In a touching finale, Mad Dog is fatally shot and Marie cries, "He's crashed out at last." Roy is finally free, for the first time in his life.
Current Status: Dead, riddled with coppers' bullets.
What to Do If You Meet: This guy won't hurt you if you cooperate.
Worthy of Note: One of Bogie's greatest.

Madeline

Alias: Judy
Born: 1930s
Died: 1958

Starred in:
Vertigo
Paramount, 1958
Director: Alfred Hitchcock
Played by: Kim Novak

Scottie Ferguson (James Stewart) and Madeline (Kim Novak) struggle on a high perch in Vertigo.

Description: Beautiful blonde. Seductive, alluring. Mysterious, provocative female.

Reason for Villainy: Detective "Scottie" Ferguson (James Stewart) has a terrible phobia of heights after nearly falling while chasing a criminal. He gets a call from an old friend, Galvin Ester, who wants him to trail his strange and beautiful wife, Madeline. She believes that the ghost of long-dead Carlotta Montez is in her body. She attempts to kill herself but Scottie saves her. They fall in love. But Madeline then impulsively flees, possessed by the ghost, and runs to the top of a tower. Scottie is unable to go up because of his vertigo and Madeline falls to her death.

Evil Powers: Her beauty and mysterious personality are a lure for men.

Weapons: Her body and face.

Occupation: Hired accomplice to murder.

Intelligence: Highly intelligent, but weird.

Strengths: Thinks she has things under control.

Weaknesses: Falls in love.

Territory: San Francisco.

Idiosyncrasies: Acts as if she's possessed by a spirit.

Friends/Enemies: Falls in love with Scottie although she has been hired by Ester to help him in a murder plot.

Evil Deeds: Accomplice to murder. Gets Scottie to fall for her.

Outcome: Scottie gets extremely depressed after Madeline's death and has a nervous breakdown. He meets Judy, a crude shop worker, who resembles Madeline. Scottie tries to recreate Madeline by having Judy change her hairstyle and her manners. Slowly Scottie realizes that Judy *is* Madeline. What he doesn't know is that she was hired by Ester to pretend to be his wife. Ester has Madeline run to the tower and then throws his real wife from top. Scottie is a witness to the "suicide" of Madeline and corroborates the whole story. But she really has fallen for Scottie. Scottie forces Judy to return to the tower where she confesses to everything. She becomes frightened and really does fall. Scottie is cured of his vertigo, but the price. . . .

Current Status: Dead.

What to Do If You Meet: Don't fall in love with blondes hired by millionaires to use you.

Worthy of Note: One of Hitchcock's greatest and a cult film par excellence. Recently re-released.

Magua

Born: 1700s
Died: 1756

Starred in:
Last of the Mohicans
United Artists, 1936
Director: George B. Seitz
Played by: Bruce Cabot

Description: Magua is a Huron, a spy in the British ranks for the French. Magua has a Mohican haircut, a beaded bag and necklace, deerskin leggings, and is bare chested. He carries a long flint-lock rifle and he is wont to force his affections on white women in distress.

Reason for Villainy: Magua is a spy among the British defending Fort William Henry on Lake George in New York. It is the time of the French and Indian wars. The Hurons are on the side of the French, and they are bloodthirsty. The French are outraged by some of the Huron excesses, but they are more interested in beating the British. Hawkeye (Randolph Scott) is an American scout wise to the ways of the wild. He is charged by Colonel Munroe (Hugh Buckler) to take his daughters Alice (Binnie Barnes) and Cora (Heather Angel) to safety at the fort. Magua has now joined the Hurons and is trailing Hawkeye and company and harasses them all the way. He yearns for Cora. He will have her if he can defeat Hawkeye and Major Heyward (Henry Wilcoxon), who are defending the comely girls. By canoe, in impenetrable forests, he stalks them. Arrows fly and rifles crack out messages of death. Who will win?

Evil Powers/Weapons: He has the Hurons behind him.

Magua (Bruce Cabot) is a Huron and a spy in the British ranks for the French in Last of the Mohicans.

Occupation: Indian, spy, woman-abuser.
Intelligence: Wise to the ways of the wild.
Strengths: He has a lot of braves.
Weaknesses: He has not considered the virtue of the woman he seeks to despoil.
Territory: Huron territory, Lake George area, French Canada.
Idiosyncrasies: Thinks he's a ladies' man.
Friends: The Hurons.
Enemies: Decency.
Evil Deeds: Kills many British and other Indians.
Outcome: Cora falls in love with the handsome young Mohican guide Uncas (Philip Reed), who has joined the party along with his father, Chinchagook (Robert Barrat). Magua traps Cora on a high cliff and threatens her either with dishonor or death. She chooses death and plunges from the cliff. Uncas, himself mortally wounded, crawls to her side and the lovers die touching hands. Thus dies the last of the Mohicans (Uncas). Hawkeye holds off the rest of the Hurons but is captured. The rest of the party, however, makes it to the fort. The French capture the fort, grant generous, civilized terms to the British, and arrange for Hawkeye's release from the Hurons who are about to torture him.
Current Status: Dead.
What to Do If You Meet: Bring a canoe.
Worthy of Note: Binnie and Heather shine as virtuous women in distress.

Mailer

Alias: The boss
Born: 1930s
Died: 1974

Starred in:
The Outfit
MGM, 1974
Director: John Flynn
Played by: Robert Ryan

Macklin (Robert Duvall), Mailer's henchman, threatens Bett in The Outfit.

Description: Mailer sometimes wears expensive clothes, but he's wont to wear sloppy jeans and workshirts in the country. He's a syndicate boss so you tell him what to wear, not me. His hair is stylishly long, his cuticles manicured. Still, there's a rough edge to this tough guy.

Reason for Villainy: Mailer runs the rackets. He's even gone legit, owning banks and other semi-honest places. So when Earl Macklin busts one of his banks, it is time to put out a contract on the fellow. Earl (Robert Duvall) survives the hit, beats up the assassin, and takes off vowing revenge on Mailer because Mailer has killed his brother. Mailer, acting through Jake Menner (Timothy Carey), dogs Macklin and his partner, Cody. It seems all the fuss is because Macklin, Cody, and the dead brother had knocked over Mailer's bank. Lesson: Only knock over legit places. Cody and Earl are determined to turn the tables and get even with the syndicate—a tall order in their position. They rob a betting parlor or two and Mailer tells Menner, "Get these guys out of my hair or you die." Menner is after them to save his own skin now. Menner's country ambush fails and Cody and Macklin kill Menner and his pals. But Mailer, the big gorgonzola, is still alive in his mansion.

Evil Powers: Mailer has the rackets and the muscle to keep you out of his hair.

Occupation: Local syndicate bigwig.

Intelligence: An organization man, but relentless. Above average on the SAT, but dropped out of dental school.

Strengths: He's got the mob, and his mansion has high security—he thinks.

Weaknesses: Underestimating the little guy.

Territory: His mansion in New Orleans and environs.

Idiosyncrasies: Can't let go.

Friends: The mob.

Enemies: Macklin, Cody.

Evil Deeds: Everything the mob does and that's plenty.

Killed by: Bett (Karen Black) is Macklin's girl. Sure she set the guy up to get hit, but she had to. He's forgiven her, and she's with him when he and Cody are confronted by Menner and his men and shoot it out. She's hit, she's down, she's—you got it—dead. (Women in these black-mood films always are dangerous and devious. It's best to not have them around. If they betrayed you once. . . .) Mailer is the next objective. The derring-do duo defeat the devious, deadly defenses of the mansion and track the frantic, cowardly Mailer from room to room, breaking a lot of crockery that Louis XIV managed not to tip over. Finally, and we do mean finally, they mercilessly cut down the mobster and, using high explosives, cream the surroundings and make good their escape. Little guys, huh. We taught them. The movie ends with the duo getting away and our villain trying out pitchforks in a warm place.

Current Status: Dead—but what great funerals mobsters have. A boon to florists.

What to Do If You Meet: Before you knock over any joints, check to see if someone shady owns the place first. It'll save aggravation.

Worthy of Note: It just proves freelancers are tougher than organization men. Can you believe this plot? Really?

Dave Mallory and the Gang

Born: Mallory born early 1900s
Died: Still living

Starred in:
Night Key
Universal, 1937
Director: Lloyd Corrigan
Played: Boris Karloff

Description: Pleasant old man with gray hair and dusty hat and clothes. Eccentric genius. Speaks softly. Harmless and meek.

Reason for Villainy: Dave Mallory is a scientist and a good one. He has invented a super alarm system and sent it on to an alarm company on a royalty basis. The company refuses to admit he's built a better device than theirs. To prove them wrong, Mallory has been using an aspect of his invention, called the Night Key, to open stores at night. The alarms won't go off because of his special jamming device. A gang then seizes Dr. Mallory's daughter and forces him to use the Night Key to enter jewelry shops and other stores filled with valuables. He cooperates with the jumpy thieves, sometimes amused by their fear his device won't work properly.

Dave Mallory (Boris Karloff) will do anything to protect his daughter, even use The Night Key.

Evil Powers: Mallory's gang has the Night Key, a device to foil all alarm systems. The city is at their mercy.

Occupation: Mallory is an inventor. The gang is made up of a bunch of opportunists.

Intelligence: Mallory's a genuis, the rest are below average.

Strengths: The Night Key's effectiveness.

Weaknesses: Mallory only cooperates to save his daughter.

Territory: The city.

Idiosyncrasies: Mallory is angry that Mr. Ranger's alarm company doesn't recognize his genius.

Friends: The daughter—he'd do anything for her.

Enemies: The gang—and the police if they jeopardize his daughter's life.

Evil Deeds: Mallory breaks into stores on his own to prove the device works. But later he uses it to aid the gang in robbing.

Outcome: Mr. Ranger, president of the burglar alarm company, must stop Mallory or his business will collapse. Who will use his alarms if they are useless? Ranger sends Travers (Warren Hull) to find Mallory. Mallory and the gang now rob at will, plundering the sleeping city anytime they wish. Travers finds Mallory and brings him to Ranger. Ranger must admit that Mallory is a genius. Once they secure Mallory's daughter, Joan, Mallory betrays the gang. Ranger finally agrees to buy the devices that Mallory has built and they all live happily ever after.

Current Status: Making things that short out other devices. The gang is in jail.

What to Do If You Meet: Mallory's a harmless old codger, humor him, say you'd like a percentage of his invention. He could make you a bundle. Say hello to his daughter.

Worthy of Note: Karloff is a pretty good joe for a villain. Nevertheless, he cooperated with evil, and as such deserves condemnation.

Moose Malloy

Alias: The Moose
Born: 1940s
Died: 1970s

Starred in:
Farewell, My Lovely
Avco Embassy, 1975
Director: Dick Richards
Played by: Jack O'Halloran

Description: Immense, mean, black-hatted, suit size 54 gangster. Bad ties, inarticulate.

Moose Malloy (Jack O'Halloran) asks Philip Marlowe if he's located Malloy's wife Velma in Farewell My Lovely.

Reason for Villainy: "I want my Velma. You find her for me Marlowe, or else!" It is in this way that Moose Malloy hires Marlowe (Robert Mitchum) to track down his missing "goil." At the same time, Marlowe is hired to find Mrs. Grayle's (Charlotte Rampling's) jewels. Marlowe beds Mrs. Grayle (who encourages him in front of her husband). She has a connection to a gangster named Burnette (Anthony Zerbe) and his gambling ship out past the three-mile limit at sea. The moody Marlowe does his thing to the beat of a dissolute jazz soundtrack while Moose shows up from time to time in a very threatening manner to inquire about progress.

Evil Powers: This gangster could crush you with his pinky. It takes a full load of slugs to slow him down.

Weapons: Uses his hamhock fists and a pistol as weapons. But most people don't fight him.

Occupation: Full time goon.

Intelligence: Really dumb! The only thing on his mind is his missing girl.

Strengths: Sheer physique and determination.

Weaknesses: Pea-brained.

Territory: Los Angeles.

Idiosyncrasies: Obsessed with Velma. But who isn't?

Friends: Marlowe (who actually likes the hulk).

Enemies: Velma—can you beat that?

Relatives: Jaws from the Bond flicks.

Evil Deeds: Cleans up the floor with lots of people, crushes heads, breaks collarbones and knuckles.

Killed by: Marlowe keeps getting back to Moose's case (because the big guy insists). He finds evidence that could solve everything, but he is slugged and beaten by a whorehouse madam for refusing to tell where Moose is hiding. (Other gangsters are hunting Moose.) More murders of people who know anything about Velma ensue. Marlowe is paid by Burnette to bring Moose on board his gambling ship, but why? It turns out that Moose has 80Gs hidden away. Moose meets Mrs. Grayle on board ship and cries out "Velma, Velma," in joy. She guns him down. The goon dies as ignorant of reality as he had lived. Marlowe manages to ice Velma with a few bullets and so it ends. Velma's motive? What rich dame wants an ex like Moose cluing everyone in on her sordid past? You figure it—dames!

Current Status: Dead.

What to Do If You Meet: There's nothing you can do. Just don't mention Velma and he'll probably thunder past.

Worthy of Note: Sylvester Stallone has a bit part as goon. One of Chandler's better stories and for once the remake is considered by some to be better than the original. The original, made in 1944, was titled *Murder My Sweet*.

The Manchurian Candidate

Alias: Raymond Shaw
Born: 1920s
Died: 1962 U.S.A.

Starred in:
The Manchurian Candidate
United Artists, 1962
Director: John Frankenheimer
Played by: Laurence Harvey

Description: Clean cut, tall, dark-haired, well-dressed, well-spoken, cultured, quiet.

Reason for Villainy: Unknown to American intelligence or himself, Raymond Shaw (and others of his company) was brainwashed when captured by Korean troops in the Korean War. Shaw is a programmed assassin working for Red agents Zilkov (Albert Paulson) and Yen Lo (Knigh Dhiegh). They have put him under an incredibly deep hypnotic trance that can be triggered by a pack of playing cards—the Queen of Diamonds means to kill. Shaw is made to murder several people, including his own family on command.

Evil Powers/Weapons: A holder of a medal of honor, which puts him above suspicion and gets him in places. When commanded to kill, he is like a robot. Uses a gun.

Occupation: Businessman, assassin.

Intelligence: Very intelligent, but he's been hypnotized by the Reds and doesn't even realize his condition.

Strengths: Willpower—to a point!

Weaknesses: Brainwashed, but good.

Territory: Korea, U.S.A.

Idiosyncrasies: Nightmares and a far away look.

Friends/Enemies: Marco (Frank Sinatra), who served with Shaw in Korea and now works for army intelligence, is his friend. He realizes that something is wrong because of his own strange nightmares. He tries to help Raymond and to stop him.

Relatives: The Jackal.

Evil Deeds: After being brainwashed in Korea, he shoots a buddy on command in a POW camp. In the U.S.A. he kills his employer, his fiancee, and her father.

Killed by: After Shaw has killed his fiancee and her father, he is visited by Marco, his old Korean War buddy who has also been having strange dreams. Shaw denies any such

Raymond Shaw (Laurence Harvey) plays solitaire, unaware that the Queen of Diamonds will trigger his brainwashed mind to kill in The Manchurian Candidate.

thoughts or dreams himself. Later, Shaw realizes that something is wrong and tries to fight it with his will, but can't. He is compelled to go to a giant political rally where he is programmed to kill the presidential candidate. (It turns out that his mother and her husband, Senator Iselin, are communist agents who plan to use the assassination to push Iselin into the presidency, giving the Communists control of America.) Shaw draws a bead on the candidate, but suddenly is able to break the brainwashing and swings the rifle over to his mother and Iselin. He pulls the trigger and the two Red agents topple over dead. Then he kills himself.

Current Status: Dead.

What to Do If You Meet: Don't play cards, the Queen of Diamonds trigger him.

Worthy of Note: Relic of the paranoid 1950s and prophetic precursor to Kennedy assassination one year later.

Raymond and Connie Marble

Alias: The dirtiest couple alive
Born: 1950s
Died: 1973

Starred in:
Pink Flamingoes
New Line—Saliva, 1973
Director: John Waters
Played by: David Lochary, Mink Stole

Description: Tie-dyed splotches in their long, flat-looking hair. He sports a handlebar moustache, she a rhinestone-studded pair of glasses. They constantly spout filth and are known for perverse insanity.

Reason for Villainy: The Marbles have lost their marbles. They have heard that Babs

Johnson (Divine) is living in a trailer nearby and she considers herself the most depraved person alive. They are the most disgusting perverts in the universe and covet the title. They prove their villainy by their acts during this mucho disgusto film. They speculate in pornography, sell heroin to elementary school children, and drive around picking up teenage hitchikers then chloroforming them and bringing them back to their cellar where they have their butler Channing (Channing Wilroy) impregnate them. The teenagers are kept alive until they give birth. The babies are then sold to undesirables, such as sadomasochistic lesbian couples, for a huge profit. Worse, they have Cookie (Cookie Mueller) infiltrate Divine's trailer. There the freako wacko discovers Mama Edie (Edith Massey), a multiple hundreds-of-pounds person living in a crib eating buckets of raw hen's eggs. Cookie has sex with Divine's confidant Crackers (Danny Mills) with a dying chicken between them. Are you ready to leave the theater yet?

Evil Powers: They want to be the most disgusting couple alive.

Occupation: Pornographers, baby sellers, kidnappers, etc.

Intelligence: They can't read, they just look at pictures.

Strengths: Insane desire to be the best perverts!

Weaknesses: Divine beats them out sometimes.

Territory: Near Boise, Idaho (Or Baltimore, Maryland)?

Raymond and Connie Marble (David Lochary and Mink Stole) covet the title of the most disgusting perverts in the universe in Pink Flamingoes.

Idiosyncrasies: They like plastic.
Friends: Pervertos.
Enemies: The super pervert Divine.
Evil Deeds: You name it.
Killed by: The hand-held color cameras used to create this film have a funny effect on the tones of pink, red, and green, making them all look off in this extremely low budget film. Also, the plot seemed to be made up as the filming went along. But as near as we can figure, the Marbles come home to find Channing dressed in Connie's clothes, mimicking her. "It's not funny," they say, locking Channing in the closet. Divine and her son, Crackers (Danny Mills), come in when they leave. They give Channing to the girls he's been torturing for months. They wreak revenge. Meanwhile, Ray and Connie, obsessed with being the dirtiest couple, are out on a foray. He goes to expose himself to women in the park (they drop their pocketbooks and he picks up some cash this way). She goes to shoplift, etc. Later, Divine has a lawn party, but the perverto guests are surprised by cops, who were tipped by Raymond and Connie. (The Marbles found their house in shambles when they returned home—courtesy of Divine and her incestuous son, Crackers.) The cops, alas, are *eaten* by the guests and the party goes on. Soon Raymond and Connie Marble are tarred and feathered and shot, admitting they are not the most disgusting people. (But they really were—don't you think?)

Current Status: Their tarred and feathered bodies are filled with bullet holes and they are buried in a swamp near the abandoned trailer.

What to Do If You Meet: Don't hitch.

Worthy of Note: Probably holds the title as the most disgusto movie ever made. See if you can sit through the whole thing without barfing.

Marie Antoinette

Alias: The Queen of France
Born: 1700s Austrian Empire
Died: 1789 Paris

Starred in:
Marie Antoinette
MGM, 1938
Director: W.S. Van Dyke II
Played by: Norma Shearer

Description: Marie is the daughter of Empress Maria Theresa and, like her mother, is a beauty. She's always clothed in the finest dresses and gowns suitable for court occasions. Like her wedding gown, they are often low cut. Real diamonds are used as sequins.

Reason for Villainy: Marie is a dreamer, out of touch with the seething masses in discontent. The peasants' lives are atrocious; they yearn for food and freedom. Such is the case in France when Marie is wed to fatty King Louis XVI. Their honeymoon night is a farce and the unmanly king (Robert Morley) fails at love. On Marie's second anniversary, Madame DuBarry sends her a cradle. The Duc D'Orleans (Joseph Schildkraut) is a fop that joins the circle. Marie loses a necklace and her heart at a gaming house with Fersen (Tyrone Power) and is looked upon for this liaison as a "wan-

Norma Shearer plays Marie Antoinette, the excessive and capricious Queen of France.

ton." Louis wants to send her back to Austria after she degrades DuBarry at a gala, but the King dies soon thereafter. She is now Queen and absolute ruler. Fersen says he will love her forever, but he must go to America. He also tells her she must be less frivolous. No one understands her sensitive nature. She's hardly started at her new job when the revolution breaks out. The people are starving. Informed that they don't have any bread, Marie asks why they can't eat cake instead.

Evil Powers: Wealth and majesty are at her feet and she ignores the clamor for reform and food from the masses.

Weapons: The French army.

Occupation: Queen.

Intelligence: Intelligent, but caught up in royal intrigues.

Strengths: She has the might of France at her fingertips.

Weaknesses: It's all going by the board.

Territory: Paris, France.

Idiosyncrasies: Wears feathers in her hair, likes betting.

Friends: Fersen and the King, sometimes.

Enemies: The masses.

Evil Deeds: While she parties, the old world crumbles and the red flag of revolution is raised by the sans-culottes.

Killed by: The revolutionaries now have horrible power. They mass in the streets, unstoppable by the army. They reach the gates, and bridge the fortresses. They are upon the royal court. Marie frantically seeks escape. She didn't bargain on this. Her rule is about to tumble and that's not the only thing. The mobs sack the palace, sweeping away the gold, burning the precious tapestries, dismembering the members of the court. Marie is captured and Louis XV's prediction "After me the Deluge" is fulfilled. Marie is firm and resolved when she approaches the guillotine. She places her head on the board and she thinks about the time she told her mother "I shall be Queen of France." That is all over now, and the sharp blade descends rapidly and the head of the Queen rolls into the dustpan of history.

Current Status: Dead.

What to Do If You Meet: She was too occupied in court affairs to stop hardened revolutionists. Keep her at parties and dilly-dallying with the fops. That way, the proletar-iat can organize and strike. Sad to see all that finery get torn though.

Worthy of Note: This movie symbolizes the villainy of not being progressive when it's called for, and the villainy of unconcern for the masses of starving people.

Martha and the Girls

Alias: The Beguiling Women
Born: 1800s
Died: Antebellum U.S.A.

Starred in:
The Beguiled
Universal, 1971
Director: Don Siegel
Played by: Geraldine Page, Elizabeth
   Hartman, Pamelyn Ferdin

Description: Martha is a solid, puritanical woman who doesn't like to show any skin to men, especially enemy Union soldiers. She's middle aged, with brown hair in a bun, and wears plain dresses all the time. The girls are various ages and mostly cute.

Reason for Villainy: Martha is head of an all-girl boarding school during the war between the states. A wounded Union soldier is found by one of the girls. Martha, at first, wants to turn him over to the Confederates. However, the soldier, John McBurney (Clint Eastwood), is charming the pants off all of them. The lonely bunch of girls become enamored with him. McBurney has it made in the shade. Edwina (Elizabeth Hartman) falls deeply in love with him and he promises to marry her but wants to undo her bloomers. She won't consent. He instead sleeps with Carol, as Edwina spies on them. Edwina pushes the soldier down a flight of stairs. Unconscious, with a leg broken, he is operated on by Martha and her buddies. They amputate

John McBurney still manages to be friendly with Martha (Geraldine Page) and her girls even after they've amputated his broken leg in The Beguiled.

Richard Mason

Born: 1910s
Died: Executed 1947

Starred in:
Conflict
Warner Bros.-First National, 1945
Director: Curtis Bernhardt
Played by: Humphrey Bogart

his leg. He awakes and is quite angry, to put it mildly, but eventually apologizes for his actions.

Evil Powers: The power of women over men.

Weapons: The girls have looks, and Martha has security for the soldier.

Occupation: Mistress of a girl's boarding school.

Intelligence: Bright females.

Strengths: They can operate on a leg, can plan, can organize well.

Weaknesses: She and the others need male companionship.

Territory: The torn United States.

Idiosyncrasies : Puritanical outlook, even though she is lusting in her heart.

Friends: The South.

Enemies: The Union, then McBurney.

Evil Deeds: Entrapment, murder.

Killed by: The girls become hateful of the way McBurney lied and used them. They see an opportunity in the mushrooms. Amy picks poisonous mushrooms and McBurney is fed the deadly stuff at a party given in honor of his engagement to Edwina. McBurney writhes around in agony and dies a horrible death. The women have ended their flirtation with the male gender and will dispose of him.

Current Status: Dear old Martha lived till age 97.

What to Do If You Meet: Don't dine there.

Worthy of Note: Here Clint is a victim—of women. Usually in other movies he's their protector.

Description: Humphrey Bogart didn't radically change his appearance in his different crime films. He's still handsome, with swept back hair and of medium height. Here, he's the ideal husband, except that he loves his wife's sister.

Reason for Villainy: Richard Mason is, on the surface and before their good friends, happily married to attractive Katherine (Rose Hobart), but he loves her sister, Evelyn Turner (Alexis Smith). He asks for a divorce and but is denied. He begs off going on a vacation with his wife and secretly plans to do away with her. Everything is planned but the best plans of mice and men. . . . Later, Mason meets his wife's car on a deserted road and strangles the lovely lady. He pushes her and her vehicle off a cliff. So much for that—or so he thinks. He reports her missing, but a string of bizarre clues that she is still alive keeps him nervous. For one thing, some of her jewelry reappears and he smells her perfume, an expensive brand, everywhere he goes. Afraid that he's going crazy, Mason goes to his wife's best friend, Dr. Mark Hamilton (Sydney Greenstreet), and asks for help. Of course, he can't tell the whole story of his obsession. He even quarrels with Evelyn, and soon they are on the outs.

Weapons: His hands.

Occupation: Ideal husband.

Intelligence: Average.

Strengths: His fingers.

Weaknesses: His mind. He thinks it's playing tricks on him.

Richard Mason (Humphrey Bogart) shares a toast with his wife and friends but is actually planning to murder the poor woman who refused him a divorce in Conflict.

Territory: The shadows near a lonely road.

Idiosyncrasies: He injured his leg in an accident, but it healed nicely. Still he faked a limp to "show" he couldn't get around.

Friends: The night.

Enemies: The truth.

Evil Deeds: Strangulation for adulation.

Killed by: Hamilton knows that Mason is lying. Hamilton had given Mason's wife a rose to wear just before she was murdered. Mason described her to police as wearing a rose before she disappeared. The only way he could have known she was wearing a rose was if he intercepted her and killed her. But Hamilton realizes this is flimsy evidence. It would be better he thinks to drive our bad guy wild with anxiety by planting his wife's jewels around where it looks like she's still active. He also sprays some of her perfume in the room before Mason arrives. He also drives Mason crazy with anonymous phone calls and the brief look at a woman who looks like his wife. Hamilton has faith that the guy will crack. Mason is jarred and finally does crack. He returns to the scene of the crime determined to get to the bottom of whether his wife is dead or not. Of course, by doing this he reveals himself as the murderer. Soon Mason is tightly bottled in a cell awaiting the fate of all who dare defy society's laws against murder.

Current Status: Paroled by liberal judge in the '60's.

What to Do If You Meet: Spray some perfume around and he'll think his wife is after him and forget all about killing you.

Worthy of Note: Greenstreet is nifty as the shifty shrink.

Mata Hari

Born: Late 1800s
Died: During World War I

Starred in:
Mata Hari
Universal, 1932
Director: George Fitzmaurice
Played by: Greta Garbo

Description: Slinky, long-legged, sexy woman. She's got an enrapturing figure, wears tight, clinging gowns and dresses of silk and sparkling material. Very female.

Reason for Villainy: Mata Hari is a spy for the Austrian Empire during World War I. She pries secrets from Allied forces officers with her feminine charms and then gives them to her "control" Adriani (Lewis Stone). The officers grovel at her lovely feet. When she dances in her wide-stepping, erotic way they will do anything to please her. She has a lover, Lieutenant Rosanoff (Ramon Novarro), who is shot down probably as the result of the information she has fed to the enemies of democracy. Remorseful, for he is blinded, she nevertheless carries out her spying duties. Mata Hari is later arrested and imprisoned. And in those days they didn't have habeas corpus or the Miranda decision. They are planning to put Mata Hari before a firing squad. She is to be shot at dawn. Such a waste of a beautiful woman. The officers can hardly bear it.

Evil Powers: Given the body she has by nature, Mata Hari uses it and accentuates her natural charm with clothes that lure men. She has the power to wrap most men about her little pinkies.

Occupation: Spy, seductress, femme fatale.

Intelligence: Mata Hari is well-educated and suave.

Strengths: Her charms.

Weaknesses: Her love for a pilot who flies against her employers.

Territory: Austro-Hungarian Empire, France, Russia—anywhere she is needed to go ply her spying trade. She was born in the exotic Dutch East Indies.

Idiosyncrasies: She takes long steps when she dances, and exposes her gorgeous legs when she sits and talks to you.

Friends: All men adore her, and Rosanoff, in particular, is her close friend and lover.

Enemies: The Allied counterspy network.

Relatives: Spy X-27 in *Dishonoured*.

Evil Deeds: Her spying results in terrible

Greta Garbo, as Mata Hari, uses her charms to pry secrets from Allied officers.

losses of men and material for the Allies in World War I.

Killed by: Mata Hari, in prison, is give one last opportunity to see her lover, the blinded pilot Rosanoff. He comes to her believing that she is in a hospital dying of a disease. He falls at her feet and she caresses him. She wants to save his feelings as much as possible, and tells him to go on. He must do that for her. He agrees. The woman that he adores, the femme fatale that cruelly betrayed him, is forever in his heart as a shining symbol of his desires. At the end, Mata Hari led out to the wall to face the firing squad.

Current Status: Shot dead by firing squad.

What to Do If Meet: Give her the secrets, it might be worth it.

Worthy of Note: The archetypical femme fatale.

Bobby Maxwell

Alias: The terrorist
Born: 1950s
Died: 1976

Starred in:
The Enforcer
Warner Bros., 1976
Director: James Fargo
Played by: De Veren Bookwalter

Description: Light brown, wild-looking hair, and strong legs for running. Often seen with a handgun or M-16 rifle. Cowboy shirts and blue jeans are his standard clothing.

Reason for Villainy: Maxwell is a psychotic Viet Nam veteran. He's also the leader of an urban terrorist group. The terrorists raid an ammo dump and steal a great deal of weaponry. This includes M-16s, grenades, bazookas, and other basic tools of the terrorist trade.

Bobby Maxwell (De Veren Bookwalter) screams at Dirty Harry Callahan who has trapped him at Alcatraz in The Enforcer.

Police officer DiGeorgio (John Mitchum) discovers the terrorists in the act of stealing, but sneaky Maxwell comes up from behind and stabs him. Fatally wounded and in the hospital, DiGeorgio tells his partner, Inspector Harry Callahan (Clint Eastwood), that he recognized Maxwell as a former cheap pimp. DiGeorgio, unfortunately, dies. Harry's new partner, Kate Moore (Tyne Daly), is a woman. What's happening to the force, he wonders. He treats her with contempt. She, however, dogs Harry's footsteps trying to be a good officer. But Harry is some super cop. He's seen jumping from roof to roof while pursuing Maxwell. Keeping up is hard. Maxwell eventually kidnaps the major (John Crawford). Harry tracks Maxwell through Big Ed, a militant black man who Harry pressures. Harry finally traps Bobby Maxwell on Alcatraz Island.

Evil Powers: Bobby Maxwell has bazookas, M-16s, and grenades, and experience in using them.

Occupation: Terrorist.

Intelligence: Maxwell is smart, but a raving maniac.

Strengths: His weapons and men, plus his combat experience.

Weaknesses: Killing Dirty Harry's partner put Harry on his case.

Territory: San Francisco and Alcatraz Island.

Idiosyncrasies: Likes overkill.

Friends: His gang of terrorists.

Enemies: Harry Callahan, a.k.a. Dirty Harry.

Relatives: The *Black Sunday* Terrorists.

Evil Deeds: Kills cops, kidnaps the mayor, extortion, illegal possesion of an arsenal, double parking, and failing to file for a gun permit.

Killed by: Harry and Kate get into a fierce gun battle with the terrorists and Bobby. Alcatraz Island is the former site of the infamous prison. It's eerie now that it's deserted and there are lots of hiding places. Maxwell knows them all, and shoots with that advantage. Maxwell climbs a tower to get some leverage on Harry. The dirty inspector uses one of the stolen bazookas to blast the villain from his perch. Bobby dies a victim of his own insanity and violence. The two partners free the mayor and he's rightfully grateful.

Current Status: Dead. When you get hit by a bazooka you're very dead.

What to Do If You Meet: Terrorists like Bobby are well-armed. Tell him you enjoy the finesse of terrorism and then back out the door. Call Dirty Harry.

Worthy of Note: A very popular film in the Dirty Harry series.

Lewt McCanles

Born: Mid 1800s
Died: Late 1800s

Starred in:
Duel in the Sun
Selznick Studios, 1946
Director: King Vidor
Played by: Gregory Peck

Description: Lewt is tall, sensual, and cruel, preferring the life of raw, violent aggression.

Lewt McCanles (Gregory Peck) and his brother Jesse are pitted against each other for the love of a woman in Duel in the Sun.

He has ties to guns, stallions, and the outdoors. He is committed to an *amor fou* with Pearl. He represents the passionate killer Cain, perhaps, of the Bible, while his brother represents Abel.

Reason for Villainy: Lewt and lovely, sensual Pearl (Jennifer Jones) are star-crossed lovers embroiled in a triangle with his brother Jesse (Joseph Cotten). Jesse is enterprising upstanding, and forthright. This appeals to Pearl. She must have Lewt's raw, love/hate, destructive passions however. They make love during storms and on the sand so much that the Catholic League of Decency had a fit before the film was released and it was toned down. Pearl is the daughter of an unfaithful Indian woman who was shot dead by her husband in a Texas border town. Pearl was sent to live with the McCanleses and the woman has now pitted brother against brother. Torn between respectability and savagery, she flees into the arms of an older man, Sam Pierce (Charles Bickford), who Lewt kills in order to force Pearl to come back to him. In the mountains, a duel of guns is fought between Pearl and Lewt. The savage lovers fire at one another, but do they hate or love?

Evil Powers/Weapons: He's got macho.

Occupation: Gunslinger, train dynamiter, ne'er-do-well.

Intelligence: Raw but clever.

Strengths: His guns, his fist and his desire.

Weaknesses: His confrontation with respectability is sure to bring trouble.

Territory: The West during the time of the early railroads.

Idiosyncrasies: He's mad over Pearl and her sensual shoulders and legs.

Friends: His brother wants to be friends.

Enemies: His brother, society, and ultimately Pearl.

Evil Deeds: Shoots everything in sight, kills his brother, blows up a train, and an all-consuming commitment to *amor fou*—crazy love.

Outcome: All good love affairs come to an end, and Lewt's and Pearl's ends here in the mountains—Pearl makes her mark with her blazing bullets, and so does Lewt. Both wounded they crawl toward each other on the sand and touch hands. It is over. They are in each other's arms for one final time. In real life they probably would have died a few inches short of one another.

Current Status: Dead, and panned by critics.

What to Do If You Meet: Don't fall in love with their type. (But we all do.)

Worthy of Note: Billed as Selznick's follow-up to "Gone with the Wind," this interesting turkey gobbled up money and doomed other dramatic epics on the shooting list. Still, it's an effective film. See it.

Nicholas Medina

Born: 1800s
Died: 1840s

Starred in:
The Pit and the Pendulum
American International, 1961
Director: Roger Corman
Played by: Vincent Price

Description: Medina is always well-dressed. He is flamboyant, of dubious taste, and a bit effeminate in a menacing way. He is tall, has a thin moustache over thin lips, and a sneering smile. A glance will tell you he's gone over the edge into madness. His hair is tousled for he is constantly running he is nervous fingers through it.

Reason for Villainy: Francis Barnard (John Kerr) journeys to the haunted and bizarre castle of his mad brother-in-law. He wants to ask that madman—who says that his sister Elizabeth, Medina's wife, died—what happened. Elizabeth, supposedly succumbed of natural causes. But her groans and screams wake Francis at night. Is she still alive? Elizabeth (Barbara Steele) is not dead, but trying to drive her "widower" mad so she can marry her lover, Dr. Leon (Antony Carbone). Complications follow as Francis tries to unravel the insane secret of the castle. Sliding doors and odd camera angles abound. Francis travels the decadent corridors of flamboyant wealth and morose taste, and at last gets himself in the clutches of Medina, who suspects him of deception. In the cellar, once used in the Inquisition, Francis is introduced to the incredibly evil pit and pendulum torture device.

Evil Powers/Weapons: Medina has the pit, and the pendulum to go with it.

Nicholas Medina's attempt to strangle his wife fails; they later meet their respective ends in his horrible torture chamber in The Pit and the Pendulum.

Occupation: Madman with a castle.
Intelligence: Reads manuals left from the Inquisition.
Strengths: He has the device in the cellar.
Weaknesses: He is flipped-out.
Territory: Likes macabre decorating schemes, plus drapes and heavy oak doors leading nowhere.
Friends: The pendulum.
Enemies: Francis.
Evil Deeds: He ties Francis to the device, pitiless use of odd music, mad love of torture and pain—of others.
Killed by/Outcome: Medina straps Francis onto the path of the slowly descending, swinging pendulum. It is razor sharp, immense in its scythe-like swing. It will eventually begin cutting his chest to ribbons—s-l-o-w-l-y. The bizarre expressionist set lends eerie color and atmosphere. Who would ever want so many spiders in one cellar? Look at all those years of webs. Naturally, the hero triumphs and the villain perishes horribly. So be it. And lustful Elizabeth gets locked—alive—in an iron maiden.
Current Status: Dead.
What to Do If You Meet: Stay out of the rooms downstairs.
Worthy of Note: Atmospheric.

Gerald Meldrick and Anya Von Duren

Born: 1900s
Died: Still alive

Starred in:
They Met In Bombay
MGM, 1941
Director: Clarence Brown
Played by: Clark Gable and Rosalind
   Russell

Gerald displays the diamond pendant they've stolen from the Duchess of Beltravers to his fellow thief in They Met in Bombay.

Description: He wears a pith helmet at times, due to the heat. She wears a kerchief over her head to keep out the sun. He has a mustache and is very handsome. She is a charming, graceful, and well-built woman. The couple dons more formal attire (tuxes and gowns) when going about on their jewel thefts.

Reason for Villainy: The pair of thieves are at odds at first. In old-time India they are both after the same prize: the fabulous diamond pendant owned by the Duchess of Beltravers (Jessie Ralph). He is posing as an investigator from Lloyd's of London, she as a member of the royal class. She manages to pull off the sensational theft, but Meldrick is clever and steals the diamond from her. Fleeing the police, they are thrown in together. They pose as an eloping couple—somewhat close to the truth—and manage to escape by boarding a tramp steamer. They are eventually discovered and the skipper, Chang (Peter Lorre), turns them in to the police inspector (Matthew Boulton). However, they manage another escape. Meldrick, realizing they are nearly broke, disguises himself as a military officer, a British captain. This gets him some necessary funds. But, before our villains can sneak away, the "Captain" is called to active duty.

Evil Powers: They are good at lying and impersonating.

Occupation: Thieves, particularly of jewels.

Intelligence: Both are swift.

Strengths/Weaknesses: Wile/fate.

Territory: India.

Idiosyncrasies: They are both charming scoundrels.

Friends: Their wit.

Enemies: The police and Chang.

Evil Deeds: They steal the diamond pendant, he impersonates an officer, they escape from the law to avoid prosecution, and they basically go around insulting society.

Outcome: Our couple are fast and tight by now. Meldrick, sent to the interior for warfare by the high command, is in love with his fellow thief, and she with him. Romantic isn't it? He engages the Japanese enemy and wins. He is decorated with the Victoria Cross, but is led to prison for his dirty deeds—for only a short stay. When released he falls into the arms of his beloved co-thief and they live happily ever after.

Current Status: Still a lovely couple.

What to Do If You Meet: Hide the family jewels.

Worthy of Note: Another great romantic romp by the great Gable. Roz is royal, also.

Dr. Josef Mengele

Alias: The Nazi
Born: 1920s
Died: 1976

Starred in:
The Boys From Brazil
20th Century Fox, 1978
Director: Franklin J. Schaffner
Played by: Gregory Peck

Description: Tall and evil Nazi doctor. Dark hair, penetrating eyes, mustache. Handsome but without feeling. Always wears a suit and tie. Sophisticated, ruthless.

Reason for Villainy: One of the most infamous of the Nazis, Dr. Mengele has escaped the demise of the Third Reich. Now operating out of Paraguay, he plots a deed as evil as Hitler's terrible vision. However, Barry Kohler, a member of the young Jewish Defender's Organization, is spying on neo-Nazis in Paraguay. After planting an electronic bug on their headquarters, he learns that Mengele is still alive and that he and his associates are planning to assassinate 94 civil servants in America and Europe before their sixty-fifth birthday. Kohler gets the info to Ezra Lieberman (Laurence Olivier), Nazi hunter. But soon, Kohler is murdered by Mengele's Nazi goons. Lieberman is left to deal with the plot himself—an old, frail man against a band of the world's most evil men.

Gregory Peck plays the evil Nazi Dr. Josef Mengele in The Boys From Brazil.

Evil Powers/Weapons: He has the powers of Nazis—psychotically cold, organized, and efficient. He works in a worldwide organization of Nazis who will obey any order without hesitation. Uses all types of weapons—knives, guns, torture—to carry out his plans.

Occupation: Nazi doctor. Experimenter, genetic manipulator, plans to bring a horde of Hitler clones into the world.

Intelligence: A scientific genius who uses his knowledge and skills for evil.

Strengths: Super organized. He will do anything to further the Nazi cause.

Weaknesses: His own inhumanity ultimately does him in.

Territory: Works out of Paraguay, but Mengele comes to New England to kill Henry Wheelock.

Idiosyncrasies: Cold, cold, cold. Hitler salute from time to time.

Friends: Other Nazis, Hitler clones.

Enemies: Lieberman, Jews, communists, homosexuals, blacks, gypsies. . . .

Relatives: Marathon Man.

Evil Deeds: In Nazi Germany, Mengele tortured and mutilated thousands of Jews in the concentration camps in order to carry out his horrifying experiments. In modern times, he has helped create Hitler clones and killed many of their fathers. Has also killed anyone, including Kohler, who gets in his way.

Killed by: Lieberman visits several men on the list that Kohler gave him. He discovers what they have in common and why Mengele is killing them off. They are all civil servants of similar economic and social backgrounds and their sons are all identical—short, arrogant, with cold blue eyes. Lieberman finds out that all the boys were adopted from an organization run by Frieda Maloney (Uta Hagen), a convicted war criminal. He sees her in prison and discovers the incredible secret. The boys, created by Mengele, are all genetic clones of Adolf Hitler and have been placed with families all over the world. Mengele's plan is to have each child grow up in an almost identical environment to Hitler and then kill his father at the same age Hitler's father died. Realizing that a Fourth Reich is in the germination stage, Lieberman rushes to the Wheelock home in New England (the next civil servant on the list). However, when he arrives,

Mengele has already murdered the man. He and the Nazi struggle, and Lieberman is shot. The Hitler clone, Billy, comes home and sees that his father has been killed. In anger, he unleashes two huge watchdogs who tear Mengele to bits. Lieberman, tired of all the bloodshed, burns the list of names. The world is on its own now, God help it.

Current Status: Mengele is dead, but his cohorts and Nazi clones are still alive.

What to Do If You Meet: Look out! Stiffen your arm and walk backwards out the door saying "Your Wienerschnitzel is burnink!"

Worthy of Note: A best selling book and an excellent movie with stellar performances by Olivier and Peck.

Can Don Winslow of the Navy turn the tables on our nation's enemies?

Enemy Agent Menlin

Born: 1900s
Died: 1942

Starred in:
Don Winslow of the Navy
Universal, 1942
Directors: Ford Beebe and Ray Taylor
Played by: John Littel

Description: This is wartime America, remember. So these guys are very cruel looking and mean. They wear cuffs on their pants and carry big pistols of foreign manufacture. The Axis is against all freedom, so their German and Japanese killers are sneering, cruel stereotypes.

Reason for Villainy: The U.S. is at war with Axis villainy. So Don Winslow, hero of many mine-sweeping and convoy-protecting jobs in the U.S. Coast Guard, is sent to Naval Intelligence to track the deadly enemy saboteurs. Menlin and friends are out to wreak havoc on tiny Tongita, where our good guys have a chemical plant and a troubled naval installation. Menlin and his cohorts often operate from his undersea cave, which is great for hijacking ships, stealing codes, etc. Winslow (Don Terry) manages to fend off the butcherous hordes of the Axis, crushing the rising-sun creeps and the swastica-sloppies quite readily. But Maitel gets the drop on Misty (Anne Nagel), an attractive helper to Don. With Lieutenant Red Pennington's help, Don triumphs again, Still, the Axis's goons slip away. The Lieutenant (Walter Sande) and Don will pursue.

Evil Powers/Weapons: All the might of the Axis—subs, guns, ships, secret base in an undersea cave, etc.

Occupation: Spies, saboteurs,

Intelligence: Just enough to click his heels, the fascist pig!

Strengths: Knows jujitsu taught by his Japanese friends.

Weaknesses: He's up against our guys.

Territory: Germany, Japan, Tongita Island.

Idiosyncrasies: Yell "Seig Heil" and he stiffens his arm.

Friends: Just the evil Axis goons.

Enemies: The moral world, the Allies.

Evil Deeds: Supports Hitler's evil grab for world domination and is assisted by the evil Empire of Japan and its suicide commandoes.

Outcome: Using the tribe of superstitious natives he gets to oppose our use of their useless island for the greater good of all, the German spy and his fellow goose-steppers meet some success. But Winslow and the forces of good triumph as the Naval Intelligence officer and his buddy infiltrate the base and fight the Axis maniacs to a stunning conclusion. One more nail in Hitler's coffin. One more triumph for Don Winslow. Plus Winslow gets the nurse.

Current Status: Dead.

What to Do If You Meet: Yell "Seig Heil." When he salutes, shoot him.

Worthy of Note: Winslow was at his best in another serial "Don Winslow of the Coast Guard," also from Universal.

Messala

Born: B.C.
Died: Circa A.D. 35

Starred in:
Ben Hur
MGM, 1959
Director: William Wyler
Played by: Stephen Boyd

Description: As a young boy, he's dark-haired, charming, and playful. As an adult, he's a ruthless Roman procurate, intense, dedicated, cruel, and good-looking.

Reason for Villainy: Ben Hur (Charlton Heston) is a wealthy citizen of Judea, which is occupied by the oppressive Romans. Under Emperor Tiberius (George Relph), the ancient kingdom in the Middle East is rife with anti-Roman sentiment. Ben Hur meets his childhood friend Messala, back from Rome for a high position in Judea. Messala wants Ben Hur's cooperation, but Ben declines. The two are now enemies. While watching a parade of the new governor, Hur's sister accidentally dislodges a roof tile which falls and injures the Roman. Ben Hur takes the blame and Messala condemns his old friend to the

The climatic moment in Ben Hur occurs as the hero grapples with Messala (Stephen Boyd) in the furious chariot race.

galleys of the Empire's warships—there he will row and row until he dies. Messala orders this sentence to win marks in Rome and to crush any doubts that he will be sympathetic to the rebels. While at sea, an enormous battle sinks the ship that Ben Hur rows on. However, a kind, high Roman official had loosened Ben Hur's chains. Hur goes about freeing many rowmen and then he rescues the admiral of the Roman fleet, Aurelius (Jack Hawkins). He also has to prevent Aurelius from killing himself for it is a disgrace to have lost the fleet. But when the two make it to shore, Rome pours out its tribute, welcoming the admiral and his new slave, Ben Hur, as victors. It seems that the enemy fleet had also been destroyed, saving Rome. Ben Hur now lives for one thing—he survives to avenge his fate as a galley slave. He vows to kill Messala somehow, and to find out what happened to his mother and sister.

Evil Powers/Weapons: He has a chariot fitted with deadly wheelblades. He has the Roman army and the power of the Roman Empire behind him, and a whip and sword.

Occupation: High-ranking Roman-occupation official in Judea.

Intelligence: Highly intelligent.

Strengths: Good chariot driver, competitive and strong.

Weaknesses: Ben Hur is better.

Territory: Judea, Rome.

Idiosyncrasies: He's two-faced.

Friends: Rome.

Enemies: Ben Hur.

Evil Deeds: He condemns his old friend Ben Hur, sends Ben Hur's family to a leper valley to be infected, and rules Judea with iron fist.

Outcome: Ben Hur eventually is adopted as the son of the famed admiral, and he is free to travel to Judea. In Judea he is given the finest horses and chariots by a sheik in order to race Messala. The sheik thinks it's amusing sponsoring a Jew to kill a Roman. The race is on. Messala whips Ben Hur, but the wheels of the chariots lock and it is Messala who tumbles to his death. Messala has the last word though, revealing to Ben Hur that his family are now lepers. Later, Ben Hur finds his family and also falls in love with his loyal crippled slave's daughter, Esther (Haya Harareet), who is a convert to Christ. To make an epic short, the leper sister and mother are cured by Christ, and Ben Hur is also a convert to the new religion of love.

Current Status: Dead from chariot-wheel mangling and horse trampling.

What to Do If You Meet: Hail Caesar.

Worthy of Note: Spectacular. The film won Academy Awards for Best Picture, Best Director, Best Actor, and Best Supporting Actor.

Frank Miller and Friends

Born: 1800s
Died: 1840s

Starred in:
High Noon
United Artists, 1952
Director: Fred Zinnemann
Played by: Ian MacDonald

Description: Typical gunfighters. Miller has his gun strapped down tight, for quick draws.

The others are lanky cowhands when doing honest work, but are sweaty gunslingers with disgusting spitting and chewing-tobacco habits.

Reason for Villainy: Miller had been in jail for a long time because Will Kane (Gary Cooper), Marshall of Hadleyville, put him there. Now he's been released and riding in on the noon train and seeking revenge. His three gang members will meet him at the station. They will help him destroy Kane. Kane, however, is not really up for a fight. He has just married Amy (Grace Kelly) and he has agreed to follow her Quaker ways of nonviolence. He will forsake the gun. But a man has to do what a man has to do. Kane realizes he will need help. He goes one by one to his best and dearest friends and is surprised to find them cowards all. Martin Howe (Lon Chaney, Jr.), an old lawman, won't do anything. Deputy Harvey Pell (Lloyd Bridges) won't help. He's been mad at Kane for keeping him from the job. Former lover Helen Ramirez (Katy Jurado) is mad at him for marrying. Scratch her. Kane's best friend, Jonas Henderson (Thomas Mitchell), is scared. But it's now 10:30 a.m. and Miller's gang meets under a dead tree and ride toward town.

Weapon: Blazing Colt .45s and .44 long barrels. In a crossfire!

Occupation: Gunslinging outlaws.

Frank Miller (Ian MacDonald) and his boys are itching to use their guns on the Marshal, if he's the man enough to stick around, in High Noon.

Intelligence: They know the odds are on their side. Their brains are in their itchy trigger fingers.

Strengths: Four against one.

Weaknesses: Kane is four times the man of this gang.

Territory: Hadleyville, the Old West, and prison.

Idiosyncrasies: Miller and his friends find it hard to fight fair.

Friends: The cowardice of the people of Hadleyville.

Enemies: Kane.

Evil Deeds: Miller's a killer, bank robber, train robber, and so are his friends.

Killed by: As the ever present clocks tick off in each scene (the movie takes the unusual path of matching the real time the events take place), the dusty town waits. All have advised Kane to run, but he won't. The townspeople stand behind locked windows and peer from cracks in doors, waiting for the slaughter. Kane's new bride forsakes him, despite Tex Ritter's soundtrack plea: "Do not forsake me oh my darlin'." The slippery judge that performed Kane's wedding waits with resignation for the groom to be blasted down, the barber nervously peers from his shop, and the town stands still. Will Kane finds himself on the deserted dusty street facing our villains. The townspeople rationalize their cowardice by thinking they are protecting the town's peaceful reputation, which will encourage investments by northerners. Still, why doesn't the marshall just ride out? Kane and the gang clash. They don't exactly stand there and shoot it out, but run and hide and fire from hidden positions. Finally, it's just Kane and Miller. Miller grabs pretty Amy as hostage after she bravely helped Kane down a man. But in a lucky break Amy twists away. Kane is wounded, but Miller is dead.

Current Status: All dead. This gang is buried on Boot Hill in marked graves that are tourist attractions.

What to Do If You Meet: There's a stage out of town one-half hour before they arrive—be on it. Take Amy.

Worthy of Note: The Academy Award for Best Actor went to Gary Cooper. In this odd Western, Kane even broke out in tears when he realized no one would help him.

Ming the Merciless

Born/Died: Mongo time

Starred in:
Flash Gordon Conquers the Universe
Universal, 1940
Director: Ford Beebe
Played by: Charles Middleton

Description: He wears the highest collars you have ever seen. He has a "Fu Manchu-" style mustache which he likes to stroke and a tremulous voice that orders the disintegration of all enemies. He wears many rings and is bald as a pumpkin. Pointy black beard.

Reason for Villainy: Ming is the absolute and cruel ruler of Mongo, an errant planet heading toward Earth and sucking the atmosphere away with an invisible ray. Flash Gordon, son of genius scientist Dr. Gordon, blasts off in an experimental rocket ship with the half-mad Dr. Zarkov and enters the stratosphere. He finds the invisible ray and crashlands on Mongo with Dale Arden, who has gone along for the ride. Flash and Dale are captured, but intrigue in the palace sets them free. Ming says Zarkov can be useful in the labs. Meanwhile, lots of wild things happen including stoking radium-furnaces with other "slaves" and fighting, then being rescued by Lionmen from Saturn.

Evil Powers/Weapons: Ming is absolute ruler. He has science at his command, and can even use his cape as a parachute if he falls off one of those unsteady "light bridges" between high buildings.

Occupation: Would-be ruler of the universe, and currently controls Mongo and Mars.

Intelligence: Super mean and pretty smart. Leaves the technical stuff to scientists.

Strengths: The death beam aimed at Earth is upsetting the air, causing storms and earthquakes.

169

Ming (Charles Middleton) sits on his mighty throne while watching Flash Gordon being brought to his knees in Flash Gordon Conquers the Universe.

Misty

Alias: Evelyn
Born: 1940s
Died: 1971

Starred in:
Play Misty for Me
Universal, 1971
Director: Clint Eastwood
Played by: Jessica Walter

Territory: Mongo, a planet unknown to us.

Idiosyncrasies: Has running battles with his defiant daughter, Aura.

Friends: His mean soldiers in armor.

Enemies: Flash, the Earthmen, and Dale.

Evil Deeds: Suppression of the legitimate democracies of Mars and Mongo.

Outcome: The story gets very fantastic with lobster-clawed monsters, secret passages behind the throne, and spectacular rocket battles in the mid-ionosphere. Flash, however, is too much for Ming. In the end, Ming walks into the disintegrator room to avoid capture. He throws himself at the mercy of the great god Taos! Was he disintegrated? See the next film.

Current Status: May be in the Phantom Zone.

What to Do If You Meet: Bring one of those nifty ray pistols that you wear on your knuckles.

Worthy of Note: Best fantasy going. See it. This film was a set of serial episodes put together and there are several versions.

Description: Misty is cute, with short dark hair, and an appealing figure. She's well spoken, middle-class type, and often wears turtleneck sweaters.

Reason for Villainy: Dave Garland (Clint Eastwood) is a DJ on a Monterey, California radio station. Late at night, a sexy voice always calls and asks him to play "Misty" by Errol Garner. He does. Later at a local bar, a woman named Evelyn (Jessica Walter) picks Dave up. She's secretly the mystery caller Misty. They bed down together. However, Dave has a steady girl and leaves Misty. Toby (Donna Mills) is Dave's artist girlfriend. Evelyn, who wants to keep seeing Dave, slashes her wrists to prove a point. This woman is psychotic and possessive. She won't accept the loss of the man she wants.

Evil Power: Misty is seductive and can appear quite warm. She is loving, sometimes. Other times the real Misty comes out—the violent killer that will stop at nothing to terrorize those who block her desires.

Weapons: A knife.

Occupation: Sexy lady, radio fan, California dreamer.

Intelligence: Above average.

Strengths: Her passion.

Weaknesses: Psychosis.

Territory: Monterey, California.

Idiosyncrasies: She lies a lot, apologizes a lot, and is possessive to a fault.

Friends: Dave—until he jilts her.

Enemies: Toby—Dave's girlfriend.

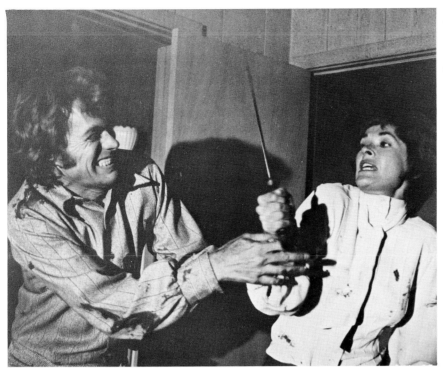

Misty (Jessica Walters) would rather kill her former lover Dave than lose him to another woman in Play Misty for Me.

Relatives: Norman Bates in *Psycho*.

Evil Deeds: She tears up the house, butchers the maid, and terrorizes Toby.

Killed by: Misty goes on a rampage and tears apart Dave's house. She even cuts up the maid. She also keeps calling the radio station requesting that Dave plays "Misty." Eventually she moves in with Toby as a roommate. When Toby isn't there she slashes Dave's picture. She later turns on Toby. Dave, however, comes in right on cue and struggles with the raging psychotic. The mad woman plunges off a cliff and that is the end of Misty.

Current Status: Dead.

What to Do If You Meet: Support mental health or else she'll kill you.

Worthy of Note: The sexiness of this film was a departure from the rough, tight-lipped Clint Eastwood we generally see. This film improved his standing.

Admiral Mitamura

Alias: The Admiral
Born: Turn of the century
Died: Still alive

Starred in:
1941
Columbia, 1979
Director: Steven Spielberg
Played by: Toshiro Mifune

Description: A dignified Japanese admiral. He wears a black Japanese outfit, a cap with a visor, and huge binoculars around the neck.

Reason for Villainy: It's December 13, 1941 and California is in a state of high anxiety after the attack on Pearl Harbor. Rumors spread that the Japanese plan to attack. The military begins preparing a defense. Major General Stillwell (Robert Stack) is given command to protect the state. He stations tanks in Los Angeles and puts cannons along the coast. Meanwhile, a Japanese submarine commanded by Admiral Mitamura surfaces just off the California coast. The admiral and his Nazi associate Von Kleinschmidt (Christopher Lee) decide to attack Hollywood. This will surely deal the Americans a crushing blow. But the question is where are they. They discover they're lost.

Evil Powers/Weapons: He commands a naval crew and has a sub and its weapons—torpedos, machine guns—at his disposal. He wants to really crush American morale.

Admiral Mitamura (Toshiro Mifune) plans to torture a captured American unless he tells him where Hollywood is, in 1941.

Occupation: Submarine commander.

Intelligence: He seems quite dumb. He can barely maneuver his sub and actually attacks the wrong target.

Strengths: Fearless warrior.

Weaknesses: Doesn't know what he's doing.

Territory: His submarine, the California coastline, and Japan.

Idiosyncrasies: Keeps asking "Is this the way to Hollywood?"

Friends: Other Japanese, Von Kleinschmidt.

Enemies: Captured Americans who won't tell him where Hollywood is.

Evil Deeds: Tries to torture American prisoners, and attacks an amusement park.

Outcome: Ward Douglas, a mild mannered coastal resident whose yard has been given the honor of housing a 40mm American cannon, located the Japanese sub off the coast and starts madly firing the cannon, blowing most of his house down. The admiral orders the submarines to return fire and blows up a large ferris wheel at an amusement park. Satisfied that he has destroyed a huge American industrial facility, the admiral heads home to Japan.

Current Status: Alive, patrolling the Pacific. He doesn't know the war is over.

What to Do If You Meet: Bow, given him the directions to Hollywood, let them worry about it.

Worthy of Note: Although a tremendous amount of cash was spent on *1941*, it didn't fare that well at the box office or with critics.

Mord

Alias: The Executioner
Born/Died: 15th century

Starred in:
The Tower of London
Universal, 1939
Director: Rowland V. Lee
Played by: Boris Karloff

Description: Tall, hulking, bald-headed executioner/torturer. Mean, mean, mean. His face is immobile as stone, and he wears a Middle Age leather outfit with a dagger in his belt. His right clubfoot is housed in a huge, black, square shoe.

Reason for Villainy: Mord is the official executioner of the Tower of London. But he's not loyal to the king. In a series of incredibly complicated double- and triple-crosses, Mord allies himself with Richard, Duke of Gloucester (Basil Rathbone), who plots to become King of England himself.

Evil Powers/Weapons: Mord has all the torture devices of the tower at his disposal, including racks, screws, ropes, swords, knives, red-hot pokers, and crushing devices. His favorite weapon is a huge ax which has beheaded many a soul.

Occupation: Torturer, executioner, throne plotter.

Intelligence: Quite intelligent for an executioner, but twisted. Sadistic. He just loves to hurt people and puts all his energy into evil and pain.

Strengths: Physically strong, fearless, with tremendous willpower.

Weaknesses: Greed and disloyalty to the crown.

Territory: Tower of London, England.

Friends/Enemies: Richard is his only "friend," if that's the word for two such evil personages. Everyone else is just fodder for his torture chamber.

Evil Deeds: Murders, plots, steals, tortures, beheads, stabs, drowns, and kills half the royal family of England (even children) in an effort to help Richard usurp the throne.

Killed by: Working with Richard, Mord kills Lord De Vene (John Wyatt) and the aging King Henry VI. Richard desires Anne Neville, whose husband, the Prince of Wales, he kills in battle. But Clarence (Vincent Price) hides her away. Mord's spies find her and she is forced into marrying Richard. Mord drowns Clarence in a huge wine barrel. After King Edward dies, Prince Edward is crowned king. Mord kills the prince and his brother in the tower. Richard is crowned the new king and tries to prevent the royal treasure from being taken to the Tudors in France. Tudor raises an army and invades England. At the climactic Battle of Bosworth, King Richard and Mord are killed and Tudor becomes the new King of England.

Current Status: Dead.

Richard and Mord (Boris Karloff) confer over whom to kill next and in what manner in The Tower of London.

What to Do If You Meet: Tell him you're a torture-device saleman and have to go out to your carriage to get some nifty items he would really like.

Worthy of Note: The extras' costumes were made of cardboard. In filming one of the battle scenes, a rainmaking device was used and all the costumes melted. The scene had to be shot from scratch.

The Mountain Men

Born: 1930s
Died: 1972

Starred in:
Deliverance
Warner Bros., 1972
Director: John Boorman
Played by: Billy McKinney, Herbert "Cowboy" Coward

Description: Filthy, ragged, ugly, half-human, muttering degenerates, inbred, murderous mountain men.

Reason for Villainy: Four middle-class businessmen—Ed Gentry (Jon Voight), Lewis Medlock (Burt Reynolds), Bobby Trippe (Ned Beatty), and Drew Ballinger (Ronny Cox)—decide to go on a he-man adventure vacation canoeing down an isolated river in the Appalachians to prove their aging virility. They first stop in a small community at the edge of the river where the dwellers warn them that the mountains are filled with "danger."

Evil Powers: They know the woods well and are very sadistic.

Weapons: Guns

Occupation: Degenerate hunters.

Intelligence: Close to nil. Just above animal, extremely demented, twisted. Good hunters.

The Mountain Men attack but Lewis is quick to retaliate with his bow in Deliverance.

Strengths: They are successful in their own environment.

Weaknesses: Too dumb to deal with the four businessmen.

Territory: Aintry county, Appalachian mountains.

Idiosyncrasies: Drool, mumble, love to perform sexual humiliations on captured tourists.

Friends: Other mountain men and women.

Enemies: Outsiders.

Relatives: The rednecks from "Easy Rider."

Evil Deeds: They torture and sexually humiliate Bobby and have probably performed countless sadistic deeds on forest animals and other outsiders. Probably killed before.

Killed by: The four businessmen head deep down the uncharted river through the rapids. Bobby and Ed are separated from the others and are captured by the hideous Mountain Men. They tie Ed up and then sexually attack the fat Bobby, forcing him to squeal like a pig. Lewis rescues them, shooting one of the mountain Men with an arrow. They escape and head downriver. However, the boat capsizes and Drew drowns; Lewis ends up with a broken leg. They are later attacked by another mountain man, but Ed shoots him down with a bow. Once they finally reach safety, changed by their horrific experience, they realize they will relive this nightmare for the rest of their lives.

Current Status: Dead, but more Mountain Men are up in those hills.

What to Do If You Meet: Stick with guided tours!

Worthy of Note: Written by James Dickey, a major poet. *Deliverance* is truly a terrifying movie. Very popular, made lots of money.

The Muranians

Born: Unknown
Died: 1935

Starred in:
The Phantom Empire
Mascot, 1935
Directors: Otto Brewer and B. Reeves Eason
Played by: Dorothy Christy, Wheeler Oakman, et al

Description: The Muranians are human-looking, but live 20,000 feet underground. They wear outlandish outfits and capes. They ride horses. They have fantastic weapons, and a TV system that can see the surface. They are strong, especially Queen Tika. Argo, her often rebellious assistant, is equally strong. Muranians have no use for weaklings.

Reason for Villainy: Gene Autry is a cowboy with an extensive ranch in the western U.S. He also has a radio broadcasting station and lots of friends. Something odd is happening though. Someone is commiting sabotage. (Maybe they don't like him singing "Back in the Saddle Again.") Anyway, it seems a gang of crooks is out to plunder the radium-laden ranch. Gene rides after them. There he finds the hidden underground city of Murania. Heavens to Betsy, those Muranians sure can ride horses. Gene is almost trapped, but his friend, Oscar (Smiley Burnett), saves him. The Muranians will destroy the people that threaten them. They later take Gene prisoner. The singing cowboy might be disintegrated!

Frankie (Frankie Darro) and Betsy (Betsy King Ross) ride to the rescue, but they also are captured. Oscar tries to disguise himself as a robot (like Woody Allen in *Sleeper*), but he is captured. Those Muranians are mean, especially Queen Tika—who's not bad looking and very leggy—and that mean old Prime Minister of Murania, Argo.

Evil Powers/Weapons: They have disintegrator rays, remote TV hookups, sliding doors in the mountains, and a lot of robots who pull death switches.

Occupation: Tika is Queen of Murania and Argo is a high politician.

Intelligence: They know how to use radium, and that's smart.

Strengths: They have horses and death rays.

Weaknesses: Gene, the singing cowboy, doesn't take any guff.

Territory: Murania (located underneath Gene's radio ranch).

Idiosyncrasies: They wear capes and collars like they are at a costume ball.

Friends: Other Muranians—until there is an underground civil war.

Enemies: Gene, the crooks, and all surface people.

Evil Deeds: The Muranians can monitor the surface with a new device called television. They also can shoot death rays and send the robots to kill you.

Queen Tika and Argo, the leaders of the Muranians, torture Gene Autry to prevent him from destroying their underground kingdom in The Phantom Empire.

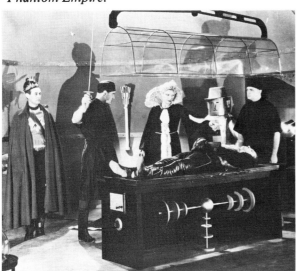

Outcome: Well, saved by the bell. The Muranians are about to have a civil war. Gene and his group take advantage of the death-ray filled confusion to reach the surface. The Muranian revolutionaries blast the kingdom to little radioactive pieces. The radio broadcasts of the singing cowboys will go on and on, thrilling the listeners with "Oh, I've got spurs that jingle, jangle, jingle" forever.

What to Do If You Meet: Ride away, report them to the A.E.C.

Worthy of Note: The West is best when left to rest. The Muranians should have known better than to tangle with good old American cowboys. Yahoooooo!

John Neville

Born: 1940s
Died: 1978

Starred in:
Eyes of Laura Mars
Columbia Pictures, 1978
Director: Irvin Kershner
Played by: Tommy Lee Jones

Description: Neville is a handsome, virile, and tough police detective. He is tall, and has dark hair and a quiet, sexy demeanor. His strong arms hold you close when you are afraid.

Reason for Villainy: Neville is investigating the strange murders that are occurring among the people of the fashion industry. The victims are all connected to the sensational and controversial fashion photographer Laura Mars. Mars (Faye Dunaway) takes her photographs amidst scenes of carnage—recreated car crashes, bloody murders, etc. Laura also has the strange, awesome gift of ESP. She can see through the eyes of the killer stalking the people in her photographs, but she cannot see

175

Detective John Neville promises to protect Laura from the murderer who's stalking her friends and models; he is actually that murderer in Eyes of Laura Mars.

the face of the killer. She knows when crimes are about to be committed and when the killer is advancing. It is a horrible talent. She confides in the detective. He begins investigating the likely suspects. Top of the list is Laura's ex-felon chauffeur (Brad Dourif). One by one Laura's models and friends are being knifed by the unseen killer. To make matters more confusing, right in the middle of the gruesome investigation, Laura and the detective start having an affair. Yet, the killing continues. The detective questions the chauffeur who says he saw something he didn't understand. Before you know it, the chauffeur is running away down the street and the detective's assistant guns him down. Was he the killer? Most people think so.

Evil Powers/Weapons: He is cunning and totally schizoid. One aspect of his personality doesn't even like the other. He's deadly because he is the least likely person to ever be suspected.

Occupation: New York City police detective.

Intelligence: Very intelligent.

Strengths: His kind side loves Laura and wants to protect her. When he's out of control, he's a mad killer.

Territory: New York City fashion world.

Idiosyncrasies: One part of him is nice and gentle, the other . . . watch out!

Friends/Enemies: Laura is both.

Evil Deeds: He kills many models.

Outcome: Neville didn't want the chauffeur to die. He is upset that death is treated so casually. It is a terrible thing, not to be taken lightly. Laura is relieved, however, now that the chauffeur—the alleged killer—is dead. Suddenly her eyes begin working again, and she sees the killer. This time, though, the killer is watching her. She locks the door. Neville soon arrives at Laura's apartment. Yet, she will not let him in because she is afraid. Determined to get inside, the detective smashes through Laura's window. He holds her close and says he will protect her. But then he starts mumbling about his prostitute mother torturing him as a child, his loneliness, and his anger at women. Then we come to understand that he's a fruitcake. His good side starts battling the evil side. He hands Laura his gun and begs her to shoot him, the killer. She holds the gun against him as he helps her squeeze the trigger.

Current Status: Both personalities are quite dead.

What to Do If You Meet: Support mental health.

Worthy of Note: Great flick, and an unusual variation on a theme. A sexy and taut drama.

Nuclear War

Born: 1945
Died: Still threatening

Starred in:
On The Beach
United Artists, 1959
Director: Stanley Kramer

Description: It's a million times more deadly than a meltdown; it is the end of

Peter and Mary search for hope in each other even as nuclear war fall-out begins to reach Australia in On the Beach.

humanity. Nuclear War is always threatening, and its huge capacity for destruction will grow daily until the world settles its differences. In this film, Nuclear War has occurred.

Reason for Villainy: It all started in 1945 with the dropping of nuclear bombs on Hiroshima and Nagasaki. It has now gone so far that the nations armed with nuclear weapons have all fired their weapons. As the film begins, we see the results of World War III. It is 1964 and the Northern Hemisphere is obliterated by radioactive fallout from exploded atomic bombs. The radiation is slowly drifting toward Australia, which has been untouched as yet. But it is also doomed. A United States submarine and its crew, led by Captain Dwight Towers (Gregory Peck), surface in Sidney harbor. Thinking all life has ceased north of the equator, the submarine men are startled to hear radio signals from San Diego. The sub takes off to the U.S., but, once there, discovers that the signal is just a Coke bottle rolling against a telegraph key. The sailor that went ashore had to wear a radiation suit. So much for life after a Nuclear War in America. Back in Australia, the populace prepares for the coming fallout—and the end of all life on Earth.

Evil Powers/Weapons: 10,000 independently targeted reentry vehicles atop ICBM rockets, plus scads of bombers and cruise missiles. A mistake could start the whole thing off.

Occupation: Nuclear threat.

Intelligence: Starting World War III is not very intelligent.

Strengths: The most destructive weapon man could devise.

Weaknesses: Man's inability to make peace with his fellow man.

Territory: Everywhere.

Idiosyncrasies: It's all so foolish.

Friends: Paranoia.

Enemies: Sanity.

Relatives: Nuclear Meltdowns.

Evil Deeds: Hiroshima and Nagasaki were destroyed by nuclear attack. Will the whole world be destroyed like them?

Outcome: The doctors in Australia begin handing out medication that will ease the pain of death, which is slow and painful due to radiation. But life goes on. The best wines are doled out and people begin to party. Some people are desperately trying to accomplish their life goals, while others just continue what they have always done. Julian Osborne (Fred Astaire) races his car in a grand prix. There have never been such daredevils. What do they have to lose? Peter (Anthony Perkins) and Mary (Donna Anderson) give a big party. She shouts that there must be hope. But they are forced to give their little baby the death medicine to prevent it from suffering. Cynical Moira (Ava Gardner) confesses to Dwight Towers that she wants to be with him and not die alone. Towers, however, can't get it through his head that his whole family is dead in Connecticut. Towers eventually accepts Moira's love. But it all will come to a dramatic conclusion. Soon they all commit suicide in their own way. The world is empty. The end—really the end!

Current Status: Nuclear War is an ever-present possibility.

What to Do If You Meet: Be at ground zero, and don't survive. It will be hell.

Worthy of Note: This was Fred Astaire's first dramatic role. It also proved to be a most disturbing film. You keep hoping that someone will invent a cure for radiation, but it's too late. The only way to cure nuclear war is to prevent it.

The Octopus 179
Odd Job 180

Judge
  Quincannon 186
Hank Quinlan 187

Nurse Rached 188
Captain Juan
  Ramon 189

The Passengers 181
Grand Duke
  Peter 182
Phantom of the
  Paradise 183
Hjalmar Poelzig 184
Pretty Poison 185

Raven 190
Lonesome Rhodes 191
Rico 192
Johnny Rocco 193
Rochefort 194
Roy and the
  Driver 195

The Octopus

Alias: Mr. Chase
Born: 1900
Died: 1938

Starred in:
The Spider's Web
Columbia, 1938
Directors: Ray Taylor, James W. Horne
Played by: Charles Wilson

The Octopus sits and waits for his arch-rival the Spider in The Spider's Web.

Description: The Octopus wears a false right hand sticking out of his shiny robe, but no one knows that. He can reach for and shoot with his *real* right hand from under the robe. He is fully masked as the Octopus, but as Chase, he is a dark-suited industrialist of average height and weight with brown hair. Who would suspect?

Reason for Villainy: The Octopus is the head of a ruthless criminal organization that is terrorizing the nation—especially the transportation industry—with explosives. In his secret identity as the Spider, Richard Wentworth battles back as the nemesis of the underworld, who sometimes goes beyond the law killing criminals and leaving their foreheads red with a spider cartouche.

In his pursuit, Wentworth (Warren Hull) assumes the disguise of Blinky McQuade, a notorious criminal, and infiltrates the Octopus's organization. Wentworth discovers a bus is to be blown up. With his loyal Sikh chauffeur Ram Singh (Kenneth Duncan), the Spider rescues the bus passengers. Naturally, as is the Spider's luck, the police implicate him in the bombing. But the mad attacks of the Octopus on the nation's transportion goes on. Why?

Evil Powers/Weapons: He's got his gang, his guns, and his disguised, radio voice of terror. Who can stop him?

Occupation: Master criminal and industrialist.

Intelligence: Eight times smarter than you or I.

Strengths: His mad drive for power and his "secret" right hand.

Weaknesses: He's up against the Spider and his twin .45s.

Territory: The city.

Idiosyncrasies: He wears that silly outfit.

Friends: No one except the gang.

Enemies: Richard Wentworth, Ram Singh.

Evil Deeds: Kills hundreds of innocent people by blowing up buses, derailing trains, etc.

Outcome: Wentworth finds some special radio equipment used by the slippery Octopus to give his mad radio warnings to the nation. The millionaire, disguised as the Spider, Master of Men, finds a sealed-off wing in Chase's warehouse. Chase, it seems, plans to control all commerce in the U.S.A. The Spider finds the Octopus at his radio microphone and the Octopus extends his secret hand with a gun. But the Spider's flaming .45s are faster and burn the Octopus to death. He discovers that the dead Octopus is none other than industrialist Chase. Wentworth retrieves his long-suffering mistress/fiancee, Nita Van Sloan (Iris Meredith), and they are off for a tryst.

Current Status: Dead.

What to Do If You Meet: Walk, don't take the bus.

Worthy of Note: *Spider, Master of Men*, by Richard Wentworth, is a purpleprose classic. Read the series for illuminating metaphors and daring action. One of the best of the serials. See also *The Spider Returns*, a 1941 serial by Columbia. There Nita is played by Mary Ainslee. Top notch.

Oddjob

Born: 1930s
Died: 1964

Starred in:
Goldfinger
United Artists, 1964
Director: Guy Hamilton
Played by: Harold Sakata

Oddjob is the henchman of Goldfinger. His innocuous bowler hat is actually a deadly throwing weapon.

Description: Oddjob is Oriental, strongly built like a sumo wrestler, but usually attired in formal wear. He wears a bowler hat that has an unusual feature: It is a throwing weapon. He sports a moustache, a pair of killer hands, and neatly parted hair with a recent trim.

Reason for Villainy: Oddjob is the henchman of Goldfinger, an international master criminal. Auric Goldfinger (Gert Frobe) is planning to break into Fort Knox—where the U.S. stores its gold reserves. There he will detonate a nuclear device, making all the gold radioactive and cornering the market with his vast store of gold. James Bond (Sean Connery), top British secret agent, meets Goldfinger in Miami Beach and foils him in a game of crooked poker. Then Bond walks out with Goldfinger's girl, Jill Masterson (Shirley Éaton). Later, she is found dead of gold-paint poisoning (her body is covered with the gold). "M", Bond's boss, calls him to London. He is sent out on Goldfinger's trail. Bond discovers that Goldfinger intends for Pussy Galore (Honor Blackman) to fly over Fort Knox with a bunch of private planes and saturate the place with debilitating gas.

Evil Powers/Weapons: Oddjob's hat makes him deadly. Also watch out for his hands.

Occupation: Henchman, helper, and sometimes caddy for Goldfinger.

Intelligence: Not brilliant, but knows who's got the gold.

Strengths: His hat.

Weaknesses: James (007) Bond doesn't like his ladies killed by hats.

Territory: Switzerland, Miami, Kentucky.

Idiosyncrasies: Is familiar with golf. He wears formal wear on most occasions.

Friends: Goldfinger, Chang, Pussy Galore—for a while.

Enemies: Bond and the world.

Evil Deeds: Kills both men and women with his hat, and plays (and cheats) at golf.

Killed by: There is a grotesque confrontation in Fort Knox between superagent Bond and Oddjob. Somehow Bond manages to avoid being skewered by the hat. Bond also has trouble with Pussy Galore, but once she's defeated in a knock-down, drag-out karate fight with our hero, they make love—now that's English! Later, a buzz saw is about to render Bond unattractive, but he wisecracks his way out of that. Oddjob, however, meets his end when his hat gets stuck in a metal fence and he tries to retrieve it. James Bond touches a live electric cable to the metal, and Oddjob meets his electrifying finish.

Current Status: Shockingly dead.

What to Do When You Meet: Tell him you love his hat.

Worthy of Note: Bond, of course, has radar and chariot blades on his Aston-Martin sportscar, but that's old hat (sorry). What's new in this film is the great villainy of Oddjob.

The Passengers

Born: 1800s
Died: Still alive

Starred in:
Murder on the Orient Express
Paramount, 1974
Director: Sidney Lumet
Played: Ingrid Bergman, Wendy Hiller,
   Vanessa Redgrave, Michael York,
   Jacqueline Bisset, Anthony Perkins,
   Lauren Bacall, Rachel Roberts, Sean
   Connery

*The Passengers on the train are all suspected of
Murder on the Orient Express.*

Description: They are all passengers aboard the famous *Orient Express.* However, they are of varied backgrounds, classes, and nationalities. What do they have in common? One thing and one thing alone, and Belgian detective Hercule Poirot must find out what that one common thread is.

Reason for Villainy: In 1934, aboard the train moving from Istanbul to Calais, an odd group of passengers are making a deadly journey. Aboard the train is famous detective Hercule Poirot (Albert Finney). American business tycoon Ratchett (Richard Widmark) asks Poirot to protect him. Someone is out there trying to kill him. Ratchett is a sleazy character—and Poirot is not a bodyguard—so the famed investigator refuses. Later, Ratchett is found murdered. He had been drugged and repeatedly stabbed in his compartment. Poirot is honor-bound to investigate. He finds all the passengers are related in one way or another to one event—the kidnapping of an infant some years earlier. Even Ratchett's valet Beddoes (John Gielgud) had been the chauffeur of the kidnap victim's family. Odd. More odd is the fact that all the passengers have alibis. Unless . . . . No, it couldn't be, it's too fantastic, and yet . . .

Evil Powers/Weapons: They all have a hand in it.

Occupation: Various and sundry. Revengers all.

Intelligence: They are fiendishly clever.
Strengths: They stick together and feel justice is on their side.
Weaknesses: Hercule Poirot is the only man in the world who can solve the bizarre murder.
Territory: The *Orient Express* train.
Idiosyncrasies: They all are characters.
Friends: Each other.
Enemies: Ratchett and Hercule Poirot—except that he is a man that wants justice.
Evil Deeds: They take turns stabbing the evil Ratchett in his drugged sleep. After all, he had murdered the poor, innocent child he kidnapped.
Outcome: Well, it's all unfathomable to ordinary men, but Poirot cracks the case. Hercule calls all the passengers together. He proposes an incredible thing, based on the one clue that each and everyone of the passengers knew of and were related to that famous kidnapping. Hercule proposes that all the stab wounds—of different depths—were made one by one by each passenger in a pact to kill Ratchett. The problem is that they won't admit it and no one would ever believe such a story. There had been a ruse too—a conductor's uniform was stolen. It could be, says the justice-loving Poirot, that someone did come aboard and kill Ratchett. In the interest of real justice, he will conclude that this is indeed what happened. He will not mention his bizarre theory to the authorities. The passengers are all relieved and thank Poirot. Sometimes justice is served in strange ways.

Current Status: Never killed again, but they do get together and have a party once a year.

What to Do If You Meet: Have a drink with them.

Worthy of Note: A brilliant adaptation of Agatha Christie's story to the screen.

Grand Duke Peter

Born/Died: 1800s

Starred in:
The Scarlet Empress
Paramount, 1934
Director: Josef von Sternberg
Played by: Sam Jaffe

Description: He has a nonending, silly grin. He's also quite mad. He is often seen with his toy soldiers or drilling his real Hessian troops in the palace. He is wild-haired and wide-eyed, and demented.

Reason for Villainy: Princess Sophia Frederica (Marlene Dietrich) is betrothed to Grand Duke Peter, heir to the throne of Russia. She travels to the brutish, illiterate court with her escort Count Alexi (John Lodge), who she is very fond of. She can't wait, however, to see the magnificent Peter. Empress Elizabeth (Louise Dresser), Peter's mother, is a rambunctious, ill-mannered, bossy woman who orders Sophia to change her name to Catherine and produce an heir as soon as possible after her marriage to Peter. Then, Catherine is finally introduced to her future husband. He is a drooling idiot who the empress orders about like a slave. Catherine is miserable. Peter, even after the marriage, still prefers the company of Countess Elizabeth (Ruthelma Stevens), a black-haired firebrand who wants the throne. Discovering that her friend Alexi is now one of the empress's bedmates, Catherine becomes heartbroken and

The insane Grand Duke Peter (Sam Jaffe) wants his Empress to look good while holding court in The Scarlet Empress.

turns to the captain of the guards and bears a boy child by him. Peter progressively goes off his noggin and all of Russia is uneasy that he will gain the throne.

Evil Powers/Weapons: When he is czar, his proclamations lead to an insane reign of terror.

Occupation: Grand Duke, czar, idiot.

Intelligence: None.

Strengths: A czar can do anything he wants.

Weaknesses: His "toy" soldiers are fed up.

Territory: The royal palace in imperial Russia

Idiosyncrasies: He's quite mad. He loves to play with his soldiers.

Friends: His troops, until they revolt.

Enemies: Catherine.

Evil Deeds: He ascends the throne and begins confiscating property, stealing from the poor to give to the rich, and basically becomes a mean, nasty monarch.

Outcome: After the Empress has died, Peter takes over the government and a reign of terror begins. He insults the church, slapping the patriarch when he is asked for a symbolic offering to the poor, and begins to confiscate his peasants property. Catherine, however, has been making allies, rallying the army behind her. Amidst his toys, Peter is strangled in his bedroom and Catherine steps in in his place. Catherine is triumphant.

What to Do If You Meet: Give him a toy soldier and run.

Worthy of Note: Surreal, man, surreal.

Phantom of the Paradise

Alias: Winslow Leach
Born: Created 1974
Died: 1974

Starred in:
Phantom of the Paradise
20th Century Fox-Rank, 1974
Director: Brian DePalma
Played by: William Finley

Description: At first, he's normal looking, almost nebbishy, but later he becomes horribly disfigured and wears a birdlike plastic, space-helmet mask, leather jump suit, black gloves, boots and cape. Red lips.

Reason for Villainy: Swan (Paul Williams), the boss of Death Records, wants a "whole new sound" to open his giant rock emporium The Palace. He hears Winslow Leach's song and picks it to be the lead of his new show. Winslow comes to Death Records where he falls in love with an aspiring singer, Phoenix (Jessica Harper). Swan steals Leach's music and frames him on a drug charge, sending him off to prison.

Evil Powers/Weapons: He is very strong and can swing on ropes. He also plays the organ expertly. He uses fire and a knife as weapons.

Occupation: Rock composer.

Intelligence: Highly intelligent. A gifted musician and songwriter.

Strengths: Gifted.

Weaknesses: Gullible, easily swayed by Swan.

Territory: The Paradise, a giant rock palace.

Friends: Falls in love with Phoenix.

Enemies: Comes to hate Swan when he realizes what he has done to him.

Relatives: Phantom of the Opera.

Evil Deeds: Kills Swan.

Killed by: While Leach is in jail, the song he wrote becomes a huge hit for Swan. Leach escapes from prison and raids Death Records to destroy the tapes. While there he gets his head stuck in a record press and is grotesquely disfigured. Leach begins wearing a strange outfit and prowls the corridors of the Palace. Swan tries to convince him to finish the score for the opening. Leach agrees only if Phoenix can sing. Swan agrees, but later imprisons Leach in a recording booth and hires Beef, a rock star, to sing. Angered, Leach escapes and disposes of Beef, and the Paradise opens with Phoenix singing. She is a huge success. That night, intoxicated with her fortune, Phoenix is seduced by Swan. Leach watches the seduction and stabs himself in anger. His wound mysteriously heals. Swan reveals that the healing occurred because Leach is under "eternal contract" to Swan and Swan is under the same contract to the devil. Neither can die. Swan later marries Phoenix (planning to have her assassinated at the wedding to thrill the huge audience). Later, Leach finds a videotape (from the devil) that makes Swan immortal and burns it. Swan withers and dies.

Having already swindled Leach once, Swan tries to get him to continue writing songs for him in Phantom of the Paradise.

Leach's knife wound also suddenly opens and he dies, too.

Current Status: Dead.

What to Do If You Meet: Tell him he's the best rock 'n' roll composer since the Beatles.

Worthy of Note: One of the best rock satires ever, and a super black comedy.

Hjalmar Poelzig

Born: Late 19th century
Died: 1934

Starred in:
The Black Cat
Universal, 1934
Director: Edgar Ulmer
Played by: Boris Karloff

Description: Cruel, devil worshipping, murderer/sadist. Swept back dark hair, cruel grin. Wears magician-type gown from neck to ankles. Huge black eyebrows and eyes.

Reason for Villainy: Newlyweds Peter and Joan Alison are traveling through Europe when they are joined by Dr. Vitus Verdegast (Bela Lugosi) who is heading to visit Hjalmar Poelzig, a former army engineer. Their car crashes in the desolate Hungarian mountains and the travelers go to Poelzig's home. Verdegast accuses Poelzig of being responsible for a military defeat years earlier which cost the lives of 10,000 men and cost Verdegast 15 years in prison. He demands to know the whereabouts of his wife and daughter, who he suspects Poelzig of abducting. Events quickly prove Poelzig to be a man of infinite evil.

Evil Powers/Weapons: Physically strong, hypnotic powers, and the leader of a devil cult with total power over its followers. He's ruthless. Uses magical spells and his torture chamber.

Poelzig (Boris Karloff) welcomes Peter Alison and Dr. Verdegast to his home in The Black Cat.

Occupation: Army engineer, devil worshipper.

Intelligence: Highly intelligent, but serves the forces of evil.

Strengths: The powers of black magic, plus his house has secret tunnels.

Weaknesses: Underestimates the anger of his victims.

Territory: Hungary.

Idiosyncrasies: Likes to play chess and hear screams.

Friends: Devil followers.

Enemies: Verdegast, who wants to avenge his wife's and daughter's murders.

Evil Deeds: Was responsible for the death of 10,000 soldiers. Holds black masses, has killed numerous people over the years, and makes human sacrifices to the devil.

Killed by: In an underground chamber, Verdegast finds the dead body of his wife preserved under glass. He goes to shoot Poelzig, but a black cat leaps in front of him, unnerving him. The newlyweds are made prisoner and Verdegast plays chess with Poelzig for Joan's release but loses. Poelzig holds a black mass where he plans to sacrifice Joan, but Verdegast and his servant, Thamal, rescue her at the last second. Verdegast also discovers the corpse of his daughter and, in a fit of rage, ties Poelzig to a rack and skins him alive. Thinking Verdegast is about to hurt Joan, Peter shoots him. Verdegast allows the couple to escape and then blows up the house to destroy the evil that dwelleth within.

Current Status: Dead, but devil worshippers have a pact with the devil and often return.

What to Do If You Meet: Get your cross and holy water and run!

Pretty Poison

Alias: Sue Ann Stepanek
Born: 1950s
Died: Still alive

Starred in:
Pretty Poison
20th Century Fox, 1968
Director: Noel Black
Played by: Tuesday Weld

Description: Beautiful, all American, typical small-town girl. Cute, long blonde hair, blue eyes, plaid skirt. As ideal an American teen as there could ever be.

Reason for Villainy: Dennis Pitt (Anthony Perkins) is released from a mental institution where he spent many years for having burned down his aunt's house. He is given a job with a lumber company in a small New England town, and begins living in a trailer. He takes pictures of everything with a small spy camera fantasizing himself as a master spy. He becomes attracted to a pretty high school majorette, Sue Ann, and tells her he works for the CIA and is investigating the lumber company because it is manned by foreign agents polluting the waters. Sue Ann, in search of excitement, quickly joins forces with Dennis and makes love with him when he asks her to prove her loyalty. He thinks he's controlling her, but almost immediately, it is she who is running the show with disastrous consequences.

Evil Powers: Her powers of persuasion and her seeming innocence make her evil totally hidden.

Weapons: She uses her body and her face to get what she wants.

Occupation: Student, high school majorette.

Intelligence: Very smart. Able to understand what makes people tick and how to use them.

Headquarters: Small lumber town in Massachusetts.

Idiosyncrasies: Craves excitement at all costs. Can only enjoy sex after violence.

Friends: Dennis.

Enemies: Her mother.

Relatives: *The Bad Seed, The Omen.*

Evil Deeds: She kills a factory guard and her mom, plus frames Dennis.

Outcome: Dennis and Sue go to the lumber mill to unscrew some bridge beams when a guard finds them. Sue Ann kills him with a wrench. They plan to flee to Mexico and get married (or so Sue says), and rush to Sue Ann's house to pack. However, Sue Ann's mother comes home and Sue Ann tries to get Dennis to kill her. When he won't, she takes out the guard's pistol and cold bloodedly shoots her mom. She sends Dennis to dispose of the body. Dennis, now terrified of Sue Ann, phones the police. When he arrives at the station, however, Sue Ann is sitting there, crying, blaming the murder all on him. They believe her, of course, and Dennis is put away. At end of the film, Sue Ann meets another young man and begins telling him how boring her foster parents are.

Sue Ann (Tuesday Weld) tries to convince her lover Dennis to murder her mother in Pretty Poison.

Current Status: Alive, and luring other young men into her evil clutches.

What to Do If You Meet: Do not go out with this girl! You'll do much better with a blind date arranged by your Aunt Emma.

Worthy of Note: One of the blackest of black comedies of the 1960s, Tuesday Weld's acting powers reached her peak. A cult classic.

Judge Quincannon

Born: 1900s
Died: 1945

Starred in:
And Then There Were None
20th Century Fox, 1945
Director: Rene Clair
Played by: Barry Fitzgerald

Description: He's a merry old judge, he is. He called for his friends, he called for his foes, he called for his enemies ten. He's always in a sweater, and when fate calls he's the first to "die." Gray-haired. A tux and tie make him the best dressed corpse in the bunch.

Reason for Villainy: A group of people have been brought together for a party of sorts on a remote island. There's a little decoration of ten little Indians in the building. Little by little, one by one, each guest is murdered. After each murder one of the Indian ornaments is broken off. Frightfully amusing. What is the one fact that links all the guests? Answer: They have all committed crimes for which they are now being summarily executed. They try all the old gambits to avoid being murdered, but nothing works. The judge is a good suspect, but he soon has a hole in the head from a bullet. The doctor pronounces him dead and soon he is gone, too. Mystery of mysteries.

Evil Powers/Weapons: The doc has connived with the judge to fake the judge's mur-

der. They planned to have the judge skulk around and find the murderer, but it's too late when the doc finds out that the murderer was the judge.

Occupation: Retired, but not inactive, judge. (He still sentences people to death!)

Intelligence: Jurisprudential.

Strengths: Clever as a bat in hell.

Weaknesses: He didn't count on love altering the sentences.

Territory: An island cut off from the world as only islands off England can be in the cinema.

Idiosyncrasies: He's a vengeful little bugger, isn't he?

Friends: The law.

Enemies: Unpunished criminals.

Evil Deeds: He takes the law into his own hands.

Outcome: It's baffling how each person is murdered because they watch out for each other so much. Finally, only the man and woman who have fallen in love with each other are left. They each logically deduce that the other has to be the killer. There is a stand off with weapons between the lovers on the beach and shots are fired. Inside the old house the judge swallows his poison—his work is done now. He presumes the one surviving lover will be executed by authorities for all the murders. But, lo and behold, arm in arm, the lovers

Four little Indians have been broken off the ornament meaning four murders have been committed. Who will be next in And Then Were None?

enter. The judge is stunned, but with his dying breath he says eight out of ten is not bad. The glass falls from his hand. Love conquers fear—and logic.

Current Status: Death is nature's way of telling you to slow down. The judge has slowed down.

What to Do If You Meet: Avoid suspicious parties on remote islands.

Worthy of Note: Remade with Fabian as the male lead. A must to avoid. See this old-time version instead. It'll make your heart sing.

Hank Quinlan

Born: 1920s
Died: 1958

Starred in:
Touch of Evil
Universal, 1958
Director: Orson Welles
Played by: Orson Welles

Description: Fat, paunchy, candy-chewing degenerate who is a crooked, callous, vindictive cop. He limps, has half-open eyes, and generally is in disarray. He has a fondness for cigars and you can tell when he's been in the room.

Reason for Villainy: This cop has turned sour on the world and the law. His wife had been murdered some time back and they never caught the guy. Now Quinlan plants evidence and uses illegal frames to "get" who he wants. It is Ramon Vargas (Charlton Heston), a good Mexican narcotics cop who is in the U.S.A. with his American wife, Susan (Janet Leigh), who makes a difference. On the border between the nations, a millionaire named Linnekar has been blown up by a time bomb. Quinlan believes a Mexican, Sanchez, did the bombing and sets about framing him. Vargas objects. Quinlan is incensed. He gets gang-

Hank Quinlan is a crooked cop who frames people to make sure that "justice" is served in Touch of Evil.

sters to go after Vargas. The gangster boss, Grandi (Akim Tamiroff), sends a gang to set Susan Vargas up as a dope addict. Quinlan, no friend to Grandi, kills him in Susan's hotel room to further expose her to prosecution. Will this guy stop at nothing?

Evil Powers/Weapons: The frame-up.

Occupation: Insane cop.

Intelligence: Clever.

Strengths: He is a cop.

Weaknesses: He goes too far.

Territory: The border area between the United States and Mexico.

Idiosyncrasies: Candy-obsessed, smokes cigars.

Friends: His cronies and his partner until they double-cross him.

Enemies: Vargas.

Evil Deeds: The frame-up is his specialty. He will do anything if you oppose him. He endangers Susan, kills Grandi, has a lot of blood on his record. His arrests are largely illegal.

Outcome: Quinlan's faithful partner, Menzies, can't take this. He finds Quinlan's cane near the murder victim, realizes what happened, and is pressured by Vargas to expose Quinlan. Menzies records Quinlan admitting his crimes. The mad cop discovers this and shoots Menzies. Menzies, with his last dying breath, also shoots Quinlan. They die and the news comes that the bomber, Sanchez, has confessed to his crimes. All has been for nothing. How ironic. Now cleared, Susan and her husband go away.

Current Status: Dead.
What to Do If You Meet: He'll frame you if you cross him.
Worthy of Note: Definitely first rate.

Nurse Rached

Alias: Big Nurse
Born: 1930s
Died: Possibly still alive

Starred in:
One Flew Over the Cuckoo's Nest
United Artists, 1975
Director: Milos Forman
Played by: Louise Fletcher

Description: Puffy-faced nurse, dressed in white nurse's outfit. Cruel, cold, compassionless. Always carries her keys.

Reasons for Villainy: To escape the horrid boredom of a prison work farm, Randle P. McMurphy (Jack Nicholson) pretends to go insane and is transferred to a mental hospital. As a "free" spirit he immediately comes into conflict with Nurse Rached, who rules over her charges like a dictator, controlling their every action. McMurphy quickly realizes that most of the patients in the hospital are not insane but emotional misfits who had hard times. Their vulnerability makes them easy victims for the sadistic hospital staff, especially Nurse Rached who delights in handing out harsh punishments for the slightest misbehavior. McMurphy tries to bring life to the patients by organizing games and fieldtrips. But Nurse Rached, seeing her power threatened, becomes determined to destroy him.

Weapons: Her staff, straitjackets, drugs, electric shock, lobotomies.

Evil Powers: Cruel and sadistic, Nurse Rached has huge power in the hospital as its head nurse.

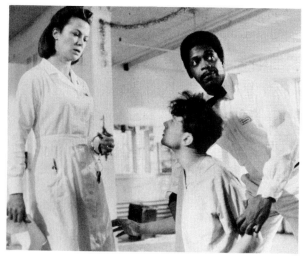

Evil Nurse Rached (Louis Fletcher) sends out another patient to be lobotomized in One Flew Over the Cuckoo's Nest.

Occupation: Chief nurse of insane asylum.

Intelligence: Quite intelligent. She sees herself as benign, trying to do what's best for the patients.

Strengths: Power of the self-righteous.

Weaknesses: Can't stand to see a spirit stronger than her own.

Headquarters: Mental hospital.

Idiosyncrasies : Keeps her thumb on the patients, and won't allow even the slightest trace of fun or individuality.

Friends: Other staff members.

Enemies: The patients, especially McMurphy.

Relatives: The staff of *The Snake Pit*.

Evil Deeds: She keeps her patients in mindless states. Through drugs and lobotomies she has also destroyed countless numbers of harmless, frightened people.

Outcome: The patients grow to love McMurphy, calling him "Mac" as he helps them grow into real people. Soon they begin disobeying Nurse Rached. In retaliation, she gives McMurphy an electric shock. McMurphy survives and plots an escape with Chief Bromden (Will Sampson), whom he befriends. Billy, a patient whom Mac tries to help, is driven to suicide by Rached. Maddened beyond control, McMurphy tries to strangle her and, in turn, is lobotomized, which transforms him into a vegetable. As an act of mercy, and to save his soul from Nurse Rached, Chief Bromden smothers McMurphy and escapes. Nurse Rached has regained control of the hospital, but lost, in a metaphysical way, her battle with McMurphy with his death.

Current Status: Nurse Rached is still alive and ruining men's minds.

What to Do If You Meet: Agree with everything she says or it's lobotomy time.

Worthy of Note: The film won five Oscars.

Captain Juan Ramon

Born: 1800s
Died: 1830s

Starred in:
The Mark of Zorro
United Artists, 1940
Director: Rouben Mamoulian
Played by: Basil Rathbone

Description: Juan is a stubborn man, and also a master fencer. He is tall and dark with pointy sideburns on his long face. He sports a sharp moustache, as do many bad guys. He wears a tight white outfit with wide sleeves—perfect for fencing movements—with a black sash belt. He has wader-type knee-high boots that are especially designed for movement.

Reason for Villainy: The Captain is the usurper of the legitimate government in Spanish-controlled California. Don Diego Vega, a.k.a. Zorro, the fox (Tyrone Power), is the son of the deposed governor. Vega has returned from Madrid and he vows revenge on the evil of Captain Ramon. However, Vega cannot outwardly oppose the new leadership of California. There is a lot of cruelty and unfair taxation, and people will help him only if he becomes the dashing Zorro—the black-clad figure that carves a Z on the walls everywhere. Vega appears to be a weakling, a coward, a silly, useless fop. Secretly he goes out in disguise and confounds the tyrant's swordsmen. Our villain puts a huge reward on Zorro's head, but who can claim it? The new evil governor (Ramon is his assistant and the real evil) has a comely daughter. Zorro falls for her, and she for him. But she hates Vega, until she discovers that they are one and the same man. They will wed when the nasty Captain Ramon is disposed of. But Ramon is a master of swordsmanship and perhaps too much a match for Zorro. Who will win?

Evil Powers/Weapons: His swordsmanship, his control of California and its troops, and his reputation.

Occupation: True tyrant of California.

Intelligence: Strategy in fencing is his forte, plus he has read Don Quixote.

Strengths: Master swordsmanship.

Weaknesses: He's up against the best—Zorro.

Territory: Spanish-held California.

Idiosyncrasies: Can't stand the letter Z.

Friends: His men.

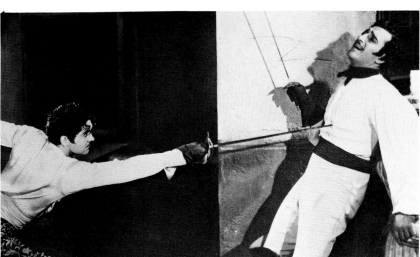

Zorro plunges through Captain Juan Ramon (Basil Rathbone) in The Mark of Zorro.

Enemies: Zorro.

Evil Deeds: Taxation without fairness, cruelty, usurpation, running through his opponents, rebellion against the crown of Spain.

Outcome: Zorro must put an end to this evil Captain, but how? First he must stop the Captain's right-hand man, Garcia. Zorro defeats Garcia so often that the half-fool decides to side with Zorro because he feels that Ramon mistreats him anyway. Our heroine is bothered by the lecherous Ramon, but Zorro interrupts the lustful lunger. He engages him in terminal swordsplay. Pierced to the heart, the evil Captain Ramon will not bother any other young senoritas again. Zorro unmasks, and there is a great fiesta. The wicked swordsman is dead.

Current Status: Run through, and dead.

What to Do If You Meet: Stick that little button on the end of his rapier.

Worthy of Note: Most versions of Zorro don't come close to this one because Rathbone was a genuine sword master.

Raven

Alias: Philip Raven
Born: Around 1910
Died: 1942

Starred in:
This Gun for Hire
Paramount, 1942
Director: Frank Tuttle
Played by: Alan Ladd

Description: He wears a raincoat with the collar up, a snap-brim hat, and a hidden gun. He makes slow, paranoid movements. Your basic shifty-eyed loser.

Reason for Villainy: Philip Raven is a psychotic gun-for-hire who is contracted by Willard Gates (Laird Cregar) to hit someone who knows that Gates's boss is selling secret formulas to the Nazis. Raven does his dirty duty and

Raven (Alan Ladd) walks calmly downstairs after having just shot someone upstairs in This Gun for Hire.

collects, but the green stuff is hot money. Detective Michael Crane (Robert Preston) tracks Raven. Meanwhile, Raven is looking to bump off Gates. On the train to L.A., Raven meets Ellen Graham (Veronica Lake), who is Crane's fiancee. The female singer has a heart for the loser and helps him hide from the coppers. Raven helps the government find out who Gates's boss is. Alvin Brewster (Tully Marshall) is the chief traitor. Raven also falls for warm, sexy Ellen. She has a soft spot for him too, within limits.

Evil Powers/Weapons: Efficient and cold killer with gun. Amoral. He will do anyone in for the right price.

Occupation: Hitman.

Intelligence: Below average, but a good hunter, tracker and killer.

Strengths: Resourceful at surviving.

Weaknesses: Depressed psychotic.

Territory: Los Angeles.

Idiosyncrasies: Loves cats. Always giving them milk.

Friends: Cats, Ellen.

Enemies: Nazis, the cops, the FBI, and his parents who pathologically mistreated him.

Evil Deeds: Has killed scores of people for money (though most of them were gangsters and killers themselves).

Killed by: Raven confronts Brewster and forces a confession at gunpoint. Detective Crane comes through the window and shoots Raven. Raven dies happy knowing he has helped the only woman who was kind and caring to him.

Current Status: Dead.

What to Do If You Meet: Tell him you want to hire him to kill someone, but need to go to the cash machine for some moola.

Worthy of Note: Really a *noir* classic. Ladd plays one of his best roles as the paranoid but somehow touching Raven.

Lonesome Rhodes

Born: 1900s
Died: Still alive, but ostracized by society

Starred in:
A Face in the Crowd
Warner Bros, 1957
Director: Elia Kazan
Played by: Andy Griffith

Description: Living media-legend Rhodes is country-bumpkin cute and smiles like hell. He has wavy light hair, an "aw shucks" self-effacing demeanor, a "homey" way of speaking, and sings insipid, friendly songs.

Reason for Villainy: Rhodes is a media-created monster. The charismatic, cornfed man is mad with power. It all begins when Marcia Jeffries (Patricia Neal), a talent scout, must come up with a format for a daytime TV program. Rhodes auditions. After all, he entertains his cornball friends with anecdotes and homilies mixed with songs, so why not?

He is a hit in Arkansas and soon is picked up by most networks. He is underestimated by his fellow TV workers. He is not as simple-minded as he seems. He starts dropping political hints to his vast TV following. He does favors for "interest groups," and then for an up-and-coming presidential aspirant. After the election he makes a callous deal to become politically powerful himself.

Evil Powers/Weapons: The voice of the media is heard throughout the land.

Occupation: TV personality, popular philosopher.

Intelligence: Clever and witty.

Strengths: His image.

Weaknesses: His real nature, if revealed.

Territory: Arkansas, then the nation via the boob-tube.

Idiosyncrasies: Cracker-barrel, down-home philosophy spouts from his mouth between silly tunes.

Friends: The people who make deals with him for plugs on his program.

Enemies: Eventually Marcia, and then the world.

Evil Deeds: He is a demagogue bent on power. He will build or destroy you depending on what you can give him in return.

Outcome: Marcia is able to understand the great threat to the world that this homey philosopher of the airwaves poses. However, the media controllers don't want to destroy his multimillion-dollar image, which makes a lot

Lonesome Rhodes (Andy Griffith) begins assuming more and more authority as a result of his successful TV show in A Face in the Crowd.

of people a lot of money. She sneaks up in the control room as he is going off the air. The mad country philosopher Rhodes is speaking off the record. He is voicing his real, hateful, manipulative opinions. Marcia leaps for the switch and turns the sound back up so the whole nation can hear his callous, greedy comments. Television technicians try to restrain her but she manages to destroy the personality she had unleashed on the world.

Current Status: Sitting by his phone waiting for a call from a producer.

What to Do If You Meet: Take his crackerbox philosophy with a little salt.

Worthy of Note: Of course, nowadays most shows are not broadcast live. The video tape revolution would have made his exposure impossible. We could be controlled by people similar to Rhodes this very moment.

Rico

Alias: Little Caesar
Born: 1890s
Died: 1920s

Starred in:
Little Caesar
First National, 1930
Director: Mervyn LeRoy
Played by: Edward G. Robinson

Description: This gangster wears a roundish, expensive hat, a camel-hair coat with velvet collar, expensive shirts and cufflinks, and diagonally striped ties. He's got a diamond pinkie ring and a sour expression.

Reason for Villainy: Rico holds up a gas station with his cohort, Joe Massaro (Douglas Fairbanks, Jr.). Rico thinks this is small time, so he dreams of Chicago and the big jobs. He heads for the Windy City and pushes his way into Sam Vettori's (Stanley Field's) gang. Sam Stanley calls him a Little Caesar. Eventually

Edward G. Robinson plays the notorious gangster Rico in Little Caesar.

he takes Vettori's place and rises toward the top of the rackets. This impresses the big boys, especially "Big Boy" himself (Sidney Blackmer). Big Boy lets Rico take over from Diamond Pete. Rico sees his meteoric rise as a triumph of his ambition and cleverness, and he is proud and never thinks negatively about his career. Crime is as natural to him as mom and apple pie is to America. His racketeers blast themselves a new niche in American myths, making the world safe for no one but the frightened men who "pay off." But Rico's star starts falling when the teetotaler begins drinking his own booze.

Evil Powers/Weapons: Rico uses his gang well. They use machine guns, run down people, and use their tommy guns effectively to make the other mobs give up territory. Rico is the boss. No one messes with Rico, see? Or they wind up in a cement overcoat talking to the fishes in the lake, you got that, see?

Occupation: Gangster.

Intelligence: Ambition rules his house. Intelligence is lacking.

Strengths: Great drive, can intimidate by pointing at you.

Weaknesses: Doesn't look to the future. He doesn't have any. Criminals will be punished.

Territory: Chicago, Chicago, what a wonderful gangster town.

Idiosyncrasies : Says "Gnnnnaaaaaa" instead of yeah.

Friends: His mobsters and his mother.

Enemies: The legitimate, hard-working suckers without diamond stickpins and fancy dames.

Evil Deeds: Extortion, murder, theft, speeding, failure to obey the directions of a traffic officer, sadism.

Killed by: Rico is an egotist, and he especially doesn't like people who talk back much. Aside from that, he's not very moral, and doesn't think twice about bumping off anyone who tries to stop him. This arrogance, of course, leads to his fall and he is shot down. Dying, he cries out incredulously, "Mother of Mercy, is this the end of Rico?"

Current Status: Dead.

What to Do If You Meet: Say you'll play ball and don't like cement coats.

Worthy of Note: When this film came out, few moviegoers had ever seen such violence. The censors were appalled, but gangster films passed if the gangster met a bad end. They seemed to serve a moral purpose. However, in 1934 the "Legion Of Decency" made such movies a no-no. Even in this film you couldn't show any details on how to commit a crime. Unlike today, films weren't protected by the First Amendment. Films were viewed by the court as "an entertainment" and subject to rigid censorship.

Johnny Rocco

Born: Early 1900s
Died: 1940

Starred in:
Key Largo
Warner Bros., 1948
Director: John Huston
Played by: Edward G. Robinson

Description: Gangster extraordinaire. Short, a braggart, and vain. He is a snarling bull terrier. He wears what he calls "high class" duds, and he has diamonds on his pinky. He smokes bad but expensive cigars, which stink up the places he's been.

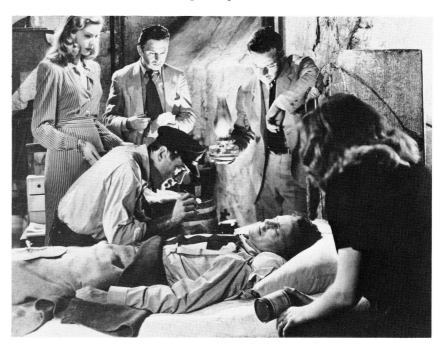

Frank McCloud helps a wounded sheriff who was shot by two desperate Indians framed by Johnny Rocco in Key Largo.

Reason for Villainy: Johnny Rocco is on the lam from the coppers. He and his gang have taken over a resort in Key Largo, Florida. Frank McCloud (Humphrey Bogart) is a guest there. He passes up an early opportunity to kill Rocco because there's no percentage in it for himself. Later, he wishes he had done the meanie in. But McCloud, a war veteran, is sick of strife and wants to weather the whole thing through, just like they plan to weather the approaching hurricane. The hurricane, cutting off his escape, panics Rocco, who likes to think he's a god. Thankfully, he isn't. A sheriff comes to look for his missing deputy, who has been killed by Rocco. Rocco, however, fingers two fearful Seminoles. When the Indians try to escape they are shot by the sheriff. McCloud decides that he has had enough.

Weapons: His guns. Without his guns he's a scaredy-cat.

Occupation: Gangster.

Intelligence: Sniveling, cowardly, and defensively clever.

Strengths: He trusts bullets and bad guys.

Weaknesses: McCloud pretends to be a bad guy, taking in this sucker.

Territory: Chicago and all points of the compass where crime is rampant.

Idiosyncrasies : Gnnnnnnnaaaaaaaa, what eccentricities, see?

Friends: Tommy guns.

Enemies: Society, decent standards and ideals, the American way.

Relatives: Could be second cousin to big Al Capone.

Outcome: McCloud tells Rocco that for a cut he will pilot a boat to Cuba—a haven for gangsters—with Rocco aboard. Instead, McCloud battles and kills Rocco, wounding himself in the struggle. Nora (Lauren Bacall) welcomes McCloud back and treats his wounds. It is here the famous line "If you want me, just whistle. You know how to whistle, don't you?" is spoken. It all goes to prove, probably, that the movie-going public demands a happy ending. So does society. Incidentally, McCloud got the gat from Rocco's spurned mistress.

Current Status: Prying gold off St. Peter's gate.

What to Do If You Meet: Don't meet him, ever.

Worthy of Note: The problems of the returning veteran was the theme of this film. But, of course, it's the atmosphere and Bogart and Bacall that get the attention here.

Rochefort

Born/Died: Royalist times

Starred in:
The Four Musketeers
20th Century Fox, 1975
Director: Richard Lester
Played by: Christopher Lee

Description: Rochefort has mustaches and wears a hat with ample feathers, as a cavalier should. Has an eyepatch on his right eye. His hair is dark and shoulder length. He wears royal purples and brilliant reds with embroidered buttonholes. Yet, he's not a fop. He's a mean swordsman in league with the evil Milady.

Reason for Villainy: Rochefort is helping Milady (Faye Dunaway) in her revenge against the gallant D'Artagnan, who thwarted her attempt to discredit the Queen (Geraldine Chaplin). Along with D'Artagnan (Michael York), she intends to bring down Constance (Raquel Welch) and the Duke of Buckingham (Simon Ward). Luring D'Artagnan with sexual favors, she tries to kill him, but he is on guard in an instant. She instructs Rochefort to go and seize Constance, the chivalrous D'Artagnan's beloved. While this is occuring, she goes to England and uses her wiles to entice the Duke. (All of this is done in sweeping scenes filled with costume and color in a magnificent tradition of epic movie-making.) She manages to plunge a long dagger into his heart. In the meantime, Constance has been taken by our villain Rochefort to a retreat high on the coast of Italy. The noble D'Artagnan hears of this and the death of his pal Buckingham. Will Rochefort and Milady triumph?

Evil Powers/Weapons: His sword, stealth, intrigue, and money. Milady is on his side with her feminine wiles.

Occupations: Swordsman, killer, intriguer.

Intelligence: Rochefort is sharp.

Strengths: The tip of his rapier.

Weaknesses: The Musketeers and D'Artagnan are after him.

Territory: Royalist France and England.

Idiosyncrasies: None.

Friends: Milady.

Enemies: D'Artagnan.

Evil Deeds: Kidnaps, abuses, murders, and plans intrigue against the crown.

Outcome: The Four Musketeers storm the retreat where Constance is being held by Rochefort. In a daring duel with D'Artagnan, Rochefort is run through quite thoroughly and he dies. Unfortunately, Constance has been murdered by Milady. But the story is not over yet. The Musketeers decide that Milady deserves a fate that no one would want. They hire a black executioner. The ghoulish beheader carries out his grim duty once a price has been set and Milady's evil days are over along with Rochefort's. This then is the end of all who oppose the Four Musketeers!

Current Status: Dead.

What to Do If You Meet: Say you don't get the point and leave.

Worthy of Note: This is the even-better-than-the-original sequel to Lester's brilliant *Three Musketeers*. Bravo.

Roy and the Driver

Alias: The Redneck Killers

Born: 1940s

Died: Still alive and killing hippie types.

Starred in:
Easy Rider
Columbia Pictures, 1969
Director: Dennis Hopper
Played by: David C. Billodeau, Johnny
   David

Roy (David C. Billodeau) and the driver wait for more hippie types to shoot in Easy Rider.

Description: Ruddy faces from sitting in the sun spouting racist garbage to one another. Hateful eyes accustomed to drawing beads on helpless animals. Spitting, cussin' incarnations of stupidity and cruelty. The older redneck wears a hat and likes to drive, the younger redneck would rather sit and shoot.

Reason for Villainy: Well, the story begins in California. Two druggie motorcycle fanatics, Captain America (Peter Fonda) and Billy (Dennis Hopper) start out for the East and their dream of freedom and fun. They have it pretty swell at first, stopping and loving along the way in friendly country-folks' places, in hippie communes, and sunny fields of flowers. Then the going gets choppy. They have to start dealing heavy drugs to support themselves. How can they hope to succeed when they finance their trip with the bad karma of dealing hard drugs? Well, they'll worry about that later. They are into symbolism in this youth-oriented, alienated tale. They even throw away their watches—time doesn't matter, man, you dig? All of this, however, catches up to them. Out there driving down those mean roads are some fearsome, hippie-hating rednecks with long guns.

Evil Powers/Weapons: These rednecks have the heavy truck, the guns, the time, and the inclination. They want to destroy non-conformity.

Occupation: Redneck killers.
Intelligence: Badass stupid.
Strengths: Have guns.

Weaknesses: Their brains.
Territory: The road.
Idiosyncrasies: Cain't hardly think none.
Friends: The bullets they use.
Enemies: Hippie types.

Evil Deeds: Shoot forest creatures, and take deadly aim at Captain America and Billy.

Outcome: Well, the killers just take the opportunity. They see the hippies on their wild bikes and decide to blast them when they get the finger from the duo. It's relatively easy, and there are no witnesses. They'll go home and have a beer and cuss out the young-generation, commie types and sleep well. They get away. No problem. Who would try to find the killers of a pair of drugged-out drifters?

Current Status: Alive and laughing, shining their guns.

What to Do If You Meet: Stay some place populous.

Worthy of Note: This was Hollywood's attempt to deal with the drugged-out end of the flower-power movement. It worked.

Colonel Saito 198
Sal and Sonny 199
Scanlon 200
The Scorpio Killer 201
The Scorpion 202
Hunt Sears 203
Alexander
    Sebastian 204
Leo Sellars 206
Ned and William
    Sharp 207
Long John Silver 208
Roger Simmons 209
Emma Small 210
Jimmy Smith and
    Gregory Powell 211

Perry Smith
    and
    Dick Hickok 212
Virgil Starkwell 213
Camilla
    Sternwood 214
Dr. Stevenson 215
Dr. Strangelove 216
The Stranger 217
Major Strasser 219
Szell 220

Colonel Saito

Born: Around 1900
Died: 1945

Starred in:
Bridge on the River Kwai
Columbia Pictures, 1957
Director: David Lean
Played by: Sessue Hayakawa

Description: The Colonel, five feet, seven inches, is tall for a Japanese man of that era. He wears a pith helmet against the insufferable Southeast Asian heat. His uniform is neat and well pressed. His manner is always precise and military.

Reason for Villainy: Colonel Saito runs a prisoner of war camp in the jungle with an iron hand. His mission is to use the Allied prisoners as workers to construct a huge bridge for Japanese supply convoys. But Colonel Nicholson (Alec Guinness) is about to flaunt the rules. He insists that his men cannot participate in helping the enemy. The Japanese military man is incensed and puts Nicholson in a sweatbox, and does various other tortures to him. Nicholson

Colonel Saito (Sessue Hayakawa) slaps the British Colonel Nicholson after he refuses to have his men work on the Bridge on the River Kwai.

won't relent. Then the wily Oriental gets a better idea. The prisoners will not work, but will design and plan the bridge from inception to completion. Nicholson agrees and he and his men throw their best efforts into the grand bridge.

However, an American has escaped from the camp and made his way to safety through the jungle. This man, Shears (William Holden), informs the Allies about the base and the bridge. Major Warden (Jack Hawkins) wants Shears to lead his men back to the prisoner camp and help blow up the bloody bridge. Shears agrees and they are off. The British prisoners are building the best damned bridge the Cinemascope wide screen has ever seen, and they aren't about to let anyone, British or otherwise, destroy it. The sheer idiocy of war won't end their great work. Or is it the sheer idiocy of their work will not be ended by the war?

The universal themes of the insanity of war, man's cruelty to man, man's heroism and need to accomplish goals, and, ultimately, the futility of accomplishing the wrong things in life made this an Academy Award winner.

Evil Powers/Weapons: He's got lots of tortures for the prisoners and, especially, Nicholson. These include near starvation and the sun-baked, tiny, sweatbox exclosure.

Occupation: Japanese military commander.

Intelligence: He's a clever war criminal.

Strengths: He's got the Japanese Empire behind him, plus his sense of duty.

Weaknesses: He's a stickler for doing a good job, even more than winning.

Territory: The Southeast Asian jungle.

Idiosyncrasies: Stays crisp in the heat.

Friends: The Emperor.

Enemies: The Allies and Nicholson.

Evil Deeds: Innumerable tortures of British prisoners.

Outcome: The commandoes come and start planting charges to blow up the bloody impressive bridge. Nicholson himself warns Saito because he can't stand to see his ultimate achievement blown apart. As a result, the Japanese spring into action and Shears is killed. Realizing what a bloody thing he's done, Nicholson and his men blow the bridge up themselves. The bridge falls in one of the best action sequences since the parting of the

Red Sea in *The Ten Commandments*. The audience sees the end of the well-constructed bridge as a bloody insanity through the eyes of a British medic.

Current Status: Dead.

What to Do If You Meet: Do anything to avoid the tiny sweatbox.

Worthy of Note: Academy Awards for Best Actor (Alex Guinness) and Best Picture were given to this film.

Sal and Sonny

Born: Around 1940
Died: 1975

Starred in:
Dog Day Afternoon
Warner Bros., 1975
Director: Sidney Lumet
Played by: John Cazale, Al Pacino

Description: Sal is five feet, nine inches tall and has a tense way of looking around as if he's paranoid. He has long hair parted in middle, sweat dangling from his nose, and speaks about the evils of cigarette smoking, and mumbles that he won't go back to prison. He also carries a mean looking sawed-off rifle. Wears loud ties. Sonny is shorter, thin, and nervous. He wears an open sport shirt and does all the negotiating. He's the sharpie.

Reason for Villainy: Based on a real incident this story takes place on a dog day summer afternoon in New York City. It all begins when Sal and Sonny, plus a third man who chickens out, attempt to rob a bank in Flatbush, Brooklyn. The problem is that the bank had just had most of its cash taken away. Worse, police begin closing in, taking up headquarters across the street. Soon Sonny suspects something is up, and he gets a call from Police Captain Moretti. Moretti asks what the hell is goin on in there, and Sonny denies that

It's a Dog Day Afternoon for these two inept bank robbers.

anything is wrong. The tellers and bank officers become hostages to the pair of desperadoes as negotiations over the phone continue. Sonny asks Sal what country he'd like to escape to. Sal says Wyoming. So it goes. It's a dog day afternoon. A camaraderie develops between Sonny and Sal and the tellers. When some are offered their freedom, they refuse, preferring to stick together. Weird. At last it is arranged for Sonny to speak to his gay lover, Leon. Leon (Chris Sarandon) swishes over to the scene and gets on the phone from across the street as young cops smirk. He's quite effeminate. As a matter of fact, it is discovered that Sonny planned the robbery to get money to pay for Leon's sex-change operation. The cops finally agree for Sonny and Sal—plus some hostages—to drive to the airport and board an escape plane. But the FBI is in on it now.

Weapons: They have guns. They have hostages. Sal is really desperate—he would rather go down in a shower of bullets than go to prison again. That puts Sonny in a bind. He'd rather not die, but instead make a deal, release the hostages, and cop a plea in court.

Occupation: Unsuccessful bank robbers.

Intelligence: Sonny is bright. Sal needs help.

Strengths: They have hostages.

Weaknesses: They really would never be permitted to carry their terror into the sky.

Territory: Brooklyn, New York City.

Idiosyncrasies: Sonny is gay and strange. Sal is a desperate loser.

Friends/Enemies: The cops are both friends and enemies. But the FBI doesn't kid around. They want them both dead.

Evil Deeds: Siege of a Brooklyn bank.

Outcome: Sonny's wife hears about the situation on the radio. She calls the bank, and so does a radio station. Everyone gets in on the act. Crazies gather in the street, some rooting for Sonny and Sal. There's pandemonium. At last the van arrives, the hostages and Sonny and Sal go to it, and they drive to the airport. The driver is an FBI agent specializing in killing. It is obvious Sonny wants it to end, but Sal is the problem. At the airport, the FBI man seizes an opportunity and blasts Sal dead with a secret gun. It is over. Sonny is led away to jail, the hostages are free. The 747 warming up on the runway cuts its engines. Another story in the bizarre city ends.

Current Status: Sal is dead. Sonny cops a plea and gets 10 years.

What to Do If You Meet: Bungling bandits are the most dangerous—especially Sal's type. He'd rather die than surrender. Stay away.

Worthy of Note: Lots of nominations. A great flick.

Scanlon

Born: 1920s
Died: 1951

Starred in:
The Racket
RKO, 1951
Director: John Cromwell
Played by: Robert Ryan

Description: Old-time, pinstriped, brute-force gangster with the style and manners of

Scanlon is gunned down after being set up by his own syndicate in The Racket.

violence. He has an aquiline nose, feisty brown eyes, and he wears the most expensive cuff links. Always has a .38 in his shoulder holster.

Reason for Villainy: In a corrupt Midwestern city, an election is scheduled. It's the mob's politicians—who might reach as high as the governor—versus the good guys. Captain McQuigg (Robert Mitchum) is a tough, no-nonsense type of cop who tears up writs of habeas corpus. He makes getting Scanlon—who is a mid-level hood—a personal vendetta. Alas, the fun of their confrontation is being ruined by modern times. A more genteel police constabulary and criminal syndicate are cozying up to one another for a more low-profile sort of detente. Scanlon and McQuigg are woefully outdated. You see, it's brute force with these guys. Personal, you get me?

Prosecutor Welch and Inspector Turck (Ray Collins and William Conrad) are part of the sinister racket. They keep trying to pry McQuigg out of his boxed-in view of things. He'd do much better promotionwise and healthwise to lay off the Racket. But nooooooooo. Yet, on the other side of the tracks, Scanlon, our villain, is having much the same trouble. Why doesn't he go for more low-profile activities, ask his underworld bosses? Why draw attention to a good thing by such nasty behavior?

Weapons: Guns, knives, and snarls.

Occupation: Racket boss, mid-level (GS-18).

Intelligence: Scanlon is bright.

Strengths: Determination.

Weaknesses: High-profile.

Territory: Midwestern city during election time.

Idiosyncrasies: Loves fighting.

Friends: The old ways.

Enemies: The modern world, McQuigg, eventually his bosses in the racket.

Evil Deeds: Scanlon, aside from the usual bumping off of rivals, flaunts the law, and that angers McQuigg.

Killed by: The bosses instigate Scanlon in his desire to eliminate another gangster. However, they withdraw their protection from Scanlon, figuring him to be too much of a risk to have around. Somebody has to be apprehended, why not this turkey? So they pass the word that it's okay to unleash McQuigg and let the guy close in on our villain. McQuigg is only too anxious to put an end to Scanlon's activities. Alone and alienated, Scanlon is cut down—but not by McQuigg. McQuigg could stop Scanlon's rub-out, but he doesn't. McQuigg is just as much out of sync with the times. Violence is the man's thing. In this film, perhaps, the villain is drawn with sympathy. His violence is straightforward. Turck's corruptness and the evil maneuverings of the racket in the halls of justice are somehow much greater evils than the aboveboard gangsterism of Scanlon.

Current Status: Pushing up daisies.

What to Do If You Meet: Say you don't care about writs of habeas corpus. Yell "clear out, punk."

Worthy of Note: Nominally this film is set in the late 1940s but harks of the 1920s. Perhaps this is the film's problem; it wants to be universal and isn't.

The Scorpio Killer

Born: 1940s
Died: 1960s

Dirty Harry shoots the Scorpio Killer in the shoulder, freeing the hostage.

Starred in:
Dirty Harry
Warner Bros., 1971
Director: Don Siegel
Played by: Andy Robinson

Description: Wild-haired, blonde youth with a sniper rifle, handgun, and ragged clothes. Wears gloves.

Reason for Villainy: Scorpio is the brutal murderer of young girls in San Francisco. He threatens to keep killing unless city officials come up with 100 grand. Dirty Harry (Clint Eastwood) delivers the dough, with his .44 magnum ready for action. At the meeting place, a monument, Scorpio makes Harry throw away the gun and proceeds to punch and kick the cop bloody. But Harry pulls a secret knife and wounds the villain, who gets away.

Evil Powers: Takes advantage of the lack of control of criminals to flaunt justice. Evil, psychotic, capable of performing any hideousness.

Weapons: His main weapon is the inefficient, mollycoddling justice system which he uses to advantage. Also carries a pistol.

Occupation: Rapist, extortionist, criminal.

Intelligence: Average, but clever at using bureaucracy against itself.

Strengths: Single minded, imaginative, violent.

Weaknesses: Taunts the wrong cop—Dirty Harry.

Territory: San Francisco.

Idiosyncrasies: Mad laughter, loves to taunt police.

Friends: Liberal judges, do-gooders, liberal sympathizers.

Enemies: Cops who go beyond the law to get him.

Evil Deeds: Extortion, snipings, torture, rape, hurting kids and mothers. Asks to be beaten by a professional sadist so he can claim police brutality against Harry.

Killed by: Harry captures Scorpio at a stadium after wounding the psycho in the leg. But the liberal judges let him go for lack of evidence. Is there a message here? Harry is forced to go after Scorpio on his own. Scorpio commandeers a schoolbus full of schoolchildren, but Harry jumps on top. Scorpio crashes bus near a quarry and grabs one of the children as protection. Harry manages to shoot Scorpio in the shoulder, knocking him to the ground and freeing the child. Harry approaches the wounded psycho who is eyeing his own gun only inches away. "I can't remember if I used up all my shots," Harry says. "Do you feel lucky?" Scorpio reaches for his pistol and Harry blows his head away.

Current Status: Dead, but hundreds more just like him are out there hunting.

What to Do If You Meet: Change all loose laws before you meet him or you won't be around to worry about it.

Worthy of Note: Harry was supposed to be played by John Wayne, who turned the part down. The character made Clint Eastwood a super superstar and a bundle of money.

The Scorpion

Alias: Professor Bentley
Born: 1911
Died: 1942

Now that the Scorpion has the statue and all the lenses, the death ray is at his disposal in the Adventures of Captain Marvel.

Starred in:
Adventures of Captain Marvel
Republic, 1941
Directors: William Witney, John English
Played by: Harry Worth

Description: As the Scorpion, he wears a full-length black robe embossed with scorpions on the forehead hood and chest. As Professor Bentley, he is a middle-aged scientist of average looks. He wears reading glasses and has self-effacing speech.

Reason for Villainy: In far-away Siam, the Malcolm Ex expedition comes upon a primitive tribe guarding a sacred cave. Inside is the guardian of the tomb, called Shazam. Billy Batson (Frank Coghlan Jr.) is confronted by the wizened guardian (Nigel de Brulier) and is given the power to become Captain Marvel, a flying superman, by merely saying the word "shazam." Meanwhile, the scientists of the expedition have found the golden scorpion statue and it has multiple special lenses, which, if focused together, make a death ray. They divide the lenses amongst them. Back in the good old U.S.A., crooks plot to steal all the lenses. They are led by the mysterious "Scorpion." It becomes obvious that one of the scientists from the expedition is the "Scorpion." But who? Finally, only one special lens remains out of the Scorpion's slimy hands. He must have it. Then he can rule the world—or blow it up.

Evil Powers/Weapons: When he gets the last lens, he will have the power of a disintegrator death ray. In the meantime, he has guns and a gang.

Occupation: Scientist and hoodlum.

Intelligence: Brilliant, but power mad.

Strengths: He has his gang.

Weaknesses: Very much in need of one more lens.

Territory: Siam, U.S.A.

Idiosyncrasies: Wears a black robe, and looks silly in it.

Friends: His gang.

Enemies: Captain Marvel, a.k.a. Billy Batson.

Evil Deeds: Steals the lenses, kills several scientists, kidnaps Betty, threatens the world.

Outcome: The Scorpion has seen Marvel change back into Billy. Puzzled, he kidnaps Billy. He now has all the lenses and fits them into the golden scorpion device. He threatens to use it on Billy and his friends, unless Billy will show him how he can turn himself into a superman. Billy nods (he is gagged). The minute the gag is removed he shouts "shazam" and he becomes Captain Marvel (Tom Tyler). He rescues his friends by doing his super fighting, and unmasks the Scorpion. Why, it's nice Professor Bentley! Curses, foiled again.

Current Status: Incarcerated, but rumored to have died in an escape attempt.

What to Do If You Meet: This scientist is only dangerous when he has the lenses. Thank heavens they are now in the arsenal of the U.S. Armed Forces, ready in case of an enemy attack.

Worthy of Note: Captain Marvel was killed by Superman some years later—in a law suit.

Hunt Sears

Alias: The AMPCO Corp. President
Born: 1930s
Died: Still alive

Starred in:
The Electric Horseman
Universal, 1979
Director: Sydney Pollack
Played by: John Saxon

Description: Tight-assed, rigid, short black hair, wears wirerim glasses, deadpan expression, $800 pinstriped suits.

Reason for Villainy: As AMPCO's head, Hunt Sear is exploiting rodeo star Sonny Steele (Robert Redford) to promote his company's cereal. Sonny must appear at countless shows, wearing garrish outfits, for publicity. In Las Vegas, Sonny must wear a flashing electric cowboy suit while riding the $12 million horse

The cold Hunt Sears (John Saxon) listens to some of his men discuss the growing public fascination with the escape of Sonny and Rising Star in The Electric Horseman.

Rising Star. Hally Martin (Jane Fonda), a reporter, quizzes Sonny about Ranch breakfast cereal, and whether he really likes it. Angry at his exploitation, Sonny confronts Sears, who tells his cronies to dump Sonny. Sonny finding out that the horse is to be dangerously drugged up for an upcoming extravaganza, rides right off the stage and into the desert to save the animal—electric lights flashing.

Evil Powers/Weapons: All the corporate powers of a megaconglomerate. Powers of money, influence, etc.

Occupation: AMPCO's chief officer.

Intelligence: Sneaky, callous, highly intelligent in a corporate, manipulative way.

Strengths: He has unlimited money.

Weaknesses: Can't accept nonconformity.

Territory: Las Vegas, U.S.A.

Idiosyncrasies: Sleeps in a suit and tie. Thinks like a robot.

Friends: Products that make money.

Enemies: Humanity and compassion.

Relatives: Leaders of the Ventana Corporation.

Evil Deeds: Tries to stop Sonny any way he can. Exploits people. Drugs horses.

Outcome: Hunt Sears realizes that if the truth about Rising Star being drugged gets out, all hell will break loose. Sears accuses Sonny of kidnapping and gets a warrant out. Hally finds Sonny, learns the truth (that he really cares about people and animals), and falls in love with him. She spreads the truth through her newspaper. After a daring series of escapes with the police in hot pursuit, Sonny and Rising Star become national media heroes. Unfortunately, Sears discovers that Ranch cereal is selling better than ever and decides to drop charges and exploit the "humanitarian" acts of Sonny, taking the credit for his link to the product. However, Sonny won't give the horse back and lets it go in the wilds.

Current Status: Alive and selling adulterated products.

What to Do If You Meet: Buy wholesome food and not the junk he advertises.

Worthy of Note: The inhumanity of corporate greed is depicted well. No wonder Jane is in this flick.

Alexander Sebastian

Born: 1900s
Died: late 1940s

Starred in:
Notorious
RKO Radio, 1946
Director: Alfred Hitchcock
Played by: Claude Rains

Description: Alexander Sebastian is a slimy, though outwardly personable, man of about forty with a secret penchant for Hitler. He is in a western hemisphere spy ring and his Rio parties are a cover for the activities of the Third Reich. No wonder he has a haughty, aristocratic demeanor. He's good looking and well-placed in society.

Reason for Villainy: Sebastian was once in love with Alicia Huberman (Ingrid Bergman), the daughter of a convicted Nazi spy. Devlin (Cary Grant) is a U.S. government agent sent to stop the Nazi ring that Sebastian heads. Devlin tests Alicia's loyalty to the U.S. and reluctantly enlists her in the fight for freedom. The gist of it is, she loves her father, but hates his ideals. She and Devlin go to Rio to break into the Nazi ring. Happily, the pair fall in love, even though Alicia pretends to be interested romantically with cunning spy Alexander Sebastian. Devlin decides to play down his true feelings for the good of his mission. Alicia and Sebastian are married and Alicia soon begins to send secret Nazi information to the U.S. agents.

Evil Powers/Weapons: Are you kidding? The Nazis weren't knitting sweaters over there in Europe, you know!

Occupation: Super Nazi spy.

Intelligence: Nazi super brain.

Strengths: The Reich is powerful, especially in South America.

Weaknesses: Devlin and Alicia are clever and true-blue patriots to the grand old flag.

Territory: Rio de Janeiro.

Idiosyncrasies: He's stupid in love. Why else would he come back to the overbearing prissy?

Friends: Schicklegruber himself. They went to art school together.

Enemies: The land of the free and the home of the brave.

Relatives: Mata Hari.

Evil Deeds: He's on Hitler's side, and you think he's a goodie? Bah, it would be better for a house to fall on him.

Outcome: The Nazi's secret seems to be in his wine cellar. To get access, Alicia asks her hubby to throw an enormous party. Alicia removes the key to the wine cellar from Sebastian's pockets. Alicia is startled when Sebastian opens her other hand to kiss it, then slowly begins to open the hand with the stolen key! She quickly wraps him in a big embrace and saves the day, and the audience's hearts. The vintage in the cellar, Devlin and Alicia find, is pure U-235, a liquid solution from which bombs are made. When Sebastian sees Devlin and Alicia near the cellar, they mask their real mission by kissing to make him jealous but less curious. Later, though, he spots a broken bottle by the U-235 and figures it out. Sebastian and his mother systematically begin to poison Alicia. The Nazis won't think they have failed and the Americans won't guess that Alicia is the victim of foul play. However, Devlin skips out on the other duty he's been assigned to and finds Alicia semi-conscious. Devlin tells her he really loves her and whisks her away in his arms. Sebastian, not

The Sebastians look like a respectable family but he is actually the head of a Nazi spy ring in Notorious.

wanting the other Nazis to know how he had let them be betrayed, helps Devlin and Alicia into a waiting car. But we all know that the Nazis will eventually find out and Sebastian and his buddies will meet their end.

Current Status: All hung up probably.

What to Do If You Meet: Yell "Seig Heil." When he stiffs his arm in salute, kick him in the shins and run.

Worthy of Note: The "key" scene is probably the best scene in any Hitchcock movie.

Leo Sellars

Born: 1940s
Died: 1975

Starred in:
Hustle
Paramount, 1975
Director: Robert Aldrich
Played by: Eddie Albert

Description: Sellars is graying, and has a sweet-looking face soured by too many angry outbursts. He is tall, well built, but he needs exercise; being a lawyer he often sits and broods. He wears a hand-tailored suit, not off-the-rack. There is strength in his character. He would be comfortable with a more active job.

Reason for Villainy: A girl is slain, or is it suicide? Lieutenant Phil Gaines (Burt Reynolds) wants to find out. The girl died from an overdose of pills and was found on a beach. Her parents identify her. The dead girl's father, Marty Hollinger (Ben Johnson), is insane with rage. He wants the guy responsible. The police lieutenant will investigate. Leo Sellars, a prominent but corrupt lawyer is identified in a photograph where the dead girl appears. Gaines thinks he's a good suspect. Sellars is also the lawyer responsible for bringing Gaines's girlfriend, Nicole (Catherine

The powerful and crooked lawyer Leo Sellars (Eddie Albert) has gotten Nicole into prostitution in Hustle.

Deneuve), into the U.S.A. Nicole, however, is a prostitute, who won't quit without guaranteed financial security. Hollinger is on the case, too, and gets beaten to a pulp while visiting the club where the dead daughter, Gloria, worked. Gaines later must tell Hollinger that his daughter was in porno films. Hollinger immediately blames Sellars.

Evil Powers/Weapons: Sellars has knowledge of what the law can and cannot do. He hides behind the law. He is into rackets and porno.

Occupation: Corrupt lawyer.

Intelligence: Criminal mind, brilliant in law.

Strengths: The careful way he conceals his activities.

Weaknesses: He can't stop a bereaved, insane father.

Territory: Los Angeles.

Idiosyncrasies: He's testy.

Friends: No one we can see.

Enemies: Lieutenant Gaines and Marty Hollinger.

Evil Deeds: He runs the rackets and is involved in porn and murder.

Outcome: Gaines is also out to get Sellars because he has gotten Nicole into prostitution. Hollinger is out for Sellars for his daughter's death. If he didn't do it overtly, Sellars is still responsible for the death. Sellars, however, has a legal way of avoiding retribution. Alienated and alone, both Hollinger and Gaines have much in common. Hollinger acts on his own, killing Sellars. The Lieutenant covers up for him by tampering with the evidence. But Gaines is killed shortly thereafter in the line of duty. This whole film twists about the guilt and innocence of various people, showing, as *Dirty Harry* does, that sometimes the law is not the right way. Justice demands going beyond the law.

Current Status: Dead.

What to Do If You Meet: He's the syndicate's lawyer—watch out.

Worthy of Note: Gaines is a less violent version, in some ways, of Dirty Harry.

Ned and William Sharp

Born: Early 1800s
Died: 1876

Starred in:
They Died with Their Boots On
Warner Bros., 1941
Director: Raoul Walsh
Played by: Arthur Kennedy and Walter
    Hampden

Description: The Sharps are sharp traders and saloon keepers. They do all they can to make life difficult for both the indians and Custer's soldiers. They also give aid and comfort to Crazy Horse and his Sioux indians in exchange for wampum. They are mean.

Reason for Villainy: George Custer and the Sharp brothers were cadets at West Point. Upperclassman Ned Sharp pulls a fast one on Custer by tricking him into lounging in the commander's quarters. From that moment until his graduation Custer is blacklisted. He does manage to meet Elizabeth (Olivia de Havilland), who wants him, but her father Samuel Bacon (Gene Lockhart) won't have the soldier as his son-in-law because of his record. Meanwhile, Custer goes off to the Civil War and distinguishes himself by making

clever moves. One incident accidentally gets him promoted to brigadier general. He is quickly given leadership of a run-down Western post, and discovers that Ned and William Sharp are traders that have kept the post's soldiers in a perpetual state of drunkenness. Perhaps this is why Crazy Horse is still on the rampage. Custer asserts his authority and throws the Sharps out. Boy, are our villains mad!

Evil Powers/Weapons: Whiskey, guns, and their hate of Custer.

Occupation: Traders, traitors, and exploiters.

Intelligence: Clever traders interested only in a buck.

Strengths: They are resourceful plotters.

Weaknesses: Custer is a formidable and clever opponent.

Territory: The West, more precisely Little Big Horn.

Idiosyncrasies: They can't wait to get even.

Friends: Disruption is their only friend.

Enemies: Custer.

Evil Deeds: They get the indians and soldiers very drunk. They also murder and conspire against the government, and, boy, do they smell.

Ned Sharp (Arthur Kennedy) and his brother are crooked traders who give General Custer a difficult time in They Died With Their Boots On.

Outcome: Custer, who was allowed to marry Elizabeth because of his heroic deeds, gets the post in shape. Custer even goes to Washington on behalf of the Indians. (This plays with history a bit.) The Sharps, however, have a plan to ruin Custer. They begin by spreading rumors that gold has been discovered in the area. The Indians, portrayed in this film as wronged people, go on the warpath when settlers start pouring into their territory looking for the gold. Custer must now make his move, but he also forces the Sharps unwillingly to Little Big Horn with him. There, in order to save the rest of the regiment, Custer maneuvers the men to stop the indians. Unfortunately, they all get trapped and die bravely, even the Sharps. Custer, of course, is the last to stand.

Current Status: Dead.

What to Do If You Meet: Call Washington and tell them to send more troops.

Worthy of Note: Nice western.

Long John Silver

Born: Pirate times
Died: Ditto

Starred in:
Treasure Island
MGM, 1934
Director: Victor Fleming
Played by: Wallace Beery

Description: Long John is identifiable by his peg leg, swarthy manner, garrulous, violent nature, and multiple, tarry dreadlocks (pigtails). You can smell him from quite a distance. A crutch and a parrot on his shoulder completes the picture.

Reason for Villainy: Long John is a pirate, flying the Jolly Roger flag, bent on booty and adventure. The tale begins at the Admiral Benbov Inn. Young Jim Hawkins has become

Long John Silver (Wallace Beery) leans on his crutch as he stands on the deck chatting in Treasure Island.

apprised that drunken Captain Belly Bones has a tale of treasure. Several shady seafarers appear and do the bloke in, and Jim discovers the secret is a map of Treasure Island. It is there that the late, not lamented, Captain Flint, a pirate, had stashed his booty in abundance. Together with his friends, Dr. Livesey and Squire Trelawney, and with the map as a guide, Jim sets off on the *Hispaniola*, paying Captain Smolett for the passage. The crew, however, are old maties of Captain Flint, and their leader is the redoubtable Long John himself. Long John befriends the young Jim, but when he causes a mutiny he betrays the boy's admiration and trust. Our villain is soon hot on the heels of the treasure. Smolett, Jim, and his friends, building a stockaded fortress, keep the pirates at bay. It seems the treasure has been moved to a cave by a hermit.

Evil Powers/Weapons: Arr, arr, he'll make you walk the plank, hang you on the yardarm, give you a treatment of the cat-o-nine tails.

Occupation: Independent sailor or pirate.

Intelligence: Crafty.

Strengths: He's relentless.

Weaknesses: He's rather slow in a marathon.

Territory: Treasure Island, the Bounding Main, and English inns of ill repute.

Idiosyncrasies: Soft-hearted meanie.

Friends: Jim, but only for awhile.

Enemies: Jim and his friends.

Evil Deeds: Plunderer of more than 20 ports, abuser of the sea lanes, and mutiny.

Outcome: Long John can't find the treasure. The mad old coot, Ben Gunn, filthier and crazier than the crew, was marooned there by Flint and only he knows where the treasure is. He befriends Jim and his friends, and together they outsmart and defeat the pirates. Long John Silver is clapped in irons by Smollett and they all sail back to England with the treasure. Long John, however, tricks Jim and escapes. Harr, harr.

Current Status: Presumably pursuing more treasure and adventure.

What to Do If You Meet: Tell him where the treasure is or he'll run you through.

Worthy of Note: Years later Robert Newton did the same film for Disney—an equally fine job.

Roger Simmons

Alias: The Contractor
Born: 1940s
Died: 1974

Starred in:
The Towering Inferno
20th Century Fox, 1974
Director: John Guillermin
Played by: Richard Chamberlain

Description: Tall and handsome electrical engineer and contractor. He wears a tuxedo in the film because he is at a banquet.

Reason for Villainy: The Glass Tower, the tallest building the world, is built in San Francisco. A gala party is thrown on the 122nd floor to celebrate its completion. Attending the party are the wealthy, the makers-breakers of San Francisco; the tower's builder, Doug Roberts (Paul Newman); the owner, James Duncan (William Holden); and the electrical contractor, Roger Simmons. During the party, Roberts discovers that Simmons (Duncan's son-in-law) has installed cheap wiring, not properly insulated, throughout the Tower to save money. A fire breaks out in a storeroom and Roberts tells Duncan, who doesn't pay attention to a "minor fire." After all, the building is equipped with the most advanced fire-fighting and detection equipment in the world.

Evil Powers/Weapons: He was given the responsibility of installing all the electricity in world's tallest building and has put thousands of lives in jeopardy by using cheap wire. Electricity is his weapon.

Occupation: Electrical engineer.

Intelligence: Highly intelligent but careless, lackadaisical.

Territory: The Glass Tower in San Francisco.

Idiosyncrasies: Doesn't take it all seriously.

Friends: Married to Duncan's daughter, Patty, who is tight with the old man.

Enemies: Doug Roberts, the architect, who finds out what Simmons has done.

Evil Deeds: Installed faulty wiring in the Glass Tower. This starts the fire that destroys the entire building and kills hundreds of people.

Current Status: Dead.

What to Do If You Meet: Don't stay in high-rises that cut costs!

Worthy of Note: The biggest budgeted of all the disaster flicks and one of the best and most harrowing.

John Duncan yells at Roger Simmons (Richard Chamberlain) in a fit of rage upon learning of his cost-cutting electrical shortcuts in The Towering Inferno.

Emma Small

Born: 1840s
Died: 1870s

Starred in:
Johnny Guitar
Republic, 1954
Director: Nicholas Ray
Played by: Mercedes McCambridge

Description: Pent-up, incredibly repressed cowgirl. Pretty, but has a very severe appearance, neurotic eyes, tight-clenched mouth, and pale face. Wears dark skirt and vest, shirt buttoned to the neck. Carries a gun.

Reason for Villainy: Johnny Guitar (Sterling Hayden), an ex-gunslinger, rides up to Vienna's (Joan Crawford's) saloon and the two quickly strike up a strong attraction, much to the chagrin of the Dancin' Kid (Scott Brady), another gunman and outlaw. Meanwhile, a stagecoach is robbed and a banker is killed. Emma Small, the dead man's sister, comes to Vienna's with a crowd of townspeople and demands that Vienna and the Dancin' Kid and his cronies (Burt, Corey, and Furley) all be arrested and hanged. She is in love with the Dancin' Kid, something she won't even admit to herself. Of course, he won't return the affection since he's hung up on Vienna. Emma tells Vienna she'll kill her someday. Vienna's reply is "I know, unless I kill you first."

Evil Powers/Weapons: Mean, sexually repressed, vicious, rumor monger. Continually tries to rouse the townspeople to go after Vienna and Johnny Guitar. She uses her tongue and her gun for her best advantage.

Occupation: Part owner of town bank, and a troublemaker.

Intelligence: Shrewd, but only of medium intelligence. Adept at manipulating others. Seems to understand the lower elements of human nature and how to use them to her ends.

Emma Small (Mercedes McCambridge) leads a posse into Vienna's saloon to get the woman she hates and has vowed to kill in Johnny Guitar.

Territory: Arizona.

Idiosyncrasies: Sexually repressed. She wants to hurt those men she's attracted to but is terrified of.

Friends: No real friends, but town men are swayed by her.

Enemies: Vienna.

Evil Deeds: Arouses townspeople against Vienna, sets her saloon on fire, kills Tom, Vienna's right hand man, hangs Turkey, and kills the Dancin' Kid.

Killed by: The Dancin' Kid and his cohorts rob the town bank and head for the hills. Emma gets the teller to swear that Vienna was involved. Emma, the marshal, and a posse ride to Vienna's and burn the place to the ground, killing her assistant Tom. They also hang Turkey, the youngest of the Dancin' Kid's gang. They are about to hang Vienna when Johnny Guitar saves her. Johnny and Vienna ride to Dancin' Kid's mountain hideout. The posse follows and, in a complicated shoot out, Emma kills the Dancin' Kid before she and Vienna have a chance to shoot it out. Vienna is wounded in the shoot out, but it is Emma who is killed and tumbles to the ground. As the posse look sheepishly on, they realize they've been manipulated by the mad little woman.

Current Status: Dead.

What to Do If You Meet: Don't mention sex or dancing.

Worthy of Note: One of the most Freudian cowboy movies ever made. Repressed and exploding emotions and sexual symbols are constantly filling the screen.

Jimmy Smith and Gregory Powell

Jimmy Smith (James Woods) has patrolman Ian Campbell in his clutches in The Onion Field.

Born: 1940s
Died: Awaiting execution

Starred in:
The Onion Field
Avco Embassy, 1979
Director: Harold Becker
Played by: Franklyn Seales, James Woods

Description: Jimmy Smith looks like some pale mask of a person. He has a skull-like quality to his face that is matched by his cohort Gregory. They both have short, cropped hair, wear jackets and mug hats, and carry handguns. They talk like criminals out of the side of their mouths.

Reason for Villainy: On the night of March 9, 1963, two patrolmen, Karl Hettinger and Ian Campbell (John Savage and Ted Danson) met up with two ruthless killers. Based on a true incident of lingering, inadequate justice, the parolees kidnap the two officers. They take them to a lonely onion field and open fire. Hettinger survives to testify against the pair. However, their trials and appeals consume years, and Hettinger slowly loses his sanity. Hettinger is left with the guilt that perhaps he is responsible for the whole situation because he surrendered his gun to the killers when he was kidnapped. Hettinger becomes a virtual

sick derelict after years of going in and out of court repeating his story again and again. Will the murderers ever be convicted, or will blind justice make a wreck out of one of their victims? The inadequacies of American justice is the dominant theme.

Evil Powers/Weapons: Sure they have guns, but better than that they have the unwitting ally in the criminal justice system.

Occupation: Killers and stick-up men.

Intelligence: Below normal to average.

Strengths: They have inadequate justice on their side.

Weaknesses: Eventually they might get executed.

Territory: Bakersfield, California and other spots on criminal escape routes.

Idiosyncrasies: They're getting to know the law better than the judges while in prison.

Friends: The parole system.

Enemies: Society and decency.

Evil Deeds: They kill Campbell and stymie justice.

Outcome: The criminals have the upper hand now. Even if they are convicted again and again, "new evidence," or "inadequate procedures" always pop up to make their appeals viable. It seems only the lawabiding are punished. At the film's end, the criminals are spending more and more time reading and writing and expecting that they will be released soon.

Current Status: They will likely get out on parole and kill again.

What to Do If You Meet: Mention that you are a lawyer.

Worthy of Note: Remember the movies about how society was really responsible for guys going wrong? Contrast those "bleeding heart" movies to this cold appraisal of law in the U.S.A. This film was based on a book by ex-policeman Joseph Wambaugh.

Perry Smith and Dick Hickok

Born: 1940s.
Died: Executed in the 1960s after several stays of sentence.

Starred in:
In Cold Blood
Columbia Pictures, 1967
Director: Richard Brooks
Played by: Robert Blake, Scott Wilson

Description: Perry Smith sports a motorcycle jacket and coxcomb hair, both black and shiny. He wears his denims too short over white socks. Dick Hickock likes plaid, comfortable suede shoes, and sports a baseball hat at times. He's tall; Smith is short.

Reason for Villainy: Smith and Hickock had alienated, lonely childhoods, and spent some time in prison for small offenses. But they had no call to drive up to the Clutter house and try to rob its non-existent treasure. They had even less motive for killing the whole family, in this story based on a true incident which occurred in 1959. They just did it because they were there, the victims were there, and they thought they could get away with it. Sick. We find out that the villains, sneaking up on the house, which is open, have heard a rumor that the family had a lot of money squirreled away. So they plan to rob it. Once inside they tie up

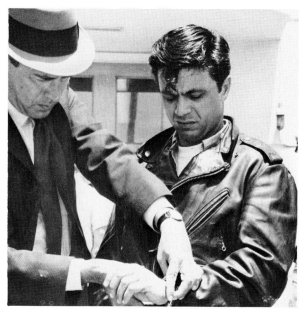

Perry Smith (Robert Blake) is finally apprehended for brutally murdering an entire family In Cold Blood.

the whole family. They find no loot, but then they decide that they should leave no witnesses. They shoot Herbert Clutter (John McLiam), Bonnie Clutter (Ruth Storey), Nancy Clutter (Brenda C. Currin), and Kenyon Clutter (Paul Hough). One at a time, as they ask for mercy, the nice members of the farm family are dispatched for no good reason.

Evil Powers: They are the personification of alienated violence.

Occupation: Felons, killers.

Intelligence: Below average, though Smith sketches well.

Strengths: Their experience with police.

Weaknesses: They are ready to believe that the other squealed to save his own skin.

Territory: The Midwestern U.S.A.

Idiosyncrasies : Penchant for senseless murder.

Friends: Stealth, tight lips.

Enemies: Prosecutors, judges, cops, the truth.

Evil Deeds: Their worst deed was killing the little girl—she begged pitifully to grow up. The kind girl even tried to be friendly to the killers and understand them.

Killed by: The pair of hideous killers are cool. They escape and wind up in Mexico for a time. Later they are arrested on a flimsy charge in Las Vegas. The police's relentless search for information on the brutal murders succeeds when a fellow con relates that he spoke of working on the Clutter place to Smith. The con told him there was a fortune there to be had. It was just bragging. The police now know who probably committed the crime. The clever investigator, Alvin Dewey (John Forsythe), puts it all together. Smith and Hickock are grilled repeatedly for answers. They are presented with a bloody footprint that police say could only be from their particular shoes (which, of course, was a bit of a lie). Individually they are told the other copped a plea. They start blaming each other. The jig is up. It is only a matter of time now as the relentless wheels of creaking justice put them on the gallows to be hanged. If anyone deserves it, they do.

Current Status: Dead.

What to Do If You Meet: They represent the increase in senseless violence in America. The search for its roots goes on. Preventing this sort of crime is hard. Lock your door.

Worthy of Note: Robert Blake later became the popular emotional and sensitive cop Baretta in the long-running TV series of the same name. What a difference from this role.

Virgil Starkwell

Alias: That loser
Born: 1930s
Died: Still on the lam

Starred in:
Take the Money and Run
Cinerama Releasing, 1969
Director: Woody Allen
Played by: Woody Allen

Description: Red-haired, thin, short, nervous looking, with dark hornrim glasses. Virgil is shifty, always twisting his head to see who's following him. He wears sneakers.

Reason for Villainy: Ever since he was a little boy trying to rob a gumball machine and getting his fingers caught, Virgil has been a criminal without great success. Trying to go straight, he spit-shines shoes, but spits too high and loses customers. As an adult, he decides to play the cello as his career, but fails because he thought the cello was a wind instrument. Returning to crime, he tries to rob a bank by passing a note saying he has a gun. But like all people who want a large withdrawal, he is sent to have the note initialed by a bank officer. Romance also eludes him until he goes walking in the park one day in order to snatch purses. One of his victims is a cheerful laundress named Louise (Janet Margolin). She steals his heart when he gives up the idea of stealing her purse. All his life he's been a loser, now he is a winner—with a loser.

Evil Powers/Weapons: He will use a gun, he will pass notes to tellers, and he will plan robberies and escapes with hardened criminals.

Occupation: Thief.

Intelligence: Average.

Strengths: He's determined.

Weaknesses: He's incompetent and nervous.

Territory: The city and the beach.

Idiosyncrasies: Talks out of the side of his mouth like a con.

Friends: The other cons and Louise.

Enemies: The relentless law, and his bungling.

Virgil Starkwell is an amazingly inept criminal in Take the Money and Run.

Evil Deeds: Robbery and escaping from prison.

Outcome: Virgil is jailed when the man he is holding up turns out to be an old school buddy and a cop. Virgil is put on a chain gang, under the authority of a mirrored-sunglass type of warden that Cool Hand Luke is familiar with (James Anderson). For once Virgil deftly—and hilariously—is able to pull a job. In this case it's escape. The chain gang has to run like hell and in sequence, too; if one falls, they all fall. Now, with five men chained hand and foot to him, Virgil decides to hide out in a farmhouse. The elderly woman who owns the farmhouse feeds them and introduces them to the local sheriff as her cousins. Of course, through all of this they stand very close together to hide their chains. A closely knit family, according to Virgil. Incredibly, the deception passes. Later, in an episode at a beach house, Virgil and Louise are cutting beans and baloney in half and living the poor but happy life. She begs him not to go back to crime, but they are starving. All in all, Virgil just keeps moving and keeps on failing at crime.

Current Status: Incarcerated, planning to escape.

What to Do If You Meet: Hand him your eyeglass case—he'll think it's a wallet and run away with it. Then buy yourself a beer. Tell everyone you met the most incompetent robber ever born.

Worthy of Note: One of Woody's best. Unpretentious, truly funny.

Camilla Sternwood

Born: 1958
Died: Institutionalized 1978

Starred in:
The Big Sleep
United Artists, 1978
Director: Michael Winner
Played by: Candy Clark

Description: Attractive, willful little sister type, always trying to be sexy and coy, and succeeding. Giggles a lot and is playful. She has straight hair in an overgrown pageboy style, wears turtleneck sweaters and hippie clothes. Likes to be naked. Likes weird stuff. Cute.

Reason for Villainy: Camilla is somehow involved in a blackmail problem. Her father, the aged General Sternwood, calls in Philip Marlowe, an American private investigator, to check out the situation. Marlowe (Robert Mitchum) arrives at the palatial estate of Sternwood, and is told that a blackmailer has some very, very dirty pictures of Camilla, who is a little wild and posed for the shots when she was not at her sharpest. Marlowe begins investigating and finds the blackmailer dead on the floor of his photo studio. He also finds Camilla there naked in a drugged stupor. Marlowe quickly gets her away from there. Sternwood thinks that Marlowe should now find a young male friend that disappeared some months ago. The convoluted trails all lead to Eddie Mars, a gangster-type nightclub owner. It seems also, Marlowe finds out, that Camilla has the hots for the aging, cynical private eye.

Evil Powers/Weapons: A gun and an insane desire to use it on people. It's a toy to her. It goes "boom" and people disappear.

Occupation: Nude model, bizarre daughter, nymphomaniac.

Intelligence: She's so flaky that it's hard to

Blackmailer Joe Brody is threatened by Camilla Sternwood (Candy Clark) in The Big Sleep.

have a rational conversation with her. She really likes to just take her clothes off.

Strengths: Lying ability.

Weaknesses: Gets into trouble too quickly.

Territory: Mansions, estate grounds, photo studios, nightclubs, big, expensive Bentleys.

Idiosyncrasies: Nymphomania.

Friends: Marlowe is trying to save her.

Enemies: Her own delusions and the violent nature of her sexuality.

Evil Deeds: Camilla shoots lots of people, in particular, the man who is missing and the subject of Marlowe's search. That handsome, honest, and respectful confidant of her father had the nerve to refuse to sleep with her when she took a walk out to the lake with him. So she killed him and pushed him into the water. Her evil deed took away her father's only close friend.

Killed by: Camilla, aside from being a murderess (which we don't know until Marlowe finds out just in time to save his own hide), is involved with some really sleazy types who have their own intrigues and murders. Marlowe is set up several times and several more murders occur in this remake of the even more complicated 1946 version (with Martha Vickers and Humphrey Bogart). Suffice to say that in the end, Marlowe is invited out to the lake for some target practice courtesy of Camilla. He's got her ticket now. She's luring him to his death. He disarms the sexy little wacko and her father says "I suppose I'll have to put her away after all." He thanks Marlowe for finding out everything. There's a big check waiting for Marlowe.

Current Status: Making paper guns in the asylum.

What to Do If You Meet: She's cute, but deadly. If you're a guy, it might be best to succumb to her animal drives. It's definitely better than a bullet.

Worthy of Note: This is a remake of the 1946 Warner Bros. hit of the same title. In that film the sex aspect is toned down. This film, however, is truer to the book by the great Raymond Chandler.

Dr. Stevenson

Alias: Jack the Ripper
Born: 1800s England
Died: A.D. 1999999999999999. . .

Dr. Stevenson (David Warner), alias Jack the Ripper, intends to make Amy his next victim if H.G. Wells doesn't give him the key to the time machine in Time After Time.

Starred in:
Time After Time
Warner Bros., 1979
Director: Nicholas Meyer
Played by: David Warner

Description: He's a suave doctor in a black cape and coat. He is often carrying a doctor's sachel. Inside are scalpels. He has long blond hair and sideburns. He walks fast and strikes hard.

Reason for Villainy: Dr. Stevenson attends a gathering of the friends of H.G. Wells. He is just in time to see Wells's latest invention, a time machine. Wells (Malcolm McDowell) is a young man with wirerim glasses and an attractive manner. His demonstration is interrupted by the police, who want Stevenson for questioning. The doctor escapes in the time machine. The police inform the guests that Stevenson is the Ripper! Wells immediately hops into the machine and goes to the same time-address, San Francisco 1979, to capture Stevenson and save future women from being ripped open. Realizing he must exchange his gold for modern currency, Wells traces Stevenson to a foreign exchange bank. He meets Amy, a teller. Amy (Mary Steerburgen) falls in love with him and vice versa. She digs Wells's quaint clothes—mod, isn't it? In the meantime, Stevenson hides out elegantly in a hotel and worships the violence on TV and in the streets. He realizes that this is his age, not Victorian England. He soon starts murdering women. This time he takes their bodies apart and strews them around the rooms that look like human butcher shops when he is finished.

Evil Powers: Wells's time machine has taken Stevenson to a new killing ground. Stevenson is at home in 1979 and can function very well there.

Occupation: Surgeon, lady-ripper.

Intelligence: Cunning and resourceful. He's up on the latest techniques for slicing flesh.

Strengths: Can run like hell, can use the time machine, and knows what he likes.

Weaknesses: Cops are on to him—they're more scientific nowadays.

Territory: 1890s England, 1979 San Francisco.

Idiosyncrasies: Likes violence on the tube.

Friends: Violent times, fog.

Enemies: The bobbies, H.G. Wells.

Evil Deeds: Disembowels pretty girls who are harlots. (In 1979 all women are considered harlots by Stevenson.)

Outcome: Stevenson eludes Wells. To get help, Wells tells his tale to the cops. They don't believe him, but think maybe he's the crazy that's been dismembering women. Later, in the museum where the time machine is a curiosity, Wells and Stevenson fight it out. The device to activate the machine is the source of contention. Amy doesn't really believe Wells's story about the machine, but when Wells overpowers the Ripper and sends him in the machine into the furthest time zone possible—to die—she does believe. The next step is for Wells to convince Amy to live back in Victorian times. She accepts Wells's hand in marriage. Our villain is somewhere in the impossibly far future, meeting his end perhaps in the final seconds of the whole universe. Incredible.

Current Status: Dead in the far, far future.

What to Do If You Meet: If you're a woman, say you're inexperienced. Act prissy. Otherwise . . .

Worthy of Note: Interesting theme based on Meyer's interest in the real H.G. Wells, a man of fantastic vision and imagination.

Dr. Strangelove

Born: 1920s
Died: May be alive in a bunker

Starred in:
Dr. Strangelove
Columbia Pictures, 1964
Director: Stanley Kubrick
Played by: Peter Sellers

Description: Wheelchair-bound, black-suited, ex-Nazi, with black sunglasses, and a

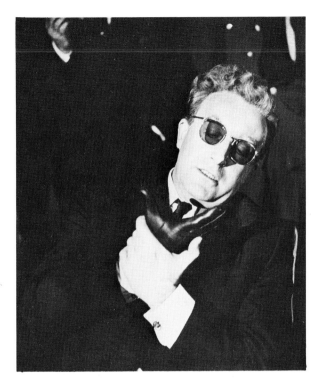

Dr. Strangelove's independent gloved hand tries to strangle him in Dr. Strangelove.

thick black glove on his right hand. A totally opportunistic operator who worked for the Nazis. He now advises the President of the United States on top policy decisions.

Reasons for Villainy: A wild-eyed, right wing Air Force general, Jack D. Ripper (Sterling Hayden), believes that the communists are "polluting our precious bodily fluids." To prevent the decline of the American "race," he takes over the controls of the jet bomber base which he commands, and sends all his bomber squadrons to attack Russia. The President calls an emergency session in which Dr. Strangelove comes to give his bizarre advice.

Evil Powers/Weapons: Powers of one of the "experts" who advise the President. Believed to be a genius by top Pentagon staff. He tries to convince the President to declare nuclear war.

Occupation: Presidential advisor.

Intelligence: Highly intelligent, totally war mad. Twisted from working for Hitler.

Strengths/Weaknesses: Physically weakened (possibly from Nazi sex orgies) and crippled, but his sharp, analytic mind makes him a force to be reckoned with.

Territory: Germany (in the 1940s), Washington, D.C. now.

Idiosyncrasies: Twitches, keeps screaming "Mein Fuehrer" when addressing the President. His gloved hand keeps rising up into a seig heil and at one point tries to strangle his own neck.

Evil Deeds: Unknown horrors in Germany. Tries to corrupt those around him here in the U.S.

Outcome: At the crisis meeting, the President gets on the phone with the Russian premier and the two try to stop World War III. All the planes are called back or shot down except one, which heads on into Russia to deliver its nuclear load. Dr. Strangelove gives a bizarre and stirring speech which the President, generals, and advisors listen to spellbound. He tells the President that if the war is going to be fought, we should go ahead with an all out strike. Then he points out that all the "important leaders" of the country should immediately go to the underground bunkers that have been built, where women, food, and beds wait for them, so that the world can be repopulated with the best gene pool. Meanwhile, the U.S. bomber evades all Russian attempts to stop it. However, the bomb the plane is carrying is stuck in its cradle. Major T.J. "King Kong" (Slim Pickens) climbs on and rides it down to an explosive finale to the tune of "We'll meet again."

Current Status: Presumed alive and living in A-proof bunkers with other top officials, and beautiful women.

What to Do If You Meet: Tell him you admire the Fuehrer and could you please come inside the bunker, just for a minute. Please!

Worthy of Note: One of the best black humor films ever made. It made director Kubrick a household name. Peter Sellers played multiple roles.

The Stranger

Born: 1947
Died: 1979

The Stranger has another victim in his clutches in When a Stranger Calls.

Starred in:
When a Stranger Calls
Warner Bros., 1979
Director: Fred Walton
Played by: Tony Beckley

Description: He's an escaped psychopath with bulging eyes, tremendous strength, a chilling voice, and has a four o'clock shadow worse than Nixon's. He wears sports clothes, but the only sport this maniac participates in is calling and saying scary things to his victims. Once inside your house he will tear you apart.

Reason for Villainy: The Stranger is calling a babysitter (Carol Kane) who is alone in the home of a couple who live in the affluent suburbs. He keeps asking "Have you checked the children?" The babysitter is scared out of her wits. She is trying to study, to watch TV, anything. He calls again, after she has checked and found the children fine in their room. She calls the police. The police say that when he calls again they will check the line and make a trace. He does call again. By this time she is so terrified that when the refrigerator ejects some ice into a tray from its automatic ice maker she nearly passes out. The police are on the line—they call her back. Get out of the house, the cops shout. They've traced the call and it's coming from the inside the house. Panicked,

she unlatches the bolts and chains on the door to escape and comes face to face with a frightening looking man. She faints. But it is only the police detective (Charles Durning). The police go upstairs where the phone is and find the children slaughtered like pigs. But the Stranger is caught. He's a real wacko.

Evil Powers/Weapons: A huge knife, a breathy voice, and the strength of five men.

Occupation: Maniac.

Intelligence: Clever at avoiding the police.

Strengths: He's fast and strong.

Weaknesses: The detective is after him relentlessly.

Territory: Smalltown, U.S.A.

Idiosyncrasies: Butchers children for fun.

Friends: He befriends some winos on skid row, but even they don't like him.

Enemies: The detective on his trail.

Evil Deeds: Butchers the children, terrorizes the babysitter when she's sixteen and again when she has her own kids.

Outcome: After years of imprisonment, he escapes, and begins threatening the now grown-up babysitter. She and her husband hire the detective, now retired, to go get him and make sure he doesn't escape again. The understanding is that the ex-cop will use lockpicks to impale the killer so that he will never live to kill again. The detective traces the killer to skid row, throws his lock-pick (a long steel needle), and misses. This puts the Stranger on the loose. He sneaks into his favorite babysitter's house and knocks out her husband. The killer takes the husband's place in bed. When she notices, she screams. The detective hiding in the house, pulls his gun and blasts the killer down. She is safe. Thank her lucky stars.

Current Status: Dead.

What to Do If You Meet: Don't check the children.

Worthy of Note: Good casting and acting make this a scary movie, but it's made rather crudely. Still, its uneven flavor has something to do with its documentary authenticity.

Major Strasser

Born: 1900s Germany
Died: 1942 in Casablanca

Starred in:
Casablanca
Warner Bros., 1942
Director: Michael Curtiz
Played by: Conrad Veidt

Description: He's neat, tall, mustached officer of the Third Reich. As senior officer in Casablanca, he must look well pressed. He wears shiny boots and his hat is on just right. Gold epaulettes and an eagle insignia on his hat complete the picture.

Reason for Villainy: Strasser is the Nazi in charge of the Reich's affairs in Vichy French Casablanca. Nominally the Vichy run the place, but Strasser really calls the shots. Rick Blaine (Humphrey Bogart) runs a night spot that is rife with anti-German sentiment. Strasser orders Captain Renault (Claude Rains) to close it. Rick is neutral and cynical He was ditched by a lover in Paris years earlier. Now she appears again. She is Ilsa Lund (Ingrid Bergman). Two criminal types, Ugart (Peter Lorre) and Señor Ferrari (Sydney Greenstreet), also hang around Rick's place. Ugart procures two special Nazi-approved travel permits and gives them to Rick. Ilsa holds a gun on Rick and threatens to use it unless she gets those passes. She explains that she ditched Rick because she found out that her husband, Victor Lazlo, whom she thought dead, was alive after all. Lazlo (Paul Henreid) has to get out of Casablanca. He's in the resistance. She makes a deal—she will stay with Rick if he lets her husband leave with one of the permits. It is impossible to describe the

Major Strasser (Conrad Veidt) is greeted by Captain Renault and his men upon his arrival in Casablanca.

poignancy of this scene—two lovers, star-crossed, trying to work it out with each other.

Evil Powers: Backed by the might of Nazi Germany.

Weapons: Terror and torture at the hands of the efficient and ruthless Nazis.

Occupation: Major in the Third Reich's army.

Intelligence: Above average, but likes Wagner more than "As Time Goes By."

Strengths: Backed by troops with an arsenal of weapons.

Weaknesses: Underestimates the will of the resistance and the will of the people against totalitarian oppression.

Territory: Vichy-controlled Casablanca.

Idiosyncrasies: Wants Sam to play "Deutchland Uber Alles." Sam doesn't know it.

Friends: He thinks his stooge, Renault, is his friend. The Reich is his biggest friend.

Enemies: Victor, and eventually Rick and Renault.

Relatives: *The Boys from Brazil.*

Evil Deeds: Countless torture interrogations and mass executions. The man is a brute and he lives high on the hog procuring the best wine and women for himself, leaving crumbs for others.

Killed by: Renault, always Strasser's stooge, catches Rick, Victor, and Ilsa at the airport. Rick gets the drop on Renault. Strasser arrives. Strasser thinks Renault a perfect stooge and Rick a cowardly American. Strasser reaches for Rick's gun, but Rick shoots Strasser dead. When the rest of the Nazis arrive, Renault says Strasser has been killed by someone he doesn't know. Ilsa and Victor take off with the passes, and Rick and Renault start a new friendship. "Round up the usual suspects," says Renault. Arrogant Nazis like Strasser think us good guys will put up with anything. But don't try to disarm an American. That's going too far. We don't like to get involved, but watch out, buddy, when we do. Like Rick in this wartime propaganda flick, all freedom lovers, including Frenchmen like Renault who grovel at Hitler's boots, eventually rally around the flag. Then it's goodbye to bad rubbish like Strasser.

Current Status: Dead, posthumously awarded the Iron Cross.

What to Do If You Meet: Give him some Vichy water with a mickey in it.

Worthy of Note: The best line in any movie ever is Rick's when Ilsa holds the gun on him: "Go ahead and shoot, you'll be doing me a favor."

Szell

Alias: The Nazi Dentist
Born: Early 20th century
Died: 1976

Starred in:
The Marathon Man
Paramount, 1976
Director: John Schlesinger
Played by: Laurence Olivier

Description: Nearly bald, *very* cruel and cold Nazi torturer. Thick glasses. Wears a suit and tie at all times.

Reason for Villainy: In New York, Babe Levy (Dustin Hoffman) trains in hopes of becoming a marathon runner. Babe's older brother, Doc (Roy Scheider), is a high ranking CIA agent who has developed a felonous relationship with Szell, an ex-Nazi who wants to obtain his dead brother's hidden diamonds (stolen from Jews in Nazi Germany). Szell's brother has been killed by an enraged Jew who recognized him as a war criminal. For a small fortune, Doc smuggles Szell into the U.S. but is then wounded by the psychotic Nazi. Doc, barely alive, crawls to his brother Babe's apartment, but dies before uttering a word. Szell, sure that Babe is in cahoots with his brother, goes after him to find the missing diamonds. The hapless Babe (who doesn't know a thing) is suddenly thrust into a world of torture, sadism, and unimaginable pain from the evil Szell.

Evil Powers/Weapons: Super-cunning and devious. He has a group of Nazi henchmen

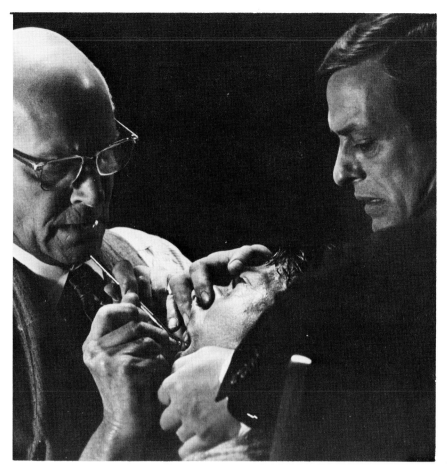

Szell (Laurence Olivier) jabs the raw nerve of his prisoner to squeeze vital information out of him in The Marathon Man.

who will torture and kill on command. He's part of the international Nazi conspiracy based in South America. He also carries a hidden fist-knife which he can whip out in an instant and uses dental tools to torture with exquisitely painful results.

Occupation: Nazi/dentist torturer.

Intelligence: Extremely intelligent and calculating.

Strengths: Determined, organized, and will stop at nothing.

Weaknesses: Can't run as fast as Babe.

Territory: Nazi Germany, South America, New York City.

Idiosyncrasies: Loves to torture. Says to Babe, over and over as he tortures him, the meaningless words, "Is it safe? Is it safe?"

Friends: Nazis everywhere.

Enemies: Babe, Jews.

Evil Deeds: Incredible atrocities committed in Nazi death camps. Torture, experimentation, vivisection. He has killed scores since the end of the war. Commits horrible acts upon Babe to extract the "truth." He uses an electric drill on the exposed raw nerve of Babe's tooth. Can there be anything worse?

Killed by: After torturing Babe, Szell realizes that he must be telling the truth about not knowing anything about any diamonds or he'd talk. Babe escapes and runs halfway across New York pursued by puffing Nazi thugs. He gets a .45 from his apartment. In the meantime, Szell finds the diamonds and stupidly visits a pawnbroker to have them assessed. The Jewish pawnbroker recognizes Szell as a war criminal, as does a woman in the street. As Szell races off to their cries, he is caught by Babe who forces the Nazi at gunpoint to an enclosed reservoir. Opening Szell's briefcase he discovers the diamonds and tells Szell, "You can keep all the diamonds you can swallow." Choking them down, Szell lunges at Babe with his hidden knife. In a struggle, however, he falls on it himself and is killed.

Current Status: Dead, but those Nazis just keep coming!

What to Do If You Meet: Seig heil!

Worthy of Note: Top cast and director. One of the best thrillers of the 1970s.

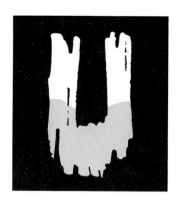

Bart Tare   223
Taxi Driver   223
Dr. Terwilliker   224
Bobby Thompson   225
Toecutter's Gang   226

Tommy Udo   227

Fred Van
  Ackerman   228
Philip Vandamm   230
Johnny Vanning   231
Mrs. Venable   232
Ventana Corp.   233
The Vigilante
  Cops   234

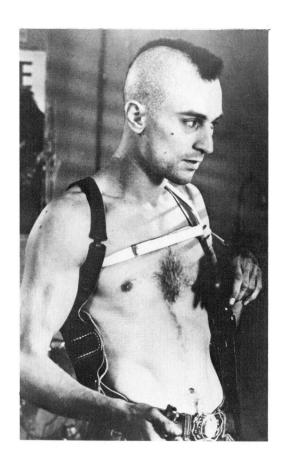

Bart Tare

Born: 1920s
Died: 1949

Starred in:
Gun Crazy
Warner Bros.-First National, 1949
Director: Joseph H. Lewis
Played by: John Dall

Bart Tare (John Dall) is a reformed juvenile delinquent who returns to a life of crime on the instigation of the woman he loves in Gun Crazy.

Description: Tall, lanky, good-looking guy with a boyish, but somehow weak, character. He wears a tweed suit.

Reason for Villainy: Sent to reform school as a young boy for stealing a pistol, Bart finally returns home and visits his friends Clyde, now the Sheriff, and Dave, a newspaperman. They go to the circus and he meets Annie Laurie Starr. It's love at first sight, and soon Bart and Laurie are married and he joins the circus. But the honeymoon soon sours as Laurie, who has had a "bad past," gets Bart to pull some bank robberies when they run out of money. His life of crime has begun again.

Evil Powers: His obsession with Laurie. He also commits evil acts and is good with a gun.

Weapons: Pistol.

Occupation: Reform schooler, part of a shooting act in the circus, and armed robber.

Intelligence: Quite intelligent, but immature emotionally.

Strengths: Excellent shooter.

Weaknesses: His love for the beautiful but "bad" Laurie.

Territory: The Midwest and West.

Idiosyncrasies: He loves guns. Ever since he was a child he has had an obsessive fascination with them. He only feels like a man when he has one.

Friends: Laurie.

Enemies: The police.

Evil Deeds: Robs banks, kills.

Killed by: After committing a number of armed robberies, the lovebirds decide to give up their life of crime. They'll go straight and Laurie will be "good." However, Laurie asks Bart to pull one more job so they'll have enough money to retire. They rob a Montana packing plant and Laurie kills two people. They escape, but the police set a trap and they can't get to their money. They flee into the mountains, but the police track them. Dave and Clyde, Bart's friends, try to persuade Bart to surrender, but Laurie tries to kill them. Bart shoots her to save his friends, but then he is cut down by police bullets when they think he's firing on them. Like Romeo and Juliet, the star-crossed lovers lie touching one another on the cold ground.

Current Status: Dead.

What to Do If You Meet: Tell him you'll show him your M-16 if he'll show you his Colt .45.

Worthy of Note: Excellent film that has reached cult status. A predecessor of *Bonnie and Clyde,* and better.

Taxi Driver

Alias: Travis Bickle
Born: 1930s
Died: Still alive

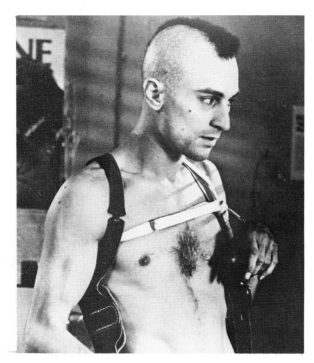

Travis Bickle, now completely insane, practices drawing his guns in front of a mirror in Taxi Driver.

Starred in:
Taxi Driver
Columbia Pictures, 1976
Director: Martin Scorsese
Played by: Robert De Niro

Description: Alienated loner with a strange, disturbed look in his eyes. Taxi driver. He wears sloppy clothes, jeans and flannel shirts. He eventually shaves his hair into a mohican.

Reason for Villainy: Travis Bickle is a demented ex-marine. He drifts through New York City at night, either driving his cab or walking the streets staring down gangs and pimps. He is obsessed with the darkness of the city. (A nightmarish vision as created by Scorsese.) He meets Betsy (Cybill Shepherd), a cute blonde campaign worker for Senator Palentine, a presidential candidate. Betsy agrees to a date, but when Travis (not having the slightest social graces) takes her to a porno film, she is disgusted and leaves. This pushes Travis over the edge.

Evil Powers: Psychotic, fearless, boiling rage capable of exploding into incredible violence.

Weapons: Uses guns and knives.

Occupation: Taxi driver, pimp killer.

Intelligence: Medium intelligence, nice guy quality, but somehow twisted into a truly deranged and vacant mind.

Strengths: Madness, self-righteousness.

Weaknesses: Paranoia, does not see things properly.

Territory: New York City streets.

Idiosyncrasies: Has a Messianic feeling about saving a young prostitute, Iris (Jodie Foster).

Friends: His only friends are two women who like him, although they are terribly frightened of him.

Enemies: He hates pimps.

Relatives: No one is quite like this guy!

Evil Deeds: Kills.

Outcome: Travis, deeply depressed from his rejection by Betsy, meets Iris, a 12-year old prostitute. He buys time with her from her pimp, Sport (Harvey Keitel), but just talks with her, trying to make her go back to school. He comes to believe he has a mission to save her! Armed with pistols, he goes to Times Square and tries to kill Senator Palentine at a political rally, but is chased away by the secret service. He goes to Iris's and, in a bloody shootout, kills Sport, and a customer. Wounded himself, Travis is taken to the hospital where the newspapers make him, a media hero.

Current Status: Alive and currently a hero. He may kill again—anyone he perceives as evil.

What to Do If You Meet: If you ride in his cab, only talk about the weather, smile a lot, give him a big tip, and don't mention sex.

Worthy of Note: One of the darkest films of the American city. Truly frightening.

Dr. Terwilliker

Alias: Dr. T
Born: 1910
Died: Perhaps

Starred in:
The 5,000 Fingers of Dr. T
Columbia Pictures, 1953
Director: Roy Rowland
Played by: Hans Conried

Description: Dr. T is an overbearing, demanding piano instructor, who callously forces young Bart to learn the piano even if it kills him. He's the meanest, biggest, and baddest teacher.

Reason for Villainy: Dr. T is causing Bart Collins to have bad dreams—to put it mildly. Bart imagines that he is in the endless mazes of the Terwilliker "Happy Finger Institute" where 500 boys are kept in cells and taught piano 24 hours a day until all of their 5,000 fingers play in one grand recital. He also dreams that Dr. T marries Bart's lovely widowed mother, Mrs. Collins (Mary Healy). Groups of darkly clad men are everywhere throwing nets at young Bart, but he escapes and invents a music absorber to destroy Dr. T's music power. Bart enlists the aid of the plumber, handsome and sweet Mr. Zabladowski (Peter Lind Hayes), who in "real" life is sweet on Mrs. Collins but getting nowhere. Bart and the plumber install the music absorber

Bart (in the cylinder) and the plumber plan on upsetting the plans of piano-obsessed Dr. Terwilliker in The 5,000 Fingers of Dr. T.

in the 500 cells for the little boys. Dr. T's terrible plans are thwarted. Or are they?

Evil Powers: He has hypnotic power over Mrs. Collins, plus he has a big institute and lots of pianos.

Occupation: Piano instructor, madman.

Intelligence: Good at reading notes.

Strengths: Metronomic willpower.

Weaknesses: Bart's one smart cookie.

Territory: Pianoland—somewhere where there is a huge Happy Fingers Institute.

Idiosyncrasies: Concerts are his life's blood.

Friends: Pianos.

Enemies: Little boys who want to play baseball.

Evil Deeds: Makes little boys practice.

Outcome: Zabladowski and Bart next go about freeing all the little boys who hate music lessons. Bart also brings the nice plumber to meet his mom. Then, suddenly, Bart wakes up (he sleeps inside the big piano) and he finds out that his mom and the plumber are off to take a ride downtown for supplies. Can marriage be far away? Happy it was all a dream, Bart grabs his baseball mitt and goes out to play. His piano-playing days are over. Perhaps he'll use his time to learn plumbing.

Current Status: Works for Lawrence Welk.

What to Do If You Meet: Say, "How do I get to Carnegie Hall?" and he'll reply, "Practice, practice . . . ," and you can run away.

Worthy of Note: The story is by Dr. Seuss and terrifying to young kids. The film was panned by some critics, but they weren't five years old—or were they?

Bobby Thompson

Born: 1945
Died: Received life imprisonment in 1969

Starred in:
Targets
Paramount, 1968
Director: Peter Bogdanovich
Played by: Tim O'Kelly

Description: Bobby is a young man with short-cropped light-brown hair and an innocent face. He is usually seen carrying a lot of rifles with scopes. He wears a white windbreaker jacket.

Reason for Villainy: Bobby has a problem. He has this urge to kill people. You might say he's gone over the edge. One day, while his father is at work, he shoots his wife, his mother, and the delivery boy. He drives off in his flashy car with lots of ammo and rifles. Meanwhile, Orlock, a famous horror film star, is calling it quits. Orlock (Boris Karloff) is convinced by his secretary, Jenny (Nancy Hseuh), and the director of his last picture, Sammy Michaels (Peter Bogdanovitch), to make a personal appearance to promote the film. They proceed to the drive-in where *The Terror* is showing. One of the reasons Orlock wants to quit is because he feels real life has become more scary than his movies. Within this timeframe, Bobby has been shooting people all over the place and now sets his sights on the drive-in theater. At the theater he begins picking people off from the back of the screen. All of this mayhem occurs because of his strange, confused thoughts. The guy needed someone to talk to, but now it's too late.

Evil Powers/Weapons: Lots of high-powered rifles and ammo.

Occupation: Unemployed, drives a convertible.

Intelligence: Smart, and has a good eye.

Strengths: He's a good shot.

Weaknesses: He can be confused by movie images.

Territory: Hollywood, drive-in movies, tops of oil tanks with good views of surrounding country, his convertible.

Idiosyncrasies : Bobby can't tell real life from film life.

Friends: His family—but that doesn't stop him from killing them.

Enemies: Orlock, the cops.

Evil Deeds: Kills innumerable people from the top of an oil tank and from behind the movie screen.

Outcome: Bobby panics when some people get their guns and start running toward the screen to kill the sniper. He runs to the side of the screen and fires wildly. He wounds Jenny. The horror star becomes enraged. He walks

Bobby Thompson (Tim O'Kelly) is well equipped with rifles and ammo, and has a great vantage point from the top of an oil tank to see his Targets.

toward the killer with the same monstrous killer-expression that his character on the screen is wearing. Bobby is confused. He fires—at the screen madman, not at the real Orlock. Orlock grabs him and the police arrive and take charge. Presumably he will be put on trial. For now, his spree is over.

Current Status: Jailed.

What to Do If You Meet: He's shooting from far away, you won't know what hit you.

Worthy of Note: Bogdanovitch's screen plea for gun control.

Toecutter's Gang

Born: 1950s
Died: 1990s

Starred in:
Mad Max
American International, 1980
Director: George Miller
Played by; Hugh Keays-Byrne, Geoff
   Parry, Tim Burns

Description: Toecutter, Bubba, and Johnny are the principals in an insane motorcycle gang that is tearing up Australia after World War III. They wear leather, helmets, and odd, post-atomic war styles of plastic and fur.

Reason for Villainy: When the Knightrider is killed, the control of the mad gang of killer-sadists goes to Toecutter. The man is insane. The gang chases a couple in a car, catches them, and rapes them both. They perform other various violent abuses and are pursued by the Bronzes, cops in souped up, 600 horse-power cars. Two of these cops, Max and Goose (Mel Gibson and Steve Bisley), are particularly effective in thwarting the gang through incredible driving and just-as-violent methods. The pair arrest Johnny (Tim Burns) when he is too stoned to get away from the scene of the crime with the rest of the gang. Of course, a judge releases him. Max turns in his badge to his boss Fifi (Roger Ward). He leaves town with his wife Jessie and their little baby. Soon they arrive at May's idyllic seaside farm. In the meantime, the gang has caught Goose and burned him in his car. He lies near death in the hospital. Before long, the gang discovers where Max and his family are hiding. They begin their terror by kidnapping the baby.

Weapons: Their cycles, knives, and guns.

Occupation: Post-atomic war motorcycle gang.

Intelligence: Brute instincts of lust and sadism.

Strengths: They are fast on their bikes.

Weaknesses: They can be run down by a souped up Bronze car.

Territory: Australia after the ultimate destructive act of man.

Idiosyncrasies: They wear different styles because they come from different backgrounds—the highest to the lowest classes.

Friends: Speed.

Enemies: Mad Max.

Evil Deeds: They kill, torture, rape. They'll do anything for kicks or money.

Killed by: Jessie manages to get her child back. When the car carrying Jessie and the rescued baby stalls, the mad gang catches up and kills them both. Mad Max now puts his uniform back on and pursues the gang. He drives through their V formation with his car

Mad Max is up against the tough, weird Toecutter and his gang in post-World War III Australia.

and plunges many of the gang off the bridge. But Max is out for Toecutter. Toecutter is forced into an oncoming truck and squashed like a bug. Max gets Johnny next. Johnny is on the side of the road robbing a motorist's corpse. Max handcuffs him to the car which will explode shortly because of its leaking fuel. Max gives Johnny a saw to file himself free—if he can—before the explosion. Max drives away and we hear and see a big boom in the distance.

Current Status: Dead, all dead.

What to Do If You Meet: Get off the road.

Worthy of Note: Endless violence and stunt driving. It made money on a small budget. Skip this one.

Tommy Udo

Alias: The Killer
Born: 1920s NYC
Died: 1947

Starred in:
Kiss of Death
20th Century Fox, 1947
Director: Henry Hathaway
Played by: Richard Widmark

Tommy Udo (Richard Widmark) and Nick Bianco are handcuffed to each other in Kiss of Death.

Description: Frail, maniacal eyes, shifty, snickering killer. He wears a suit, tie, and trenchcoat—gangster style. His sinister, falsetto baby talk chills the bones.

Reason for Villainy: Udo grew up in the tough city and turned to crime early. He discovered that he got great pleasure from torturing cats, old ladies—everyone. Hates the "screws." When Nick Bianco (Victor Mature) finds himself jobless on Christmas Eve, he robs a jewelry store and is shot by the cops. Sentenced to 20 years away from the family he was trying to feed, the D.A. offers clemency for information on his accomplices, namely Udo, but Nick refuses. Then Nick's wife commits suicide and his children are sent to an orphanage. He realizes he must get out and agrees to testify. The D.A. now goes after the vicious psychopath Tommy Udo. Nick is sprung and soon marries Nettie, who used to babysit his kids, and is in love with him. He testifies against Udo who still manages to get away with the crime. But now Udo wants Nick and his loved ones. He wants them bad.

Weapons: Fright is his main weapon. People are terrified of him. He is also backed by his mob and his .45.

Occupation: Small-time crook, hustler, pimp of violence trying to make it big.

Intelligence: Clever. His frightening speeches are meant to taunt and degrade. Understands the use of fear and human nature.

Strengths/Weaknesses: His reputation. Nobody wants Tommy Udo not to like them. The terror and fear of what he'll do to you or your family when he laughs (he-hee, he-hee-he-hee hah) makes him powerful. He has few weaknesses.

Territory: Hotel Margyery, NYC, Criminal Court Building, Sing Sing.

Idiosyncrasies: Acts like he's god on top of the world and in full control. He's also a sadist who can't stop snickering when he hurts people.

Friends: Are you kidding?

Enemies: The screws, the people he extorts money from, Nick, the D.A., and society.

Evil Deeds: Slaps people around, pushes an old lady in a wheelchair down the stairs, orders his henchmen to take people's fingers off, break people's legs, and shoots countless people, including Nick.

Killed by: Tommy Udo, planning to have his thugs blast Nick away, is goaded by Nick into doing it himself. Nick, however, has arranged for the police to show up. Nick comes face to face with the psychopathic Udo and insults him. Udo shoots him several times in the stomach. Then the cops close in and shoot it out with the mad killer, blasting him apart.

Current Status: Tommy Udo is dead.

Worthy of Note: Richard Widmark's first picture. It propelled him into superstardom.

Fred Van Ackerman

Born: 1930s
Died: Still alive, but disgraced

Starred in:
Advise and Consent
Columbia Pictures, 1962
Director: Otto Preminger
Played by: George Grizzard

Fred Van Ackerman (George Grizzard) is a young, cunning Senator hungry for power in Advise and Consent.

Description: Ackerman is a young, cunning Senator who is a rising star in the Washington, D.C. firmament. He is tall, dark, and handsome. He wears polyester suits and ties, and keeps his hair short. He has the look of a man hungry for power and self-righteous about his cause.

Reason for Villainy: Van Ackerman is the heavy in a tense drama of Washington insiders. He is opposed to the political maneuvers of Seabright Cooley (Charles Laughton), a southern conservative eager to block the President (Franchot Tone) in his desire to appoint Robert Leffingwell (Henry Fonda) as Secretary of State. The President, according to the Constitution, needs the advise and consent of the Senate to approve Leffingwell. The President plots to have Leffingwell's previous Communist party affiliation covered up. Eager to have Leffingwell's nomination approved, Van Ackerman tries to discredit the special subcommittee chairman, Brigham Anderson (Don Murray), who blocks the candidate's way. Van Ackerman digs up a pathetic homosexual lover of Anderson's from his trying Army days in the Pacific. Anonymous phone calls to Anderson's wife threaten to expose her husband unless he relents and lets Leffingwell into the high post. Although they have the same cause, Leffingwell's supporters would not stoop this low. Van Ackerman knows no conscience in the matter.

Evil Powers/Weapons: Van Ackerman is good at digging up old dirt from out of an opponent's closet. He is sneaky enough to use it.

Occupation: Senator.

Intelligence: Highly intelligent, but amoral.

Strengths: He's brilliant in maneuvers at the Capitol.

Weaknesses: His hot-shot rising-star attitude, and his amoral stance.

Territory: Washington, D.C.

Idiosyncrasies: Walks fast, thinks fast, but doesn't realize some things are above politics—like ethics.

Friends: Leffingwell's supporters are his friends, but only at first.

Enemies: Everybody in Washington after Anderson's suicide.

Evil Deeds: By digging up dirt on a brave and dedicated opponent he causes the man to take the only way out.

Outcome: Anderson is quick to arrange a meeting in a sordid gay bar with his ex-lover. He discovers that the man had told about their affair and handed over some damaging letters. Anderson is so disturbed he commits suicide. The Senate hears about it the next day. Van Ackerman is sad, but doesn't realize what the others will do now. Rather than take advantage of Van Ackerman's foul deed to push through Leffingwell, Bob Munson, Senate Majority Leader opposed to Leffingwell, releases the votes he has against the approval of Leffingwell. Cooley won't vote to throw out Leffingwell either. It is left to the Vice President, Harley Hudson (Lew Ayres) to decide on the nomination. But he receives word that the President is dead and suddenly he too refuses to approve Leffingwell. Hudson is President now and wants to think about the best man for the post. The Senate files out, Van Ackerman is censured and left alone to ponder ethics. Van Ackerman lives on, but is chastened and shunned for his dirty deed by friends who once admired his intelligence and political sense.

Current Status: Depressed.

What to Do If You Meet: Shun him.

Worthy of Note: Laughton's last picture. Burgess Meredith as the Communist party member who fingers Leffingwell was nominated for a Best Supporting Actor Award.

Philip Vandamm

Alias: The Red Spy
Born: 1920
Died: Still alive

Starred in:
North By Northwest
MGM, 1959
Director: Alfred Hitchcock
Played by: James Mason

Description: Well-dressed, middle-aged aristocrat.

Reason for Villainy: Vandamm has Roger Thornhill kidnapped from a hotel. Vandamm believes Thornhill to be CIA top agent George Kaplan. Thornhill had been using that name to elude his pushy mother. The coincidence gets him in a lot of trouble. He's interrogated. He can't spill the beans because he doesn't know beans. The Reds get him drunk as a skunk and

About to be taken away by Philip Vandamm (James Mason) and other Red spies, Roger Thornhill fakes being shot to escape in North by Northwest.

put him behind the wheel of an out-of-control car on a treacherous road. This leads to some thrills as he manages to weave down the incline wildly and stop. Of course, he's arrested for drunk driving and they don't believe his intoxication story. Once he's sober, Thornhill goes back to the hotel and tries to find the mysterious Kaplan. Kaplan's room is empty, but his clothes and possessions are there. At that moment Kaplan receives a telegram and Thornhill decides to open it.

Vandamm still believes he's Kaplan—much more than ever since his daring escape from death. He's a regular James Bond. Vandamm tries to kill our fall guy and Thornhill is left holding the bag for the death of a United Nations' speaker. The cops are after Thornhill now, too.

Back at the CIA meeting, the professor (Leo G. Carroll) is getting a laugh. He announces there is no Kaplan. He's a ploy set up by the CIA to confuse the Red spies. Thornhill is giving the CIA extra fun by making their false man all the more real.

Evil Powers/Weapons: Vandamm has a spy network, goons, pilots and planes with machine guns all behind him. Plus he's very clever.

Occupation: Vandamm is a Communist spy.

Intelligence: As clever a spy as there ever was.

Strengths: He's resolute about killing Thornhill and has the means.

Weaknesses: Thornhill is not Kaplan, and the CIA is on to Vandamm.

Territory: The mansion and the hotel in New York.

Idiosyncrasies: He's a guy that likes to sit by a fire and think.

Friends: The KGB.

Enemies: The CIA. Also Thornhill and the counteragent, Eve Kendall.

Evil Deeds: He kidnaps Thornhill and makes numerous attempts to kill him. He also tries to frame Thornhill. Vandamm fights for communism, injustice, and the Soviet way of life. In the process he has many people killed.

Outcome: Thornhill, our hero/patsy, meets Eve Kendall on a train. Eve (Eva Marie Saint) is apparently taken with our hero and he with her. But she seems to lure him to a rendezvous with his tormentors. He's out on a deserted country road, surely; nothing could happen here. But a cropdusting plane comes by and attempts to strafe him with its flaming machine guns. The bullets narrowly miss. Eve is in league with Vandamm. It was a set-up. Thornhill is a mad guy now. He finds Vandamm and Eve at an auction house. The slightest nod will make you a bidder. Vandamm has his men surround Thornhill. It looks like curtains for Thornhill, but he figures a way to escape. He bids up fantastically. He is taken into the office and offered a blank check to sign. This gets him out of the spy's way. Vandamm is foiled. The cops come to take the irrationally behaving Thornhill away. Who bids when they don't have a red cent? The cops take him to the professor, who explains that Eve was a CIA plant and that Thornhill was caught up in a trap for the Reds. Now the trap is sprung and our hero rises to the occasion and gets the girl.

Current Status: By spilling his guts to the CIA, he was eventually repatriated, or so we believe. In spy stuff, you don't ever know for sure.

What to Do If You Meet: Give Vandamm what he wants or you'll soon be intoxicated and stuck behind the wheel of a car and sent on to your doom.

Worthy of Note: Paul Newman used the same ploy of creating a disturbance to elude his pursuers in *The Prize*.

Johnny Vanning

Born: 1900s
Died: Executed in the 1930s

Starred in:
Marked Woman
Warner Bros., 1937
Director: Lloyd Bacon
Played by: Eduardo Ciannelli

Description: Vanning is a gangster during the period of prohibition. He's sneering, arrogant, and, with his bought law-enforcement people, he can afford to be. He's dark and handsome and quick to strike a blow. He goes down as one of history's most virulent men.

Reason for Villainy: Vanning is a big-time racket boss. He owns the clip joints that take suckers for all their worth and then dump them in some back alley. The hostesses in his clubs are forced to take the average Joe for a ride in order to keep their demanding jobs. Mary Dwight (Bette Davis) does not like doing this dirty work and she complains. Vanning likes her spunk, but rules are rules. Mary then lends a nice sucker enough money to avoid being beaten by Vanning's men for his gambling debt at the club. The next morning the man's body is found with Mary's number in his pocket. The district attorney (Humphrey Bogart) sees this as his chance to get Vanning and puts Mary in jail so that she can squeal on Vanning. Betty (Jane Bryan), Mary's sister, a college girl, also gets caught up in the police net.

Evil Powers/Weapons: Buys and sells judges and law officers. He has also crooked lawyers, guns, and a gang.

Occupation: Racketeer.

Intelligence: Good at adding up the take.

Strengths: His powerful organization.

Weaknesses: The D.A. is tough, and Mary is too.

Territory: The city.

that Mary will really tell all the dirt on them, decide to get even and beat her up. However, Mary recovers in order to tell all in court and the evil Vanning is sent up the river. The clip joint girls all walk away into the fog together arm in arm.

Current Status: Dead

What to Do If You Meet: Get the D.A.

Worthy of Note: Bogart's impassioned speech to the jury is really focused on the movie-going public: Stop the racketeers!

Mrs. Venable

Born: 1910s
Died: Still alive

Starred in:
Suddenly, Last Summer
Columbia, 1959
Director: Joseph L. Mankiewicz
Played by: Katharine Hepburn

Description: Mrs. Venable is living in a dream world, constantly evoking the poetic and brilliant illusion of her dead son, Sebastian, in order to shield herself from the real world. She's an attractive, handicapped, elderly lady with good clothes and gray hair. She's also very rich.

Reason for Villainy: Mrs. Venable is insistent upon the insanity of her dead son's comely cousin, Catherine. She demands that a lobotomy be performed upon the young girl, claiming she is insane for contradicting the noble tale Mrs. Venable tells of her son. In order to get her own way, Mrs. Venable is willing to make a huge donation to the Sanitorium where Catherine (Elizabeth Taylor) is kept. Dr. Cukrowicz (Montgomery Clift) is investigating Catherine's so-called insanity, thinking that perhaps he can cure her—or perhaps she is not so insane after all. Dr. Cukrowicz discovers that all of this goes back

Johnny Vanning (Ed Cianelli) is no longer sneering and arrogant as the law has put a stop to his illegal activities in Marked Woman.

Idiosyncrasies: Likes strong-willed women.

Friends: The mob.

Enemies: The D.A. and Mary.

Relatives: Johnny Udo.

Evil Deeds: Murder, racketeering.

Outcome: The charges against Vanning and his men are dropped when an out-of-town sheriff testifies that they were with him at the time of all the crimes. Another of Vanning's payoffs work. Mary, having taken the stand against Vanning, is threatened, and Betty tells Mary she can't go back to school now with an arrest record. To ease Betty's shame, Emmy Lou (Isabel Jewell), Mary's roommate convinces Betty to come to a party. To their surprise, the party is at Vanning's penthouse. Vanning and Betty quarrel and Betty is pushed off the balcony. Mary is steaming over her sister's murder. The gangsters, realizing to the incidents surrounding the idolized Sebastian's death.

Sebastian was obsessed with the savagery of the world, yet cut off from feelings himself. Catherine was with him at a Spanish seaside cafe before he died. What happened that day? Sebastian—though it's played down here—was homosexual and Catherine pimped for him.

Evil Powers/Weapons: Mrs. Venable has money, elegance, and position. She also has a dream that no one is going to spoil for her if she can stop them.

Occupation: She's rich.

Intelligence: A dreamer.

Strengths: Money.

Weaknesses: Her son is not what she would think, nor did he die as she believes.

Territory: Mansions.

Idiosyncrasies: Private elevators are a weakness.

Friends: Dr. Hochstader—he wants to give Catherine the lobotomy.

Enemies: Dr. Cukrowicz—in a way.

Relatives: Dreamers everywhere.

Evil Deeds: Planning a lobotomy for a sane person. Failing to face reality.

Mrs. Venable lives in a dream world of glory about her son, and would rather have a sane girl committed than admit the truth in Suddenly Last Summer.

Outcome: Sebastian used Catherine by having her attract young men for him. He paid them for favors—although this is only alluded to here on the big screen. He also taunted them. At the seaside cafe where Catherine and he dined in elegance, a group of starving peasant boys broke apart refuse and scraps of metal and made makeshift instruments. Later, they played their instruments in a pagan ritual as they followed Sebastian up a hill in the heat. Soon the peasant boys had surrounded him. Like the sea turtles Sebastian liked to watch being torn apart on the beaches by vultures, the peasant boys tore him apart, dismembering Sebastian. Catherine was still in shock from witnessing this event until Dr. Cukrowicz makes her face what she had seen. But Mrs. Venable does not understand, even though the truth becomes obvious to everyone else. She still insists that Catherine have a lobotomy. Catherine's mother (Mercedes McCambridge), her brother, George (Gene Raymond), and the doctor all agree that Catherine is sane. It's Mrs. Venable who is not facing reality. They humor her and she becomes tired. She then rides her private elevator upstairs again. She hasn't understood a word of truth. Her poet son lives on in her mind.

Current Status: Still alive in fantasy land.

What to Do If You Meet: Take away the elevator.

Worthy of Note: One of the more successful translations of Tennessee Williams's work to the screen.

Ventana Corp.

Born: Incorporated 20th century
Died: Still diversified

Starred in:
The China Syndrome
Columbia-EMI, 1979
Director: James Bridges

Spokespeople for the Ventana Corporation try to cover up the company's lack of responsibility in The China Syndrome.

Description: A giant corporation with its tentacles wrapped around the power-generating industry. It has reactors pumping out the amps. It seeks profits at the expense of safety and humanity. It is evil.

Reason for Villainy: The corporation is interested in keeping the world from knowing how corrupt and incompetent they are. They belittle the danger of nuclear power plants. There is an emergency. A fast thinking employee, Jack Godell (Jack Lemmon), is able to avert disaster by frantic action in the control room. Two reporters, Kimberly Wells (Jane Fonda) and Richard Adams (Michael Douglas), witnessed the accident and filmed it. They are told by their station that it can't be shown as it would panic people unnecessarily. Jack Goddell wants to find out what went wrong. He finds cheap, faulty valves. He realizes the corporation is a threat to us all. He gives the two reporters x-ray pictures of the faulty equipment, and Richard tells his soundman to rush it to the public hearing on the new Ventana power plant. The soundman is forced off the road and is killed by Ventana's goons.

Evil Powers/Weapons: The ability to kill us all in its search for profits. If an accident did occur, they might not tell us. We would find out when we turn out the lights and discover we glow.

Occupation: Nuclear power company.

Intelligence: The corporation has thousands of company officers, spokesmen, and technicians working for it, who are all watching out for their jobs.

Strengths: Money, political pull.

Weaknesses: The media could expose them. If they can't cover up their mistakes, they could lose a big pile of dough.

Territory: KXLA country around Los Angeles.

Idiosyncrasies: They buy two-bit valves for a billion-dollar plant.

Friends: Public ignorance.

Enemies: The truth, reporters, whistle-blowers.

Relatives: The Watergate Conspirators in *All the President's Men.*

Evil Deeds: Kills the guy with the x-ray pics, falsifies records on safety, kills Godell, lies to the government and people, covers up, criminal negligence.

Outcome: Jack Godell wants the story to come out. He seizes the nuclear reactor's control room and barricades himself in with hostages. He is interviewed by the media but appears to be insane. Ventana's security men break in and shoot him dead. Ventana lives on, endangering us all with the potential of a meltdown. In a meltdown, the reactor material gets so hot—a million degrees—that it could ooze through the floor and theoretically melt its way to China, hence the name The China Syndrome. Of course, once below the shielding, deadly radiation kills for miles around.

Current Status: Still incorporated, but undergoing a merger.

What to Do If You Meet: If you get a job from this outfit, find out if they still do the kinds of things that endanger us. Blow the whistle to the media. But be prepared to meet your maker if you do.

Worthy of Note: Two weeks after this film was released, Three Mile Island's nuclear reactor blew its cork. The picture had some eerie counterparts in the real situation. Box office zoomed.

Vigilante Cops

Alias: Death squad
Born: 1950s
Died: Incarcerated 1973

Starred in:
Magnum Force
Warner Bros., 1973
Director: Ted Post
Played by: David Soul, Kip Niven, Robert Urich, Tim Matheson

Description: Four tough, young motorcycle cops and their commander-in-secret, Lieutenant Briggs. The young cops are hard and deadly shots. They wear all leather motorcycle togs and carry .357 Magnums. Helmets and reflective sunglasses make them indistinguishable.

Reason for Villainy: These cops, and their boss, are disgusted that some criminals get away with their crimes. They vow to do the job that the courts don't. In the beginning, we see Harry Callahan (Clint Eastwood) investigating a rash of killings of criminals. He is an inspector, and his superior, Lieutenant Briggs (Hal Holbrook) orders him off the case. After all, Harry tends to shoot first, ask questions later. They have enough bodies to contend with. Meanwhile, it becomes apparent that the killings are the work of some odd gang. Harry, on the police firing range, notices some young cops are supermarksmen with .357 Magnums. He borrows one cop's gun, fires it so he can retrieve the bullet for ballistics match-up. Sure enough, the bullet from Officer Davis's (David Soul's) gun is a match for a deadly bullet in a victim. Another cop investigating the case, Charlie McCoy (Mitchell Ryan), who Harry first suspected, is gunned down. This gang kills cops, too. Harry confronts the Vigilante cops, who say they are doing a needed job.

Evil Powers/Weapons: They have motorcycles, guns, badges. They are expert shots plus they have someone higher up covering for them.

Occupation: Killer cops out to take the law into their own hands.

Intelligence: Smart and fast.

Strengths: They have badges of the law. With their helmets on it's hard to tell them from other cops.

Weaknesses: Harry is after them.

Territory: San Francisco.

Idiosyncrasies: Robot-like actions.

The Vigilante cops have decided to take the law into their own hands and get rid of crooks themselves in Magnum Force.

Friends: Lieutenant Briggs.

Enemies: Dirty Harry.

Evil Deeds: They kill plenty of crooks and pimps. When the other cops start closing in on them, they kill them, too.

Outcome: Dirty Harry Callahan explains to them that what they are doing is murder. They refuse to believe him and say their job is necessary. Harry later goes to the mailbox and finds an explosive charge there. He calls Briggs. Briggs takes a ride with Harry to convince him to lay off the death squad. He won't. Briggs pulls a gun. Harry now knows that Briggs is the mastermind of the killer cops. Harry slams Briggs's head against the dashboard and leaves him on the street. He's now after the other cops. The Vigilantes and Harry meet on the pier. One by one, Harry throws them in the water, shoots them, and beats them to a pulp. The Vigilante Cops are out of commission.

Current Status: In jail, not popular with other criminals.

What to Do If You Meet: Speed away, don't pull over. It's not a ticket they have for you—it's bullets.

Worthy of Note: Mean movie.

Mr. Wabash 237

Josey Wales 238

Walker 239

Matty Walker 240

Wallich Town
Bigots 241

Walter and Phyllis 242

Wicked Witch of
the West 243

The Wild Bunch 244

Wilkes and the
Patients 246

Peter Willems 246

Professor
Willingdon 247

Zampano 248

Mr. Wabash

Born: 1930s
Died: 1975

Starred in:
Three Days of the Condor
Paramount, 1975
Director: Sydney Pollack
Played by: John Houseman

Mr. Wabash (John Houseman) is the benign looking man who is actually behind all the killings in Three Days of the Condor.

Description: Mr. Wabash is a man of mystery—ostensibly a mild-mannered bureaucrat, secretly the head of a CIA within the CIA that has mind-boggling power and an army of hit men and double-agents. There is nothing remarkable about his appearance, although he does dress well and speaks softly.

Reason for Villainy: It seems like any other day for Turner (Robert Redford), a low-level CIA office worker at a computer center. Well, not exactly ordinary. Turner had reported a slip in security to his superiors. When he returns from a coffee break, he discovers everyone in his office has been machine-gunned dead. Suspecting the KGB or terrorists, he calls his superiors once again. Wabash makes things difficult for Turner. All the confusion makes Turner suspicious and paranoid. With his gun and his wits he quickly slips away into the New York City streets, becoming a non-entity and a man hunted by evil. It seems his CIA group, "The American Literary Historical Society," had been hit deliberately by the organization itself for some unknown reason.

Turner, becoming desperate, kidnaps Kathy (Faye Dunaway), an innocent shopper, and hides out in her house, trying to convince her he's not an ordinary rapist killer, but that the CIA is after him.

Evil Powers/Weapons: They're everywhere—watch out. Wabash's men dress as mailmen, but they deliver bullets into your gut.

Occupation: Intelligence officer.

Intelligence: Intelligence is his game.
Strengths: Secrecy and violence.
Weaknesses: He has been found out.
Territory: CIA safehouses and his home in the suburbs.
Idiosyncrasies: Human life is expendable to him.
Friends: His operatives.
Enemies: Turner.
Evil Deeds: In a blatant disregard for innocent lives, he orders the elimination of secretaries and clerks at the low-level CIA center. What else has the man done?
Outcome: Turner is a shifty character. He boggles Wabash and his men by tapping into the main switch-boards at the CIA and routing calls to hundreds of locations. Wabash can't trace a single call. He knows now that Turner is a formidable enemy. Turner is also a ladies' man and eventually romances and wins over his hostage. But Turner is soon discovered and Wabash sends one of his friendly "mailmen" to Kathy's house. A package she didn't expect arrives. At the last second, Turner notices that

the mailman is wearing non-regulation sneakers and manages to escape before the Brooklyn Heights apartment is riddled with bullets. Turner's section head, Higgins (Cliff Robertson), catches up to Turner after this incident but he has already given the whole story to the New York Times. Higgins says they won't print it. Turner thinks they will. After all, the newspaper industry is independent—ISN'T IT?

Current Status: Dead. The CIA doesn't like independent actions.

What to Do If You Meet: Check out all mailmen.

Worthy of Note: Max Von Sydow, as assassin "Joubert," is particularly good here, but see him in some of the Bergman movies!

Josey Wales

The Outlaw Josey Wales has all the weapons he needs to avenge the murder of his family.

Born: Pre-Civil War
Died: Post-Civil War

Starred in:
The Outlaw Josey Wales
Warner Bros., 1976
Director: Clint Eastwood
Played by: Clint Eastwood

Description: Long brown hair, short beard, range riding clothes, cowboy hat, two huge pistols, and, of course, that icy Eastwood face.

Reason for Villainy: Wales's family is murdered by bluecoat marauders during the Civil War. Josey goes to join Confederates with vigilante Fletcher (John Vernon). He's very effective in killing Union soldiers and the bluecoats come to fear him. Tricked into surrendering with amnesty, all of Josey's band surrender and are slaughtered. He escapes and picks up two Indians, Little Moonlight and Lone Watie. They head to Texas and more trouble. The three eventually come upon a ranch with settlers and Josey falls in love with Laura Lee (Sondra Locke).

Evil Powers: Wants to destroy those Unioners who hurt people.

Weapons: Good shot with his long, long pistols.

Occupation: Cowboy, Confederate irregular, outlaw, homesteader.

Intelligence: Can't read none, but sure can outsmart people, especially Yankees.

Strengths: Honest, hard working.

Weaknesses: Thinks he can stand alone—until he finds a new family.

Territory: Southern and Western U.S.A.

Idiosyncrasies: Cynical, but brave. He likes Indians.

Friends: Indians, women, children, honest folk.

Enemies: Union soldiers, bounty hunters.

Evil Deeds: Forced to kill lots of soldiers and bounty hunters during the Civil War. Now there's a price on his head.

Outcome: Wales, now bunking down with the family of settlers and Indians, expects a new attack by Union soldiers and fortifies the house and arms everyone in sight. Captain Terrell, who is after Wales, attacks but all his men are killed. Terrell escapes the massacre but Josey goes after him, finally running him through with a sword.

Current Status: Lived to a ripe old age and had many grandchildren.

What to Do If You Meet: Don't try to collect the bounty or you'll be less one head.

Worthy of Note: Clint shows emotion in this film, actually crying when his son is killed!

Walker

Born: 1930s
Died: Still alive

Starred in:
Point Blank
MGM, 1967
Director: John Boorman
Played by: Lee Marvin

Description: Tall and lanky. His face is frozen with the betrayed look he had when he "died." He doesn't stand still long enough for anyone to get a good look at him. A middle-aged organization man gone wild.

Reason for Villainy: Walker is a "good" bad guy because one can identify with his desire for revenge on his attempted murder. Walker is lured to Alcatraz Island, now deserted where he is set up by his wife Lynne (Sharon Acker). There he is shot at point blank, hence the title of the film. However, he doesn't die. His killer, Reese (John Vernon), goes off with Walker's wife as his life ebbs away. But wait, he is alive, and, boy, is he mad. He finds a man, Yost (Keenan Wynn), who wants to help Walker collect the thousands in loot that Reese and Walker had stolen from the syndicate. Reese will not be the first target. Walker first fills his betrayer/wife's bed full of bullets. She's not there at the time of the attack, but later takes her life with pills. One down, more to go. It's not just Reese that Walker wants, it's also Carter, Fairfax, and Brewster, all big syndicate bosses. They have

the money and he wants it. Chris (Angie Dickinson) was Lynne's friend. Walker uses her to seduce Reese in a penthouse. Reese is so scared of the "dead" Walker when he appears in the penthouse that he falls from the building. So much for him.

Evil Powers/Weapons: Walker is like a ghost—everywhere and nowhere. He is motivated by one of the most primitive urges—revenge. He can use both ends of a gun, plus his fists and feet.

Occupation: Mobster.

Intelligence: Wiser now that he's been betrayed.

Strengths: Insane desire for revenge.

Weaknesses: He's up against too many people.

Territory: Alcatraz Island, Los Angeles, the West Coast in general.

Idiosyncrasies : Flamboyant ties, thinks with his mouth open.

Friends: Chris.

Enemies: The mob, especially Reese.

Evil Deeds: Murder, attempted murder, beatings, robberies, escape, littering, jaywalking.

Outcome: Walker next tries to get his money from Carter (Lloyd Bochner). Walker is set up, but Carter's sniper kills Carter instead. Walker then makes his way to Brews-

Walker (Lee Marvin) threatens Carter to find out where the money he had stolen from the syndicate has been secreted in Point Blank.

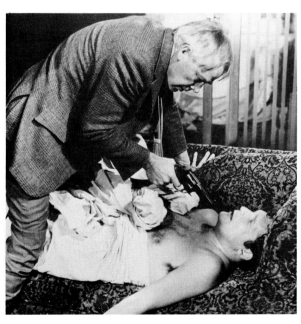

ter's house. Brewster (Carroll O'Connor) tells him that the dough is on Alcatraz Island, which is another trap. But our "dead" man goes there and the strange Yost, his ally, kills Brewster for him and tells Walker to pick up his money. It seems Yost is really Fairfax, but he's no friend of the gangster. Our anti-hero slips away into the shadows. He wasn't after any money—just revenge.

Current Status: Slipped away.

What to Do If You Meet: Never mention the name Lynne.

Worthy of Note: Some nice camera work. It allowed the viewer to share Walker's alienated psychosis.

Matty Walker

Alias: Mary Ann
Born: 1940s
Died: She really didn't die

Starred in:
Body Heat
Warner Bros., 1981
Director: Lawrence Kasdan
Played by: Kathleen Turner

Description: She's sultry, dark-haired, mysterious, hot, sensuous, desirous, and dangerous.

Reason for Villainy: Ned Racine (William Hurt), a stud and lawyer, and more than a little crooked, meets sultry Matty Walker (Kathleen Turner) at an outdoor concert. The setting is Miranda Beach, Florida during a heat wave. She disappears, but he finds her days later at a bar and they decide to leave together. He follows her to her mansion, but she throws him out. As she begins to fondle herself, Ned smashes through the French doors and they begin their romance with hot sex. She eventually talks him into killing her husband—a small

and mean type, she says—and the lawyer is crazy enough to do it. Racine drives to Miami and rents a place to establish an alibi. When he returns in another car, he clubs hubby to death and they dump the body. Maybe he'll be rich now. They agree not to meet for a long while—till it blows over.

Evil Powers/Weapons: She's not who she says she is—she's not even the person she's not. But she's so sexy you'd do anything for her.

Occupation: Femme fatale; conspirator; user and abuser of love, sex, and other people; heroine of the existential dread; alienation incarnate; and evil extraordinaire.

Intelligence: Too tricky for words.

Strengths: Hidden desires, twisted aspirations cleverly disguised and overlaid with sex.

Weaknesses: Perhaps none. Unless evil is a weakness unto itself.

Territory: Florida, other places unknown, and, finally, Tahiti.

Matty Walker (Kathleen Turner) uses her sex appeal to seduce Ned Racine into murdering her husband in Body Heat.

Idiosyncrasies: You never know when she'll stick it to you, but you still go on.

Friends: Racine is mad about her.

Enemies: Racine will never stop searching for her. His problem is he has to do it from prison.

Evil Deeds: Countless betrayals of men, conspiracy and murder, deception, and bad sportsmanship. Worst of all, an enormous insincerity regarding the act of love. But she is hot. Her temperature actually runs about 100 degrees. No wonder she's hot to touch.

Outcome: The dead husband, Edmund (Richard Crenna), had altered his will shortly before his demise in a fire (arranged by the sex-mad couple). The will leaves it all to Matty. Worst of all for Racine is that his name is signed on the will as the man who made the changes. Yes, Matty made the changes without telling Racine. Still in the clear, but now they are being watched. Racine soon begins to suspect all is not as it seems. This woman is devious; what else doesn't he know? Peter Lowenstein, Racine's friend, and the prosecution's attorney, warns Racine to stay away from her. Despite the warning, he can't. The prosecutor, for friendship, reveals that on the night of the murder many unanswered calls were made to Racine's Miami address, plus Edmund's glasses are missing and an anonymous source is threatening to produce them and incriminate Racine. Most stunning is the revelation from a legal acquaintance that Racine accidentally meets in a bar. This man says that Matty had been asking about Racine a year earlier. So the entire relationship had been a set up. The sex, the whole thing, was calculated to string him into the crime. He confronts her and she admits it, but says she is now really in love with him. Phoooey, he knows better. He even knows that a man was paid by her to rig a bomb in the boathouse that he had been expected to enter to look for the mysterious missing glasses. He forces her to walk to the boathouse to test her innocence. She appears to enter as he shouts a warning. The boathouse is blown up and the mangled body of the beauty is found. Racine is off to jail, for all clues point to him as a psycho murderer. He's not convinced, however, that she is dead, even though dental records proves it's Matty Walker's body. In jail, Racine sends for Matty's high school yearbook. The face of the Matty Walker he knew is not the same as in the picture. The name Mary Ann Simpson appears by the picture of the woman he knew. A triple triple-crosser. Where is she now? The fade out of the film shows her in the South Pacific, rich and suntanned.

Current Status: Hot.

What to Do If You Meet: Use your intuition and marry a sweet, old-fashioned dame.

Worthy of Note: Our vote for best recent mystery film. This steamy film of *film noir* excellence marked the debut of a new director. An auspicious debut.

Wallich Town Bigots

Born: Different ages
Died: Still alive

Starred in:
Billy Jack
Warner Bros., 1972
Director: Tom Laughlin
Played by: Bert Freed, Clark Howat, David Roya

Description: Group of bigoted, redneck-cowboy types and lawmen from Wallich, Arizona. Wear cowboy boots, Stetsons, jeans.

Reason for Villainy: These folks are just plain mean and narrow minded. They don't like other races or race mixing. Ex-Green Beret and karate expert Billy Jack returns to his Indian reservation near Wallich. He tries to protect the Indians, the wild horses that Posner (the town boss) catches and slaughters, and Jean Roberts's Freedom School, which takes in troubled kids of any race. (He and Jean are lovers.) The townspeople (particularly the men) hate the school and everything it stands for. Mike, a deputy sheriff, beats up his daughter Barbara when she confesses she's pregnant. Barbara runs away to the Freedom School. In Wallich, Freedom School students are thrown out of an ice cream parlor. Bernard, Posner's son, throws flour on the kids and attacks Martin, a pacifist Indian. Billy Jack arrives and is also attacked by Posner and his goons, but he manages to get in some good shots before the sheriff stops the fight.

Evil Powers: Power of small-town bigots—ostracism, bullying, assaults.

Weapons: Fists, fear, guns, knives.

Occupation: They have different jobs, but a lot of them just sit around spitting in the dust and trying to look mean.

Intelligence: Dumb, provincial, close-minded, prejudiced.

Territory: Wallich, Arizona.

Idiosyncrasies: Enjoy sadistic games, bullying, picking on kids, yelling racial insults. They are impotent, insecure men who get their rocks off by looking down on others.

Friends: Each other.

Enemies: All others, particularly Indians, blacks, Mexicans, hippies, and, of course, Billy Jack.

Relatives: The Mountain Men of *Deliverance*, rednecks of *Easy Rider*.

Outcome: Jean is raped by Bernard. She doesn't tell Billy Jack, fearing he'll kill the vicious son of the town boss. Bernard convinces Mike that Barbara's baby (which she

loses in miscarriage) was fathered by Martin, and Mike kidnaps the Indian and beats him. Martin escapes but Bernard kills him. Billy Jack, realizing that Bernard has raped Jean and killed Martin, goes after him. Bernard wounds him, but Billy kills him with a karate blow. Then Mike attacks him, but Billy kills him, too. Billy positions himself in a church refusing to surrender unless Barbara is put in Jean's custody and the school gets funding for the next 10 years. Billy's demands are agreed to and he surrenders and is driven to jail. But he has broken Posner's grip of fear on the Freedom School and dealt a blow to the bigots.

Current Status: Alive, still racist.

What to Do If You Meet: Chew tobaccy, spit, and say, "If there's one thing I can't stand it's miscegenation."

Worthy of Note: Independently produced and rejected at first by big movie companies. The film went on to make millions for Tom Laughlin and made him a legend

Walter and Phyllis

Alias: Walter Neff
Phyllis Dietrichson
Born: 1920s
Died: 1940s

Starred in:
Double Indemnity
Paramount, 1944
Director: Billy Wilder
Played by: Fred McMurray and
Barbara Stanwyck

Description: He's a dapper, middle-aged insurance salesman who wears a suit and carries a valise. She's a sexy housewife in velour dresses. Brilliant blonde hair.

Reason for Villainy: Phyllis gets it on with Walter, her husband's insurance man. They

The Wallich town bigots close in on Billy Jack but get more than they bargained for in his lethal feet.

Walter and Phyllis (Fred McMurray and Barbara Stanwyck) are lovers who plot to murder her husband after Walter has sold him a huge insurance policy in Double Indemnity.

trick him into securing some policies on his life and do the poor fellow in. But soon after the murder, Walter decides to kill his co-conspirator because he realizes she used him and doesn't really love him. He also believes she has another lover.

Evil Powers: Legerdemain, skullduggery.

Weapons: Duplicity.

Occupation: Insurance salesman and housewife.

Intelligence: Highly intelligent pair, but totally amoral.

Strengths: Their planning is good.

Weaknesses: They keep secrets from one another and cheat.

Territory: Los Angeles.

Idiosyncrasies: Walter and Phyllis are always whispering to one another, lying.

Friends: One another—to a point.

Enemies: Barton Keyes, a co-worker, is suspicious of Walter.

Relatives: The couple in *The Postman Always Rings Twice.*

Evil Deeds: They bump off Phyllis's husband, insurance fraud, adultery, and then they try to kill each other.

Outcome: Phyllis's and Walter's distrust of each other grows so much that they finally shoot it out. (Classic thieves-falling-out stuff.) As Phyllis lays dying she says she really does love Walter. Later Walter dictates a confession in his office and keels over.

Current Status: She's shot dead, he's electrocuted.

What to Do If You Meet: Don't sign any insurance policies handed to you by a new lover (or an old wife). It could mean your life.

Worthy of Note: The electrocution of Walter Neff was cut from the film before release. Based on a true story that occurred in New York in 1927.

Wicked Witch of the West

Born: Ancient witch
Died: Water melts her down

Starred in:
The Wizard of Oz
MGM, 1939
Director: Victor Fleming
Special Effects by: A. Arnold Gillespie
Played by: Margaret Hamilton

Description: Wicked witch, black clothing, cape, huge, black cone-shaped hat. Clawed, gnarled hands, huge nose.

Reason for Villainy: The Wicked Witch of the West occupies the darker parts of the mythical land of Oz. When Dorothy (Judy Garland) is whisked up inside her Kansas farmhouse by a tornado, she is carried far "over the rainbow" to the land of Oz. When she emerges from the house, she discovers that the house has squashed the evil Wicked Witch of the East into a wafer. Her sister, the Witch of the West, shows up on the scene and is furious. She wants revenge on Dorothy. But just in the nick of time, Glinda, the Good Witch of the North, protects Dorothy by giving her a pair of magic ruby slippers. The Wicked Witch of the West, cackling madly, flies off on her broom vowing revenge.

Evil Powers/Weapons: She flies on a broom, has magic spells, dematerializes, uses a crystal ball, and controls a flying army of killer monkey men.

Occupation: Meanest witch in the valley.

Intelligence: Moderate intelligence, but has extra sensory perceptions.

Strengths: All the powers of a top witch. Invulnerable to weapons.

Weaknesses: Allergic to water.

Territory: Secret cave high in the mountains of Oz.

Idiosyncrasies: She cackles and sneers.

Friends: Her only friend was her sister and she's flat as a pancake now.

Enemies: Hates Dorothy, Toto, the Scarecrow, the Tin Man, and the Cowardly Lion.

Evil Deeds: Tries to destroy Dorothy and her friends by setting all kinds of traps. She has the monkey men set the scarecrow on fire. She terrorizes Oz and the Munchkins. Kidnaps Dorothy.

Killed by: After popping out of Munchkinland, the Wicked Witch of the West keeps an eye on Dorothy waiting for the right moment to attack. Dorothy, meanwhile, makes friends with the Tin Man, the Cowardly Lion, and the Scarecrow and they all set off for Emerald City to find the great and powerful Wizard of Oz, who can send Dorothy back to Kansas. The Wicked Witch taunts the group throughout their journey and eventually makes them drift into a field of poisoned poppies. The Good Witch intervenes and coats the poppies with snow which kills the poison. Once inside Emerald City, the group finds the Wizard who promises help if they'll bring him the Wicked Witch's broom. When the four head off to get it, the witch attacks again, kidnapping Dorothy with her flying monkey men and bringing her to her secret headquarters. The others come to rescue her. When the witch catches the others rescuing Dorothy, she plans to torture them. Her first victim will be the Scarecrow. The Wicked Witch sets her broom afire with plans of burning the Scarecrow. Dorothy, in an effort to save her friend, goes to extinguish the broom with a bucket of water. The water hits the witch instead and she begins to melt. "Look, what you've done to my beautiful wickedness," she screams. Within seconds, she is goo. Later, still looking

The Wicked Witch of the West (Margaret Hamilton) is out to get Dorothy whose house inadvertently squashed her sister, the Wicked Witch of the East, in The Wizard of Oz.

for a way to get back to Kansas, Dorothy is told by the Good Witch to merely click the heels of her ruby slippers three times and say, "There's no place like home." In a matter of seconds she's back in her bed in Kansas. Was all of this real or just a dream?

Current Status: Dead, but she has another sister who's taken her place.

What to Do If You Meet: Tell her you know where that blasted dog Toto is.

Worthy of Note: One of the absolute best films of all time. The Wicked Witch of the West has undoubtedly filled many a youngster's head with a nightmarish visions, as is the wont of a good villain.

The Wild Bunch

Born: 19th century
Died: 1913

Starred in:
The Wild Bunch
Warner Bros./Seven Arts, 1969
Director: Sam Peckinpah
Played by: William Holden, Ernest
    Borgnine, Ben Johnson, Jaime Sanchez,
    Warren Oates

Description: A gang of eight violent outlaws who plunder whatever will bring them cash, e.g., banks and Wells Fargo. They wear Army uniforms but later switch to cowboy clothes. Of course, they ride horses and carry plenty of guns.

Reason for Villainy: It's 1913, and these eight men in Army uniforms decide to rob the railroad office in San Rafael, Texas. Ambushed by bounty hunters, the robbers shoot their way out, killing loads of bystanders. Five of the bank robbers escape—Pike Bishop (William Holden), the leader; Dutch (Ernest Borgnine), his right hand man; Hector and Lyle Gorch (Ben Johnson, Warren Oates); and Angel (Jaime Sanchez), a young Mexican. Their loot turns out to be steel washers and, with the bounty hunters on their trail, the Wild Bunch heads down into Mexico.

Evil Powers/Weapons: Mean fighters, tougher than everyone around them. Fists, guns, dynamite, rapid-fire guns.

Occupation: Bank robbers, killers.

Intelligence: Different intelligences but all are smart and tough. They are survivors. Pike is very smart and an excellent planner. He's perceptive and knows how other men operate.

Strengths: They stick together and are fearless.

Weaknesses: Their macho image, plus they don't care if they live or die.

Territory: Texas, Mexico.

Idiosyncrasies: Each man has his own peculiarities, but they all like wine and women. Angel wants to help the revolutionaries of his country, Mexico, who are fighting evil and corrupt leaders.

Friends: Each other.

Enemies: Mapache, the Mexican warlord, and Deke Thornton (a man who once rode with them and now leads the bounty hunters who are constantly on their trail).

The Wild Bunch decide they've had enough and walk through the fort to blast General Mapache.

Relatives: *The Dirty Dozen, Quantrill's Riders.*

Evil Deeds: Rob banks, shoot innocent bystanders, rob trains, kill half a Mexican fort.

Killed by: They arrive in Aqua Verde, a fort run by Mapache (Emilio Fernandez), a cruel general. Angel shoots Mapache's girlfriend who is sitting on Mapache's lap, and the Wild Bunch is almost shot by the general's troops. But instead they make a deal to rob an American train and steal guns for Mapache. They rob the train and turn over the weapons, except for one box which Angel gives his guerilla buddies. Mapache seizes Angel for this and tortures him horribly. The Wild Bunch show up at the fort to save him, but can do nothing. The Bunch spends the night with some women and the next morning decide on revenge. Armed with rifles they walk up to Mapache and his troops and begin blazing away. An incredible firefight erupts in which half the fort and the four remaining Wild Bunch members are shot to pieces. In death they have somehow performed a heroic, if not bloody, deed and killed a tyrant.

Current Status: Dead, riddled with bullets.

What to Do If You Meet: Tell 'em you're a macho cowboy and ask if you may join them.

Worthy of Note: One of the best, most violent of cowboy movies. The film also did incredibly well at the box office. Resurrected Peckinpah's sagging career.

Wilkes and the Patients

Alias: The mean attendant
Born: 20th century
Died: Still alive

Starred in:
Shock Corridor
Allied Artists, 1963
Director: Samuel Fuller
Played by: Chuck Robertson

Description: Wilkes is a tough-looking mental ward attendant in a white uniform. He has shiny, well-combed hair and is articulate. He is strongly built and the patients fear him.

Reason for Villainy: Wilkes, though we don't discover it until the end, has murdered a man named Sloane in the institution. In this wonderfully sleazy picture, Johnny Barrett (Peter Breck) is an investigating reporter. Barrett fakes insanity by having his girl friend claim she's his sister and that he raped her. That gets Dr. Cristo to put him in the asylum. Perfect cover. But immediately Johnny starts going crazy. Also helping him along are the crazies of the Shock Corridor. The patients—Pagliacci, who sits on him and feeds him chewing gum; a black man who is a white supremacist spouting KKK nonsense; and a slew of others—help drive Johnny over the edge. Wilkes is afraid that Johnny will find out something since all the patients know Wilkes killed Sloane. Wilkes is relieved when Johnny is given shock therapy because it fogs the brain. But in a lucid moment Johnny tells on Wilkes.

Evil Powers/Weapons: Wilkes has access to the electroshock room, and no one would believe the murder story from the loonies.

Occupation: Male attendant.
Intelligence: Below average.
Strengths: He's in a good position to cover up his crime.
Weaknesses: Johnny's on his case.
Territory: Mental ward.

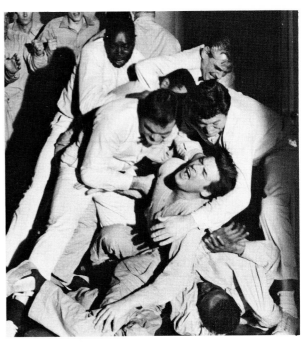

The inmates of Wilkes's ward subdue undercover reporter Johnny Barrett in Shock Corridor.

Idiosyncrasies: He's interested in crazy women.
Friends: The patients, but only sometimes.
Enemies: Johnny.
Outcome: When Dr. Cristo learns that Wilkes committed the murder, he removes him from his position. But the sex abuser's nemesis, Johnny, is completely bonkers now and retreats within himself. He stands and stares at walls, mumbles; he's a mess. He actually believes his girl is his sister. Johnny will remain in the funny farm for the rest of his life.
Current Status: In jail.
What to Do If You Meet: Tell him you're seeing a therapist privately and don't believe in electroshock treatments anyway.
Worthy of Note: Fuller did *House of Bamboo* and *The Big Red One*, which also had a great asylum scene.

Peter Willems

Born: 1800s
Died: Still alive at the end

Starred in:
Outcast of the Islands
United Artists (Lopert), 1951
Director: Sir Carol Reed
Played by: Trevor Howard

Description: In Singapore he is completely together, wearing a tie and clean white suit. Under the influence of the tropical, lusty hell, however, he degenerates into loose, ragged clothes with his shirt open down the front. A comparable moral decay has occurred in this tall, dark, and handsome man.

Reason for Villainy: Peter is dismissed from his clerk's job in Singapore. A trader, Captain Lingard (Ralph Richardson), takes him on in Simbar, where he has a lucrative monopoly. Soon, however, Peter comes under the influence of a sarong-wearing, slinky native girl, Aissa (Kerima) and her boss, native leader Babalatchi (George Couloris). Babalatchi wants to take over Lingard's trading monopoly but needs Willems's knowledge of the operations to pull it off. Through Aissa's slinky ways, Willems joins the natives and betrays Lingard.

Evil Powers/Weapons: His knowledge.

Occupation: Trader's clerk.

Intelligence: Smart, but passion leads to his fall.

Peter Willems (Trevor Howard) double-crosses his boss to help another man gain the trading monopoly in Outcast of the Islands.

Strengths: He knows the trade routes and other necessary things for taking over business.

Weaknesses: Aissa and alcohol.

Territory: Singapore and points east.

Idiosyncrasies: He has an infatuation with a native girl who doesn't even speak his language.

Friends: The captain, until he betrayed him.

Enemies: The captain, once he betrayed him.

Evil Deeds: Betraying Lingard and taking up with Aissa. Willems is filled with lust for Aissa. Her sexuality and the native allure corrupt his soul and his body.

Outcome: They have succeeded in ruining Lingard, but they also are left to stew with each other in a love/hate relationship.

Current Status: Steamy sulking.

What to Do If You Meet: Bring extra white shirts.

Worthy of Note: From the Conrad novel, with some liberties taken.

Professor Willingdon

Born: 1910 or thereabouts
Died: 1950

Starred in:
Seven Days to Noon
London Films, 1950
Director: John and Roy Boulting
Played by: Barry Jones

Description: The professor is bald with frizzy gray hair at the temples. He has a wide-eyed stare and starts skipping shaves, ending up with a face full of stubble. He wears a woolen suit and tie against the cold London air and he can't be reasoned with.

The clean-shaven Professor Willingdon walks unnoticed in spite of the huge wanted posters bearing his picture in Seven Days to Noon.

Reason for Villainy: On a Monday morning, a postman delivers an ordinary envelope to the prime minister. It contains a threat by an eminent scientist to blow up London. The scientist, Professor Willingdon, has stolen an atomic bomb and plans on using it unless the government ceases construction of all nuclear weapons. The letter gives the authorities until noon of the following Sunday to decide. A search is begun at once to determine if the threat is for real. Meanwhile, the professor is hiding out at the home of an aging musical actress, Goldie (Olive Sloane), who "entertains" gentlemen. She doesn't know what's in the professor's suitcase. Time is running out; the evacuation of London begins.

Evil Powers/Weapons: He's got the bomb.
Occupation: Atomic scientist turned peace hungry extremist.
Intelligence: $E=MC^2$ smart!
Strengths: He's got the bomb.
Weaknesses: He's got problems.
Territory: London.
Idiosyncrasies: Will blow up London for peace.
Friends: Nuclear bomb.
Enemies: The authorities.
Evil Deeds: Have bomb, will travel.

Outcome: In the shadow of Big Ben, on the last gloomy Sunday for London, the professor is prepared to flip the switch. Can he be stopped? In this case, as Goldie flees under the wail of the siren, the man is apprehended and the all-clear signal warbles through the sky. Is there a message here? Ban the bomb was the slogan at the time of the threat.
Current Status: Dead.
What to Do If You Meet: Handle his packages gently.
Worthy of Note: The Boulting Brothers, who produced this film, also produced *I'm Allright Jack* nine years later. That film made a star of Peter Sellers.

Zampano

Alias: The Great Zampano
Born: 1900s
Died: 1960s

Starred in:
La Strada
United Artists, 1954
Director: Federico Fellini
Played by: Anthony Quinn

Description: Super strongman Zampano is as hefty as a strongman should be, and is often seen breaking chains at fairs. He has short-cropped black hair, muscles galore, and fierce eyes.
Reason for Villainy: Zampano is a cruel brute. He has submerged his humanity in the desperate desire to make enough money to live on La Strada—the road. He drives his motorcycle—wagon—home throughout Italy, putting on his act. But he is lonely. He negotiates with an extremely starving family and purchases their half-wit daughter to assist him and keep him company. But now she will have to endure his heavy handed scolding. Still, she

does whatever he wishes and is happy somehow no matter how cruel he is. He believes she is not worthy of him, but it is obviously the other way around. She is a weak-minded, not-so-pretty young thing, but he is a lout. Zampano and Gelsomina (Guilietta Masina) travel the country until they are near Rome. Rome's wealth and decadence lure Zampano. He also becomes embroiled in a controversy with another performer, Matto the Fool (Richard Basehart), who vies for Gelsomina's attention. She won't desert Zampano though, even if Matto offers her better treatment. Later, at a crossroad where Zampano and Matto inadvertently meet, they fight to end their hatred of each other. It is Matto who is killed.

Evil Powers/Weapons: Strong, brutish, callous.

Occupation: Strongman, a one-man show.

Intelligence: Oafish illiterate.

Strengths: His muscles.

Weaknesses: His brain.

Territory: Italy during hard times.

Idiosyncrasies: Slowly thinking, quickly acting.

Friends: Gelsomina.

Zampano (Anthony Quinn) fails to appreciate his simple-minded companion until he loses her in La Strada.

Enemies: Matto.

Evil Deeds: His poor treatment of Gelsomina is unforgivable.

Outcome: Zampano is disgusted with Gelsomina's constant crying after the murder. He believes she was in love with the enemy, and the sensitive and devoted Gelsomina is dumped from Zampano's pathetic life. He continues to ply his trade for several months, slowly realizing what he has lost. Gelsomina's memory comes to haunt him. He tracks the girl down to a small village of poor people. He learns, to his great anguish, that she died shortly before. The oxlike Zampano is broken. He's destroyed the love of his life. He goes on, but he is not up to it, his act is increasingly pathetic. He is without his soul. His soul also died with the gentle devoted companion he scorned.

Current Status: It is rumored he died of a broken heart several years later.

What to Do If You Meet: Keep out of reach.

Worthy of Note: The saddest movie ever made.

Actor Index

A

Acker, Sharon 239
Adair, Jean 35
Albert, Eddie 206
Alexander, John 35
Alexander, Terrence 117
Allan, Richard 142
Allen, Corey 36
Allen, Woody 213
Amagula, Nanjiwarra 48
Anderson, Donna 177
Anderson, James 214
Andes, Danny 13
Andress, Ursula 76
Andrews, Dana 144
Angel, Heather 150
Arness, James 54
Astaire, Fred 177
Astor, Mary 103
Atherton, William 113
Attenborough, Richard 117
Atwill, Lionel 91
Autry, Gene 174
Aylmer, Felix 68
Ayres, Lew 55, 230

B

Bacall, Lauren 181, 194
Badel, Alan 121
Banks, Leslie 22
Barnes, Binnie 150
Barrat, Robert 150
Basehart, Richard 249
Bass, Alfie 135
Baxter, Anne 67, 83
Beatty, Ned 173
Beatty, Warren 34
Beaumont, Hugh 110
Beck, Michael 143
Beckley, Tony 218
Bedoya, Alfonso 74
Beery, Wallace 208
Begley, Ed 81
Bendix, William 110
Bennett, Joan 147
Bergen, Polly 40
Berghof, Herbert 71
Bergman, Ingrid 181, 204, 219
Best, Edna 22
Bettger, Lyle 52
Bickford, Charles 162
Billodeau, David C. 196
Bird, Norman 117
Bisley, Steve 227
Bisset, Jacqueline 181
Black, Karen 151
Blackman, Honor 180
Blackmer, Sidney 69, 192
Bleeker, Harry 127
Bochner, Lloyd 239
Bogart, Humphrey 46, 74, 98, 103,
    148, 158, 194, 219, 231
Bogdanovitch, Peter 226
Bookwalter, De Veren 160
Borgnine, Ernest 72, 245
Boulton, Michael 164
Boyd, Stephen 167
Boyle, Peter 71
Brady, Scott 210
Brando, Marlon 93, 98, 126, 131, 140
Breck, Peter 246
Bridges, Lloyd 168

Brodie, Lea 131
Bromley, Hunt 102
Bronson, Charles 72
Brook, Faith 131
Brown, Jim 72
Bryan, Jane 231
Brynner, Yul 66, 129
Buckler, Hugh 150
Bujold, Genevieve 96
Bull, Peter 97
Buono, Victor 25
Burnette, Smiley 174
Burns, Marilyn 138
Burns, Tim 226
Burr, Raymond 51
Burstyn, Ellen 41
Burton, Richard 111
Busby, Tom 72

C

Caan, James 99
Cabot, Bruce 149
Cagney, James 107, 124
Caine, Michael 63
Calhern, Louis 69, 75
Campus, Victor 133
Capucine 47
Carbone, Antony 163
Cardinale, Claudia 47
Carey, Harry Jr. 54
Carey, Timothy 151
Carnovsky, Morris 46
Carroll, Leo G. 230
Carruthers, Ben 72
Carson, Jack 35
Cassavettes, John 72
Cavanagh, Paul 21
Cazale, John 56, 199
Chamberlain, Richard 48, 209
Chaney, Lon Jr. 168
Chaplin, Geraldine 194
Charisse, Cyd 16
Chiles, Lois 77
Chin, Tsai 94
Christy, Dorothy 174
Ciannelli, Eduardo 231
Cioffi, Charles 39
Clark, Candy 214
Clery, Corinne 78
Clift, Montgomery 232
Cobb, Lee J. 16, 93
Cochran, Steve 124
Coghlan, Frank Jr. 203
Collins, Ray 200
Connery, Sean 76, 180, 181
Conrad, William 200
Conried, Hans 225
Cook, Elisha Jr. 103
Cooper, Gary 168
Cooper, Stuart 72
Cotten, Joseph 139, 142, 162
Couloris, George 247
Coward, Herbert "Cowboy" 173
Cox, Ronny 173
Crawford, Joan 25, 210
Crawford, John 118
Cregar, Laird 191
Crenna, Richard 241
Currin, Brenda C. 212
Curtis, Tony 27, 83, 116

D

Dall, John 223
Daly, Tyne 161
Daniell, Henry 101
Dano, Frankie 175
Danson, Ted 211
Darrieux, Danielle 71
da Silva, Howard 110
David, Johnny 196
Davies, John Howard 89
Davies, Rupert 114
Davis, Bette, 25, 59, 84, 231
Dean, James 36
de Brulier, Nigel 203
de Havilland, Olivia 55, 105, 207
Deneuve, Catherine 206
De Niro, Robert 224
Dern, Bruce 132
Dhiegh, Knigh 154
Dickinson, Angie 239
Dietrich, Marlene 182
Divine 155
Donat, Robert 69
Douglas, Kirk 26, 44, 53, 83, 129
Douglas, Michael 97, 234
Dourif, Brad 176
Dowling, Doris 111
Dresser, Louise 182
Dru, Joanne 54
Dunaway, Faye 34, 58, 60, 175, 194
Duncan, Kenneth 179
Durning, Charles 218
Duvall, Robert 57, 132, 151
Dwyer, Hilary 114

E

Eastwood, Clint 157, 161, 170, 202,
  235, 238
Eaton, Shirley 180
Eggar, Samantha 130
Eythe, William 95

F

Fairbanks, Douglas Jr. 192
Fawcett, Farrah 44
Ferdin, Pamelyn 157
Fernandez, Emilio 245
Ferrer, Jose 28
Ferzetti, Gabrielle 33
Field, Stanley 192
Finley, William 183
Finney, Albert 181
Fitzgerald, Barry 186
Fletcher, Louise 188
Flynn, Errol 104
Fonda, Henry 136, 229
Fonda, Jane 39, 204, 234
Fonda, Peter 196
Fontaine, Joan 65, 68
Forbes, Bryan 117
Forrest, Steve 59
Forsythe, John 213
Fox, Edward 121
Franz, Arthur 51
Freed, Bert 241
Frobe, Gert 180

G

Gable, Clark 31, 163
Gam, Rita 90
Garbo, Greta 159
Gardner, Ava 177
Garfield, John 92
Garland, Judy 243
Gatliff, Frank 63
George, Gladys 107
Gibson, Mel 227
Gielgud, John 181
Gilman, Sam 140
Gleason, Jackie 100
Granger, Farley 19
Grant, Cary 35, 205
Grayson, Eunice 76
Green, Nigel 63
Greenstreet, Sydney 102, 158, 219
Griffith, Andy 191
Griffith, Melanie 118
Grizzard, George 228
Guard, Dominick 20
Guerra, Ray 13
Guinness, Alec 28, 88, 135, 198
Gulpilil 48

H

Hackman, Gene 34, 49, 118
Hagen, Uta 165
Hamilton, Margaret 243
Hampden, Walter 71, 207
Hansen, Gunner 137
Harper, Jessica 183
Harrison, Susan 116
Hartman, Elizabeth 157
Harvey, Laurence 154
Hasso, Signe 95
Hawkins, Jack 117, 167, 198
Hayakawa, Sessue 198
Harareet, Haya 168
Hayden, Sterling 75, 210, 217
Hayes, Peter Lind 225
Healey, Mary 225
Heggie, O.P. 70
Henreid, Paul 219
Hepburn, Katharine 98, 232
Heston, Charlton 66, 167, 187
Hill, Roger 143
Hiller, Wendy 181
Hobart, Rose 158
Hoffman, Dustin 221
Holbrook, Hal 235
Holden, William 81, 198, 209, 245
Holloway, Stanley 135
Holm, Celeste 84
Holt, Tim 74
Homolka, Oscar 29
Hopkins, Bo 113
Hopper, Dennis 52, 196
Hough, Paul 212
House, Billy 128
Houseman, John 237
Howard, Leslie 50
Howard Trevor 139, 247
Howat, Clark 241
Hseuh, Nancy 226
Hudson, John 53
Hull, Josephine 35
Hull, Warren 152, 179
Hurt, William 240
Huston, John 60
Huston, Walter 74

I

Ireland, John 52
Ives, Burl 57

J

Jaeckel, Richard 72
Jaffe, Sam 75, 182
James, Sidney 135
Jarratt, John 20
Jewell, Isabel 232
Johnson, Ben 54, 140, 206, 245
Johnson, Rita 123
Jones, Barry 247
Jones, Jennifer 162
Jones, J. Paul 30
Jones, Robert Earl 141
Jones, Tommy Lee 175
Jordan, Richard 71
Jory, Victor 30
Jurado, Katy 168
Jurgens, Curt 126

K

Kane, Carol 218
Karloff, Boris 36, 101, 152, 172, 184, 226
Karlweis, Oscar 71
Keach, James 122
Keach, Stacy 122
Keaton, Diane 56
Keays-Byrne, Hugh 226
Keitel, Harvey 44, 244
Keller, Marthe 133
Kelley, David Patrick 143
Kelly, Grace 168
Kelly, Jim 108
Kelly, Paul 107
Kemper, Charles 54
Kennedy, Arthur 207
Kerima 247
Kerr, John 163
Kiel, Richard 77, 125
Kinski, Klaus 13
Krauss, Werner 42
Kwouk, Burt 78

L

Ladd, Alan 110, 190
Lake, Veronica 111, 190
Lambert, Anne 20
Lancaster, Burt 52, 115
Landi, Elissa 69
Lane, Priscilla 107
La Rue, Frank
LaRue, Jack
Laughton, Charles 31, 123, 229
Laurie, Piper 100
Lazenby, George 33
Leachman, Cloris 45
Leaver, Philip 109
Lee, Bernard 139
Lee, Bruce 108
Lee, Christopher 94, 171, 194
Leigh, Janet 83, 187
Lemmon, Jack 234

Leslie, Joan 148
Libbey, Fred 54
Littel, John 166
Livesey, Roger 117
Lochary, David 155
Locke, Sondra 238
Lockhart, Gene 52, 207
Lockwood, Margaret 109
Lodge, John 182
Lom, Herbert 78, 88
Lonsdale, Michael 77, 121
Lopez, Trini 72
Lorre, Peter 22, 35, 103, 164, 219
Lugosi, Bela 101, 184
Lukas, Paul 109
Lupino, Ida 148
Lynn, Jeffrey 107

M

MacDonald, Ian 168
Macready, George 124
Maitland, Colin 72
Malden, Karl 93, 139
Mamo 32
Margolin, Janet 213
Marlowe, Hugh 84
Marshal, Alan 64
Marshall, Herbert 60
Marshall, Tully 190
Marshall, Zena 76
Martin, Lori 40
Marvin, Lee 72, 126, 239
Masina, Guilietta 249
Mason, James 70, 131, 230
Massey, Edith 155
Massey, Raymond 35, 50
Matheson, Tim 235
Mature, Victor 228
Mayo, Virginia 52
McCambridge, Mercedes 210, 233
McCormick, Myron 100
McDowell, Malcolm 14, 216
McGee, Patrick 14
McKinney, Billy 173
McLiam, John 212
McMurray, Fred 242
Meeker, Ralph 45
Merrill, Gary 84
Middleton, Charles 169
Mifune, Toshiro 171
Miles, Vera 136
Milland, Ray 89, 123
Miller, Marvin 46
Mills, Danny 156
Mills, Donna 170
Milner, Marty 116
Mineo, Sal 36
Mr. T 134
Mitchell, Thomas 55, 168
Mitchum, John 161
Mitchum, Robert 39, 71, 153, 200, 214
Monroe, Marilyn 142
Montgomery, Robert 64
Moore, Kieron 117
Moore, Roger 77, 131
Morley, Robert 98, 156
Morse, Helen 20
Movita, 32
Mueller, Cookie 155
Murphy, Mary 127
Murray, Don 229

N

Nagel, Anne 166
Nash, Mary 91
Neal, Patricia 115, 191
Nelligan, Kate 85
Nelson, Margaret 20
Newman, Paul 100, 114, 141, 209
Newton, Robert 88
Nicholson, Jack 60, 188
Niven, David 47
Niven, Kip 235
Novak, Kim 148
Novarro, Ramon 159

O

Oakman, Wheeler 174
Oates, Warren 245
Oberon, Merle 50
O'Brien, Edmond 81, 124
O'Connor, Carroll 240
Ogilvy, Ian 162
O'Halloran, Jack 153
O'Kelley, Tim 225
Olivier, Lawrence 26, 65, 165, 220
O'Malley, Kathleen 54
Osceola, Cory 57
O'Sullivan, Maureen 21, 123
O'Toole, Peter 28, 111

P

Pacino, Al 56, 99, 199
Page, Geraldine 157
Parks, Michaels 131
Parry, Geoff 226
Patrick, Nigel 117
Paulson, Albert 154
Peck, Gregory 40, 102, 147, 161, 164, 177
Pellicer, Pina 140
Perkins, Anthony 131, 177, 181, 185
Peters, Jean 142
Phillips, Robert 72
Pickens, Slim 140, 217
Plummer, Christopher 57
Pollard, Michael J. 34
Power, Tyrone 156, 189
Preston, Robert 147, 190
Price, Vincent 113, 144, 162, 173

Q

Quayle, Anthony 136
Quinn, Anthony 148

R

Raft, George 51
Rains, Claude 28, 104, 204, 219
Ralph, Jessie 164
Rampling, Charlotte 153
Ranieri, Massimo 130
Rathbone, Basil 104, 172, 198

Raymond, Gene 233
Reagan, Ronald 30
Redford, Robert 141, 203, 237
Redgrave, Michael 109
Redgrave, Vanessa 181
Reed, Philip 150
Relph, George 167
Rennie, Michael 71
Rey, Fernando 49, 129
Reynolds, Burt 173, 206
Richardson, Ralph 247
Richmond, Kane 91
Rigg, Diana 33
Rivera, Cecilia 13
Roberts, Rachel 19, 181
Robertson, Chuck 246
Robertson, Cliff 238
Robinson, Andy 202
Robinson, Edward G. 66, 128, 192, 193
Robinson, Karen 20
Rodgers, Gaby 45
Rogers, Jean 91
Rojo, Helena 13
Ross, Betsy King 175
Roya, David 241
Russell, Rosalind 64, 163
Russo, Robert 113
Ryan, Mitchell 235
Ryan, Robert 67, 72, 150, 200

S

Saint, Eva Marie 93, 231
Sakata, Harold 180
Salvatori, Renato 130
Sampson, Will 188
Sanchez, Jaime 245
Sande, Walter 166
Sanders, George 68, 85
Sarandon, Chris 199
Savage, John 211
Savalas, Telly 33, 40, 72
Saxon, John 108, 203
Scheider, Roy 221
Schildkraut, Joseph 156
Scott, Lizabeth 46
Scott, Randolph 150
Seales, Franklyn 211
Sellers, Peter 47, 216
Sen, Ong Chi 60
Serna, Pepe 113
Sharif, Omar 29
Shaw, Robert 133, 140, 141
Shayne, Konstantin 128
Shearer, Norma 156
Sheen, Martin 131
Shepard, Sam 40
Shepherd, Cybill 224
Simmons, Jean 26
Simpson, Mickey 54
Sinatra, Frank 154
Sloane, Olive 248
Smith, Alexis 158
Smith, Howard I. 57
Soul, David 235
Spardlin, G. D. 56
Stack, Robert 67, 171
Stallone, Sylvester 134
Stanwyck, Barbara 242
Steele, Barbara 163
Steenburgen, Mary 216

Stefanelli, Simonetta 99
Steiger, Rod 93
Stephenson, Henry 89
Stephenson, James 60
Stewart, James 149
Stewart, Paul 45
Stole, Mink 155
Stoler, Shirley 27
Stone, Lewis 159
Storey, Ruth 212
Strasberg, Lee 56
Strode, Woody 26
Sullivan, Francis L. 88
Sutherland, Donald 39, 72, 85, 112

T

Tamiroff, Akim 187
Taylor, Elizabeth 232
Taylor, Robert 16, 68
Terry, Don 166
Tierney, Gene 88, 144
Tobey, Kenneth 53
Toler, Sidney 91
Tone, Franchot 31, 229
Torn, Rip 96
Tottenham, Merle 64
Turner, Kathleen 240
Turner, Lana 92
Tyler, Tom 203

U

Urich, Robert 235
Ustinov, Peter 26

V

Valli, 139
Van Cleef, Lee 52
Veidt, Conrad 219
Vernon, John 238, 239
Voight, Joh 173

W

Walburn, Raymond 69
Walker, Robert 18, 72
Wallach, Eli 43
Walter, Jessica 170
Ward, Roger 227
Ward, Simon 194
Warner, David 216
Warren, Jennifer 118
Webb, Clifton 144
Webber, Robert 72
Weirgraf, John 71
Weissmuller, Johnny 21
Welch, Raquel 194
Weld, Tuesday 185
Welles, Orson 128, 139, 187
Whitty, Dame May 64, 109
Widmark, Richard 96, 181, 227
Wilcoxon, Henry 150
Williams, Paul 183
Wilroy, Channing 155
Wilson, Charles 179

Wilson, Scott 212
Wood, Natalie 36
Woods, James 211
Worden, Hank 54
Worth, Harry 203
Wyatt, John 173
Wynn, Keenan 239

Y

Yamaguchi, Shirley 67
York, Michael 181, 194
Young, Loretta 128
Yung, Sen 91

Z

Zerbe, Anthony 153

Movie Index

A

Adventures of Captain Marvel 203
Adventures of Robin Hood, The 104
Advise and Consent 228
African Queen, The 97
Aguirre, The Wrath of God 13
All About Eve 83
And Then There Were None 186
Apocalypse Now 131
Arsenic and Old Lace 35
Asphalt Jungle, The 75

B

Beckett 111
Beguiled, The 157
Ben Hur 167
Big Clock, The 123
Big Sleep, The 214
Billy Jack 241
Black Cat, The 184
Black Sunday 132
Blue Dahlia, The 110
Body Heat 240
Body Snatcher, The 101
Bonnie and Clyde 34
Boys from Brazil, The 164
Bridge on the River Kwai 198

C

Cabinet of Dr. Caligari, The 42
Cape Fear 39
Casablanca 219
Charlie Chan in Panama 91
China Syndrome, The 233
Chinatown 60
Clockwork Orange 14
Coma 96
Conflict 158
Conqueror Worm, The 113
Count of Monte Cristo,The 69

D

Dark Mirror, The 55
Day of the Jackal 121
Day of the Locust, The 112
Dead Reckoning 46
Deliverance 173
Dirty Dozen, The 72
Dirty Harry 202
Dr. No 75
Dr. Strangelove 216
Dog Day Afternoon 199
Don Winslow of the Navy 166
Double Indemnity 242
Duel in the Sun 161

E

Easy Rider 196
Electric Horseman, The 203
Enforcer, The 160
Enter the Dragon 108
Eye of the Needle 85
Eyes of Laura Mars 175

F

Face in the Crowd, A 191
Face of Fu Manchu, The 94
Farewell, My Lovely 153

ffolkes 131
Five Fingers 70
5,000 Fingers of Dr. T, The 225
Flash Gordon Conquers the Universe 169
Four Musketeers, The 194
French Connection, The 49
Friends of Eddie Coyle, The 71

G

Godfather, The 211
Godfather Part II, The 56
Goldfinger 180
Gun Crazy 223
Gunfight at the O.K. Corral 52
Gunfighter, The 102

H

High Noon 168
High Sierra 148
Honeymoon Killers, The 27
House of Bamboo 67
House on 92nd St., The 95
Hud 114
Hustle 206
Hustler, The 100

I

In Cold Blood 212
Ipcress File, The 63
Ivanhoe 68

J

Johnny Guitar 210

K

Key Largo 193
Kiss Me Deadly 45
Kiss of Death 227
Klute 39

L

Lady Vanishes, The 109
Last of the Mohicans 149
La Strada 248
Last Wave, The 48
Laura 144
Lawrence of Arabia 28
Lavender Hill Mob, The 135
League of Gentlemen, The 117
Letter, The 59
Light at the Edge of the World, The 129
Little Caesar 192
Long Riders, The 122

M

Macomber Affair, The 147
Mad Max 226
Magnificent Seven, The 43
Magnum Force 235
Maltese Falcon, The 102
Manchurian Candidate, The 154
Man Who Knew Too Much, The 22
Marathon Man, 220
Marie Antoinette 156
Mark of Zorro, The 189

Marked Woman 231
Mata Hari 159
Mommie Dearest 58
Moonraker 77
Murder on the Orient Express 181
Mutiny on the Bounty 31

N

Niagara 142
Night Key, 152
Night Moves 118
Night Must Fall 64
1941 171
North by Northwest 230
Notorious 204

O

Oliver Twist 88
One-Eyed Jacks 139
One Flew Over the Cuckoo's Nest 188
On Her Majesty's Secret Service 33
Onion Field, The 211
On the Beach 176
On the Waterfront 93
Outcast of the Islands 247
Outfit, The 150
Outlaw Josey Wales, The 238

P

Party Girl 16
Phantom Empire, The 174
Phantom of the Paradise 183
Picnic at Hanging Rock 19
Pink Flamingoes 155
Pink Panther, The 47
Pink Panther Strikes Again, The 78
Pit and the Pendulum, The 162
Play Misty for Me 170
Point Blank 239
Postman Always Rings Twice, The 92
Pretty Poison 185
Prisoner of War 29

R

Racket The 200
Rebecca 65
Rebel Without a Cause 36
Red Light 51
Resurrection 40
Roaring Twenties, The 107
Rocky III 134

S

Saturn 3 44
Scarlet Empress, The 182
Scarlet Pimpernel, The 50
Seven Days to Noon 247
Shadow, The 30
Shock Corridor 246
Spartacus 26
Spider's Web, The 179
Spy Who Loved Me, The 125
Sting, The 140
Stranger, The 128
Strangers on a Train 18
Suddenly Last Summer 232
Sweet Smell of Success 115

T

Take the Money and Run 213
Targers 225
Tarzan and His Mate 21
Taxi Driver 224
Ten Commandments, The 66
Texas Chainsaw massacre, The 137
They Died With Their Boots On 207
They Met in Bombay 163
Thief, The 89
Third Man, The 139
This Gun for Hire 190
Three Days of the Condor 237
Time After Time 216
Touch of Evil 187
Towering Inferno, The 209
Tower of London, The 172
Treasure Island 208
Treasure of the Sierra Madre 74
Turning Point, The 81

V

Vertigo 148
Vikings, The 83

W

Wagonmaster 54
Warriors, The 143
What Ever Happened to Baby Jane? 25
When a Stranger Calls 218
White Heat 124
Wild Bunch, The 245
Wild One, The 126
Wind Across the Everglades 57
Wizard of Oz 243
Wrong Man, The 136

Director Index

A

Aldrich, Robert 25, 45, 72, 206
Allen, Woody 213

B

Bacon, Lloyd 231
Becker, Harold 211
Beebe, Ford 166, 169
Benedek, Laslo 126
Bernhardt, Curtis 158
Billington, Kevin 129
Black, Noel 185
Bogdanovitch, Peter 225
Boorman, John 173, 239
Boulting, John 247
Boulting, Roy 247
Brando, Marlon 139
Brewer, Otto 174
Bridges, James 233
Brooks, Richard 212
Brown, Clarence 163

C

Capra, Frank 35
Clair, Rene 186
Clouse, Robert 108
Conway, Jack 21
Coppola, Francis Ford 56, 98, 131
Corman, Roger 162
Corrigan, Lloyd 152
Crichton, Charles 135
Crichton, Michael 96
Cromwell, John 46, 200
Curtiz, Michael 104, 219

D

Dassin, Jules 87
Dearden, Basil 117
Del Ruth, Roy 51
DeMille, Cecil B. 66
DePalma, Brian 183
Dieterle, William 81
Donen, Stanley 44

E

Eason, B. Reeves 174
Eastwood, Clint 170, 238
Edwards, Blake 47, 78
English, John 203

F

Fargo, James 160
Farrow, John 123
Fellini, Federico 248
Fitzmaurice, George 159
Fleischer, Richard 83
Fleming, Victor 208, 143
Flynn, John 150
Ford, John 54
Forman, Milos 188
Foster, Norman 91
Frankenheimer, John 132, 154
Friedkin, William 49
Fuller, Samuel 67, 246
Furie, Sidney J. 63

G

Garnett, Tay 92
Gibbons, Cedric 21
Gilbert, Lewis 77, 125
Glenville, Peter 111
Guillermin, John 209

H

Hamilton, Guy 180
Hathaway, Henry 95, 142, 227
Herzog, Werner 13
Hill, George Roy 122, 140
Hill, Walter 143
Hitchcock, Alfred 18, 22, 65, 109, 136, 148, 204, 230
Hooper, Tobe 137
Hopper, Dennis 196
Horne, James W. 30, 179
Hunt, Peter 33
Huston, John 74, 75, 97, 102, 193

K

Kasdan, Lawrence 240

Kastle, Leonard 27
Kazan, Elia 93, 191
Kershner, Irvin 175
King, Henry 102
Korda, Zoltan 147
Kramer, Stanley 176
Kubrick, Stanley 14, 26, 216

L

Laughlin, Tom 241
Lean, David 28, 88, 198
Lee, Rowland V. 69, 172
LeRoy, Mervyn 192
Lester, Richard 194
Lewis, Joseph H. 223
Lloyd, Frank 31
Lumet, Sidney 181, 199

M

Mackendrick, Alexander 115
Mamoulian, Rouben 189
Mankiewicz, Joseph L. 70, 83, 232
Marquand, Richard 85
Marshall, George 110
Marton, Andrew 29
McLaglen, Andrew V. 131
Meyer, Nicholas 216
Miller, George 226

P

Pakula, Alan J. 39
Peckinpah, Sam 245
Penn, Arthur 34, 118
Perry, Frank 58
Petrie, David 40
Polanski, Roman 60
Pollack, Sydney 203, 237
Post, Ted 235
Preminger, Otto 144, 228

R

Ray, Nicholas 16, 36, 57, 210
Reed, Sir Carol 139, 247
Reeves, Michael 113

Richards, Dick 153
Ritt, Martin 114
Rossen, Robert 100
Rouse, Russell 89
Rowland, Roy 225

S

Schaffner, Franklin J. 164
Schlessinger, John 112, 220
Scorsese, Martin 224
Seitz, George B. 149
Sharp, Don 94
Siegel, Don 157, 202
Siodmark, Robert 55
Spielberg, Steven 171
Stallone, Sylvester 134
Sturges, John 43, 52

T

Taylor, Ray 166, 179
Thompson, J. Lee 39
Thorpe, Richard 64, 68
Tuttle, Frank 190

U

Ulmer, Edgar 184

V

Van Dyke, W. S. II 156
Vidor, King 161
von Sternberg, Josef 182

W

Walsh, Raoul 107, 124, 148, 207
Walton, Fred 218
Waters, John 155
Weir, Peter 19, 48
Welles, Orson 128, 187
Wiene, Robert 42
Wilder, Billy 242
Winner, Michael 214
Wise, Robert 101
Witney, William 203
Wyler, William 59, 167

Y

Yates, Peter 71
Young, Harold 50
Young, Terrence 75

Z

Zinnemann, Fred 121, 168

Studio Index

A

Allied Artists 246
Allied Film Makers 117
American International 113, 162, 226
Associated Film Distribution 44
Atlantic Releasing 19
Avco Embassy Films 153, 211

B

Bryonston Pictures 137

C

Cineguild 88
Cinerama Releasing 27, 213
Columbia-EMI 233
Columbia Pictures 28, 30, 46, 93, 126,
   171, 175, 179, 196, 198, 212, 216,
   224, 225, 228, 232

D

Decla-Film-Ges 42

E

Ealing Films 135
Eon Productions 77

F

First National 192

G

Gainsborough Pictures 109

H

Horizon-Romulus 97

L

London Films 22, 50, 139, 247

M

Mascot 174
MGM 16, 21, 29, 31, 64, 68, 72, 75,
   92, 96, 150, 156, 163, 167, 208, 230,
   239, 243
MGM/United Artists 134

N

National-General 129
New Line-Saliva 155
New Yorker Films 13

P

Paramount 52, 56, 58, 60, 66, 71, 81,
   98, 110, 111, 112, 114, 123, 132, 139,
   143, 148, 181, 182, 190, 206, 220,
   225, 237, 242

R

Reliance Films 69
Republic 203, 210
RKO 18, 200
RKO Radio 54, 101, 128, 204

S

Selznick Studios 161
Seven Arts 94

T

20th Century Fox 49, 67, 70, 83, 87,
   91, 95, 100, 102, 142, 144, 164, 185,
   186, 194, 209, 227
20th Century Fox-Rank 183

U

United Artists 33, 43, 45, 47, 51, 65,
   75, 78, 83, 85, 89, 115, 125, 131, 147,
   149, 154, 168, 176, 180, 188, 189,
   214, 247, 248
Universal 40, 51, 63, 121, 131, 140,
   152, 157, 159, 166, 169, 170, 172,
   184, 187, 203
Universal-International 26, 39

W

Warner Bros. 14, 25, 35, 36, 39, 57,
   74, 102, 104, 107, 108, 118, 122, 124,
   136, 160, 173, 191, 193, 199, 202,
   207, 216, 218, 219, 231, 235, 238,
   240, 241
Warner Bros.–First National 59, 148,
   158, 223
Warner Bros.–Seven Arts 34, 245
World Northal 48